JOURNAL FOR THE STUDY OF THE OLD TESTAMENT
SUPPLEMENT SERIES
317

Editors
David J.A. Clines
Philip R. Davies

Executive Editor
Andrew Mein

EUROPEAN SEMINAR IN HISTORICAL METHODOLOGY
3

Editor
Lester L. Grabbe

Sheffield Academic Press

Did Moses Speak Attic?

Jewish Historiography and Scripture in the Hellenistic Period

edited by
Lester L. Grabbe

Journal for the Study of the Old Testament
Supplement Series 317

European Seminar in Historical Methodology 3

Copyright © 2001 Sheffield Academic Press

Published by Sheffield Academic Press Ltd
Mansion House
19 Kingfield Road
Sheffield S11 9AS
England
www.SheffieldAcademicPress.com

Typeset by Sheffield Academic Press
and
Printed on acid-free paper in Great Britain
by Biddles Ltd
www.biddles.co.uk

British Library Cataloguing-in-Publication Data

A catalogue record for this book is available
from the British Library

ISBN 1-84127-155-1

CONTENTS

Dedication   7
Abbreviations   8
List of Contributors   13

Part I
INTRODUCTION

LESTER L. GRABBE
Introduction   16

Part II
ARTICLES

RAINER ALBERTZ
An End to the Confusion? Why the Old Testament
Cannot Be a Hellenistic Book!   30

HANS M. BARSTAD
Deuteronomists, Persians, Greeks, and the Dating of the
Israelite Tradition   47

BOB BECKING
The Hellenistic Period and Ancient Israel: Three
Preliminary Statements   78

ROBERT P. CARROLL
Jewgreek Greekjew: The Hebrew Bible Is All Greek to Me.
Reflections on the Problematics of Dating the Origins of
the Bible in Relation to Contemporary Discussions of
Biblical Historiography   91

PHILIP R. DAVIES
Judaeans in Egypt: Hebrew and Greek Stories   108

LESTER L. GRABBE
Jewish Historiography and Scripture in the Hellenistic
Period   129

LESTER L. GRABBE
Who Were the First Real Historians? On the Origins
of Critical Historiography   156

DAVID M. GUNN
The Myth of Israel: Between Present and Past   182

NIELS PETER LEMCHE
How Does One Date an Expression of Mental History?
The Old Testament and Hellenism   200

KAI PELTONEN
A Jigsaw without a Model? The Date of Chronicles   225

Part III
OTHER CONTRIBUTIONS

THOMAS L. THOMPSON
The Bible and Hellenism: A Response   274

NIELS PETER LEMCHE
The Old Testament—A Hellenistic Book?   287

Part IV
CONCLUSIONS

LESTER L. GRABBE
Reflections on the Discussion   320

Index of References   341
Index of Authors   346

To the Memory of Professor Robert P. Carroll (1944–2000)

This volume was in the press when news came of Robert Carroll's sudden death on 12 May 2000. This was a great loss to scholarship as well as a personal tragedy for many friends and colleagues in the 'Academy' (as he liked to refer to it) on both sides of the Atlantic.

Robert first made his name in the area of prophecy. His work on Jeremiah has been controversial, but it is difficult to find another commentary on the book which throws the particular perspective on the text that his does; there are many of us who feel that his Jeremiah commentary will go down in the history of biblical interpretation as a twentiethth-century classic. More recently his work on *Ideologiekritik* was very much relevant to the work of the European Seminar in Historical Methodology, of which he was an active member. The essay in this present volume is typical of his combative—and entertaining—style. Even when you disagreed with him, you learned something. Several times I pressed him to be clearer on his views about history, but his reply was that he had to write several more papers before he could say. Unfortunately, that developed position will never emerge, but his papers arising out of our debates are a part of the Seminar's developing thoughts.

Many of us owe a good deal to Robert as a friend. He was an interesting and informative conversationalist about all sorts of matters, academic and otherwise. He was generous with his time: to take up invitations to contribute to publications and to give lectures in far-flung areas of the world, to write references, to read the work of others, and to serve the cause of biblical scholarship in innumerable ways. Above all, he was a great drinking companion, than which no higher praise can be given.

Lester L. Grabbe

ABBREVIATIONS

AB	Anchor Bible
ABD	David Noel Freedman (ed.), *The Anchor Bible Dictionary* (New York: Doubleday, 1992)
ABRL	Anchor Bible Reference Library
AfO	*Archiv für Orientforschung*
AGJU	Arbeiten zur Geschichte des antiken Judentums und des Urchristentums
AHw	Wolfram von Soden, *Akkadisches Handwörterbuch* (Wiesbaden: Harrassowitz, 1959–81)
AnBib	Analecta biblica
ANEP	James B. Pritchard (ed.), *Ancient Near East in Pictures Relating to the Old Testament* (Princeton: Princeton University Press, 1954)
ANET	James B. Pritchard (ed.), *Ancient Near Eastern Texts Relating to the Old Testament* (Princeton: Princeton University Press, 1950)
ANRW	Hildegard Temporini and Wolfgang Haase (eds.), *Aufstieg und Niedergang der römischen Welt: Geschichte und Kultur Roms im Spiegel der neueren Forschung* (Berlin: W. de Gruyter, 1972–)
AOAT	Alter Orient und Altes Testament
ArOr	*Archiv orientálni*
ATD	Das Alte Testament Deutsch
BA	*Biblical Archaeologist*
BAR	British Archaeological Reports
BASOR	*Bulletin of the American Schools of Oriental Research*
BEATAJ	Beiträge zur Erforschung des Alten Testaments und des Antiken
BBB	Bonner biblische Beiträge
BETL	Bibliotheca ephemeridum theologicarum lovaniensium
BibInt	*Biblical Interpretation: A Journal of Contemporary Approaches*
BibOr	Biblica et orientalia
BWANT	Beiträge zur Wissenschaft vom Alten und Neuen Testament
BZAW	Beihefte zur *ZAW*
CAD	Ignace I. Gelb *et al.* (eds.), *The Assyrian Dictionary of the*

	Oriental Institute of the University of Chicago (Chicago: Oriental Institute, 1964–)
CANE	J. Sasson (ed.), *Civilizations of the Ancient Near East* (4 vols.; New York: Simon & Schuster, 1995)
CBET	Contributions to Biblical Exegesis and Theology
CBQ	*Catholic Biblical Quarterly*
CBQMS	*Catholic Biblical Quarterly*, Monograph Series
ConBOT	Coniectanea biblica, Old Testament
CPJ	V.A. Tcherikover, A. Fuks and M. Stern (eds.), *Corpus Papyrorum Judaicarum* (3 vols.; Cambridge, MA: Harvard University Press; Jerusalem: Magnes Press, 1957–64)
CRBS	*Currents in Research: Biblical Studies*
CRINT	Compendia rerum iudaicarum ad Novum Testamentum
DBAT	*Dielheimer Blätter zum Alten Testament*
DDD	K. van der Toorn, B. Becking and P.W. van der Horst (eds.), *Dictionary of Deities and Demons in the Bible* (Leiden: E.J. Brill; Grand Rapids: Eerdmans, 2nd rev. edn, 1999)
DTT	*Dansk teologisk tidsskrift*
EI	*Eretz-Israel*
EPRO	Etudes préliminaires des religions orientales
ESHM	European Seminar in Historical Methodology
EvT	*Evangelische Theologie*
ExpTim	*Expository Times*
FAT	Forschungen zum Alten Testament
FOTL	The Forms of the Old Testament Literature
FRLANT	Forschungen zur Religion und Literatur des Alten und Neuen Testaments
FTS	Freiburger theologische Studien
GAT	Grundrisse zum Alten Testament
HAE	Handbuch der Althebräischen Epigraphik
HAT	Handbuch zum Alten Testament
HSM	Harvard Semitic Monographs
HTR	*Harvard Theological Review*
HUCA	*Hebrew Union College Annual*
IEJ	*Israel Exploration Journal*
JAOS	*Journal of the American Oriental Society*
JBL	*Journal of Biblical Literature*
JEA	*Journal of Egyptian Archaeology*
JJS	*Journal of Jewish Studies*
JNES	*Journal of Near Eastern Studies*
JNSL	*Journal of Northwest Semitic Languages*
JQR	*Jewish Quarterly Review*
JR	*Journal of Religion*
JSOT	*Journal for the Study of the Old Testament*
JSOTSup	*Journal for the Study of the Old Testament*, Supplement Series

JSPSup	*Journal for the Study of the Pseudepigrapha*, Supplement Series
KAT	Kommentar zum Alten Testament
LCL	Loeb Classical Library
LSJ	H.G. Liddell, Robert Scott and H. Stuart Jones, *Greek-English Lexicon* (Oxford: Clarendon Press, 9th edn, 1968)
NBL	*Neues Bibel-Lexikon*
NCB	New Century Bible
NEB	Neue Echter Bibel
NedTTs	*Nederlands theologisch tijdschrift*
NTOA	Novum Testamentum et orbis antiquus
OBO	Orbis biblicus et orientalis
ÖBS	Österreichische Biblische Studien
OBT	Overtures to Biblical Theology
Or	*Orientalia*
OTG	Old Testament Guides
OTL	Old Testament Library
OTS	Oudtestamentische Studiën
PW	August Friedrich von Pauly and Georg Wissowa (eds.), *Real-Encyclopädie der classischen Altertumswissenschaft* (Stuttgart: Metzler, 1894–)
RB	*Revue biblique*
REJ	*Revue des études juives*
RLA	*Reallexikon der Assyriologie*
RSV	Revised Standard Version
SBAB	Stuttgarter Biblische Aufsatzbände
SBB	Stuttgarter biblische Beiträge
SBLDS	SBL Dissertation Series
SBLMS	SBL Monograph Series
SBLRBS	SBL Resources for Biblical Study
SBLSBS	SBL Sources for Biblical Study
SBLSCS	SBL Septuagint and Cognate Studies
SBLSS	SBL Semeia Studies
SBLTT	SBL Texts and Translations
SBLWAWS	SBL Writings from the Ancient World Series
SBT	Studies in Biblical Theology
SDOAP	Studia et documenta ad iura orientis antiqui pertinentia
SHANE	Studies in the History of the Ancient Near East
SHCANE	Studies in the History and Culture of the Ancient Near East
SJLA	Studies in Judaism in Late Antiquity
SJOT	*Scandinavian Journal of the Old Testament*
ST	*Studia theologica*
TBü	Theologische Bücherei
ThW	Theologische Wissenschaft: Sammelwerk für Studium und Beruf

TOTC	Tyndale Old Testament Commentaries
VT	*Vetus Testamentum*
VTSup	*Vetus Testamentum*, Supplements
WBC	Word Biblical Commentary
WMANT	Wissenschaftliche Monographien zum Alten und Neuen Testament
ZAH	*Zeitschrift für Althebräistik*
ZAR	*Zeitschrift für Altorientalische und Biblische Rechtsgeschichte*
ZAW	*Zeitschrift für die alttestamentliche Wissenschaft*
ZDMG	*Zeitschrift der deutschen morgenländischen Gesellschaft*
ZDPV	*Zeitschrift des deutschen Palästina-Vereins*
ZPE	*Zeitschrift für Papyrologie und Epigraphik*

LIST OF CONTRIBUTORS

Rainer Albertz is Professor of Old Testament at the Westfälische Wilhelms-Universität in Münster.

Hans M. Barstad is Professor of Biblical Studies at the University of Oslo.

Bob Becking is the Professor of Old Testament Studies at the University of Utrecht.

Robert P. Carroll was Professor of Hebrew Bible and Semitic Studies at the University of Glasgow.

Philip R. Davies is Professor of Biblical Studies at the University of Sheffield.

Lester L. Grabbe is Professor of Hebrew Bible and Early Judaism at the University of Hull.

David M. Gunn is the A.A. Bradford Professor of Religion at Texas Christian University, Fort Worth, Texas.

Niels Peter Lemche is Professor of Theology at the University of Copenhagen.

Kai Peltonen is Docent of Old Testament Exegetics at the University of Helsinki.

Thomas L. Thompson is Professor of Theology at the University of Copenhagen.

Part I

INTRODUCTION

INTRODUCTION

Lester L. Grabbe

Τί γὰρ ἐστι Πλάτων ἢ Μωυσῆς ἀττικίζων;
For what is Plato but Moses speaking Attic?

This volume publishes the papers of the European Seminar on Methodology in Israel's History from the 1998 (Cracow) and 1999 (Helsinki) sessions. Both these sessions were devoted broadly to the Hellenistic period, and the spread of topics indicates the breadth of subject. Also reprinted here is an article by Niels Peter Lemche that formed an important part of the debate (see 'Reflections on the Discussion' for further information [pp. 321-24 below]).

About the European Seminar in Historical Methodology

This is the third volume produced by the Seminar. Since some readers may not have read volume 1,[1] which explained the purpose of the Seminar, or may have forgotten the rationale behind it, it might be useful to give a reminder here. The purpose of the Seminar is to discuss the methodological issues surrounding the writing of the history of Israel/ Palestine/Southern Syria during the First and Second Temple periods, that is, the Iron Age to the early Roman Empire. For purely pragmatic reasons, regular membership is limited to scholars working in Europe; however, for our discussion in this volume we have several invited guest papers and hope to include more in the future. Current members of the Seminar include the following:

Rainer Albertz (Germany)
Hans M. Barstad (Norway)
Bob Becking (Netherlands)
Philip R. Davies (UK)

1. Lester L. Grabbe (ed.), *Can a 'History of Israel' Be Written?* (JSOTSup, 245; ESHM, 1; Sheffield: Sheffield Academic Press, 1997).

Diana Edelman (UK)
Josette Elayi (France)
Lester L. Grabbe (UK)
Ulrich Hübner (Germany)
Knud Jeppesen (Denmark)
E. Axel Knauf (Switzerland)
Niels Peter Lemche (Denmark)
Mario Liverani (Italy)
Andrew Mayes (Ireland)
Hans-Peter Müller (Germany)
Nadav Na'aman (Israel)
Herbert Niehr (Germany)
H.M. Niemann (Germany)
Ed Noort (Netherlands)
Thomas L. Thompson (Denmark)
David Ussishkin (Israel)
Helga Weippert (Germany)
Manfred Weippert (Germany)
Keith Whitelam (UK)

Is This a 'Postmodernist' Seminar?

I have heard our Seminar characterized once or twice as 'postmodernist', though only orally, to the best of my knowledge, and not in print. I cannot speak for all members of the Seminar, especially since some of them do some of their work in a postmodernist context. Nevertheless, I can say that the Seminar as a whole is not postmodernist, and some members of the Semnar would wholeheartedly reject the term 'postmodernist' as applied to themselves. In the first volume of papers coming from the Seminar, Hans Barstad discussed in detail the implications of postmodernism (among other trends) for historical research.[2] He pointed out that postmodernist study has some relevant contributions to make to the debate, and I agree with him, but he certainly did not recommend that the postmodernist agenda (some postmodernists would reject the concept of having an agenda—though whether rightly or wrongly can be debated) should be wholeheartedly embraced. On the contrary, he suggested, on the one hand, that it was already being superseded and, on the other hand, that older questions and issues were still very much in the picture.

2.   'History and the Hebrew Bible', in Grabbe (ed.), *Can a 'History of Israel' Be Written?*, pp. 37-64.

The debate about postmodernism continues in a vigorous fashion among professional historians, at least in some parts of the Academy in English-speaking scholarship.[3] One of the main advocates for a post-modern perspective in history, Keith Jenkins,[4] has recently produced a 'postmodernist reader' that tries to bring together some of the most influential articles in the debate.[5] In a long introduction he tries to lay out the main issues, with a defence of his own approach. One can find a similar advocacy of postmodernism, though perhaps less flamboyantly presented, by Alun Munslow.[6] But the past few years have been especially characterized by a strong resistance movement against postmodernism. Joyce Appleby, Lynn Hunt and Margaret Jacob produced a book which might appear at first to have postmodern agenda in its assault on the way 'outsiders' (women and other minorities) have been excluded or neglected.[7] Yet a good part of their text is a strong attack on such postmodern gurus as Foucault and Derrida. A book achieving widespread circulation in the UK is Richard J. Evans's *In Defence of History*,[8] which is written for a non-technical readership. It actually tries to explain clearly the different approachs of recent writers on historiography and is not just an assault on the postmodern, but it ultimately rejects it as the way forward even if the relevance of some aspects of postmodernism is accepted.

A wide-ranging attack on a number of recent trends in history-writing, as the title *The Killing of History* already makes quite plain, has

3.   How to define or characterize 'postmodernism' as it applies to history is not an easy task since postmodernists themselves often seem to avoid a positive statement of their historical method. For example, the Introduction to Keith Jenkins's recent 'postmodernist reader' (see note 5 below) spends a lot of time defining the way most historians do history, but then treats postmodernism only as a critique of this.

4.   See, e.g., his *Re-Thinking History* (London: Routledge, 1991); also most recently, *Why History? Ethics and Postmodernity* (London: Routledge, 1999) (my thanks to Robert Carroll for drawing my attention to this latter work).

5.   Keith Jenkins (ed.), *The Postmodern History Reader* (London: Routledge, 1997).

6.   *Deconstructing History* (London: Routledge, 1997).

7.   *Telling the Truth about History* (New York: W.W. Norton, 1994). See the extensive reviews by Raymond Martin, Joan W. Scott and Cushing Strout in *History and Theory* 34 (1995), pp. 320-39.

8.   Richard J. Evans, *In Defence of History* (London: Granta Books, 1997). See the review by Wulf Kansteiner in *History and Theory* 39 (2000), pp. 218-29.

been carried out by Keith Windschuttle.[9] He covers more than post-modernism, and such figures as Derrida are mentioned mainly in passing; however, he has a long chapter attacking Foucault whom he sees as the main culprit in undermining traditional study of history. Although the title and style might suggest an irresponsible blunderbuss attack on ill-defined targets, the book makes some effective points despite some shortcomings.[10] C. Behan McCullagh has tried to steer a middle way by recognizing that the critics have not always presented the arguments of the postmodernists fairly and by himself giving due weight to the postmodernist positions; nevertheless, taking into consideration the valid points about subjectiveness and the place of language in reality, he still concludes that historical knowledge is possible.[11] Interestingly, this debate comes at a time when R.G. Collingwood's major work on the philosophy of history, a manuscript left at his death and thought destroyed, has recently surfaced and has now been published.[12]

Thus, there is at present among historians no uniform answer to the question of the value—or not—of postmodernism in historical study. Therefore, it would hardly be surprising if different members of the Seminar chose varying approaches to the question. But the fact is that different participants are likely to have quite divergent views on the question, and as a collective we are definitely *not* a 'postmodern seminar'.

Is this a 'European School'?

While recently reading a paper on history at the Society of Biblical Literature conference in Boston, a North American scholar referred to the 'European School', apparently with the European Seminar in mind. I think the members of the Seminar, as well as those who have been observers at our discussions, will be quite surprised to hear this. The term 'school' usually implies a common view or perspective. The

9. *The Killing of History: How Literary Critics and Social Theorists Are Murdering our Past* (New York: The Free Press, 1997).

10. See the review by Daniel Gordon, 'Capital Punishment for Murderous Theorists?', *History and Theory* 38 (1999), pp. 378-88.

11. C. Behan McCullagh, *The Truth of History* (London: Routledge, 1998).

12. R.G. Collingwood, *The Principles of History and Other Writings in Philosophy of History* (ed. W.H. Dray and W.J. van der Dussen; Oxford: Oxford University Press, 1999).

common perspective of the Seminar is, I believe, twofold: (1) that we think the subject of history and ancient Israel is one worth spending time on and debating; and (2) that there is no quick and easy answer to the issue of Iron Age Palestine's history nor of its relationship to the contents of the biblical text. Beyond this common interest, however, there is a great variety of viewpoint, and there have been some sharp exchanges and vociferous disagreements over the four years that we have been meeting. I think we would all agree that the term 'school' is entirely inappropriate. We sit around the same table, and we publish papers between the same set of covers, but as the present volume makes quite clear these papers—far from taking a unified position—in fact form a vigorous debate.

What we seem to be—at least at present—is unique. We are not aware of another group trying to thrash out questions of historical methodology in a forum which takes in a diversity of views. This is a pity, since many biblical scholars and archaeologists think the subject of the Bible and history is important, yet there is little formal discussion on the subject. Polemics there are aplenty, not to mention sermonizing to the converted. What is lacking is genuine discussion. The European Seminar was founded to create a forum for discussing methodology, with a deliberate diversity of perspective between members. To label the Seminar a 'school' is nothing short of a travesty. The Seminar is not a partisan exercise but an attempt to have the proper face-to-face debate that seems to be lacking elsewhere.

Summary of the Contributions

Rainer Albertz, in 'An End to the Confusion?', has written an *Auseinandersetzung* with Niels Peter Lemche, reacting to both the latter's article of 1993 and his contribution to this volume (see below). Albertz is disappointed that after six years, Lemche's far-reaching thesis about the composition of the Bible in the Hellenistic period has not been developed further. First, the cultural development of society is not a precondition for literary production; on the contrary, a crisis may serve to start its creation. Secondly, Hellenistic culture was more of a threat to national identity of Near Eastern cultures than fertile soil for its growth. Thirdly, the Hellenistic period was not the first climax of development in ancient Israel/Judah, the first being in the eighth century BCE. Although Lemche does deal with some potential objections, this is mainly superficial. Where he really falls down is in not giving a historico-sociological context for the writing of the biblical books. Albertz is conscious that his own socio-historical scenario of how the Pentateuch might have been written in the Persian period is subjective, but Lemche needs to produce a similar explanation for his thesis. Is his theory just a joke, after all? Albertz spends the rest of his article on a refutation of Lemche, focusing on the Deuteronomistic history (which must be earlier than Zerubbabel's disappearance) and on the Pentateuch (the account of Hecataeus of Abdera especially, but also some other indications, show the Pentateuch was complete by the beginning of the Greek period).

Hans Barstad's 'Deuteronomists, Persians, Greeks, and the Dating of the Israelite Tradition' is also in some sense a critique of Lemche, though his approach is to discuss the broader question of the chief influence on the 'Deuteronomic school'. He is especially concerned with the question of whether the Deuteronomic sections of the Bible show influence from Greek models. He argues that the biblical material is more closely related to ancient Near Eastern models, and most of the essay is devoted to demonstrating this by surveying the 'common theology of the ancient Near East' under the headings of law, treaty, war, king and god. The Bible also represents an *Einheitskultur* which has been passed down through a (at least in part) long scribal tradition. Thus, much of the *material* is older and has a long history, whenever the compositions (which are themselves hard to date) were made. However, it is unlikely that either the Deuteronomistic history or even the Chronicler was influenced by Greek models.

Bob Becking, in 'The Hellenistic Period and Ancient Israel', first asks whether there is evidence for Israel in the Hellenistic period. His answer is that there is some; a 'history of Israel' in this time can be written, though it will be a tentative enterprise, perhaps a 'proto-history'. He next asks whether the Bible is a Hellenistic book, noting that the final form of the text does not exclude earlier recensions. He discusses the 'lock-and-key' method of dating texts in which the key is the text either in its original form or its final form, with the reconstructed history as background to either form of the text. There is a problem in that more than one historical context can usually be found for the text in question. The Bible as a whole is not a Jewish book but a Yahwistic book, which implies it was not created in the Hellenistic period. Another area of debate is the dating of the Hebrew language in the text.

The language of the Lachish and Arad ostraca is very similar to the language of Kings and Jeremiah, thus favouring a pre-Hellenistic date. Several early Hellenistic texts (e.g. Hecataeus of Abdera, Demetrius the Chronographer, Artapanus) provide evidence that parts of the Pentateuch were already in existence. The final question is about historical consciousness in the Hellenistic period. If the Bible is a Yahwistic book, it cannot be used for Jewish historical consciousness in this period; rather, we should look at various books of the Apocrypha and Pseudepigrapha.

Robert Carroll, in 'Jewgreek Greekjew', continues his series of articles exploring the question of historiography. He argues that we should begin with Qumran, because it is here that we first have attested witnesses to the biblical text. He also gives a useful reminder of the distinction between the writing of the books, their collection into a body, and their final canonization as Jewish scriptures. This process took place mainly in the Second Temple period, though the final part of canonization may well be post-Second Temple. Most or all of the Hebrew Bible was thus produced in the Greek period or later. The books may have been written in Hellenistic times, but the collection was most likely in the Roman period; however, the concept of an original, definitive text may be post-Gutenburg. The old saying, 'Absence of evidence is not evidence of absence', is trotted out to justify sheer speculation, but it is almost always applied selectively and arbitrarily. The Bible's account of its own origins (e.g. the Moses and Ezra traditions) is part of its own myth. We do not know when the Bible *as bible* came into existence: to start with the Hellenistic period is the beginning of wisdom, but we should not stop there. It is intriguing that the biblical writers misdirect the reader and conceal the scaffolding used to produce their stories. For example, the Chronicler does not write about the temple of his own time (the Second Temple) but about Solomon's temple—as if to substitute an ideological view of the past for the present reality. The Bible did not come from heaven but from the contested practices, debates and issues in the past. The writers seem at best interested in producing stories about the past, which is hardly our category of history.

Philip Davies, in 'Judaeans in Egypt', wants to illustrate the problems of growth in the tradition and the question of context by focusing on the exodus story. It is often overlooked that there is not just one story but a number. The present story in the Hebrew Bible is conventionally thought to be composed of more than one account, each of which had a different perspective. In addition to the Israelite versions, however, there was an Egyptian version. The fullest form of this latter is given by Manetho who speaks of the 'shepherds' (Hyksos) who were driven out of Egypt and founded Jerusalem. Then centuries later the Egyptians gathered the lepers in the country, but these revolted and called in the 'shepherds'. Both groups were defeated by Amenophus and driven out. Another version is that of Hecataeus of Abdera whose account has similarities to Manetho's but not the anti-Judaic bias. One could of course argue for the primacy of the biblical account (though which one?), but a case can just as easily be made for the opposite. We do not know when the canonical version arose and cannot assume it is the earliest. The versions of Manetho and Hecataeus have elements that cannot be derived from the book of Exodus. There is a strong theme of hostility between Egypt and Israel throughout the Bible, which may have given rise to the story. In fact, it is likely that the versions of the story were shaped by interaction with one another over the centuries. The exodus story could fit a number of backgrounds, from Amarna to the Achaemenids. It might not come from any of the various events, but all remain possibilities.

Lester Grabbe, in 'Jewish Historiography and Scripture in the Hellenistic Period', surveys our sources for the early Hellenistic period (pre-Maccabaean). The primary sources are Hecataeus of Abdera, the Zenon papyri, some inscriptions of Ptolemy II, and Ben Sira. We also have a decree of Antiochus III quoted by Josephus, which looks authentic for the most part. Finally, there is the Tobiad romance which is difficult to evaluate, though most scholars think it fits the period pretty well in its main points. The principal conclusions are that the Jews formed an ethnic/religious community centred on the temple in Judah, headed by the high priest. Especially significant were two families, the priestly Oniads and an old aristocratic family of the Tobiads. The question of scripture is raised by Ben Sira who seems to know the Pentateuch, the Deuteronomistic History and the Prophets in much the form they exist today. Since it is unlikely that he would have accepted a recently assembled and edited collection as having such authority, the suggestion is that these parts of the Bible were already in roughly their present shape by the end of the Persian period. This gives greater weight to Hecataeus's reference to a 'law of Moses' as a written book. The trauma of the destruction of the temple and the loss of the monarchy would have been an important catalyst to put tradition into written form. On the other hand, there is little indication of Greek influence or allusions in Genesis to 2 Kings or the Prophets. Portions of the Old Testament are indeed Hellenistic, but significant sections were already likely to have been completed in their major outlines by the Persian period.

In a further essay, 'Who Were the First Real Historians?', Grabbe enters the debate about who were the first to write history. Depending on your definition of history, you can argue that the Deuteronomistic History was an example of history-writing or you can deny it. Unfortunately, some definitions are tendentious and would actually exclude the work of many modern historians from the genre of history-writing. If we ask who were the first *critical* historians (and some would confine their definition of history-writing to this), the answer is definitely the Greeks. This does not mean that every Greek or every Roman historian is a good example of critical historical writing, since the classical historians range from Thucydides to those who were little more than compilers with no critical sense. Nevertheless, it was the Greeks who first asked critical questions. In that sense, the material in the Hebrew Bible (with perhaps some exceptions such as Qohelet) is naive and uncritical, however useful some sections may be for modern historians.

David Gunn has contributed a guest paper, 'The Myth of Israel', addressing three issues. He first examines the question of determining dating and provenance of texts by finding an appropriate context. Although the Maccabaean context is plausible, the evidence is rather vague, and others have found other contexts which also seem to be plausible. Lemche's argument (pp. 218-19 below) that texts should be dated by the youngest element within them is fine in theory, but there are problems with it. Why should not 'old' elements still have value as historical data? A second problem is found in Thompson's recent book, the 'Taliban argument'. The arguments about the ideological and sectarian voice of the text are convincing, but does the sectarian voice dominate everything? Despite the presence of the sectarian voice, the texts are not obviously sectarian, and it is not clear who the various parties are if the Primary History is read in a Hellenistic context. Finally, there is the question of reading the texts in Thompson's own terms. The Christian reading is one that could be pursued but not here. The example chosen is the Zionist reading of the texts as history and the conclusions deduced from this reading. The revisionist approach undermines this ideological reading. It may be that Lemche and Thompson overstress the ideological significance of exile as marking the decisive break between 'old Israel' and 'new Israel'.

Niels Peter Lemche first set out a major thesis in his 1993 article, 'The Old Testament—A Hellenistic Book?'; this article is reprinted here (pp. 287-318) and summarized (pp. 321-24 below). For this volume he has produced a programmatic essay, 'How Does One Date an Expression of Mental History?', emphasizing that the past dating of texts by historical referents constitutes circular reasoning. The Old Testament constitutes the literary remains of a rich civilization and is unlikely to be orally composed or transmitted literature. Philip Davies's 'biblical Israel' is actually two Israels: an 'old Israel' (the people of the covenant in stone) and the 'new Israel' (the people of the covenant written on the heart), divided by the Babylonian exile. The old Israel is a creation of the biblical authors, but the new Israel is also a creation: a utopian programme for the future, with the 12 tribes settled around Yhwh's temple on Zion. The laws of the Book of the Covenant have affinities with Mesopotamian law codes, but law-code writing in Mesopotamia ranged probably from the third millennium to after the coming of the Greeks. They were not primarily legal but wisdom/academic. The Persian period has been a popular place to situate the literary work, but it is a 'black box', and to put the writing of the Bible there is to create an unfalsifiable hypothesis. There are Near Eastern elements in the text, but the text, like an archaeological stratum, should be dated by the youngest material within it. The question is whether the Hellenistic material in the book is an integral part of it or was just inserted at a late stage. Some recent authors have compared the Deuteronomistic History with Herodotus, but Livy is actually closer than Herodotus. History, subsumed under rhetoric, was an integral part of the academic curriculum. The Seleucid Empire would be a likely place for the amalgamation between Mesopotamia and Greek tradition, with the centre perhaps in Mesopotamia, though it could be a place in Syria such as Damascus.

In his contribution as a guest, Kai Peltonen ('A Jigsaw without a Model?') continues his well-known work on Chronicles, devoting his attention in this article to the question of dating. He first of all surveys the various opinions, showing that neither internal evidence nor external evidence is decisive in deciding on the dating for the books (which varies from the early Persian period to the time of the Maccabees, though there is something of a consensus on the late fourth century). He then focuses on two recent attempts at finding a historical and ideological context. The first is J. Weinberg who sees the books as growing out of the *Bürger-Tempel Gemeinde* (citizen-temple community), their being an exposition of the views of one particular group in the community. Chronicles would have been composed about the time of Nehemiah. The other recent interpretation is that of Rainer Albertz who revives the theory that the books arose out of the schism between Jerusalem and Samaria/Shechem. The books of Chronicles would have been composed in the early Hellenistic period (c. 330–250 BCE). Both positions have a good deal in common, especially that Chronicles is scribal literature and was aimed at the Judaean elite. Albertz's suggestion has more merit, however, though his position is also not without problems: the main two are the dating of the Samaritan schism and the question of whether 'insider' literature would be addressing the problem of schism. There are also no clear references to the Samaritans or 2 Kings 17 in Chronicles. If the dating of Chronicles is the early Hellenistic period, then it is not dealing with problems of Hellenization but with those left over from the Persian period.

Thomas Thompson has contributed a response to some of the papers. It is difficult to summarize a response of this nature, but some of the main points seem to be as follows: He applauds Robert Carroll for giving the appropriate place of departure, setting out what we know and do not know. The Dead Sea Scrolls are indeed the *terminus a quo*; if we want to trace the pre-history of the text, we need to take into account other literary productions. Not surprisingly, perhaps, Thompson agrees substantially with his colleague Niels Peter Lemche, noting that he is back where he started in the late 1960s: with the amphictyony. He also approves of the 'Taleban argument'. However, he does have one criticism: Lemche should be pressed to define what he means by 'Hellenistic intellectual content' when discussing texts. Thompson find most problems with the views of Lester L. Grabbe, though he focuses primarily on three stated principles of history research given at the beginning of the latter's essay in this volume. If we work on the basis of probability, an assumption of 50 per cent probability becomes only 25 per cent when taken to the next stage which is also taken to be 50 per cent probable. However, Grabbe does better in practice than in theory, though he makes the common false assumption that West Semitic names in the texts must be Jewish. Thompson objects to Grabbe's use of the grandson's colophon for dating the work of Ben Sira. In responding to Philip Davies, Thompson notes that he seems to be talking of

Carroll's 'bogus sources'. Although he contrasts Davies favourably with Grabbe, he ultimately doubts that Davies's 'history of a story' is possible. What we have is not a history of a story but a set of variants—not even so much stories as motifs that travel around. Davies's 'two-tradition' hypothesis can blind us to the fact that there are no less than six variants of the story in Exodus alone. What he has done is take us outside the field of history to one of comparative literature. Thompson accepts David Gunn's criticism that his use of the term 'tradition' is ill-defined but was trying to allow for many possibilities. Rather than one version of a story being primary and another secondary, one often finds that both variants are secondary stages in a longer, ongoing process; it was this fact that informed Thompson's use of the term 'tradition'. He disagrees with Gunn that the problem is one of dating but thinks they are not that far apart. However, where he and Gunn do differ is over the 'theology of the way' motif (whose significance Gunn downplayed) which Thompson sees as pervasive in the biblical literature where it colours the primary voices and is idealistic and socially utopian. Gunn's efforts to suggest alternative ideologies in the text seem to reflect aspects of this intellectual discourse more than real departures from this world view.

Part II

ARTICLES

AN END TO THE CONFUSION?
WHY THE OLD TESTAMENT CANNOT BE A HELLENISTIC BOOK!

Rainer Albertz

A Review

Eight years ago, Niels Peter Lemche published an article with the provoking and promising title 'The Old Testament—A Hellenistic Book?'[1]
It provokes by dating the Old Testament literature as late as possible,
but at the same time it promises to solve the riddle of the complicated
literary history of the Old Testament and the lack of historical evidence.
Taking the author's radical historical criticism into account, the reader
is eager to learn about his solution: if almost nothing can be said about
the pre-exilic period, if the Exile is a mere myth, and the Persian period
is stamped by a political and cultural decline, then the most fertile Hellenistic period—hoped for by anyone reading the title—could perhaps
not only provide the appropriate cultural background for the emergence
of the main bulk of the Old Testament literature, but also offer a well-
documented historical basis on which its origin can be solidly reconstructed. Of course, the question mark must not be overlooked. Scholars
are used to presenting their new theses cautiously. But normally the
reader can be sure that an author who titles an article in this way is
personally nearly completely convinced by his thesis.

However, having read the article, the reader is confused and disappointed. He has not heard any single positive argument for the thesis
that the bulk of Old Testament literature actually originated in the Hellenistic period. What is pointed out is only the assumption that the
Hellenistic period provides the better chance for literary activity than
the Persian, because of its general cultural uprise. To quote Niels Peter
Lemche: 'It should never be forgotten that the revitalization of the
ancient Near East only became a fact after the Greek takeover... It is

1.   *SJOT* 7 (1993), pp. 163-93 (reprinted pp. 287-318 below).

my impression that we now, finally, get a glimpse of a society in which great literature may have been composed, kept and loved...' In his view, there is 'a lot of evidence that says that the Hellenistic Age was the formative period of early Jewish thought and literature as witnessed by the Old Testament itself'.[2]

Anyhow, this argument is doubtful. First, even if we admit that the cultural development of a society to a specific point of literacy is to be seen as a condition of the emergence of literature, especially when it happened for the first time, it will no longer be a necessary prerequisite in societies that had already been developed and perhaps suffered some decline. On the contrary, it is often a period of crisis that promotes literary production, especially the danger that a tradition may be lost completely.[3] The enterprise to write down the national history of Babylonia by Berossos and Egypt by Manetho, mentioned as parallel to Old Testament historical literature by Lemche in his present paper (pp. 200-24 below), I would like to interpret against this background. And in my view the same is true for the Deuteronomistic History, but dating it in the exilic period.[4]

Second, the Hellenistic culture was more a threat to the national identity of the Near Eastern cultures than it was a fertile topsoil for their literatures, as can be seen by the Chronicler's History, which is prob-

2. Lemche, 'The Old Testament', pp. 186-87 (= p. 312 below). Looking for this evidence, the reader is told in p. 187 n. 45 (= p. 312 n. 45 below): 'So far, the theme of discussion has been the historical literature. That the writings are mostly Hellenistic literature seems self-evident in the light of the present discussion, and there is no need to elaborate further on this here.' Even the persistent reader cannot find any evidence in the Deuteronomistic History or the Pentateuch that these are regarded as having been composed in the Hellenistic Period. On the contrary, there is no single anachronistic motive that clearly hints at the Hellenistic period. Niels Peter Lemche is not right in claiming that there is a scholarly consensus about the Hellenistic origin of most of the writings. That is definitely wrong concerning the book of Lamentations, Proverbs and Job, partly wrong for the book of Psalms and possibly true only for the book of Daniel, Qohelet and Song of Songs. In Lemche's opinion the collections of the pre-exilic prophets 'predate the appearance of a larger historical narrative of the kind found in the Pentateuch and the Deuteronomistic History', but that must be disputed for parts of their books, e.g. Isa. 24–27 and Zech. 9–14 are probably of Hellenistic origin.

3. That can be explicitly proved for the early Israelite prophetic tradition, cf. Isa. 8.16-18; 30.8.

4. Rainer Albertz, 'Wer waren die Deuternomisten? Das historische Rätsel einer literarischen Hypothese', *EvT* 57 (1997), pp. 319-38.

ably composed in the early Hellenistic era since it does not show any
Hellenistic influence.[5] It must be regarded as intentionally a-Hellenistic.
We possess only a very little Jewish literature written in the third and
early second centuries BCE that shows some kind of Hellenistic influence such as Qohelet, *1 Enoch*, Jesus Sirach and Daniel, but even this is
not specific enough to derive it from certain Hellenistic sources or
authors.[6] Moreover, Jesus Sirach tries to formulate a specific Jewish
philosophy against the Hellenistic challenge. Thus the flourishing Hellenistic culture was not so much a 'revitalization' of but a threat to the
Jewish intellectual and literary tradition.

Finally, in contrast to the view presented by Lemche, the Hellenistic
period was not the first climax of cultural development in ancient Israel
and Judah. Admittedly, there was high progress in agricultural production of Palestine under the the Ptolemies as the Zenon papyri and the
Tobiad novel testify.[7] The consequence was an increasing density of
Jewish population, which forced many Jews to emigrate to Alexandria
and other Hellenistic cities. In the third century Hecataeus of Abdera
was wondering about the extraordinary Jewish fertility rate.[8] But as

5.   See Rainer Albertz, *A History of Israelite Religion in the Old Testament
Period*, II (Louisville, KY: Westminster/John Knox Press, 1994), pp. 554-56, and
the article of Kai Peltonen in this volume (pp. 225-71 below).

6.   Cf., e.g., Otto Kaiser, 'Judentum und Hellenismus: Ein Beitrag zur Frage
nach dem hellenistischen Einfluß auf Kohelet und Jesus Sirach', in *idem* (ed.), *Der
Mensch unter dem Schicksal: Studien zur Geschichte, Theologie und Gegenwart-
sbedeutung der Weisheit* (BZAW, 161; Berlin: W. de Gruyter, 1985), pp. 135-53;
Yehoshua Amir, 'Doch ein griechischer Einfluß auf das Buch Koheleth?', in *idem*
(ed.), *Studien zum antiken Judentum* (BEATAJ, 2; Frankfurt: Lang, 1985), pp.
35-50; Reinhold Bohlen, 'Kohelet im Kontext der hellenistischen Kultur', in
L. Schwienhorst-Schönberger (ed.), *Das Buch Kohelet: Studien zur Struktur,
Geschichte, Rezeption und Theologie* (BZAW, 254; Berlin: W. de Gruyter, 1997),
pp. 249-73; N. Lohfink, 'Die Wiederkehr des immer Gleichen: Eine frühe Synthese
zwischen griechischem und jüdischem Weltgefühl in Kohelet 1, 14-11', in *idem*
(ed.), *Studien zu Kohelet* (SBAB, 26; Stuttgart: Katholisches Bibelwerk, 1998),
pp. 95-124; Hans Volker Kieweler, *Ben Sira zwischen Judentum und Hellenismus*
(BEATAJ, 30; Frankfurt: Lang, 1992); John J. Collins, *Jewish Wisdom in the
Hellenistic Age* (Louisville, KY: Westmister/John Knox Press, 1997), etc.

7.   See my survey of the sociological developments of the Hellenistic period in
Palestine, in *History of Israelite Religion*, II, pp. 534-44.

8.   Cf. Menachem Stern (ed.), *Greek and Latin Authors on Jews and Judaism*.
I. *From Herodotus to Plutarch* (Jerusalem: Israel Academy of Sciences and
Humanities, 2nd edn, 1976), p. 29: 'He [Moses] required those who dwelt in the

archaeological remains testify, there was an earlier high climax in the eigth century BCE.[9] And even the Persian period was not as bad as Lemche wants to make us believe. I am afraid that he has read too much in Xenophon's *Anabasis*[10] and too little in the Persepolis tablets[11] and the Elephantine papyri[12] to present a fair assessment. The latter sources reveal to us the sophisticated bureaucratic and effective organization of the Persian empire from which the Judaean community profited. Thus, from the general viewpoint of cultural development there is no reason why large parts of the Old Testament liturature could not have been written in earlier ages: in the Persian period or in the Babylonian and Assyrian period up to the eighth or even ninth centuries.

As well as this cultural argument, Lemche tried only to refute 'some objections of a more serious kind' against the possibility that the bulk of Old Testament literature, especially the historical literature, could originate so late.[13] The first objection deals with the differences in style and content between a kind of 'literature' like the Chronicler on the one hand, and the Yahwist (Lemche still believes in his existence!), the

---

land to rear their children, and since the offspring could be cared for at little costs, the Jews were from the start a populous nation'. His explanation of this fact is to be understood by his Greek perspective, which presupposes a highly developed urban society and contrasts it with a rural ideal.

9. Cf. Magen Broshi and Israel Finkelstein, 'The Population of Palestine in Iron Age II', *BASOR* 287 (1992), pp. 47-60, who estimates the population of the entire country in the eighth century BCE to have been about 400,000 people, a climax that was not reached again before the Hellenistic-Roman period.

10. Cf. Lemche, 'The Old Testament', p. 186 (= p. 312 below): 'The report by Xenophon thus hardly indicates that the adversaries of the Greeks were citizens in an efficiently governed state or empire!' It is a little bit strange that Niels Peter Lemche, who is so critical of the ideological view of biblical texts, takes this boasting adventure story of a Greek to be an objective 'primary source' for the conditions in the Persian Empire.

11. Cf. Heidemarie Koch, *Es kündet Daraeios der König...Vom Leben im persischen Großreich* (Kulturgeschichte der antiken Welt, 55; Mainz: Zabern, 1992), who concludes the information given in these tablets as follows: 'Dabei ist man immer wieder erstaunt, wie wohlorganisiert, aber auch wie "modern" in vielerlei Hinsicht das damalige persische Reich war' (p. 6).

12. Cf. Bazael Porten and Ada Yardeni, *Textbook of Aramaic Documents from Ancient Egypt* (4 vols.; Jerusalem: Bazael Porten, 1986, 1989, 1993, 1999). To get a first impression of the highly developed and specific tax and distribution system in Persian Egypt see, e.g., C3.7 and A6.2 (EP 26).

13. Lemche, 'The Old Testament', pp. 187-89 (= pp. 313-15 below).

book of Joshua, and 'not least the engaging stories of the books of Samuel' on the other hand. The second objection concerns the difference between the 'acknowledgeable Hellenistic' Hebrew, shown by the books of Qohelet or the Songs of Songs, and the 'standard Hebrew' in most Old Testament books. The third objection refers to the opinion that the Hebrew writings must be much older than their Greek translations, taking the Hellenistic dating of the Septuagint for granted.

Lemche does not have many arguments against these objections. He argues correctly that differences in style, content and perhaps even language[14] must not necessarily be explained by diachronic arguments; there is always the possibility of explaining such differences by the various milieus the authors of the texts come from. Moreover, the differences might have something to do with the authors' personal ability. Thus Lemche's explanation can be quite simple: 'the persons responsible for publishing the books of Chronicles were less able narrators than the Deuteronomistic Historians'.[15]

Apart from such problematical value judgments, I think Lemche is right in reckoning on the possibility of different groups being responsible for publishing different literatures in the same period. I tried to prove that something similar happened in the Persian period, when laymen and priestly intellectuals composed the Pentateuch arguing about the foundation of beliefs of the Jewish community. I tried to identify these intellectuals as commissioners of the two self-governmental councils of Persian Judah, the council of the elders and the congregation of the Priests, in order to explain why their work could be acknowledged by the whole community so easily. And I explained this literary activity in the framework of authorization of local legislation in

14. The language argument that the 'standard Hebrew' used, e.g. in the Deuteronomistic History and the book of Jeremiah on the one hand, corresponds with the Hebrew testified by the Lachish-letters dated by stratification in the early sixth century BCE and, on the other hand, differs clearly from the Hebrew in the book of Qohelet, showing specific features which are further developed in the rabbinic literature, cannot be put aside as easily as Lemche does; see the discussion below.

15. Lemche, 'The Old Testament', p. 188 (= p. 314 below). The example is a little bit awkward, because the fact that the Chronicler used the Deuteronomistic History for his composition forced a diachronic explanation in this case, whatever the space between them might have been. In my view, the style of the Chronicler, characterized by many allusions to and quotations from other religious texts, has nothing to do with the authors' literary ability, but is to be seen as the feature of a learned scribal class (see Albertz, *History of Israelite Religion*, II, p. 553).

the Persian Empire.[16] Of course, I am aware of the objections which can be raised against this socio-historical scenario,[17] but I think it is a hypothesis worth discussing.

However, what I really miss in Lemche's thesis is any attempt at doing a similar detailed socio-historical reconstruction. The reader of his article wants to know the following: who are the groups in the Hellenistic period? Who can be related to the different literary layers of the Pentateuch and the Deuteronomistic History? How can the different milieus they come from be determined in the Jewish-Hellenistic society? What are the interests of these authors in writing their texts? What are the reasons for mingling their writings together in a collective work? How is it possible that their writings gained such high acknowledgment from and authority for all Jewish groups so quickly, as is testified, for example, by the existence of many copies—19 for Deuteronomy alone!—in the library of the Qumran about 50 to 100 years later? But the reader looking for an answer to all these questions finds nothing in the article but is instead fobbed off with a nice little joke: 'Lemche's famous "three pub hypothesis" ', arguing that the Pentateuch came into being over a very short time in the latter part of the 3rd century BCE in three pubs in a Jewish suburb in Babylon'.[18] Assuming that the three pubs according to the Pentateuch sources 'Y', 'E' and 'P' actually existed, even then crucial questions are not answered. Who sent these

---

16. Albertz, *History of Israelite Religion*, II, pp. 466-93.

17. Cf. Udo Rüterswörden, 'Die persische Reichsautorisation der Thora: Fact or Fiction', *ZAR* 1 (1995), pp. 47-61. Even if the evidence for the Persian 'imperial authorization' is weaker than I assumed, there will be still the fact that, following the view of Ezra 7, the execution of the Jewish law—brought by Ezra from Persia—was supported by the authority of the Persian king (v. 26). Such an offensive collaboration with a gentile king in order to regulate even the holiest Jewish affairs would never has been invented if there was no cooperation at all. Not by chance, Rüterswörden refrained from discussing Ezra 7. Considering the criticism of Josef Wiesehöfer, ' "Reichsgesetz" oder "Einzelfallgerechtigkeit"? Bemerkungen zu P. Freis These von der achaimenidischen "Reichsautorisation" ', *ZAR* 1 (1995), pp. 36-46, we should perhaps restrict the Persian authorization to certain regions. But his argument that the Persians confirmed only those local regulations as far as their fiscal and administrative interests are concerned is overstated. The stele in Xanthos, the Passover letter in the Elephantine papyri and Ezra 7 clearly deal with cultic affairs too.

18. See 'How Does One Date an Expression of Mental History?', pp. 223-24 below.

guys into the pubs for some months? Who forced them to come out
with a common result? Most importantly, who paid for all the gallons
of beer they drank? Thus Lemche shows the possibility that literary
works or layers, which differ considerably in style and content, can
originate in the same age, but he fails to prove that, or how, the major
part of Old Testament literature actually came into being during the
Hellenistic age.

In his book *The Canaanites and their Land*[19] Lemche has given some
vague ideas about several possibilities relating to whether the Pentateuch was written in Egypt, Mesopotamia or Palestine. In his opinion,
the exodus motive was not invented in the Hellenistic age, because
already Hosea and Deutero-Isaiah referred to it, but it fitted the framework of the Hellenistic era well when a big Jewish diaspora existed in
Egypt. Concerning the prominence of the exodus theme in the Pentateuch, Lemche thinks 'that programme of these narratives was directly
aimed at the Jews of Egypt, the intention being to persuade these Jews
to return to their own country'.[20] However, other motives of the Pentateuch as Abraham's wandering out of Ur in Chaldea pointed to
Mesopotamia, and again other motifs to a Palestinian origin. Thus
Lemche finished his considerations with a *non liquet*: 'It is actually
impossible to decide with certainty in which place, Egypt, Jerusalem or
Mesopotamia, the historical books of the Old Testament were composed and edited'.[21] Thus the question of whether a plausible hypothesis about the origin of the historical books of the Bible in the Hellenistic era can be formulated is set aside to the future.

Ten or eight years passed. We all hoped that Niels Peter Lemche
would elaborate his ideas a little bit more. But if you read his article
below (pp. 200-24), you will see that it contains almost no additional
argument to support his hypothesis. He refers to an article of Jan-Wim
Wesselius about relations between the 'Primary History' of the Hebrew
Bible (Gen. 1–2 Kings 25) and Herodotus.[22] But even if one is ready to
accept Wesselius' parallels drawn on a high level of abstraction,[23]

---

19. *The Canaanites and their Land: The Tradition of the Canaanites* (JSOTSup,
110; Sheffield: JSOT Press, 1991).

20. *The Canaanites and their Land*, p. 167.

21. *The Canaanites and their Land*, p. 169.

22. 'Discontinuity, Congruence and the Making of the Hebrew Bible', *SJOT* 13
(1999), pp. 24-77.

23. Wesselius compares Israel's passing through the Reed Sea (Exod. 14) with

nothing is gained for a Hellenistic date for the Pentateuch and the Deuteronomistic History.[24] Knowing this, Lemche argues that in his view the Roman historian Livy seems more close to the historical writings of the Old Testament than Herodotus. But this remark does not help because Livy lived after the Hellenistic era (57 BCE–17 CE), and a claimed general similarity is no proper argument that can be used for dating. It must be emphasized: a Hellenistic dating cannot be supported by a Persian one. If Wesselius is right, then Lemche will be wrong and vice versa.

During all these years, I have to state, Lemche has not worked out any historical reconstruction of the Hellenistic period. In spite of his methodological demand that the non-biblical sources should be stressed over the biblical ones, he does not discuss what we can learn about Judaism in the Hellenistic age from Greek authors such as Theophrastus or Hecataeus of Abdera. I am no longer sure whether Niels Peter Lemche is interested in Israelite and Jewish history at all, apart from deconstructing it. For the period when the formative historical development of Judaism took place, according to his view, he has no historical imagination. The only point where I could see a little respect for the historical reality in his essay below is his concession that the pubs, where the Pentateuch might have been written, were not situated—as he

Xerxes's crossing of the Hellespont on two bridges of boats (Herodotus 7.54-56), the use of genealogies, and the division of both works into books, cf. 'Discontinuity', pp. 38-47. Anyhow, Wesselius overlooks the main difference between Greek and Israelite historiography: the absence of an self-revealing author, who comments on the reported events, in the latter; cf. the detailed argument of Erhard Blum, 'Ein Anfang der Geschichtsschreibung? Anmerkungen zur sog. Thronfolgegeschichte und zum Umgang mit Geschichte im alten Israel', *TRUMAH* 5 (1996), pp. 9-46. Thus it is highly improbable that Israelite historiography can directly be derived from the Greek one. A similar objection has to be raised against Flemming A.J. Nielsen, *The Tragedy in History: Herodotus and the Deuteronomistic History* (JSOTSup, 251; Copenhagen International Seminar, 4; Sheffield: Sheffield Academic Press, 1997), who is mentioned by Lemche too. Stressing the resemblances between both histories Flemming overlooked the important differences. And his proof that there were some similarities concerning the idea of tragedy and some other concepts, as interesting as they might be for cross-cultural studies, of their own cannot provide any evidence that both works must be written during the same period (so p. 164). Why should not similar ideas emerge in different cultures during different ages? For dating we need less ambigious arguments.

24. Wesselius argues for a date between 440 and 350 BCE, cf. 'Discontinuity', p. 47.

told us before, in the suburbs of Babylon—but of Seleucia, because the old capital was gradually abolished in the third century BCE and replaced by a new one.

Additionally, I have to state that Niels Peter Lemche has failed so far to formulate any literary-historical thesis worth talking about concerning the origins and redaction of the historical books of the Bible. Niels Peter Lemche rightly argued in his essay below against the black box model, used to put the bulk of the Old Testament literature into a dark age: 'The "black box" concept makes everything possible and allows the scholar to propose all kinds of theories that cannot be controlled. The procedure is illegitimate as it provides us with a hypothesis that cannot be falsified.'[25] I have tried to bring some light in the darkness of the Persian period, but I cannot see that Niels Peter Lemche has tried to do anything similar in favour of the Hellenistic period. His refusal to elaborate his vague ideas is met by his own reproach: an unelaborated hypothesis 'is illegitimate', because it 'cannot be falsified'.

The reader understands and smiles now: the confusion has come to an end. It was just a joke.

A Refutation

Having shown that Niels Peter Lemche did not offer any evidence for the assumption that the historical books of the Bible originated in the Hellenistic period, I will try to find some convincing arguments that they could not have emerged in this era, but must have been written earlier. Of course I am aware of the fact that by elaborating a thesis I expose myself to the danger of being refuted, but I think that is our job as biblical scholars.

In my view the Deuteronomistic History (Deut. 1–2 Kings 25) is the easier case: as used and interpreted by Chronicles, which can roughly be dated in the late Persian or the early Hellenistic period,[26] it must be a text which originated earlier. Moreover, since the Chronicler conceded so much importance to it, there was probably a longer interval of time between the two works during which the latter could win a considerable authority. These considerations correspond with the dating we can establish on the basis of the Deuteronomistic History itself. At its end it mentions an event that must have been of crucial importance for its

25. See his essay below, p. 216.
26. Cf. Albertz, *History of Israelite Religion*, II, p. 545 and Peltonen in his present essay below, pp. 225-71.

authors (2 Kgs 25.27-30): Jehoiachin's release out of a Babylonian prison, in which he might have been thrown in connection with the murder of Gedaliah by a member of the royal family (Jer. 41.1-2).[27] This event not only establishes a clear *terminius post quem*, the accession year of Evil-Merodach in 562 BCE, but also offers the possibility of narrowing the *terminus ante quem*: since this hopeful report about Jehoiachin's release is to be understood in the context of the exilic dispute—whether Jehoiachin or one of his sons (Zerubbabel) should ever reign in Judah again or not when the opportunity for a new beginning should arise (Jer. 23.27-30; Hag. 2.20-23)—then this passage could not be written after the dispute was negatively decided by the historical events, that is, when Zerubbabel disappeared from the scene in 518 BCE or, at the latest, at the end of the sixth century BCE.[28] Since there is not any anachronistic hint in the Deuteronomistic History which points to a later date than the sixth century, it can be dated in the last third of this century with a high degree of probability.

Compared with that, the date of the Pentateuch is the more serious problem. I think there are good arguments that exclude its origin during the second part of the third century. First, the oldest scrolls of the books of Pentateuch, which are found in Qumran, are dated up to the midst of the third century BCE on paleographical grounds.[29] Second, the translation of the Pentateuch into Greek, which according to the Aristeas letter took place under the reign of Ptolemy II Philadelphos (285–246 BCE), is to be dated around the midst of the century. That does not only

27. For the reasons and more details cf. Rainer Albertz, *Die Exilszeit* (Biblische Enzyklopädie, 7; Stuttgart: W. Kohlhammer, forthcoming).

28. Cf. the scenario I outlined in 'Wer waren die Deuteronomisten?', pp. 325-37, which I have elaborated further in my article 'Die verhinderte Restauration', which will be published in the forthcoming Festschrift for Rolf Rendtorff. According to André Lemaire, 'Zorobabel et la Judée à la lumière de l'épigraphie (Śn du VIe s. av. J.-C.)', *RB* 103 (1996), pp. 48-57, esp. pp. 56-57, who identified the names of two postexilic seals with a son and a daughter of Zerubbabel, the leadership of the Davidides did not fail suddenly, but ran down more slowly. In my opinion his interpretation can be disputed. However, at the end of the sixth century the royal family has disappeared from the political stage of Judah anyway. The establishment of a non-monarchic constitution is testified in the midst of the fifth century.

29. Cf. 4Q Exod^e, 4Q paleoDeut^s and Johann Maier, *Die Qumran-Essener: Die Texte vom Toten Meer* (2 vols.; Munich: Reinhard, 1995), II, pp. 17, 28. Even if paleographical arguments can fail sometimes, we should not doubt the judgments of the experts generally!

presuppose that the Hebrew text of the Pentateuch existed but also that it had already won the authority to be the foundation charter of the Jews, even for those who lived in Alexandria. Thus the Pentateuch could not be written immediately before that date as Lemche has argued. Finally, the language argument is still of some weight in this connection; the lack of typical features of Hellenistic Hebrew in the Pentateuch points to a pre-Hellenistic date for its completion.

In my view the books of Chronicles presuppose the Pentateuch too. In 1 Chronicles 1–7 parts of its genealogical skeleton are used; and I have tried to show in detail how the Chronicler adjusted the older Deuteronomistic History to the younger legislation of the Pentateuch.[30] I think that can be an argument not only for the existence of the text but also for the 'canonical' authority of the Pentateuch at the end of the Persian or the beginning of the Hellenistic period. Moreover, I argued that the composition of the Pentateuch was probably far developed in the midst of the fifth century BCE, because Nehemiah's mission (444–432) shows clear similarities to the Dtn./Dtr. and priestly legislation of the Pentateuch.[31] And if we date Ezra's mission (Ezra 7) to the seventh year of Artaxerxes II (398 BCE), his execution of the 'law of God of Heaven' can be interpreted as the event that finished the canonical process of the Pentateuch. However, these arguments are not unambigious, I admit.

Therefore I will introduce here an additional argument for my thesis that the Pentateuch cannot have originated in the Hellenistic period, but must have been composed earlier. It has the advantage of coming from a non-biblical source so that it gives us the opportunity to find some external evidence. I am referring to the report on the Jews given by Hecataeus of Abdera, transmitted to us by Diodorus Siculus through the Bibliotheca of Photius.[32] Hecataeus lived at the beginning of the Hellenistic period, his report being dated about 300 BCE.

---

30. Cf. Albertz, *History of Israelite Religion*, II, pp. 610-13.

31. Cf. Albertz, *History of Israelite Religion*, II, pp. 503-504. Neh. 13.25-27 refers to the dtn./dtr. prohibition of mixed marriages (Deut. 7.3; cf. 1 Kgs 11); Neh. 13.4-13 presupposes the relation of priests and Levites, typical for P (cf. Num. 18.25-32).

32. See Stern (ed.), *Greek and Latin Authors*, I, pp. 20-34, esp. pp. 26-29. The source has been already introduced in the discussion of the Seminar by Lester L. Grabbe (see pp. 131-33 below), but so far it has not been discussed in the literary-historical context.

On the one hand, Hecataeus's report in part differs widely from what we know about Israelite history and Jewish customs from biblical and ancient Near Eastern sources: after the Jews were expelled from Egypt because of a pestilence and driven into later Judaea, which was utterly uninhabited at that time (§§1-2), their leader Moses founded Jerusalem as well as some other cities, established the temple, drew up their laws and ordered their political institutions (§3). He installed all the priests, who should not only carry out the temple services but also function as judges and guardians of laws and customs (§§4-5). In order to do all their duties without any distraction they possessed a larger quantity of land than ordinary people (§7). They elected one colleague whom they regarded as superior in wisdom and virtue to be the high priest in order to act as messenger between the people and God's commandments in the assemblies. For this reason, according to Hecataeus, the Jews never had a king (§5). On the contrary, it was Moses who led out military expeditions against the neighbouring tribes and made provision for warfare in a later phase of their history (§6). Moreover, in providing for a good and cheap education of Jewish children, he made sure that the Jews became a populous nation all the time (§8).

Obviously in this presentation of Jewish history the whole period of the Israelite and Judaean kingdoms is omitted. Moses, not David, is seen to be the founder of Jerusalem. He also plays the role of Joshua to some extent. Next to him the authority of the priests and especially the high priest is most prominent. The claim that the priests owned land property contradicts the regulations made in Num. 18.23-24; Deut. 10.9; 12.12; 18.1.

On the other hand, Hecataeus's report corresponds in many interesting details with what we particularly know about postexilic Judaism. It mentions the—ideal—division of the whole people into 12 tribes (§3; cf. Num. 1; 7; 26, etc.), the aniconic and monotheistic concept of God (§4), the fact that Jewish regulations for cult and daily life differed from those of other nations (cf. Lev. 18.1-5, 24-30, etc.) and had—in the eyes of a Greek—an unnatural (ἀπάνθρωπον) and intolerant (μισόξενον) touch (§4), and the—ideal—custom to distribute equal allottments of land to all private citizens and to prohibit them from selling their individual plots in order to prevent the oppression of the poorer classes (§7, cf. Lev. 25, esp. v. 23; Ezra 47.21–48.29). These details are astonishingly reliable.

How can this contradiction be explained? The reliable details make it

highly probable that Hecataeus used some authentic Jewish information, maybe in a written or in a oral form. One part of the differences
can clearly be explained by the fact that Hecataeus portrayed, of course,
the emergence of Judaism from a Greek perspective: according to the
concept of Greek colonization Moses is described as the head of a
colony (ἀποικία, cf. §3), who not only founded the new cities, but also
functioned as founder of the cult, legislator (νομοθέτης, cf. §6), admin-
istrator of the political institutions (πολιτεία, cf. §3), army commander
and distributor of land (§7). Also most of his rationalizing reasons and
explanations he introduced can be derived from his Greek background.[33] This Greek outlook testifies to the authenticity of Hecataeus's
report, which was possibly a little bit reworked and shortened by
Diodorus Siculus, but never underwent any Jewish reinterpretation.[34]

However, the *interpretatio graeca* does not explain the main differences. These must have to do with a specific Jewish self-portrait presented to Hecataeus by his Jewish informer or source.[35] Obviously, this
informer or source promoted a priestly perspective as has often beeen
noted. But much more important is the fact that in this priestly perspective of the present—postexilic—Jewish reality in Judah, the capital,
the cult, the law and and all cultic and political institutions were

33. Cf. W. Jaeger, 'Greeks and the Jews: The First Greek Records of Jewish
Religion and Civilization', *JR* 18 (1938), pp. 127-43; Doron Mendels, '*Hecataeus
of Abdera* and a Jewish "patrios politeia"', *ZAW* 95 (1983), pp. 97-110, esp. pp. 98-
102; and more generally Wolfgang Leschhorn, *Gründer der Stadt: Studien zu einem
politisch-religiösen Phänomen der griechischen Geschichte* (Palingenesia, 20;
Stuttgart: Steiner Verlag, Wiesbaden, 1984), pp. 83-117; Irad Malkin, *Religion and
Colonization in Ancient Greece* (Leiden: E.J. Brill, 1987), pp. 1-13. However, it
must be noted that the picture drawn of Moses also differs from the role of a Greek
οἰκιστήρ in so far as his mission to found Jerusalem is not induced by a divine
oracle and he is not venerated by the colony in a founder's cult after his death.

34. In contrast the Hecataeus tradition, transmitted by Josephus in *Apion* 1.183-
204, is totally reworked by Jews, cf. Stern (ed.), *Greek and Latin Authors*, I, pp. 21-
24, 35-44.

35. So rightly M. Stern and O. Murray, 'Hecataeus of Abdera and Theophrastus
on Jews and Egyptians', *JEA* (1973), pp. 159-68; and Mendels, 'Hecataeus of
Abdera', pp. 101-109. In addition, John Dillery, 'Hecataeus of Abdera: Hyperbor-
eans, Egypt, and the *Interpretatio Graeca*', *Historia* 47 (1998), pp. 255-75, convincingly argues against the opinion that the *interpretatio graeca* of Hecataeus pre-
vents his proper understanding of the foreign culture. On the contrary, it is to be
seen as his serious effort to transfer important informations about Oriental societies
to his own Greek one.

directly derived from the foundation history under the leadership of Mose. This foundation history began with the Exodus from Egypt and ended with the immigration to Palestine, but ignored totally all the history from Joshua to Zedekiah. I think this specific concept can easily be explained: we are dealing with a kind of Judaism which was strictly based on the Pentateuch,[36] but had deliberately excluded the Deuteronomistic History from its foundation charter.[37]

This thesis can be supported by several additional observations. First, according to Hecataeus's report the exclusion of Israel's state history concerns the denial of any Israelite kingship in connection with his description of the prominent status of the priests. This agrees not only with the anti-monarchic tendency of the Pentateuch itself,[38] but also with the non-monarchic constitution of the postexilic Judaean community.[39] Especially the priestly layers of the Pentateuch aim to establish the independence of the priests from the king and the quasi-monarchic status of the high priest by the decree of Moses (Lev. 8-9),[40] similar to the description of Hecataeus.

Second, the portrait painted of Moses in Hecataeus's report—to be the legislator not only with regard to the warfare, but also and most prominently with regard to the cult, its rites and its sacrifices—presupposes the combination of deuteronomic (cf. Deut. 20) and priestly legislation (cf. Exod. 25-31; 35-40; Lev. 1–16) in the Pentateuch. That means, as far as we can see on the basis of literary-criticism, its final redaction must already have taken place.[41]

---

36. The parallels to the books to Ezra–Nehemiah, which Mendels, 'Hecataeus of Abdera', pp. 100-107, stresses, do not disprove this conclusion, because the books Ezra and Nehemiah testify to a Torah-based Judaism as well. That the immigration of Israel to Palestine looks more like the picture of how the return from the Exile is described by the book of Ezra—as Mendels pointed out correctly ('Hecataeus of Abdera', p. 99)—has to do with the mythical kind of the Torah concept where the founding past and the postexilic present, neglecting any historical distance, are directly jointed together.

37. With the exception of the book of Deuteronomy, of course. The end of the foundation charter was located directly after the death of Moses.

38. R. Albertz, *History of Israelite Religion*, II, pp. 471-74, 484-86.

39. Cf. Albertz, *History of Israelite Religion*, II, pp. 446-47.

40. See Albertz, *History of Israelite Religion*, II, pp. 485-86.

41. Since the deuteronomic legislation (Deut. 12–26) and the pre-priestly Sinai story (Exod. 19–24; 32–34) show only a little interest in the temple, sacrifices and cultic affairs, Hecataeus's report cannot refer to this earlier stage of the Penta-

Third, the manner in which the function of the high priest is described by the report corresponds to the idea of revelation unfolded in the Pentateuch. According to Hecataeus the high priest acts as a messenger (ἄγγελος) to the people of God's commandments (§5). In their assemblies it is his duty to announce what is ordained and to expound the commandments. What is meant here, becomes clear by the following information, that all Jewish laws were appended with the statement: 'These are the words that Moses heard from God and declares unto the Jews' (§6). That means: All revelation, given by God, is necessarily mediated by Moses. There is no heavenly revelation apart from him. The high priest is not an immediate messenger of God,[42] but the mediator between God's commandments (τοῦ θεοῦ προσταγμάτων), declared by Moses, and the people. In other words, the high priest is committed to the Pentateuch, especially to its laws. Thus his duty is only to announce (ἐκφέρειν) the right commandment of the Pentateuch to the people in a specific situation or, in the case that there were competing regulations in the Pentateuch, or instances that did not fit the commandments exactly, to interpret (ἑρμενεύειν, cf. §6) the legislation of the Pentateuch by supplementing it with his oral Torah.

In the Pentateuch God's extraordinary revelation to Moses which cannot be compared to any other experience, even a prophetic one is stressed throughout (Num. 12.1-16; Deut. 34.10-11) against priestly and prophetic claims. At the conclusion of the laws in the Pentateuch we can indeed find a subscription similar to the sentence that Hecataeus cited: 'These are the commandments which the Lord gave Moses for the Israelites on Mount Sinai' (Lev. 27.34; cf. Num. 36.13). Especially in the priestly legislation of the Pentateuch, the laws are often headed

---

teuchal tradition. Moses did not become the founder of the whole cult before the Priestly Code or better the Priestly Composition, which according to Erhard Blum, *Studien zur Komposition des Pentateuch* (BZAW, 189; Berlin: W. de Gruyter, 1990), pp. 219-85; 361-82, constituted not the very last, but the latest important redaction of the Pentateuch.

42. So the formulation of Mal. 2.7, taken as a reference by Mendels, 'Hecataeus of Abdera', p. 106, overlooking the difference. But the specific formulation in Hecataeus's report must not be levelled. It testifies to his effort to describe the theological concept of his Jewish informer or source as correctly as possible! Astonishingly enough the passage was completely misunderstood by Francis R. Walton, 'The Messenger of God in Hecataeus of Abdera', *HTR* 48 (1955), pp. 255-57, who thinks that Hecataeus ascribes a prophetic function to the high priest. Thus Hecataeus on this point seems to be more sophisticated than his modern commentators!

with the stereotyped formula 'The Lord spoke to Moses and said: Speak to…',[43] and so are describing the revelation through Moses again and again. Also this formula is intentionally very close to what is cited by Hecataeus. The demand to Aaron in particular, who represents the high priest, and his sons (which means the priest in general), 'to teach the Israelites all decrees which the Lord has spoken through Moses' is given in Lev. 10.11, ending a conflict in which the priesthood has acted in an unauthorized manner (10.1-10). Thus as far as the priests are concerned, there is nearly a total agreement between the priestly concept in the Pentateuch and the priestly self-understanding transmitted by Hecataeus.

There are only two possible objections which can be raised against the thesis that the Judaism which Hecataeus referred to is already committed to the Pentateuch. The first is the absence of all political officials in the picture of Israelite history presented by Hecataeus, and the second is the violation of the command that priests should not possess any land (Num. 18.23-24; Deut. 10.9; 12.12: 18.1). Concerning the first objection it has to be stated that the absence of any functions for laymen is really peculiar, as we know from other sources that besides the 'congregation of priests' headed by the high priest there existed in Persian times, attested in the second half of the fifth century BCE at least, a 'council of elders' which claimed the political leadership of the Judaean community. This claim was also rooted in the Pentateuch by the story that the spirit of Moses came over the 70 elders so that they shared his authority concerning leadership (Num. 11.4-34).[44] The denial of the political and religious claims of the leading laymen in the Jewish community may be partly to do with the one-sidedness of the Jewish informer or source Hecataeus depends on. But it is also possible that in the late Persian and early Hellenistic period the status of the priests, especially the high priest, has become more prominent than in the earlier Persian era. Thus in the Judaean community attested by Hecataeus

---

43. Lev. 4.1; 7.22, 28; 12.1; 17.1; 18.1; 19.1; 22.1; 23.1, 9, 23; cf. similar Lev. 1.1; 16.1; 25.1; 27.1, etc. Sometimes in these formulas Aaron is mentioned together with Moses and both are ordered by God to teach the people; cf., e.g., Lev. 11.1; 15.1, but this does not offend the outstanding authority of Moses in principal, because those cases are restricted to typical priestly instructions for the people. Each time that priestly affairs are concerned, God's commandments are mediated by Moses only!

44. Albertz, *History of Israelite Religion*, II, pp. 446-47, 479-80.

the balance of power was probably already shifting in the direction of a hierocracy, which became manifest in the later Hellenistic period.[45]

Concerning the second objection we must be reminded of the fact that the reality often disagrees with religious demands, especially if there were economic interests against them. Even in this specific case there existed the possibility of justifying priestly land possession in some way, because this was explicitly allowed by the priestly prophet Ezekiel in his vision of an ideal future (Ezek. 45.4-5; 48.10-14). Admittedly, the support of priests and Levites was regulated by the Pentateuch (Lev. 1–7; 24.5-9; Num. 18) in contrast to Ezekiel's picture, but the possibility that the priests came to a compromise solution in order to guarantee the temple service is not totally inconceivable, if we regard the basis of their theology.

Thus we can conclude: Hecataeus's report is a reliable source of Judaism in the late Persian and the early Hellenistic period in so far as we take its Greek shape and the one-sidedness of his Jewish informer into account.

Concerning the disputed Hellenistic origin of the Pentateuch, first the report definitely refutes the opinion that only in the Hellenistic period did the Exodus tradition take on the status of a foundation myth of Israel. It clearly testifies instead that the Exodus must have reached this status earlier, at the latest in the Persian period. Secondly, the report makes it completely unlikely that the Pentateuch was not composed before Hellenistic times. On the contrary, it attests a kind of Judaism which is already based on and shaped by the Torah. Thus not only the last redaction but also the 'canonical' acknowledgment of the Pentateuch had actually happened before, in the Persian period. The date for the final enforcement about 400 BCE assumed above is also supported by the report of Hecataeus of Abdera.

Thus the rhetorical question which Nils Peter Lemche put in the title of his article must be denied: the Old Testament, at its core, is not a Hellenistic book, definitely not.

---

45. Cf. Albertz, *History of Israelite Religion*, II, pp. 448, 535-36.

DEUTERONOMISTS, PERSIANS, GREEKS, AND THE DATING OF THE ISRAELITE TRADITION

Hans M. Barstad

1. *Introductory Remarks*

Recently, we have been witnessing a later and later dating of more and more of the texts of the Hebrew Bible. Obviously, to anyone interested in the use of these texts as possible sources for information about the history of Palestine during the Iron Age the question of dating is of vital importance. For this reason it may be worthwhile to take a closer look at recent trends in this field.

However, before we start examining recent developments more closely, we should not fail to remind ourselves that 'late dating' is not something new in biblical scholarship. Even if we cannot by a long way talk about any consensus, many 'moderate' scholars have for a long time dated the greater part of the Hebrew Bible to the Persian period. When the Hellenistic period is referred to, the book of Daniel of course springs to mind.[1] It remains a fact, however, that several other biblical texts have also been dated, with varying success, to 'the Hellenistic era'. The texts in question are as follows: Isaiah 24–27, Isaiah 65–66, Joel, Jonah, Habakkuk, Zephaniah, Haggai, Zechariah 9–14, Malachi, Psalms, Job, Proverbs 1–9, Ruth, Song of Songs, Qohelet, Lamentations, Esther, Ezra and Nehemiah, and Chronicles.[2]

---

1. J.J. Collins, *Daniel: A Commentary on the Book of Daniel* (Hermeneia; Minneapolis: Fortress Press, 1993), pp. 34-38.

2. Isaiah 24–27: W.R. Millar, *Isaiah 24–27 and the Origin of Apocalyptic* (HSM, 11; Missoula, MT: Scholars Press, 1976), pp. 16-17. Isaiah 65–66: For Hellenistic datings of Isa. 65–66 see B. Schramm, *The Opponents of Third Isaiah: Reconstructing the Cultic History of the Restoration* (JSOTSup, 193; Sheffield: Sheffield Academic Press, 1995), pp. 17-18. Joel: S. Bergler, *Joel als Schrift-interpret* (BEATAJ, 16; Frankfurt: Peter Lang, 1988), p. 363. Jonah: J. Limburg, *Jonah: A Commentary* (OTL; London: SCM Press, 1993), p. 28 n. 18. Habakkuk: G. Fohrer, *Einleitung in das Alte Testament* (Heidelberg: Quelle & Meyer, 11th rev.

From the references just given we understand that it is nothing new in itself to date large portions of the texts of the Hebrew Bible to the Hellenistic period. Yet if we compare recent studies in the field with earlier contributions, there are some conspicuous differences. Clearly, there is now a much more consistent and deliberate dating to the Hellenistic era. Moreover, the late dating now appears to embrace also the *historical* traditions of the Hebrew Bible. This particular circumstance, seemingly, also affects the view on the historical trustworthiness of the texts. Whereas it was felt earlier that the Deuteronomistic History, despite its ideological bias, contained at least some reliable historical information from pre-exilic Israel, this is to a lesser degree the case today.[3] One

edn, 1969), pp. 499-500. Zephaniah: P.R. House, *Zephaniah: A Prophetic Drama* (JSOTSup, 69; Bible and Literature Series, 16; Sheffield: Almond Press, 1988), p. 13. Haggai: C.L. Meyers and E.M. Meyers, *Haggai, Zechariah 1–8: A New Translation with Introduction and Commentary* (AB, 25B; New York: Doubleday, 1987), p. lxx. Zechariah 9–14: O. Kaiser, *Einleitung in das Alte Testament: Eine Einführung in ihre Ergebnisse und Probleme* (Gütersloh: Gütersloher Verlagshaus, 1969), pp. 222-24. Malachi: A.E. Hill, *Malachi: A New Translation with Introduction and Commentary* (AB, 25D; New York: Doubleday, 1998), p. 77. Psalms: M. Treves, *The Dates of the Psalms: History and Poetry in Ancient Israel* (Pisa: Giardini, 1988). Job: For scholars who have dated Job to the Hellenistic period, see J. Lévêque, 'La datation du livre de Job', in J. Emerton (ed.), *Congress Volume, Vienna 1980* (VTSup, 32; Leiden: E.J. Brill, 1981), pp. 206-19 (209 n. 13). Proverbs 1–9: R.E. Murphy, *The Tree of Life. An Exploration of Biblical Wisdom Literature* (ABRL; New York: Doubleday, 1990), p. 19. Ruth: J.M. Sasson, *Ruth: A New Translation with a Philological Commentary and a Formalist-Folklorist Interpretation* (The Biblical Seminar, 10; Sheffield: Sheffield Academic Press, 1989), p. 240. Song of Songs: For a dating of Song of Songs to the Hellenistic era, see M.H. Pope, *Song of Songs. A New Translation with Introduction and Commentary* (AB, 7C; New York: Doubleday, 1977), pp. 25-26. Qohelet: See J.L. Crenshaw, *Ecclesiastes: A Commentary* (OTL; Philadelphia: Westminster Press, 1987), p. 50. Lamentations: C. Westermann, *Die Klagelieder: Forschungsgeschichte und Auslegung* (Neukirchen–Vluyn: Neukirchener Verlag, 1990), p. 57. Esther: C.A. Moore, *Esther: Introduction, Translation, and Notes* (AB, 7B; New York: Doubleday, 1971), pp. lvii-lx. Ezra and Nehemiah: O. Kaiser, *Einleitung in das Alte Testament: Eine Einführung in ihre Ergebnisse und Probleme* (Gütersloh: Gütersloher Verlagshaus, 1969), pp. 149-50; H.G.M. Williamson, *Ezra, Nehemiah* (WBC, 16; Waco, TX: Word Books, 1985), p. xxxvi. Chronicles: For scholars who have dated Chronicles to the Hellenistic period, see S. Japhet, *I and II Chronicles. A Commentary* (Old Testament Library; London: SCM Press, 1993), p. 24. See also K. Peltonen, pp. 225-71 below.

3.   Needless to say, not everyone would agree about these developments.

important result of this particular development is the recent attempt to look for and to find Greek influence in, for example, the Deuteronomistic History. A few quotations may illustrate this development.

A scholar such as Lemche writes: 'The writers who invented the "history of Israel" seem to have modelled their history on a Greek pattern'.[4]

And Bolin:

> Very little of the HB [Hebrew Bible], either in content or composition, is to be found in any historical era earlier than the Persian Period. What I have attempted to demonstrate is that the Persian Period is not the place to look for the writing of the biblical texts. Rather, the bible itself points us to the beginning of the Hellenistic period for that process.[5]

And Nielsen:

> The fact that the similarities between the Herodotean and the Deuteronomistic historiography also include the tragic ornamentation of the course of history supports the assumption that the Hellenic literary tradition, which Herodotus was part of, influenced the Deuteronomistic history. Thus it becomes probable that DtrH [the Deuteronomistic History] was written at a time and in a milieu where the Hellenistic influence was important in the Israelite or more correctly, the Jewish tradition.[6]

And Wesselius:

> The most likely scenario for the origin of Primary History therefore seems to be that a Jewish author (alternatively, leader of a group of authors) who was well versed in Greek literature set out to write a history of his own people at some time in the third quarter of the fifth century BCE or a little later...such a person may not have been very common in the Persian era, but a few decades later, still before or a short time after the conquests of Alexander the Great, it was considered conceivable that there would be Jews who would know the Greek language and

Among several recent negative reactions, see, for instance, F.E. Deist, 'The Yehud Bible: A Belated Divine Miracle?', *JNSL* 23.1 (1997), pp. 117-42; N. Na'aman, 'The Contribution of Royal Inscriptions for a Re-Evaluation of the Book of Kings as a Historical Source', *JSOT* 82 (1999), pp. 3-17.

4. N.P. Lemche, 'The Old Testament—A Hellenistic Book?', *SJOT* 7 (1993), pp. 163-93 (183).

5. T.M. Bolin, 'When the End is the Beginning: The Persian Period and the Origins of the Biblical Tradition', *SJOT* 10 (1996), pp. 3-15 (14-15).

6. F.A.J. Nielsen, *The Tragedy in History: Herodotus and the Deuteronomistic History* (JSOTSup, 251; Copenhagen International Seminar, 4; Sheffield: Sheffield Academic Press, 1997), p. 164.

culture very well, so there is no reason why such a combination of religion and knowledge would have been possible earlier.[7]

From the quotations above it may appear that something 'new' has
entered the discussion concerning the Hebrew Bible and its 'late' dating. It is now felt that even the Deuteronomist(s) are building on Greek
literary models and consequently, that it, has become necessary to make
comparisons between the historiography of the Hebrew Bible and Greek
sources, above all Herodotus's *Historiae*.[8]

For my own part, I do not think that it is completely without value to
make comparisons between the Deuteronomistic History and Herodotus;
however, we have to know what we are doing. The real danger starts
when we claim that the biblical texts are *modelled* on Greek prototypes.
Undoubtedly, there are similarities between the Pentateuch and Herodotus, and the Deuteronomistic History and Herodotus. The issue here is
not that this is not the case. Having read Herodotus I can easily see that
there are similarities. It is, however, the nature of these similarities that
must concern us here. We may, for instance, find even more similarities
between the Deuteronomistic History and the Icelandic sagas. For my
own part, I have pointed to some really striking parallels between the
Deuteronomistic history and the history of Ireland at the end of the
nineteenth and the beginning of the twentieth centuries.[9] This, though,
is not problematic: because of the distance in time no one would claim
that the Deuteronomistic History was modelled on Irish or Icelandic
prototypes!

When dealing with comparisons, we may, tentatively, attempt to sort
out parallels into 'historical' or 'typological'. When we make historical

---

7.   J.-W. Wesselius, 'Discontinuity, Congruence and the Making of the Hebrew
Bible', *SJOT* 13 (1999), pp. 24-77 (45). In his article, Wesselius discusses the
Primary History (= the Pentateuch and the Deuteronomistic History), Nehemiah,
Ezra and Daniel. He compares, in detail, the Primary History and Herodotus's *His-
tories* (pp. 38-48 and *passim*), and concludes that it is modelled on Herodotus, and
written between 440 and 350 BCE.

8.   Obviously, this is not as 'new' as some may believe. Among those scholars
who have compared Herodotus's work to the historiography of the Hebrew Bible
particular mention should be made of J. Van Seters. See his *In Search of History:
Historiography in the Ancient World and the Origins of Biblical History* (New
Haven: Yale University Press, 1983), *passim*.

9.   H.M. Barstad, 'History and the Hebrew Bible', in Lester L. Grabbe (ed.),
Can a 'History of Israel' Be Written? (JSOTSup, 245; ESHM, 1; Sheffield: Sheffield Academic Press, 1997), pp. 37-64 (56-57).

comparisons we compare things within the 'same' historical, linguistic or literary context ('culture', 'social system', 'civilization'). Typically, comparisons made between Assyrian laws and the laws of the Hebrew Bible would fall under this category. We should, however, always keep in mind that a historical comparison should *not* be excessively interested in questions of origin or in whether this or that particular phenomenon is the result of cultural diffusionism. Such views, apparently highly popular in earlier days, will as a rule be too speculative to be really prolific. Mostly, they are also based on inadequate 'evolutionist' views of how cultures grow and develop.

With 'typological' comparisons I mean in the present context comparisons which may be made between literary phenomena appearing in quite different contexts, and from no matter how distant periods of time or localities. Similarities in separate cultures would, as far as we know, in the majority of cases not follow historic–genetic connections, but rather be the result of how the human brain works and of how humans, for some reason, behave in 'similar' manners in 'similar' situations. Parallels between the Deuteronomistic History and the history of Ireland at the end of the nineteenth and the beginning of the twentieth centuries should be classified as 'typological'. As for similarities between biblical historiographical texts and Herodotus's *Historiae* these are undoubtedly far too general to be of any real relevance in a discussion about provenance and influence.[10] This fact should be recognized no matter whether

---

10. Nielsen has pointed to many interesting similarities between tragedy in Herodotus's *Historiae* and in the Deuteronomistic History. However, since tragedy is also a feature of ancient Hebrew literature, it is not possible to say that tragedy in the Hebrew Bible is modelled on Greek prototypes. Many authors have discussed tragedy in the Hebrew Bible. Important works, also used by Nielsen, are D.M. Gunn, *The Fate of King Saul: An Interpretation of a Biblical Story* (JSOTSup, 14; Sheffield: JSOT Press, 1980), and, more thorough, J.P. Fokkelman, *Narrative Art and Poetry in the Books of Samuel: A Full Interpretation based on Stylistic and Structural Analyses. II. The Crossing Fates (I Sam. 13–31 & II Sam. 1)* (Studia Semitica Neerlandica, 23; Assen: Van Gorcum, 1986). For further references, see M.A. Powell, *The Bible and Modern Literary Criticism: A Critical Assessment and Annotated Bibliography* (Bibliographies and Indexes in Religious Studies, 22; New York: Greenwood Press, 1992), pp. 468-69 (index, under 'tragedy'). We should not fail to notice, however, that it has also been claimed that Greek and Hebrew tragedies are completely different literary modes. See N. Frye, *The Great Code: The Bible and Literature* (San Diego: Harcourt Brace Jovanovich, 1983), p. 181. If

one believes that the influence goes from Herodotus to the Bible (cf. the examples which I have referred to above) or from the Hebrew Bible to Herodotus.[11]

2. *Deuteronomy*

The book of Deuteronomy is vital as a background for any understanding of the Deuteronomistic History, irrespective of the view one takes on the relationship between Deuteronomy and the books of Joshua, Judges, Samuel and Kings, or the relationship between the 'Priestly Work' (Genesis, Exodus, Leviticus, Numbers) and Deuteronomy and the Deuteronomistic history. It is not, on any account, possible to go into any details on such problems here. Nor is it possible to touch upon the many difficult problems relating to dating, composition or literary development of Deuteronomy.[12]

accepted, such an assertion of course makes all assertions about Hellenistic influence in this particular area meaningless.

11. For this reason the view of Mandell and Freedman that Herodotus was influenced by Genesis–Kings (= Primary History), dated exactly to 561–560 BCE, when composing his *Historiae*, is equally to be rejected. Mandell and Freedman believe that Herodotus had access to an Aramaic translation of Genesis–Kings. See S. Mandell and D.N. Freedman, *The Relationship between Herodotus' History and Primary History* (South Florida Studies in the History of Judaism, 60; Atlanta: Scholars Press, 1993).

12. There are many useful surveys of the history of research in recent contributions on Deuteronomy and the Deuteronomists. For a survey of the older literature, see H.D. Preuss, *Deuteronomium* (Erträge der Forschung, 164; Darmstadt: Wissenschaftliche Buchgesellschaft, 1982). See further M.A. O'Brien, *The Deuteronomistic History Hypothesis: A Reassessment* (OBO, 92; Freiburg: Universitätsverlag, 1989), pp. 2-23; T. Römer and A. de Pury, 'L'historiographie deutéronomiste (HD): Histoire de la recherche et enjeux du débat', in A. de Pury, T. Römer and J.-D. Macchi (eds.), *Israël construit son histoire: L'historiographie deutéronomiste à la lumière des recherches récentes* (Le Monde de la Bible, 34; Geneva: Labor et Fides, 1996), pp. 9-120; G.A. Knoppers, *Two Nations under God: The Deuteronomistic History of Solomon and the Dual Monarchies*. I. *The Reign of Solomon and the Rise of Jeroboam* (HSM, 52; Atlanta: Scholars Press, 1993), pp. 1-50; E.T. Mullen, *Narrative History and Ethnic Boundaries: The Deuteronomistic Historian and the Creation of Israelite National Identity* (Semeia Studies; Atlanta: Scholars Press, 1993), pp. 1-18; H.A. Kenik, *Design for Kingship: The Deuteronomistic Narrative Technique in 1 Kings 3:4–15* (SBLDS, 69; Chico, CA: Scholars Press, 1983), pp. 1-26.

In its *present* context Deuteronomy forms a part of the great story of the Israelite people in antiquity. In Exodus, Leviticus, Numbers and Deuteronomy we find the account of the prophet and law-giver Moses who leads God's chosen people out from Egypt, through the desert to the borders of Canaan, the promised land. In Deuteronomy, the ardous travelling has come at an end, and the Israelites, camping east of the River Jordan, are soon to enter their new homeland.

Yet, the narrative parts of Deuteronomy are modest, almost exclusively restricted to the story of the death of Moses in ch. 34. What we actually find in Deuteronomy is a *speech* made by Moses. Since his audience is now on the verge of entering the promised land, the speech contains those laws and regulations, given by God, that must be observed in the new land. The speech, in fact, is nothing but a law book, with implicit and explicit exhortations.

In the very centre of the story of the Israelites and their relationship to the 'national god' YHWH we find the firm belief that YHWH has elected the Israelites among all the inhabitants of the earth to be his particular favourite and property. Consequently, these traditions also play an important persuasive part in the speech of Moses. We find retrospective glances at the promises to the patriarchs Abraham, Isaac and Jacob, the escape from Egypt, the covenant at Mount Sinai and the desert wanderings. The most distinguished promise to the Israelites, however, is the promise of the land of which they are now about to take possession.

The legal materials that we find in the Hebrew Bible—both in Deuteronomy and in the Priestly writings—are, whatever else they may be, also the *conditions* agreed upon in the covenant between YHWH and his people. However, it follows from Deuteronomy (Deut. 30; cf. also Josh. 24) that it is up to the Israelites themselves to make the choice between YHWH—with a good quality life in the promised land—and other deities with disasters and loss of land as the ultimate consequence.

Another characteristic feature of Deuteronomy—and clearly as important as the different laws and regulations—are threats of punishment and promises of reward. Deuteronomy stands as the prologue to the history of the elected people in the promised land, which is also the story of their covenant with YHWH. In the prologue, the conditions for the use of the land are clarified. If the Israelites in their new land obey the laws and commandments of YHWH and worship him as their sole deity, they shall be blessed and have a prosperous life. If they do not they shall be cursed. The worshipping of other deities is regarded as particularly abominable. The punishment is depicted in some detail: sickness, crop failure, defeat, siege, invasion, looting, and deportation from the promised land. The importance of the loss of land aspect of Deuteronomy can hardly be exaggerated.

3. *The Deuteronomistic History*

When using the designation the 'Deuteronomistic History' in the present context I do not necessarily adhere to the theories of Martin Noth nor to any of the several variant theories among his successors. Nor do I wish to discuss whether there actually ever existed a coherent, written history in ancient Israel prior to this document as we now have it. It may well have been, or it may not. Those interested in such questions should rather consult the vast secondary literature on the topic.[13] For our immediate purpose, it suffices to say that with the expression the 'Deuteronomistic History' in the present essay I refer simply to the biblical books of (Deuteronomy), Joshua, Judges, 1–2 Samuel and 1–2 Kings. What we find here is a large, independent and mostly consistent literary work, characterized by its prose style and the constant repetition of certain theological main points through the use of certain set phrases.

The significance of this highly ideological work is clearly seen also from its length, which amounts to approximately 25 per cent of the Masoretic Text! Furthermore, the period dealt with also attests to the importance of the work. Joshua–Kings tell the story of the Israelite people from the conquest of the promised land until the fall of Jerusalem in 586 BCE. According to conventional scholarly chronology this means a period of about 700 years. And those are not any 700 years! The Deuteronomistic History wants to tell the story of the Israelites throughout the whole period of their national existence in Canaan, the land given to them by YHWH their god. The Deuteronomistic History gives us the story of the Iron Age kingdoms of Israel and Judah from

---

13. See the literature referred to above. A short but succinct survey from the historiographical point of view (with literature) is found in B.O. Long, *1 Kings with an Introduction to Historical Literature* (FOTL, 9; Grand Rapids: Eerdmans, 1984), pp. 2-8. The most recent contribution to the discussion is that of H.N. Rösel, *Von Josua bis Jojachin: Untersuchungen zu den deuteronomistischen Geschichtsbüchern des Alten Testaments* (VTSup, 75; Leiden: E.J. Brill, 1999).

the time of their foundation to the time when they ceased to exist as sovereign states.[14]

It is impossible—and unnecessary—to give a full review of the contents of Joshua to Kings in the present context. Only a few, major points may be made. Above all, the Deuteronomistic History is a book about a people and their God in their land (formerly belonging to the Canaanites), given to them by their God. And most of all, perhaps, it informs us about the *leaders* of this people! In the book of Judges, for instance, the Israelites are depicted as a body completely without a will of their own, badly in need of a strong leader. Under good 'judges' the Israelites worship YHWH as their god and obey his laws and regulations. When the leader dies they leave YHWH and start worshipping the despicable Baalim of the Canaanites. As a result of this, YHWH must punish the people he has elected for himself. He lets the enemy win on the battlefield. The people regret their sins, and they pray to YHWH for forgiveness. Their prayers are granted, and YHWH sends another 'judge' to save the Israelites from the enemy. After the death of the new leader the story repeats itself: the Israelites forsake YHWH and indulge in the worshipping of other deities. Here, in a nutshell, we find the 'philosophy of history' of the Deuteronomists. As we see, this represents a contemporary, theological interpretation of history rather than any attempt to convey past reality in a positivistic fashion.

However, the political leaders whom the Deuteronomists despise the most are the kings. A major theme in their history is the strongly negative view of so many of the Israelite and Judaean kings. This may be perceived already in the books of Samuel, a text reflecting the transition period between the charismatic 'judges' and the establishment of kingship, but above all in the books of Kings. According to the Deuteronomists, it is primarily the kings who are responsible for provoking the wrath of YHWH and for his various castigations of his people in the land, leading up to the final punishment: the sacking of Jerusalem, and the taking away of the whole of the Judaean population into exile to Babylonia.

The particular Deuteronomistic view penetrates all of the story of the Israelites from Joshua to Kings. Major historical disasters are partic-

14. The use of words like 'king', 'nation' and 'state' in the present context may appear anacronistic. I do not, however, want to take up this discussion here. This is not because I feel comfortable using these words without any definitions, but simply because this (rather imprecise) language usage reflects much of the current debate.

ularly stressed. In 1 Kings 1–11 we may read the story of King Solomon. Great importance is attached to the story of the building of the
temple in Jerusalem. According to the Deuteronomists, cultic activity
can only take place at the Jerusalem temple. Nevertheless, Solomon is
punished by YHWH for his sins, and after his death his grand kingdom
is dissolved and divided into two parts: the northern kingdom of Israel
and the southern kingdom of Judah. In later tradition the time of
Solomon should always be regarded as the golden age in Israel's past.
The next catastrophe takes place in 722 BCE with the siege and conquest of Samaria by the Assyrians and the end of the northern kingdom.
Finally, with the Babylonian invasion and the fall of Jerusalem in 586,
the greatest disaster of all in the eyes of the Deuteronomists took place:
Judah now ceased to exist as a nation in her own right.

The angle is widely theological. All the misery that has befallen the
Israelites has come about as a result of their violation of the covenant
with YHWH. They did not worship YHWH as their sole God, nor did
they follow his law.

The theological overtones appear in a narrative pattern that is strongly
schematized. Since in the eyes of the Deuteronomists it is the kings that
are to blame for what has happened, they are portrayed as good or, for
the most part, as bad. They are characterized, for instance, in the following way: 'King X did evil (or right) in the eyes of YHWH'. A good
king would typically pull down the altars of foreign gods, worship
YHWH as his only god, and follow the commandments given to the
people by Moses. A bad king would be punished for not following
YHWH.[15] Thus, the books of Kings are not about the kings in any
ordinary sense, but about good and bad kings. A king either followed
YHWH or he did not.

Moreover, the kings of Israel, the northern kingdom, had rebelled

---

15. See in general G.E. Gerbrandt, *Kingship According to the Deuteronomistic
History* (SBLDS, 87; Atlanta: Scholars Press, 1986). A typical bad king would be
King Manasseh of Judah, whose story we find in 2 Kgs 21. See P.S.F. van Keulen,
*Manasse through the Eyes of the Deuteronomists: The Manasse Account (2 Kings
21:1–18) and the Final Chapters of the Deuteronomistic History* (OTS, 38; Leiden:
E.J. Brill, 1996). One of the heroes of the Deuteronomists, of course, is King Josiah
of Judah. See J. van Dorp, *Josia: De voorstelling van zijn koningschap in II
Koningen 22–23* (Utrecht: University of Utrecht, 1991); E. Eynikel, *The Reform of
King Josiah and the Composition of the Deuteronomistic History* (OTS, 33; Leiden:
E.J. Brill, 1996).

against the Davidic dynasty, and were all, consequently, evil. For this reason the punishment of Israel occurred already in 722 BCE when the ungodly capital of Samaria was sacked by the Assyrians (2 Kgs 17.6-8; RSV):

> In the ninth year of Hoshea the King of Assyria captured Samaria, and he carried the Israelites away to Assyria, and placed them in Halah, and on the Habor, the river of Gozan, and in the cities of the Medes. And this was so, because the people of Israel had sinned against the Lord their God, who had brought them up out of the land of Egypt from under the hand of Pharaoh king of Egypt, and had feared other gods, and walked in the customs of the nations whom the Lord drove out before the people of Israel, and in the customs which the kings of Israel had introduced.[16]

The Deuteronomists present the history of Israel from the conquest of the land to the exile as a long, coherent account about the elected people who entirely and at all times *broke* the contract with YHWH, their god.

From beginning to end the books of Joshua, Judges, Samuel and Kings tell the story of covenant violation, rebellion and apostasy. The final catastrophes that struck Israel and Judah are described as the heavy price that had to be paid for the many infringements upon YHWH's commandments revealed to the Israelites before they entered the land, and that are now to be found in the book of Deuteronomy.

4. The 'Common Theology' of the Ancient Near East

When taking a closer look at the contents of Deuteronomy and the Deuteronomistic History we find many 'similarities' between genres, phraseology and motifs of these texts and those of the ancient Near Eastern literary heritage. Such correspondences are so many and so striking that there can be but little doubt that all of these texts belong within a wider, common cultural sphere! Such observations, of course, are not new at all, but have been made ever since the first discoveries of texts from ancient Mesopotamia after the middle of the nineteenth century. Ever since those early days, a steady stream of new texts have been discovered at numerous sites in Iraq, Egypt, Syria, and elsewhere. Many of these texts have been made available to scholars without an

---

16. On the historical circumstances behind the fall of Samaria, see B. Becking, *The Fall of Samaria: A Historical and Archaeological Study* (Studies in the History of the Ancient Near East, 2; Leiden: E.J. Brill, 1992).

expert knowledge of the ancient Semitic or Egyptian languages. In view of recent claims that the Hebrew Bible is modelled on Greek proto-types, it becomes vital to remind ourselves of how deeply embedded are the traditions of the Hebrew Bible in the 'surrounding cultures'. With a few exceptions, the flavour and mentality of the biblical texts are through and through 'oriental', and not 'Greek'. It was this that led Morton Smith, in a now classic work, to talk about 'the common theology of the ancient Near East'.[17]

A proper evaluation of the significance of 'the common theology of the ancient Near East' is essential for any sound understanding of the growth and nature of the texts and traditions of the Hebrew Bible. Since, however, the literature is vast and possible examples over-whelming, only a few illustrations can be given in the present context.[18]

---

17. M. Smith, 'The Common Theology of the Ancient Near East', *JBL* 71 (1952), pp. 135-47. I mention Smith here because his article has somehow become a classic. Apparently, the 'commonness' concerns not only 'theology', but also literary and historiographical traditions and laws, as well as social and economic conditions. Another classic is the book by B. Albrektson, demonstrating beyond doubt how the view that historical events were regarded as divine actions was commonplace in the ancient Near East, and not exclusive to the Hebrew Bible the way some scholars had thought (B. Albrektson, *History and the Gods: An Essay on the Idea of Historical Events as Divine Manifestations in the Ancient Near East and in Israel* [ConBOT, 1; Lund: C.W.K. Gleerup, 1967]).

18. The examples which I shall discuss below would, naturally, be those most relevant to historiography. However, it is important to be aware of the fact that *all* the literary genres of the Hebrew Bible, so to speak, have ancient Near Eastern pro-totypes. On prophecy, see M. Weippert, 'Aspekte israelitischer Prophetie im Lichte verwandter Erscheinungen des Alten Orients', in G. Mauer und U. Magen (eds.), *Ad bene et fideliter seminandum. Festgabe für Karlheinz Deller zum 21. Februar 1987* (AOAT, 220; Neukirchen–Vluyn: Neukirchener Verlag, 1988), pp. 287-319; H.M. Barstad, 'No Prophets? Recent Developments in Biblical Prophetic Research and Ancient Near Eastern Prophecy', *JSOT* 57 (1993), pp. 39-60; M. Nissinen, *References to Prophecy in Neo-Assyrian Sources* (State Archives of Assyria Studies, 7; Helsinki: The Neo-Assyrian Text Corpus Project, 1998). On wisdom, see S. Weeks, *Early Israelite Wisdom* (Oxford Theological Monographs; Oxford: Clarendon Press, 1994). However, ancient Near Eastern wisdom, too, has been regarded as an impor-tant influence on the book of Deuteronomy. See W.W. Hallo, 'Biblical Abomina-tions and Sumerian Taboos', *JQR* 76 (1985), pp. 21-40. For more specific genres such as Song of Songs, see M. Nissinen, 'Love Lyrics of Nabû and Tasmetu: An Assyrian Song of Songs?', in M. Dietrich and I. Kottsieper (eds.), *'Und Mose schrieb dieses Lied auf': Studien zum Alten Testament und zum Alten Orient für Oswald Loretz zur Vollendung seines 70. Lebensjahres mit Beiträgen von Freunden,*

a. *Law*

As mentioned above, the book of Deuteronomy consists of a speech made by Moses. The speech contains those laws and regulations given by God which must be kept when the Israelites enter the promised land. Similarly, in the Priestly tradition (Exodus–Numbers) the laws are given to the Israelites through Moses at Mount Sinai on their journey from Egypt to Canaan. The laws that Moses gives the Israelites in Deuteronomy (and in Exodus–Numbers) are not the laws of Moses but the laws of God. The notion that the major deity is also the lawgiver represents a typical example of 'the common theology of the ancient Near East'.

Here, one illustration must suffice. On the upper part of the Louvre Hammurabi stela (the best preserved and most complete edition of Hammurabi's law) there is a scene where the sun-god Shamash sits on his throne and presents the law to King Hammurabi who stands before him. The fact that the illustration covers almost one-third of the stela indicates the importance of the iconography of the deity as law-giver for a proper understanding of the situation.[19] The parallel to YHWH and Moses is obvious. The main point is the underlining of the deity as the protector of the king and his people. The fact that the laws that are referred to, both on the Louvre stela and in Deuteronomy (or in Exodus–Numbers), must be much older than the 'literary compositions' in which we may now find them, appears not to have bothered the 'authors' of our two texts.

In addition to such overarching parallels, there are of course also well-known similarities between legal systems and individual laws, far too numerous to be dealt with in any detail in the present context.[20]

Schülern und Kollegen (AOAT, 250; Münster: Ugarit-Verlag, 1998), pp. 585-634. For the city lament, see P. Michalowski, *The Lamentation over the Destruction of Sumer and Ur* (Mesopotamian Civilizations, 1; Winona Lake, IN: Eisenbrauns, 1989).

19. M.T. Roth, *Law Collections from Mesopotamia and Asia Minor* (Society of Biblical Literature, Writings from the Ancient World, 6; Atlanta: Scholars Press, 1995), p. 73.

20. See, e.g., S.M. Paul, *Studies in the Book of the Covenant in the Light of Cuneiform and Biblical Law* (VTSup, 18; Leiden: E.J. Brill, 1970); R. Sonsino, *Motive Clauses in Hebrew Law: Biblical Forms and Near Eastern Parallels* (SBLDS, 45; Chico, CA: Scholars Press, 1980); D.P. Wright, *The Disposal of Impurity: Elimination Rites in the Bible and in Hittite and Mesopotamian Literature* (SBLDS, 101; Atlanta: Scholars Press, 1987); R. Westbrook, *Studies in Biblical*

b. *Treaty*

One important factor in Deuteronomy and in the Deuteronomistic history is the view that YHWH has attached himself to his people through a contract/treaty/covenant. Scholarly discussions (of varying quality) about the relationship of ancient Near Eastern treaties to similar phenomena in the Hebrew Bible have convincingly shown how deeply rooted such ideas are in a common culture.[21]

From Deuteronomy we may also learn how closely connected the divine laws are to the covenant. In fact, the laws form a part of the very treaty terms: if the Israelites obey the laws and commandments of YHWH and worship him as their only god, they shall be blessed and prosper. If they do not they shall all be cursed. Elaborate curse catalogues are found in chs. 28–32 in Deuteronomy (cf. also Lev. 26). Again, the literature of the 'surrounding cultures' shows us that curses (i.e. threats of punishment) in which gods are asked to bring evil on those who break their oath are characteristic of Mesopotamian (and West Semitic) treaties, and common in all periods from Sumerian to late Babylonian times.[22]

and Cuneiform Law (Cahiers de la Revue Biblique, 26; Paris: J. Gabalda, 1988); M. Malul, *The Comparative Method in Ancient Near Eastern and Biblical Legal Studies* (AOAT, 227; Neukirchen–Vluyn: Neukirchener Verlag, 1990), with special weight on the laws of the Goring Ox; E. Otto, 'Die Ursprünge der Bundestheologie im Alten Testament und im Alten Orient', *Zeitschrift für Altorientalische und Biblische Rechtsgeschichte* 4 (1998), pp. 1-84; F.C. Fensham, 'Widow, Orphan, and the Poor in Ancient Near Eastern Legal and Wisdom Literature', *JNES* 21 (1962), pp. 129-39; J. Greenfield, 'Adi baltu—Care for the Elderly and its Rewards', *AfO* 19 (1982) = *Vorträge, gehalten auf der 28. Rencontre Assyriologique Internationale, Wien 6–10 Juli, 1981*, pp. 309-316.

21. There is a vast literature on the topic. Cf. D.J. McCarthy, *Treaty and Covenant: A Study in Form in the Ancient Oriental Documents and in the Old Testament* (AnBib, 21A; Rome: Pontifical Biblical Institute, rev. edn, 1978); E.W. Nicholson, *God and his People: Covenant and Theology in the Old Testament* (Oxford: Oxford University Press, 1986).

22. D.R. Hillers, *Treaty-Curses and the Old Testament Prophets* (BibOr, 16; Rome: Pontifical Biblical Institute, 1964). For a useful survey of different curses, see F. Pomponio, *Formule di maledizione della Mesopotamia preclassica*, I (Testi del Vicino Oriente antico, 2; Brescia: Paideia, 1990). For a short treatment of the biblical covenantal blessing promises, see C.W. Mitchell, *The Meaning of BRK 'to Bless' in the Old Testament* (SBLDS, 95; Atlanta: Scholars Press, 1987), pp. 36-44; F.C. Fensham, 'Malediction and Benediction in Ancient Near Eastern Vassal-Trea-

Like many other ancient Near Eastern traditions, the treaty tradition turned out to be of remarkable longevity, following standard forms for centuries. Many of the same elements which we may find in the earlier treaty literature are found also in a Punic document as late as the third century BCE.[23]

c. *War*

Any reader of the Hebrew Bible must be struck by the great role played by the deity in relation to war, and the numerous occurrences of holy war descriptions. YHWH himself is described as a great warrior.[24] From Deuteronomy and the Deuteronomistic History we learn how the enemies of Israel were also the enemies of the god of Israel, and how YHWH assisted his people in times of war (cf. Josh. 8.1; 10.11; 24.11-12; Judg. 4.14-16; 1 Sam. 17.45-47; 23.4-5; 2 Sam. 5.22-25; 2 Kgs 3.17-20; 6.15-18; 7.5-7). Quite unlike what we find with the Greeks, holy war permeated ancient Israelite society. Especially following the publication of Weippert's pioneering study in 1972[25] scholars have been engaged in comparing holy war in the Hebrew Bible with ancient Near Eastern war traditions. The many similarities in phraseology and ideology are striking indeed.[26]

ties and the Old Testament', *ZAW* 74 (1962), pp. 1-9. More specialized is M.L. Barré, 'An Analysis of the Royal Blessing in the Karatepe Inscription', *MAARAV* 3 (1982), pp. 177-94.

23. M.L. Barré, *The God-List in the Treaty between Hannibal and Philip V of Macedonia: A Study in Light of the Ancient Near Eastern Treaty Tradition* (The Johns Hopkins Near Eastern Studies; Baltimore: The Johns Hopkins University Press, 1983).

24. P.D. Miller, Jr, *The Divine Warrior in Early Israel* (HSM, 5; Cambridge, MA: Harvard University Press, 1973); M.C. Lind, *Yahweh is a Warrior: The Theology of Warfare in Ancient Israel* (Scottdale, PA: Herald Press, 1980).

25. M. Weippert, ' "Heiliger Krieg" in Israel und Assyrien: Kritische Anmerkungen zu Gerhard von Rads Konzept des "Heiligen Krieges im alten Israel" ', *ZAW* 84 (1972), pp. 460-93.

26. On the role of the deity in defeating the enemy, see in general K.L. Younger, Jr, *Ancient Conquest Accounts: A Study in Ancient Near Eastern and Biblical History Writing* (JSOTSup, 98; Sheffield: JSOT Press, 1990), *passim*. The image of the fighting god who hastens to help his people on the battlefield was widespread in the ancient Near East. Cf. M. Weinfeld, 'Divine Intervention in War in Ancient Israel and in the Ancient Near East', in H. Tadmor and M. Weinfeld (eds.), *History, Historiography and Interpretation: Studies in Biblical and Cuneiform Literatures* (Jerusalem: Magnes Press, 1983), pp. 121-47. On wars fought directly on divine

d. *King*

Obviously, there is no such thing as a monolithic king ideology to be found either in the Hebrew Bible or in the ancient Near East.[27] Also, when using a word like 'ideology' in the present context former discussions concerning 'divine kingship' easily come to mind. Needless to say, this should be avoided. However, we must not let the unfortunate exaggerations and over-interpretations of former times keep us from seeing highly relevant, important parallels between texts in the Hebrew Bible and texts from the ancient Near East. Such similarities are so copious and so striking that they can only be explained as a result of close cultural interdependency.

In the Hebrew Bible and in the literature of the surrounding countries the king was installed by the deity. As God's representative on earth, the king was also responsible for the prosperity and welfare of his people. From the short survey of the contents of Deuteronomy above we notice how YHWH's punishment for breaking the covenant consisted, above all, of military attacks by enemy armies or the destruction of the agricultural economic system. Similarly, if the elected people did not violate the covenant, the reward would be the keeping up of the agricultural production and victory over the enemy. There are numerous texts in the Hebrew Bible that attest to this theology. For the present

initiative, see B. Oded, ' "The Command of the God" as a Reason for Going to War in the Assyrian Royal Inscriptions', in M. Cogan and I. Eph'al (eds.), *Ah, Assyria... Studies in Ancient Near Eastern Historiography Presented to Hayim Tadmor* (Scripta Hierosolymitana, 32; Jerusalem: Magnes Press, 1991), pp. 223-30. On the need for consulting prophets in Assyria during military campaigns, see M. Nissinen, *References to Prophecy in Neo-Assyrian Sources* (State Archives of Assyria Studies, 7; Helsinki: The Neo-Assyrian Text Corpus Project, 1998), pp. 164-65 and *passim*. Another important work by Nissinen is 'Die Relevanz der neuassyrischen Prophetie für die alttestamentliche Forschung', in M. Dietrich and O. Loretz (eds.), *Mesopotamica—Ugaritica—Biblica: Festschrift für Kurt Bergerhof zur Vollendung seines 70. Lebensjahres am 7. Mai 1992* (AOAT, 232; Neukirchen–Vluyn: Neukirchener Verlag, 1993), pp. 217-58. A recent study by S.B. Parker synthesizes for the first time the West Semitic evidence relating to war events, comparing it to details in the Deuteronomistic History. See S.B. Parker, *Stories in Scripture and Inscriptions: Comparative Studies on Narratives in Northwest Semitic Inscriptions and the Hebrew Bible* (New York: Oxford University Press, 1997). Of particular importance in this connection is the Mesha inscription.

27. For a survey, see most recently J. Day (ed.), *King and Messiah in Israel and the Ancient Near East: Proceedings of the Oxford Old Testament Seminar* (JSOTSup, 270; Sheffield: Sheffield Academic Press, 1998).

purpose, I would like to draw attention to the last part of the story of the temple building of King Solomon in 1 Kings 8. The whole story abounds in interesting parallels to ancient Near Eastern texts.[28] Here, however, I quote only 1 Kgs 8.33-40 (RSV).

> When thy people Israel are defeated before the enemy because they have sinned against thee, if they turn again to thee, and acknowledge thy name, and pray and make supplication to thee in this house; then hear thou in heaven, and forgive the sin of thy people Israel, and bring them again to the land which thou gavest to their fathers. When heaven is shut up and there is no rain because they have sinned against thee, if they pray toward this place, and acknowledge thy name, and turn from their sin, when thou dost afflict them, then hear thou in heaven and forgive the sin of thy servants, thy people Israel, when thou dost teach them the good way in which they should walk; and grant rain upon thy land, which thou hast given to thy people as an inheritance. If there is famine in the land, if there is pestilence or blight or mildew or locust or caterpillar; if their enemy besieges them in any of their cities whatever plague, whatever sickness there is; whatever prayer, whatever supplication is made by any man or by all thy people Israel, each knowing the affliction of his own heart and stretching out his hand toward this house; then hear thou in heaven thy dwelling place, and forgive, and act, and render to each whose heart thou knowest, according to all his ways (for thou, thou only, knowest the hearts of all the children of men); that they may fear thee all the days that they live in the land which thou gavest to our fathers.[29]

As an example from Mesopotamia the letter from the scholar scribe Adad-shumu-uṣur to Ashurbanipal (668–c. 630 BCE) illustrates well

---

28. The whole of the text of the temple building in 1 Kgs 5–9 is modelled on ancient Near Eastern prototypes, providing us with yet another fascinating illustration of 'the common theology of the ancient Near East'. See on this the thorough study by V. Hurovitz, *I Have Built You an Exalted House: Temple Building in the Bible in Light of Mesopotamian and North-West Semitic Writings* (JSOTSup, 115; American Schools of Oriental Research Monograph, 5; Sheffield: JSOT Press, 1992).

29. Hurovitz, *I Have Built You an Exalted House*, pp. 291-300, provides interesting extra-biblical parallels to the prayer of Solomon. However, all of his examples are restricted to house-building prayers. For a detailed study of Solomon's prayer and its role in the composition of the Deuteronomistic History, see E. Talstra, *Solomon's Prayer: Synchrony and Diachrony in the Composition of I Kings 8, 14–61* (Contributions to Biblical Exegesis and Theology, 3; Kampen: Kok Pharos, 1993).

how the king was responsible for the prosperity and welfare of his people:

> Ashur, [the king of the gods], called the name of [the king], my lord, to the kingship of Assyria, and Shamash and Adad, through their reliable extispicy, confirmed the king, my lord, to the kingship of the world. A good reign—righteous days, years of justice, copious rains, huge floods, a fine rate of exchange! The gods are appeased, there is much fear of god, the temples abound; the great gods of heaven and earth have become exalted in the time of the king, my lord. The old men dance, the young men sing, the women and girls are merry and rejoice; women are married and provided with earrings; boys and girls are brought forth, the births thrive. The king, my lord, has revived the one who was guilty and condemned to death; you have released the one who was imprisoned for many [ye]ars. Those who were sick for many days have got well. The hungry has been sated, the *parched* have been anointed with oil, the needy have been covered with garments.[30]

From Solomon's prayer in 1 Kgs 8.22-53 we learn many interesting details concerning the role of the king in securing prosperity for his people. The prayer forms a part of the larger temple building text of Solomon (1 Kgs 5–9), which has important covenant overtones. However, probably the most important feature of this text is its role in relationship to the securing of the royal dynasty! This may be seen from the words of Solomon in 1 Kgs 8.25-26:

> Now therefore, O Lord, God of Israel, keep with thy servant David my father what thou hast promised him, saying: There shall never fail you a man before me to sit upon the throne of Israel, if only your sons take heed to their way, to walk before me as you have walked before me. Now therefore, O God of Israel, let thy word be confirmed, which thou hast spoken to thy servant David my father.

That it is the Davidic dynasty that is reconfirmed in our text may be seen clearly also from YHWH's answer to Solomon in 1 Kgs 9.1-9. I quote here only vv. 4-7 (RSV):

> And as for you, if you will walk before me, as David your father walked, with integrity of heart and uprightness, doing according to all that I have

---

30. The translation (ABL 2) is taken from S. Parpola, *Letters from Assyrian and Babylonian Scholars* (State Archives of Assyria, 10; Helsinki: Helsinki University Press, 1993), pp. 177-78. For other examples, including some earlier ones from ancient Sumer, see: H.H. Schmid, *šalôm 'Frieden' im Alten Orient und im Alten Testament* (Stuttgarter Bibelstudien, 51; Stuttgart: Katholisches Bibelwerk, 1971), pp. 30-44.

commanded you, and keeping my statutes and my ordinances, then I will establish your royal throne over Israel for ever, as I promised David your father, saying: There shall not fail you a man upon the throne of Israel. But if you turn aside from following me, you or your children, and do not keep my commandments and my statutes which I have set before you, but go and serve other gods and worship them, then I will cut off Israel from the land which I have given them; and the house which I have consecrated for my name I will cast out of my sight; and Israel shall become a proverb and a byword among all peoples.

From the short survey of the contents of the Deuteronomistic History above it appeared how the kings of Israel (the northern kingdom) had rebelled against the Davidic dynasty, and were all, consequently, depicted as evil. For this reason the punishment of Israel had already happened by 722 BCE when the wicked capital Samaria was destroyed by the Assyrian army. The philosophy of history lying behind this description is typical of the ancient Near East. In Mesopotamian texts, the view that the fate of the dynasty or kingdom is determined by the behaviour of its founder is well known.[31]

However, it was not only the behaviour of the archetypal dynastic founder that affected the events (Jeroboam was a crook, Israel fell; David was pious, Judah stood). As we noticed in the overview of the Deuteronomistic History above the course of history was dependent also upon single rulers. This was the case in Mesopotamia, too.[32] For instance, in the Middle Assyrian poems of Adad-Nirari I and Tukulti-Ninurta I, both telling the story of the battles between Assyria and Kassite Babylonia, led by the Kassite kings Nazi-Maruttash and Kash-tiliash IV, we read how the wilfulness of the Babylonian Kassite kings provoked the rage of the Mesopotamian gods who then came to the rescue of the Assyrians.[33]

31. The phenomenon has been treated thoroughly by C.D. Evans, 'Naram-Sin and Jeroboam: The Archetypal *Unheilsherrscher* in Mesopotamian and Biblical Historiography', in W.W. Hallo, J.C. Moyer and L.G. Perdue (eds.), *Scripture in Context. II. More Essays on the Comparative Method* (Winona Lake, IN: Eisenbrauns, 1983), pp. 97-125. Cf. also E. Osswald, 'Altorientalische Parallelen zur deuteronomistischen Geschichtsbetrachtung', *Mitteilungen des Instituts für Orientforschung* 15 (1969), pp. 286-96, and, more recently, P.S. Ash, 'Jeroboam I and the Deuteronomistic Historian's Ideology of the Founder', *CBQ* 60 (1998), pp. 16-24.

32. As noted also by Evans, 'Naram-Sin and Jeroboam', pp. 111-13.

33. J. Proseckýå, 'Quelques réflexions sur les textes historiques littéraires akkadiens', *ArOr* 64 (1996), pp. 151-56 (154).

More dramatic, of course, is the case of the last neo-Babylonian king Nabonidus as *Unheilsherrscher*, leading to the fall of the mighty city of Babylon to Cyrus. A quotation from the Cyrus cylinder may well illustrate this point:

> Marduk, the great lord, the protector of his people, joyfully looked at his [Cyrus's] good deeds and at his righteous heart. He ordered him to march to his city Babylon. He made him to take the road to Babylon and marched at his side like a friend and companion. His large troops whose number, like the waters of a river, could not be established, paraded at his side, their weapons girded on. Without combat or battle, he caused him to enter Babylon, his city. He saved Babylon from oppression. He delivered into his hands Nabonidus, the king who did not worship him.[34]

e. *God*

It is well known that there are many similarities between YHWH and the deities of the ancient Near East. Yet again, this is something that clearly points towards a strong ancient Near Eastern influence rather than a Hellenistic one on the traditions of the Hebrew Bible. For instance, the several similarities between the religious hymns and prayers of the Hebrew Bible and those of the ancient Near East have been known for a long time and can hardly escape the attentive reader browsing through the standard collections.[35] One observation here would concern the rich, common terminology used for the deity in Israel and in the ancient Near East. As one example, I may single out the widely used epithet 'king'.[36] Another well-known example would be the influence of ancient Near Eastern ideas of creation on the biblical book of Genesis.[37] More relevant to the present discussion and to what has been

---

34. The translation is that of P.-A. Beaulieu, in his *The Reign of Nabonidus King of Babylon 556–539 B.C.* (Yale Near Eastern Researches, 10; New Haven: Yale University Press, 1989), p. 225.

35. See A. Falkenstein und W. von Soden, *Sumerische und akkadische Hymnen und Gebete* (Zürich: Artemis, 1953); M.-J. Seux, *Hymnes et prières aux dieux de Babylonie et d'Assyrie* (Littératures anciennes du Proche-Orient, 8; Paris: Cerf, 1976).

36. For the Hebrew Bible, see the thorough study by M.Z. Brettler, *God is King: Understanding an Israelite Metaphor* (JSOTSup, 76; Sheffield: JSOT Press, 1989). For an example from Assyria, see A. Livingstone, 'Assur', in K. van der Toorn, B. Becking and P.W. van der Horst (eds.), *Dictionary of Deities and Demons in the Bible* (Leiden: E.J. Brill, 1995), cols. 200-203 (200-201).

37. Cf. the useful collection of essays in R.S. Hess and D.T. Tsumura (eds.), *'I

dealt with above are the many similarities between circumstances relating to the national god and his land.[38]

Well known from the Deuteronomistic history is the notion of the deity favouring his people. Above, I referred to the characteristic curse language of the treaty. Related to this curse language are statements about divine vengeance and destruction. If the people did not follow the will of the deity they would be punished.[39] This particular feature of Deuteronomy is shared with the rest of the ancient Near East.[40]

It has been claimed that ancient Israel constituted a monotheistic culture wheras the religions of the surrounding countries were polytheistic. This, I believe, was not actually the case, and represents at best an

Studied Inscriptions from before the Flood': Ancient Near Eastern, Literary, and Linguistic Approaches to Genesis 1–11 (Sources for Biblical and Theological Studies, 4; Winona Lake, IN: Eisenbrauns, 1994). Pages 75-282 deal with the relationship of Gen. 1–11 to ancient Near Eastern traditions.

38. D.I. Block, *The Gods of the Nations: Studies in Ancient Near Eastern National Theology* (Evangelical Theological Society Monographs, 2; Jackson, Mississippi: Evangelical Theological Society, 1988), gives a useful survey of connections between deities, territories and nations in ancient Israel and in ancient Near Eastern societies. Unfortunately, the study is sometimes tainted with 'bibliocentric' value judgments.

39. On this topic, see H.G.L. Peels, *The Vengeance of God: The Meaning of the Root NQM and the Function of the NQM-Texts in the Context of Divine Revelation in the Old Testament* (OTS, 31; Leiden: E.J. Brill, 1995). Peels also has a useful survey of extra-biblical examples (pp. 29-42). His conclusion, however, (pp. 284-87) that *nqm* is not a part of the covenantal language in the Bible fails to convince. Since *nqm* is a West Semitic word, one may consult *AHw*, I, p. 311 *(ḫalāqu D b)* and *CAD* VI p. 39 *(ḫalāqu 3 e)* for references to Akkadian texts where the deity threatens to destroy the land. For a concrete example, compare the behaviour of Marduk in the Erra epos. See L. Cagni, *The Poem of Erra* (Sources from the Ancient Near East, 1.3; Malibu: Undena, 1977), p. 33 n. 36. For other ancient Near Eastern examples of the punishing of the deity, see G. Goossens, 'La philosophie de l'histoire dans l'Ancien Orient', in J. Coppens, A. Descamps and E. Massaux (eds.), *Sacra Pagina: Miscellanea Biblica Congressus Internationalis Catholici de Re Biblica* (BETL, 12–13; Paris: J. Duculot, 1959), pp. 242-52 (245-46).

40. After the final punishment and the sacking of Jerusalem, postexilic national trends eventually developed a theology of the return to the land from the diaspora. It is very interesting to note that even this particular motif, so well known from the Hebrew Bible, also formed a part of 'the common theology of the ancient Near East'. See G. Widengren, 'Yahweh's Gathering of the Dispersed', in W.B. Barrick and J.R. Spencer (eds.), *In the Shelter of Elyon: Essays in Honor of G.W. Ahlström* (JSOTSup, 31; Sheffield: JSOT Press, 1984), pp. 227-45.

oversimplification. All the evidence available today points towards the fact that belief systems in Israel and other Near Eastern cultures in the Iron Age *were fairly similar*, with several different deities. It was only at a very late stage in Judah that YHWH was worshipped as the sole deity.[41] This circumstance is reflected also in many texts of the Hebrew Bible. Well known is the prohibition against the worshipping of foreign deities in Exod. 20.3: 'You shall have no other gods besides me'. It is easily forgotten that in order to be of any relevance this prohibition must presuppose a polytheistic situation. Similarly, we noticed above the heavy weight that Deuteronomy and the Deuteronomistic History put on the prohibition against the worshipping of 'foreign' gods. Here, too, we have clear indications of the polytheistic landscape of Israel in earlier days. Finally, we should not fail to mention also the prophetic literature. The prophetic literature abounds in polemical statements against 'foreign' deities.[42] One may here consult the following selection of texts: Isa. 2.6; 27.9; Jer. 7.31; 11.13; Ezek. 6.6; 8.14; Hos. 8.4-6; Amos 8.14; Jon. 2.9; Mic. 1.7; Hab. 2.18-19; Zeph. 1.4-5; Zech. 10.2.

When we consider the vast evidence in the Hebrew Bible for the worshipping of deities other than YHWH, it becomes clear that the bulk of these texts must reflect circumstances prior to the Hellenistic era. In Hellenistic times, the belief system of Judaism simply would not require such a massive preoccupation with deities other than YHWH. On the other hand, we should not be led to believe that the kind of 'practical monotheism' which we do encounter in the present, late form of the Hebrew Bible is influenced by Greek thoughts. For instance, in eighth-century Assyria we have an example that illustrates the favouring of one god when we read in an inscription: 'Have confidence in Nabu, do not trust another god!'[43] And while in Assyria, one should not

41. Cf. W. Dietrich and M.A. Klopfenstein (eds.), *Ein Gott allein? JHWH–Verehrung und biblischer Monotheismus im Kontext der israelitischen und altorientalischen Religionsgeschichte* (OBO, 139; Freiburg: Universitätsverlag, 1994); R.K. Gnuse, *No Other Gods: Emergent Monotheism in Israel* (JSOTSup, 241; Sheffield: Sheffield Academic Press, 1997).

42. The present author has written a monograph on this phenomenon in the book of Amos: H.M. Barstad, *The Religious Polemics of Amos: Studies in the Preaching of Am 2:7B–8, 4:1–13, 5:1–27, 6:4–7, 8:14* (VTSup, 34; Leiden: E.J. Brill, 1984). The study is an attempt to use the book of Amos as a source for the history of Israelite religion in the Iron Age.

43. F. Pomponio, *Nabû: Il culto e la figura di un dio del Pantheon babilonese*

fail to notice the striking similarities between YHWH and the god Ashur.[44] In Deuteronomy it is demanded of the Israelites that they shall centralize their cultic activities at the temple in Jerusalem.[45] Also the god Ashur is through and through Assyrian, and has no temples unrelated to his cult in the city of Ashur. The origin of Ashur is unknown as is the origin of YHWH. Unlike all the other major deities in Mesopotamia Ashur is, like YHWH, without family or consort.[46] In Deuteronomy (Deut. 5.8; 4.15-19; cf. also Exod. 20.4) we find a strong prohibition against the production of sculptured images. Similarly to YHWH, and unlike most deities in the ancient Near East, the god Ashur also did not have an anthropomorphic representation.[47]

5. *A Hebrew Einheitskultur*

As we have just seen, the content of the Deuteronomistic History is saturated through and through with an ideology which we can call 'the common theology of the ancient Near East': a god who acts in history, a 'national' god who rewards and punishes his people, etc. Consequently, the ancient Israelites did not create anything that was relatively new. The 'scribes' that wrote what we now find in our Hebrew Bibles formed themselves into part of a common international arena. This

ed assiro (Studi Semitici, 51; Rome: Istituto di studi del Vicino Oriente, University of Roma, 1978), p. 69.

44. The above examples are taken from W. Mayer, 'Der Gott Assur und die Erben Assyriens', in R. Albertz (ed.), *Religion und Gesellschaft. Studien zu ihrer Wechselbeziehung in den Kulturen des Antiken Vorderen Orients* (Veröffentlichungen des Arbeitskreises zur Erforschung der Religions- und Kulturgeschichte des Antiken Vorderen Orients, 1; AOAT, 248; Münster: Ugarit-Verlag, 1997), pp. 15-23 (15).

45. A recent study on this topic is E. Reuter, *Kultzentralisation: Entstehung und Theologie von Dtn 12* (BBB, 87; Frankfurt: Anton Hain, 1993).

46. At a later time, Ashur is connected with several goddesses, for instance Ishtar of Ninive. At an earlier stage as well YHWH was worshipped with a female deity, Ashera. The first to argue convincingly for this was S.M. Olyan, *Asherah and the Cult of Yahweh in Israel* (SBLMS, 34; Atlanta: Scholars Press, 1988). By now, the literature on this topic is vast. Cf. N. Wyatt, 'Ashera', in van der Toorn, Becking and van der Horst (eds.), *Dictionary of Deities and Demons*, cols. 183-95.

47. See, in addition to Mayer 'Der Gott Assur', also T.N.D. Mettinger, *No Graven Image? Israelite Aniconism in its Ancient Near Eastern Context* (ConBOT, 42; Stockholm: Almqvist & Wiksell, 1995), pp. 42-44. Mettinger is building on research done by Mayer.

point is extremely important and highly relevant to recent discussions regarding the dating of the ancient Israelite traditions. It has, however, not always been sufficiently appreciated. If what we find in the Hebrew Bible in fact represents nothing but a variant of what we may also find throughout the neighbouring cultures we shall have to reckon with the strong possibility that the biblical traditions may also go back a long time. I am not taking into consideration at all here the question of historical reliability in a positivistic fashion. My only point is that it is quite likely that the traditions that made up the *raw materials* for the Deuteronomistic writer(s) may be rather ancient. They were most certainly not created overnight in Persian or Hellenistic scribal centres, but represent centuries of development.

Here, I believe that we are well advised to take Mesopotamia and Mesopotamian traditions as a model. Despite an enormous amount of tablets, written in several different languages, the actual number of literary genres and works that were handed down from generation to generation was fairly insignificant.

In other words, we are not dealing with newly invented, very different or independent literary creations. Rather, all of the literature belongs to the same 'tradition stream' or *Einheitskultur*, the bulk of which must have been known to most of the ancient Near Eastern civilized world.[48] Since we are in the lucky position to have Mesopotamian literary documents available from several centuries it is possible here to follow the various stages in the development of a literary work from an early stage to its final, 'canonical' form.[49] This, of course, we are unable to do with the traditions of ancient Israel, and it remains a fact that the critical analysis of the biblical traditions has, from time to time, been somewhat speculative.

However, even if we do not possess today the same confidence in our

---

48. Compare the following statement by A.L. Oppenheim about Ashurbanipal's (668–627 BCE) 20,000-tablet strong library in Niniveh, now in the British Museum: 'We are entitled to assume that the topical range of Assurbanipal's collections is representative of the main body, if not the entire content, of the scribal tradition' (A.L. Oppenheim, *Ancient Mesopotamia: Portrait of a Dead Civilization* [Chicago: University of Chicago Press, 1964], p. 15). See also the remarks by E. Weidner, 'Die Bibliothek Tiglatpilesers I', *AfO* 16 (1952–53), pp. 197-215, and by E. Reiner, 'Another Volume of Sultantepe Tablets', *JNES* 26 (1967), pp. 177-211 (177).

49. As it has been done with regard to the Gilgamesh Epic. See J.H. Tigay, *The Evolution of the Gilgamesh Epic* (Philadelphia: University of Philadelphia Press, 1982).

own perspicaciousness as former generations when it comes to the possibility of reconstructing the tradition process, we should not let this lead us to doubt the antiquity of these traditions nor to believe that they arose for the first time in Persian or Hellenistic times. Although we should not be naive and think that the handing down of the traditions over several centuries could happen entirely without this process making its mark on the *traditum*, constantly changing the tradition.

Also the different texts of the Bible represent, in my view, an *Einheitskultur*. Recently, there has been much talk about the 'intertextuality' of the Hebrew Bible. In fact, this constitutes nothing new. Even if there apparently are great differences between the Deuteronomists and the Chroniclers, both scribal groups deal with the same persons, topics and events. And it is not difficult to recognize biblical wisdom genres no matter whether they appear in the book of Proverbs or in other biblical texts. Nor is it problematical to identify hymnic compositions, whether they are to be found in the book of Psalms, in the prophetic literature, or scattered around in the historiographical books of the Bible. It was, for instance, the discovery that there were so many similarities between the prophetic books and the book of Psalms that led Mowinckel many years ago to the conviction that the prophets had been attached to the cult, and that they should be regarded as 'cultic prophets'.[50] More recently, the interest in intertextuality has become more conscious, not least as a result of the important book by Fishbane published in 1985.[51]

6. *Scribes, Sources and Diachronic Growth*

The creation of the Hebrew Bible at all stages in its history, 'from the Iron Age to the Middle Ages', reflects, in some way or another, a scribal milieu. Scribal institutions were responsible for 'looking after' the literary heritage of a society.[52] Scribal institutions were also important in

---

50. S. Mowinckel, *Psalmenstudien. III. Kultprophetie und prophetische Psalmen* (Videnskapsselskapets Skrifter. II. Hist.-Filos. Klasse 1922, 1; Kristiania: Jacob Dybwad, 1923).

51. M. Fishbane, *Biblical Interpretation in Ancient Israel* (Oxford: Clarendon Press, 1985).

52. One should not, however, forget the vast economic implications of literacy and its significance for the development of the bureaucracy that made urbanism possible. See H.J. Nissen, P. Damerow and R.K. Englund, *Archaic Bookkeeping:*

Iron Age Palestine, especially in Jerusalem, where they were responsible for the creation of the traditions which we find today in the Hebrew Bible.[53] Unfortunately, we do not know much about these activities. It may be, for instance, that the royal court was responsible for historiographical and annalistic works, and the temple for religious law. This however, is pure guesswork.

One major discussion in relation to the question of literacy in ancient Israel concerns the problem of 'schools'. In this particular area, there has been much disagreement among biblical scholars.[54] Frankly, I do not feel that we can actually ever give a good answer to this question. The evidence for Palestine is simply too scarce. Also, I have a feeling that scholars sometimes have the mediaeval scriptorium or the modern school system of Europe at the back of their minds when debating the issue. For what is a 'school'? Is it not also a 'school' when a single

---

Early Writing and Techniques of Economic Administration in the Ancient Near East (trans. P. Larsen; Chicago: University of Chicago Press, 1993); R.F.G. Sweet, 'Writing as a Factor in the Rise of Urbanism', in W.E. Aufrecht, N.A. Mirau and S.W. Gauley (eds.), *Urbanism in Antiquity: From Mesopotamia to Crete* (JSOTSup, 244; Sheffield: Sheffield Academic Press, 1997), pp. 35-49.

53. W.G. Dever, 'Social Structure in Palestine in the Iron II Period on the Eve of Destruction', in T.E. Levy (ed.), *The Archaeology of Society in the Holy Land* (London: Leicester University Press, 1995), pp. 417-30. Dealing with the Persian period is E. Ben Zvi, 'The Urban Center of Jerusalem and the Development of the Literature of the Hebrew Bible', in Aufrecht, Mirau and Gauley (eds.), *Urbanism in Antiquity*, pp. 194-209. The early Iron Age in Jerusalem, unfortunately, is not so well known. See A. Mazar, 'Jerusalem and its Vicinity in Iron Age I', in I. Finkelstein and N. Na'aman (eds.), *From Nomadism to Monarchy: Archaeological and Historical Aspects of Early Israel* (Jerusalem: Yad Izhak Ben-Zvi, 1994), pp. 70-91.

54. A. Lemaire, *Les écoles et la formation de la Bible dans l'Ancien Israël* (OBO, 39; Fribourg: Editions universitaires, 1981); F.W. Golka, 'Die israelitische Weisheitsschule oder "Des Kaisers neue Kleider"', *VT* 33 (1983), pp. 257-70; E. Puech, 'Les écoles dans l'Israël préexilique: données épigraphiques', in J. Emerton (ed.), *Congress Volume Jerusalem 1986* (VTSup, 40; Leiden: E.J. Brill, 1988), pp. 189-203; M. Haran, 'On the Diffusion of Literacy and Schools in Ancient Israel', in Emerton (ed.), *Congress Volume Jerusalem 1986*, pp. 81-95; D.W. Jamieson-Drake, *Scribes and Schools in Monarchic Judah: A Socio-Archaeological Approach* (JSOTSup, 109; The Social World of Biblical Antiquity, 9; Sheffield: Almond Press, 1991); G.I. Davies, 'Were there Schools in Ancient Israel?', in J. Day, R.P. Gordon and H.G.M. Williamson (eds.), *Wisdom in Ancient Israel: Essays in Honour of J.A. Emerton* (Cambridge: Cambridge University Press, 1995), pp. 199-211.

village scribe (if there ever was such a person) lets his sucessor into the intricacies of scribality? More important to us is the fact that scribality and literacy were 'widespread'. The corpus of ancient Hebrew inscriptions from the Iron Age, the earliest *possibly* going back to the tenth century BCE, is fast growing.[55]

Even if the Deuteronomistic History is rather to be likened with a history theology, a religious salvation history, or whatever one chooses to call it, rather than with history in a 'positivistic' fashion, we should not be led to believe that the Deuteronomists were pure fiction writers who actually *invented* their material as they went along. Any such procedure would be far from both the practice and mentality of the ancient Near Eastern cultures. Literary production in the ancient Near East and in ancient Israel is determined above all by its stereotyped language and different sets of conventional literary types. A superb knowledge of the conventional literature—oral and written—combined with an ability to reuse and to put together various materials from the indigenous literary traditions for contemporary purposes were the hallmarks of the good literati also in Palestine. The results of their work are now on display in the selection of texts found in the Hebrew Bible, reflecting at the same time the *Einheitskultur* of ancient Israel.

Moreover, the Deuteronomists were tradition cultivators who worked with and built upon whatever traditions were available to them. What these traditions looked like in the period(s) prior to the Deuteronomists we can hardly say. We may guess, of course, as many scholars have done before us,[56] but one is quite often left with the feeling that it is very difficult to get beyond mere speculation and gain any certainty in the matter. We do find in the texts of the Hebrew Bible, however, quite a few vestiges pointing to the process of diachronic growth. Since these are well known to the scholarly world, I shall here refer only to one example in the book of Samuel. Many others could have been mentioned.[57]

55. See J. Renz, *Die althebräischen Inschriften*. I. *Text und Kommentar* (Handbuch der althebräischen Epigraphik, 1; Darmstadt: Wissenschaftliche Buchgesellschaft, 1995).

56. For literature, see the notes on Deuteronomy and the Deuteronomists above.

57. For a short, yet illustrating, survey of the study on diachronic growth in Judges see R.H. O'Connell, *The Rhetoric of the Book of Judges* (VTSup, 63; Leiden: E.J. Brill, 1996), pp. 347-66.

From a compositional point of view, the books of Samuel make a fairly variegated impression on the reader. It appears that the author must have used various sources.[58] The best known example is probably the story of Saul's accession to the throne in 1 Samuel 8–12. The different sources that constitute this story in its final state make Samuel on the one hand protest vehemently against the introduction of the monarchy, and on the other support it strongly. Typically Deuteronomistic is the statement in 1 Sam. 8.6-7: 'It displeased Samuel when they said, Give us a king to rule us. Samuel prayed to YHWH, and YHWH said to Samuel, Listen to the voice of the people, and everything that they say to you for they have not rejected you. It is me they have rejected to be king over them.' This highly negative attitude towards kingship, so typical of the Deuteronomists, appears in strong contrast to the rest of the story of King Saul where there is no end to Samuel's enthusiasm when it comes to making Saul a king. Obviously, we catch here a glimpse of the author's 'source selection procedure'.[59]

7. *The Persistence of the Tradition*

A common objection against the reliability of historical traditions found in the Hebrew Bible is that they were written down a very long time indeed after the events that they purportedly describe took place. There are, however, many indications that the traditions of the ancient Near East were extremely tenacious of life. This fact should not be confused with a false belief in 'the unchangeable East'. We do know that even if the 'same' traditions were used, the adaption to new situations could sometimes change the stories completely.[60] At the same time, we know

---

58. It is important that we do not forget about this, particularly in these days when there is so much talk about the 'unity of the text'. Brettler has reminded us of this in his recent, useful article on the sources in another text from Samuel: M. Brettler, 'The Composition of 1 Samuel 1–2', *JBL* 116 (1997), pp. 601-612.

59. Again, we should not confuse this procedure with the recovery of 'reliable' historical documents. See on this the important study by P.S. Ash, 'Solomon's? District? List', *JSOT* 67 (1995), pp. 67-86. Here Ash both demonstrates how 1 Kgs 4.7-19 (a text that used to be regarded as being of high historical trustworthiness) is based on a pre-existing source used by the Deuteronomists, but is totally without any historical value in relation to the time of Solomon.

60. One needs only to compare the Chronistic and the Deuteronomistic descriptions of King David to see my point here. For further perspectives, see L.L. Grabbe, 'Reconstructing History from the Book of Ezra', in P.R. Davies (ed.), *Second*

from Mesopotamia that the basic structures of the economic administrative system did not change much at all for the better part of 3000 years![61] And above we noticed how the contractual relationship between a deity and his people is attested through two millennia.

Probably more relevant to the present discussion on scribal responsibility for the growth and development of the Hebrew Bible is another example involving Sumerian. From Mesopotamia we know that Sumerian continued to live on as a scribal language long after it had ceased to be a spoken language. As a matter of fact Sumerian outlived even Akkadian as a literary language, and Sumerian religious texts were used as late as the first century BCE in Parthian Babylon.[62] Even if Sumerian had long since been replaced by Akkadian, which was replaced by Aramaic, which was replaced by Greek, and even if Sumerian was badly understood throughout the whole of the first millennium BCE we notice with great interest how the scribal system not only transmitted, but even *used* 2000-year-old cultic hymns written in Sumerian for theological purposes. What this at least tells us is that the scribal schools of Mesopotamia were able to take proper care of their own literary traditions!

I believe that this fact is not without relevance as well to the transmission of ancient Hebrew texts. I am, of course, not claiming that we have 2000 years or so of handing down of ancient Hebrew traditions before the fall of Judah in 586 BCE, but I believe that the mere fact that such activity went on in other, related cultures makes it plausible that some of the traditions which we may find, for instance, in the Deuteronomistic history may also go back a long time. This would apply quite independently of what happened later to these traditions in their different 'final' compositions, be it from Persian, Hellenistic, Roman or mediaeval times.

8. *Final Remarks*

As we know, there are major problems involved in attempting to date biblical texts. For my own part, I have always felt the dating of these

---

Temple Studies 1: Persian Period (JSOTSup, 117; Sheffield: JSOT Press, 1991), pp. 98-106.

61. Nissen, Damerow and Englund, *Archaic Bookkeeping*, p. 10.

62. P.-A. Beaulieu, 'Antiquarian Theology in Seleucid Uruk', *Acta Sumerologica* 14 (1992), pp. 47-75 (47).

texts to be a very rickety business indeed, and I have strong doubts about its feasibility. For instance, in most cases, I do not believe that it is possible to say of a text whether it belongs to the 'Persian' or to the 'Hellenistic' era.

A particular feature of the dating discussions are that they are sometimes not very thorough, and often based on superficial or arbitrary evidence. It is also unclear, in many cases, whether a scholarly dating to a certain period applies to all of a text or only to a part or parts of it. Also, it is not always stated whether the dating concerns the time of the final composition, or whether it is felt that some of, or most of, the materials which we may find in the texts may go back to earlier sources.

From what I have attempted to show above, it follows that I find it quite likely that biblical texts were produced over fairly long periods of time, often by reusing older materials. From Qumran we know that there were many different 'proto-Masoretic' text traditions in circulation. Quite possibly, Nevi'im was fixed as late as during the first centuries before and after Christ, and Kethuvim around the end of the first century after Christ. The standardization of the Masoretic Text is, as we know, an even later phenomenon.[63] If the information which we may find in (say) a Hellenistic text does go back to a period prior to the final composition, the dating of the final composition may be less interesting to the historian of Iron Age Palestine who wants to use these texts as sources. Whether the information found in the texts does yield reliable information on the history of Iron Age Palestine or not has to decided in each and every case.

Any claim that the Deuteronomistic History (or the Chronicler, for that matter) is influenced by Greek historiography must be regarded as highly problematic. As we have seen above, the flavour and mentality of the vast majority of our texts are ancient Near Eastern, *not* Greek.

In addition to this decisive factor, yet another argument against any form of Greek influence needs to be referred to. The very views on his-

---

63. On these and other problems in relation to the Masoretic Text, see E. Tov, *Textual Criticism of the Hebrew Bible* (Minneapolis: Fortress Press, 1992), pp. 27-30, 187-97. Cf. also B. Albrektson, 'Reflections on the Emergence of a Standard Text of the Hebrew Bible', in J.A. Emerton (ed.), *Congress Volume Göttingen 1977* (VTSup, 29; Leiden: E.J. Brill, 1978), pp. 49-65. Rather relevant in this connection are the different text forms of the book of Jeremiah. See E. Tov, *The Text-Critical Use of the Septuagint in Biblical Research* (Jerusalem Biblical Studies, 8; Jerusalem: Simor, 2nd edn, 1997), pp. 243-45.

tory and historiography in ancient Greece and in the ancient Semitic worlds are radically different. I am here not only thinking of the totally different historiographical concerns of the Greeks and the Semites. With regard to such concepts as 'past', 'future' and 'time', as well as when it comes to making distinctions between notions such as 'truth' and 'fiction', the ancient Semitic and ancient Greek worlds were far, far apart.[64]

64. See, e.g., P.G. Bietenholz, *Historia and Fabula: Myths and Legends in Historical Thought from Antiquity to the Modern Age* (Brill's Studies in Intellectual History, 59; Leiden: E.J. Brill, 1984), p. 4; D.O. Edzard, 'La vision du passé et de l'avenir en Mésopotamie: Période paléobabylonienne', in A. de Pury (ed.), *Histoire et conscience historique dans les civilisations du Proche-Orient Ancien: Actes du Colloque de Cartigny 1986* (Les Cahiers du CEPOA, 5; Leuven: Peeters, 1989), pp. 157-66; A. Momigliano, *The Classical Foundations of Modern Historiography* (Berkeley, CA: University of California Press, 1990), pp. 18-21; P.-A. Beaulieu, 'Antiquarianism and the Concern for the Past in the Neo-Babylonian Period', *The Canadian Society for Mesopotamian Studies* 28 (1994), pp. 37-42 (40); J.-J. Glassner, *Chroniques mésopotamiennes: Presentées et traduites par...* (Paris: Les Belles Lettres, 1993), pp. 19-20, and *passim*. Glassner's book (pp. 19-47) has an excellent chapter on Mesopotamian historiography. See also by the same author 'Les temps de l'histoire en Mésopotamie', in Pury, Römer and Macchi (eds.), *Israël construit son histoire*, pp. 167-89.

THE HELLENISTIC PERIOD AND ANCIENT ISRAEL:
THREE PRELIMINARY STATEMENTS

Bob Becking

The Hellenistic period is like a distant constellation, not away in the sky but buried deep down in the past. Its traces of light, and darkness, only reach us after more than 2000 years. How do we look at these traces? Do we see what we want to see or do we see what was really there?

Evidence for Israel in the Hellenistic Period

The Hellenistic period is here demarcated as the period between the rise of Alexander the Great and the Roman conquest of Palestine. One can, of course, dispute this demarcation, for instance by referring to the fact that in the Roman period the Hellenistic culture as such continued in Palestine. My demarcation has been made only to limit the period under discussion.

As can be assumed, a series of events took place in the area of Palestine/Israel during this period. These events can be reconstructed based on the available evidence. This means that a history of Israel in the Hellenistic period can be written from a variety of evidence. Written sources in Greek, Latin, Hebrew and Aramaic are lying on the desk to help perform this task. It is not my purpose here to survey all the available evidence.[1] What I have in mind are texts such as the Zenon papyri; Josephus, *Antiquities of the Jews*; Agatharchides of Cnidus;[2] 1–

---

1. They are displayed and discussed by, e.g., H.W. Attridge, 'Historiography', in M.E. Stone (ed.), *Jewish Writings of the Second Temple Period* (CRINT, 2; Assen: Van Gorcum, 1984), II, pp. 157-84; *idem*, 'Josephus and his Work', in Stone (ed.), *Jewish Writings*, pp. 185-232; E. Ferguson, *Backgrounds of Early Christianity* (Grand Rapids: Eerdmans, 2nd edn, 1993), pp. 406-479; Lester L. Grabbe, *Judaism from Cyrus to Hadrian* (London: SCM Press, 1994), pp. 171-311.

2. Josephus, *Ant.* 12.1.1. §§3-10; *Apion* 1.22 §§209-212; see also M. Stern

2 Maccabees; *3–4 Maccabees*; Polybius, *History*; the remains of the writings of Nicolaus of Damascus;[3] some Qumran scrolls; Demetrius the Chronographer; Strabo, *Geography*; Appian, *The Syrian Wars*. It is, probably, superfluous and redundant to say that all these sources are biased: they relate and reveal. They not only relate the events—in a selection made by the authors—but they also reveal their writers' perception of the event(s), since they implicitly, and sometimes explicitly, are written with a specific worldview or symbol system in mind. In addition, it can be assumed that a variety of written evidence served political and/or ideological purposes. The lengthy account of the Tobiad family in Josephus,[4] for instance, has been interpreted as a piece of pro-Ptolemaic Jewish propaganda written by Onias IV.[5] Nevertheless, by careful and conscious comparison a narrative history can be reconstructed from the evidence.[6] It is probably superfluous and redundant to say that every such history is imbued by the worldview of its present-day author.[7] Objective history in the sense of an indisputable report on past events is impossible.[8]

(ed.), *Greek and Latin Authors on Jews and Judaism*. I. *From Herodotus to Plutarch* (Jerusalem: Israel Academy of Sciences and Humanities, 1986), pp. 104-109; B. Bar-Kochva, *Pseudo Hecateus, 'On the Jews': Legitimizing the Jewish Diaspora* (Hellenistic Culture and Society, 21; Berkeley: University of California Press, 1966), pp. 74-75 and the essay by Lester L. Grabbe in this volume (pp. 129-55 below).

3.   See Stern (ed.), *Greek and Latin Authors*, I, pp. 227-60; B.Z. Wacholder, *Nicolaus of Damascus* (University of California Publications in History, 75; Berkeley: University of California Press, 1962).

4.   *Ant.* 12.4.1-11 §§157-236.

5.   See J.A. Goldstein, 'The Tales of the Tobiads', in J. Neusner (ed.), *Christianity, Judaism and Other Greco-Roman Cults* (SJLA, 12.3; Leiden: E.J. Brill, 1975), pp. 85-123, with the critical remarks by Grabbe, *Judaism*, p. 175, and his essay in this volume (pp. 129-55 below).

6.   On the concept of narrative history see A.C. Danto, *Analytical Philosophy of History* (Cambridge: Cambridge University Press, 1968); F.R. Ankersmit, *Narrative Logic: A Semantical Analysis of the Historian's Language* (Den Haag: Mouton, 1983); and the remarks by H.M. Barstad, 'History and the Hebrew Bible', in L.L. Grabbe (ed.), *Can a 'History of Israel' Be Written?* (JSOTSup, 245; ESHM, 1; Sheffield: Sheffield Academic Press, 1997), pp. 37-64, esp. pp. 54-60.

7.   See on this, e.g., R.G. Collingwood, *The Idea of History: Revised Edition with Lectures 1926–1928* (Oxford: Oxford University Press, 1994); M. Stanford, *The Nature of Historical Knowledge* (Oxford: Basil Blackwell, 1987); E.A. Knauf, 'From History to Interpretation', in D.V. Edelman, *The Fabric of History: Text,*

Archaeology has revealed a variety of evidence on the period under consideration,[9] for example, building remains, various artifacts, coins,[10] destruction layers, inscriptions. Among the inscriptions special mention should be made of a bilingual inscription from Dan[11] and an Aramaic ostracon excavated at Jerusalem containing six Greek loanwords.[12] This archaeological evidence sheds light on the events related in written evidence. I will not enter into a discussion on how and when archaeological evidence contradicts written evidence, but only note that what we know from archaeology is that it enriches and also modifies the historical narrative.[13]

In sum: the question 'can a history of Israel in the Hellenistic period be written?' will be answered by me in a positive mode: yes, it can. It will, however, be a tentative enterprise. The problem is that most of the evidence comes from outside, from Greek and Latin sources. The most informative Jewish source, Josephus, is comparatively late. This implies that it might be better to depict this 'history of Israel in the Hellenistic period' as a proto-history, the definition of proto-history being the representation of a culture mainly based on external evidence. I will not write or summarize this history here, but only point to an important

Artifact and Israel's Past (JSOTSup, 127; Sheffield: JSOT Press, 1991), pp. 26-64; Barstad, 'History and the Hebrew Bible', pp. 37-64.

8.   Objectivity versus subjectivity is a topic abundantly discussed by historians. Here, I only refer to K. Mannheim, *Wissenssoziologie: Auswahl aus dem Werk* (Neuwied: Luchterhand, 1970), and the essays in J. Rüsen (ed.), *Historische Objektivität: Aufsätze zur Geschichtsphilosophie* (Kleine Vandenhoeck Reihe, 1416; Göttingen: Vandenhoeck & Ruprecht, 1975).

9.   See, e.g., R. Arav, *Hellenistic Palestine: Settlement Patterns and City Planning 337–31 B.C.E.* (Oxford: BAR, 1989); H.-P. Kuhnen, *Palästina in griechisch-römischer Zeit* (Handbuch der Archäologie Vorderasien, 2.2; Munich: Beck, 1990).

10.   See Y. Meshorer, *Ancient Jewish Coinage. I. Persian Period through Hasmonaeans* (New York: Amphora, 1982); Y. Meshorer and S. Qedar, *The Samarian Coinage* (New York: Amphora, 1991; this book will be replaced by a new enlarged edition); O. Mørkholm, *Early Hellenistic Coinage: From the Accession of Alexander to the Peace of Apamea (336–188 B.C.)* (ed. P. Grierson and U. Westermarck; Cambridge: Cambridge University Press, 1991); L. Mildenberg, *Vestigia Leonis: Studien zur antiken Numismatik Israels* (NTOA, 36; Fribourg: Universitätsverlag; Göttingen: Vandenhoeck & Ruprecht, 1998).

11.   Edited by A. Biran, 'Tel Dan', *RB* 84 (1977), pp. 256-63.

12.   Edited by F.M. Cross, 'An Aramaic Ostracon of the Third Century B.C.E. from Excavations in Jerusalem', *EI* 15 (1981), pp. *67-*69.

13.   See the useful synthesis in Grabbe, *Judaism*, pp. 204-220, 269-311.

pattern: from the evidence available, it is clear (at least to me) that ancient Israel in the Hellenistic period had a multidimensional identity. This complexity is mainly caused by the variety of answers given to the coming of the Hellenistic culture to the area.

Is the Bible a Hellenistic Book?

The view that the Old Testament was created in a late period has been advocated strongly these last years by Diebner,[14] Lemche[15] and Thompson.[16] I purposely use the verb 'create' here, since I have the idea that the scholars just mentioned do not defend the thesis that the Hebrew Bible received its final redaction in the Hellenistic period. Their view, if I understand them correctly, is that the Hebrew Bible was fabricated in the Hellenistic period and that the text cannot be used for the reconstruction of the history of ancient, that is, pre-exilic, Israel. The idea that the Enneateuch has been written on the model of Herodotus's *Historiae* was first suggested by Van Seters,[17] and has been elaborated by Nielsen[18] and Wesselius.[19] Their view also implies a late creation of the Hebrew Bible.

This challenging view has caused some disturbance and commotion. It should not, however, be treated as an established fact or an invariable result of scholarly research.[20] It should be seen as a proposal and has the form and the character of a hypothesis, It needs to be tested against the available evidence. Besides that some implications and not a few

---

14. In an abundance of articles in *Dielheimer Blätter zum Alten Testament*.

15. N.P. Lemche, 'The Old Testament—A Hellenistic Book?', *SJOT* 7 (1993), pp. 163-93; *idem*, *The Israelites in History and Tradition* (Library of Ancient Israel; Louisville, KY: Westminster/John Knox Press, 1998).

16. T.L. Thompson, *The Bible in History: How Writers Create a Past* (London: Jonathan Cape, 1999).

17. J. Van Seters, 'Histories and Historians of the Ancient Near East: The Israelites', *Or* NS 50 (1981), pp. 137-85.

18. F.A.J. Nielsen, *The Tragedy in History: Herodotus and the Deuteronomistic History* (JSOTSup, 251; Copenhagen International Seminar, 4; Sheffield: Sheffield Academic Press, 1997).

19. J.W. Wesselius, 'Discontinuity, Congruence and the Making of the Hebrew Bible', *SJOT* 13 (1999), pp. 24-77.

20. I am not sure, though, if 'invariable results of scholarly research' really exist.

complications will be discussed here. My remarks and observations are given in a haphazard order.

Bibliophobia

As Hans Barstad has argued, the view that the Hebrew Bible is a Hellenistic book is based on one form or another of *bibliophobia*.[21] This point of view is a conceivable reaction to too much *bibliophilia* in the historiography of Ancient Israel.[22] A historian, however, has, almost by definition, an ambiguous stand towards a source: the historical trade asks for distrust, while the art of reconstruction asks for trust. I would like to opt for a balance between these two sides. In my view it would be methodically sound to trust the historicity of events related in a source until other evidence has given the proof that a certain event could not have taken place. Or to say the same in another way: I take elements from the biblical story for historical trustworthiness, conditionally however: (p)[23] is true under the condition that (p) fits the general historical framework of its time and until (p) is falsified by other evidence. The lack of other evidence is not a falsification of (p) as has been argued repetitively by scholars like Lemche, Thompson and Smelik;[24] that would be asking for verification, which from a theoretical point of view never adds new information to a hypothesis. In sum, I agree with Barstad that the Hebrew Bible contains historically trustworthy references to events earlier than the Hellenistic period.

Does the Final Form Exclude Earlier Recensions?

The Hellenistic Hebrew Bible hypothesis seems to suppose that a late date excludes the tradition-historical possibility that these texts contain older material that can be used for a reconstruction of previous periods

21. Hans M. Barstad, 'The Strange Fear of the Bible: Some Reflections on the "Bibliophobia" in Recent Ancient Israelite Historiography', in L.L. Grabbe (ed.), *Leading Captivity Captive: 'The Exile' as History and Ideology* (JSOTSup, 278; ESHM, 2; Sheffield: Sheffield Academic Press, 1998), pp. 120-27.

22. See also the discussion Simple Simon and Naive Nelly have with Crafty Cathy and Shifty Bill in B. Halpern, 'Biblical or Israelite History?', in R.E. Friedman and H.G.M. Williamson (eds.), *The Future of Biblical Studies: The Hebrew Scriptures* (SBLSS; Atlanta: Scholars Press, 1987), pp. 103-139.

23. (p) can stand for any event referred to in the Hebrew Bible: 'Sargon II conquered Samaria in 723 BCE', for instance.

24. K.A.D. Smelik, *Converting the Past: Studies in Ancient Israelite and Moabite Historiography* (OTS, 28; Leiden: E.J. Brill, 1992), esp. pp. 1-34.

in the history of Israel. Here we meet massive problems that are difficult to solve. I am fully aware of the fact of how difficult it is to reach a consensus about the content of an earlier version of a text or a story. It can be assumed that the redactor or editor of the final form made a selection of elements and events known to him (or seldom her). This selection and also the arrangement of the material has been steered by the worldview or belief system of the editor. This implies that texts, in their final form, inform us on worldviews from the period in which they were finally composed. Despite these difficulties, I find it methodically sound at least to leave open the possibility that even late texts contain references to earlier times.

On Dating Texts

On what kind of arguments are texts dated? And what are we doing when we are dating texts? As an argument in favour of a Hellenistic emergence of the Hebrew Bible it has been said that historical patterns in the Hellenistic period would fit the tendencies in the biblical narratives better than historical patterns in earlier periods. The tension between Seleucids and Ptolemies, for instance, would have been used as a model for the dichotomy between northern Israel and southern Judah in the narratives of ancient Israel.[25]

In doing so, the lock-and-key method is applied. An exemplary application of this method can be found in Hardmeier's monograph on 2 Kings 18–20.[26] The text—either in its original or in its final form—is to be considered as a key. The reconstructed history of the time in which a narrative was written or in which it received its final form is to be seen as a lock in which the key can be turned. Meaning and significance can be read from what happens when the key is turned in the lock. For instance, Hardmeier construes the original narrative in 2 Kings 18–20 as the 'Erzählung von der Assyrischen Bedrohung und der Befreiung Jerusalems'.[27] Reading this ABBJ as a literary composition, the following picture arises: the fact that apparently two Assyrian

---

25. Lemche, 'The Old Testament', pp. 163-93; Lemche, *Israelites in History and Tradition*; Thompson, *Bible in History*, pp. 3-4, 196-99.

26. C. Hardmeier, *Prophetie im Streit vor dem Untergang Judas: Erzählkommunikative Studien zur Entstehungssituation der Jesaja und Jeremiaerzählungen in II Reg 18–20 und Jer 37–40* (BZAW, 187; Berlin: W. de Gruyter, 1990).

27. This 'Report on the Assyrian Threat and the Deliverance of Jerusalem' will be referred to by the German acronym ABBJ.

campaigns against Judah/Jerusalem are mentioned is not suggested by historical data about two campaigns, nor by the assumption that two sources depicting the same event have been conflated in the final narrative, but should be resolved at the narrotological level. The narrator has built in an element of complication: after Hezekiah's payment of tribute an Assyrian withdrawal is expected but does not take place immediately. The significance of this complication becomes clear when the key is turned in the lock. Hardmeier argues that the final years before the fall of Jerusalem to the Babylonians should be seen as the historical context of the ABBJ-narrative. On the level of historical reconstruction it should be noted that a temporary withdrawal by the Babylonian forces in 588 BCE was provoked by a march of Egyptian troops to relieve the beleaguered Judaean capital.

A few remarks about this lock-and-key method need to be made. First, there is the possible pitfall of circular reasoning, especially when the key has been smoothed literary-critically, since in that process historical arguments also have a part too. Second, there will always be another lock that fits the key. The Maccabaean age, for instance, could provide a historical context for the ABBJ narrative as well. This implies that also on a secondary occasion the rereading of the text could provoke a significant meaning. Third, our knowledge of historical processes in ancient Israel is both limited and biased. It should be noted that the 'lock' is by definition a reconstructed lock. The story on Israel in the Hellenistic period indicated above is not a representation of what really happened, but a re-enactment of the modern historian. Though based on the evidence available this reconstruction will always express the symbol system of its constructor.[28]

Dating texts is, in my view, not a historical, but a hermeneutical enterprise. Reading a text against a reconstructed or assumed historical pattern yields significance, and not historical evidence. The 'key-and-lock' procedure, tentative as it will remain as long as hard evidence about the person of the author or the original date of the composition are lacking, is an important, probably the most important, way in the process of interpreting texts.[29] Hardmeier, for instance, does not supply

---

28. Thompson, *Bible in History*, seems to be aware of this problem. He, however, does not elaborate this awareness.

29. See also my paper read at the meeting of the International Organization for the Study of the Old Testament in Oslo 1998: 'No More Grapes from the Vineyard?

any historical evidence, but offers a nice proposal for the interpretation of the Hezekiah story.

All these remarks imply that the procedure for dating biblical texts remains highly tentative. From the point of view of historical methodology, it still is possible to formulate—within the boundaries of these limitations—the 'key and lock', although in a way that is still open to debate.

For me, this implies that the fact that biblical texts can be read against a Hellenistic background does not mean that they were written then. You can also read certain parts of the Hebrew Bible against the background of the Dutch revolt against Spain in the sixteenth century. This reading does supply meaning, but would anyone argue that the Hebrew Bible was written in Amsterdam when converting to Protestantism around 1678 or printed in Leyden when opening its Faculty of Theology in the same period? In sum, the 'key-and-lock' method cannot produce an argument *pro* or *contra* a Hellenistic emergence of the Hebrew Bible.

Yahwistic or Jewish?

A date of the final redaction, composition, fabrication or creation of the Hebrew Bible in the Hellenistic period has one important implication that should not be overlooked. When the texts were written in that period, the Hebrew Bible would be a document of Judaism since Judaism, in one form or another, had by that time become the religion of the Jewish people. In my view, however, the Hebrew Bible is a Yahwistic book expressing the religious ideas of Yahwism, in one form or another, and not yet of Judaism.

Although Yahwism and Judaism have much in common, they are not identical and should be treated as two different forms of religion. Traditionally, the exile is taken as the watershed between the two forms. With Diana Edelman, I assume a complex process of transition from Yahwism(s) to Judaism(s): from 'national Yahwism' or 'First Temple Yahwism' via 'Intertemple Yahwisms'[30] and 'Second Temple Yah-

---

A Plea for a Historical-Critical Approach in the Study of the Old Testament', in: A. Lemaire and M. Sæbø (eds.), *Congress Volume: Oslo, 1998* (VTSup, 80; Leiden: E.J. Brill, 2000), pp. 123-41.

30. Indicating the various forms of religion of those in exile and those who remained in the land from 587 to 515 BCE.

wism' to 'Early Judaism'.[31] Although her labels for the various periods in the development of religion in Ancient Israel can be discussed, her proposal is very helpful. It is not my purpose here to discuss these shifts in detail or to elaborate on the differences between Yahwism and Judaism. In my view, the Hebrew Bible, except for some relics of pre-monotheistic Yahwism, refers to Edelman's first three forms.[32]

In case the Hebrew Bible was composed in the Hellenistic period it would contain: (1) references to the religious struggles of that time; (2) the polarity between 'good' and 'bad' would have been defined in the polarity between 'pure' and 'impure', and not so much in the ethical terms as is now the case; and (3) the idea of divine providence that as a concept borrowed from Stoic philosophy is expressed, for example, in *Wis.* 14.3; 17.2; *3 Macc.* 4.21; 5.30; Josephus, *Ant.* 13.5.9 §§171-72; *m. Ab.* 3.16 but that is absent in the Hebrew Bible.[33] Therefore, it is possible to assume the view that the Hebrew Bible in its final form, except the book of Daniel, was written during the complex process from Yahwism(s) to Judaism(s) using and rewriting older, sometimes pre-'exilic'/Iron Age II–III material. I would advocate the assumption that the Pentateuch and also the Deuteronomistic History received their final form in this process of religion in crisis and on the move, with one of its aims to document the traditional Yahwistic religion. This assumption excludes an emergence in the Hellenistic period.

The Hebrew Language

At the meeting in Lahti, the history of the Hebrew language was discussed. Challenged by a question posed by Timo Veijola, Niels Peter Lemche formulated a multidimensional synchronic theory of language. Veijola had stressed the differences between classical Hebrew, as it can be found in the Hebrew Bible, and the Hebrew from the second century

---

31. D.V. Edelman, 'Introduction', in D.V. Edelman (ed.), *The Triumph of Elohim: From Yahwisms to Judaisms* (CBET, 13; Kampen: Kok Pharos, 1995), pp. 23-24.

32. See also R. Albertz, *Religionsgeschichte Israels in alttestamentlicher*, II (GAT, 8; Göttingen: Vandenhoeck & Ruprecht, 1992); K. van der Toorn, *Family Religion in Babylonia, Syria and Israel: Continuity and Change in the Forms of religious Life* (SHCANE, 7; Leiden: E.J. Brill, 1996).

33. See, e.g., J. Mansfeld, 'Providence and the Destruction of the Universe in Early Stoic Thought', in M.J. Vermaseren (ed.), *Studies in Hellenistic Religions* (EPRO, 78; Leiden: E.J. Brill, 1979), pp. 129-88; R.L. Gordon, 'Pronoia', in *DDD*, pp. 664-67.

BCE known from, for example, the Qumran documents and the book of Ben Sira. Whereas Veijola would explain these differences in a diachronic way—the differences witnessing the development of the Hebrew language[34]—Lemche would opt for another view. He thinks that in a given society various forms and dialects of a language can be used alternatively: What is called 'classical Hebrew' was the dialect of the scribes of the Hebrew Bible, while at Qumran another variant of the same language was dominant.[35] If this latter possibility is correct, a diachronic view is unnecessary.

In this connection I would like to refer to the linguistic evidence from epigraphy. The ostraca from Arad[36] to a lesser degree, but especially the Lachish letters[37] show semantically and syntactically a form of Hebrew that in its complexity is comparable to the 'standard Hebrew' in which, for instance, the books of Kings and the book of Jeremiah are written. Albright has used this evidence as an argument for a pre-exilic layer in the so-called Deuteronomistic History.[38] Although this conclusion is an act of overinterpreting the evidence that classical Hebrew did not develop that much in the 50 or so years between the era of Josiah and the early exilic period, the observation can still be used as an argument for the hypothesis that around 600 BCE a form of classical Hebrew was

---

34. As has been done by, e.g., A. Hurvitz, *A Linguistic Study of the Relationship between the Priestly Source and the Book of Ezekiel: A New Approach to an Old Problem* (Cahiers de la Revue Biblique, 20; Paris: J. Gabalda, 1982); *idem*, 'The Historical Quest for "Ancient Israel" and the Linguistic Evidence of the Hebrew Bible: Some Methodological Observations', *VT* 47 (1997), pp. 301-315.

35. This is how I understand Lemche's remarks.

36. Editio princeps: Y. Aharoni, *Arad Inscriptions* (Jerusalem: Israel Exploration Society, 1981). See also A. Lemaire, *Inscriptions Hébraïques. I. Les ostraca* (Paris: Cerf, 1977), pp. 147-235; K.A.D. Smelik, *Historische Dokumente aus dem alten Israel* (Kleine Vandenhoeck-Reihe, 1528; Göttingen: Vandenhoeck & Ruprecht, 1987), pp. 94-107; J. Renz, *Die althebräischen Inschriften* (HAE, 1.1; Darmstadt: Wissenschaftliche Buchgesellschaft, 1995), pp. 347-403.

37. Editio princeps: H. Torczyner, *Lachish I: The Lachish Letters* (London: Oxford University Press, 1938). See also Lemaire, *Inscriptions Hébraïques*, I, pp. 85-143; Smelik, *Historische Dokumente*, pp. 108-121; Renz, *Die althebräischen Inschriften*, pp. 405-440.

38. W.F. Albright, *The Biblical Period from Abraham to Ezra* (New York: Harper Books, 1963), pp. 45-46. F.M. Cross, *Canaanite Myth and Hebrew Epic* (Cambridge, MA: Harvard University Press, 1973), pp. 274-89; R.D. Nelson, *The Double Redaction of the Deuteronomistic History* (JSOTSup, 18; Sheffield: JSOT Press, 1981), pp. 26-27, did repeat this argument in favour of a pre-exilic Dtr[1].

spoken and written that is also attested in the books of Kings.[39]

To me this implies three things: (1) that the emergence of the books of Kings from the period of Babylonian overlordship over Judah is still plausible; (2) that a diachronic explanation of the linguistic variance in Hebrew is to be preferred over a synchronic one; and (3) that the linguistic evidence cannot be used as an unsolicited argument in favour of a Hellenistic date.

Evidence from Hellenistic Authors

Against a Hellenistic dating of the Hebrew Bible pleads the fact that in the Hellenistic period texts were written that imply the existence of (parts of) the Hebrew Bible. Around 300 BCE, Hecataeus of Abdera composed an account of Judaean history and constitution.[40] His account is far from an accurate history of ancient Israel and seems to reflect practices of his day. Nevertheless, various features in his story—such as the Exodus event, Moses as a law-giver and investigator of a monotheistic and aniconic cult—imply the existence of (parts of) the books of Exodus, Leviticus and Numbers.[41] This leads me to the assumption that what we now call the Pentateuch is not to be seen as a late fabrication, but rather as the result of a long process of redaction and that it already existed, in one form or another, before the Hellenistic period. This assumption can be reinforced from similar observations on the remains of the writings of Demetrius the Chronographer and Artapanus. Demetrius lived in the last part of the third century BCE. The

---

39. The argument is reinforced by the analyses of I. Young, *Diversity in Pre-Exilic Hebrew* (FAT, 5; Tübingen: Mohr Siebeck, 1993); S.L. Gogel, *A Grammar of Epigraphic Hebrew* (SBLRBS, 23; Atlanta: Scholars Press, 1998), pp. 233-92.

40. Apud Diodorus Siculus, 40.3; text, translation and discussion in Stern (ed.), *Greek and Latin Authors*, I, pp. 20-35. See also *Ep. Arist.* 31; Josephus, *Apion* 1.183-204; D. Mendels, 'Hecateus of Abdera and a Jewish "patrios politeia" of the Persian Period', *ZAW* 95 (1983), pp. 96-110; Grabbe, *Judaism*, pp. 173-74 and pp. 129-55 below; Bar-Kochva, *Pseudo-Hecateus*, pp. 7-43; P.R. Davies, *Scribes and Schools: The Canonization of the Hebrew Scriptures* (Library of Ancient Israel; Louisville, KY: Westminster/John Knox Press, 1998), pp. 102-106. See also Rainer Albertz, pp. 30-46 above.

41. Concluding, on the basis of absence of references to the patriarchs in Hecataeus, that Genesis traditions did not yet exist around 300 BCE is an example of overcharging the evidence and of too positivistic a historical method. The only thing that can be concluded is that Hecataeus, or his Judaean/Jewish informant, was not much interested in matters primeval, *pace* Davies, *Scribes and Schools*, p. 105.

fragments of his writings on Israelite history[42] make clear that he used the Old Greek translation of the Pentateuch as a source.[43] From Artapanus, *On the Jews*, written in the third century BCE, only a few fragments in Eusebius, *Praeparatio Evangelica*, have been preserved.[44] Artapanus has accommodated traditions on Abraham, Joseph and Moses to Hellenistic culture and history-writing.[45] His text, however, presupposes the Pentateuch. These examples might even turn round the argument by assuming that if the Hebrew Bible was a fabrication from Hellenistic times, the book might have looked similar to the evidence just discussed.

Historical Consciousness in the Hellenistic Period
(Some Sketchy Remarks)

What view(s) on history did Jews have in the period under consideration? An implication of my point of view would be that for a *histoire de mentalité* the Hebrew Bible cannot be used as a source of information for Jewish historical consciousness during the Hellenistic period.

This means that we have to look for other evidence. The so-called rewritten biblical stories from the Hellenistic period would be helpful for a reconstruction.[46] Next to that the historical exposés in various apocryphal and pseudepigraphical texts should be looked at.

In my view the narration of history in these texts mainly serves the ideological intentions of various groups within Judaism. History is not narrated for its own sake or just for fun, but rather to strengthen reli-

42. Edition, translation and commentary: C.R. Holladay, *Fragments from Hellenistic Jewish Authors*. I. *Historians* (SBLTT, 20; Pseudepigrapha Series, 10; Atlanta: Scholars Press, 1983), pp. 51-91; see also Attridge, 'Historiography', pp. 161-62.

43. See esp. J. Freudenthal, *Hellenistische Studien: Alexander Polyhistor und die von ihm erhaltene Reste jüdischer und samaritanischer Geschichtswerke* (2 vols.; Breslau, 1874–75), I, pp. 39-40; P.W. van der Horst, 'The Interpretation of the Bible by Minor Hellenistic Jewish Authors', in M.J. Mulder (ed.), *Mikra* (CRINT, 2.I; Assen: Van Gorcum: 1985), pp. 528-32; Grabbe, *Judaism*, p. 236.

44. See Holladay, *Fragments*, I, pp. 189-243; Stone (ed.), *Jewish Writings*, pp. 166-68.

45. See, e.g., van der Horst, 'Interpretation', pp. 148-52; Grabbe, *Judaism*, p. 237.

46. See on them, e.g., G.W.E. Nickelsburg, 'The Bible Rewritten and Expanded', in Stone (ed.), *Jewish Writings*, pp. 89-156.

gious and political claims. This is clear in the stories in Daniel and 1
Esdras. From this point of view historical flashbacks in 1 and 2 Maccabees can be read as supporting the Maccabaean programme. Ben
Sira's outline of the past (44.1–50.24) could be seen as a good example
of summarizing history for ideological aims. In addition to that there is
an increasing tendency to narrate in a schematic way. Here the historical 'narrative' serves apocalyptic strategies.[47] In this connection, I
would like to refer to the famous Apocalypse of Weeks in *1 Enoch*
(91.1-10, 18-19; 92.1–93.10; 91.11-17), where history is in that way
reduced to a scheme where no narration is left.

---

47. See, e.g., R.G. Hall, *Revealed Histories: Techniques for Ancient Jewish and
Christian Historiography* (JSPSup, 6; Sheffield: JSOT Press, 1991).

JEWGREEK GREEKJEW: THE HEBREW BIBLE IS ALL GREEK TO ME. REFLECTIONS ON THE PROBLEMATICS OF DATING THE ORIGINS OF THE BIBLE IN RELATION TO CONTEMPORARY DISCUSSIONS OF BIBLICAL HISTORIOGRAPHY

Robert P. Carroll

STEPHEN: As a matter of fact it is of no importance whether Benedetto Marcello found it or made it. The rite is the poet's rest. It may be an old hymn to Demeter or also illustrate *Caela enarrant gloriam Domini*. It is susceptible of nodes or modes as far apart as hyperphrygian and mixolydian and of texts so divergent as priests hai-hooping round David's that is Circe's or what am I saying Ceres' altar and David's tip from the stable to his chief bassoonist about his almightiness. *Mais, nom de nom,* that is another pair of trousers. *Jetez la gourme. Faut que jeunesse se passe. (He stops, points at Lynch's cap, smiles, laughs)* Which side is your knowledge bump?
THE CAP: *(With saturnine spleen)* Bah! It is because it is. Woman's reason. Jewgreek is greekjew. Extremes meet. Death is the highest form of life. Bah!

James Joyce[1]

...it is the nature of interpretation to send us back to the problems raised by interpretation itself, to asking the questions for whom, for what purpose, and why such an interpretation is more convincing in this context than in that. Interpretation, knowledge, and, as Matthew Arnold said, culture itself are always the result of contests and not simply a gift from heaven.

Edward Said[2]

Texts do not give direct evidence for the construction of a history of any world of the past asserted by their authors, but rather for the history and perspective of the authors' own world as implied in the texts' projec-

---

1. James Joyce, *Ulysses* (London: Bodley Head, 1960), p. 622.
2. Edward Said, *Covering Islam: How the Media and the Experts Determine How We See the Rest of the World* (London: Routledge & Kegan Paul, 1981), p. 161.

tions. This world is rather Greco-Roman than Hellenistic. We should be dating not traditions but the historical contexts of *texts*. These are first known from Qumran in the second century BCE, in contexts which clearly show that the formation of biblical books is still in process. No Bible as such existed in the Hellenistic period, only some very specific texts and collections of them. The analysis and interpretation of these texts is our primary historical source for understanding Hellenism in Asia. The intellectual worlds of the Old and New Testament text-traditions hold a common perception, distinguishable at most as older and younger contemporary witnesses of a common tradition

Thomas L. Thompson[3]

This essay should be read and understood as a further episode in my own personal exploration of basic issues of historiography in relation to the Bible or, in other words, circumlocutions in the direction of rein-venting the wheel as it relates to contemporary biblical studies and its continued obsession with the subject of history and the Bible.[4] At the outset it might be wise to be absolutely honest and open: I do not have, nor know of, any *real hard information* on when the Hebrew Bible was first written. That is, knowledge or information on either when its vari-ous scrolls were first committed to writing or when such written scrolls were first assembled into a collection approximating to what later was to become known to us today as one of the canons of the Bible. Ben Sira's reference to 'the reading of the law and the prophets and the other books of our fathers' (Prologue to Ben Sira) is interesting but remarkably and profoundly uninformative (cf. Ecclus 44–50 for further

---

3.   Thomas L. Thompson, *The Bible in History: How Writers Create a Past* (London: Jonathan Cape, 1999), p. 254.

4.   It therefore continues the arguments set out in Robert P. Carroll, 'Madonna of Silences: Clio and the Bible', in Lester L. Grabbe (ed.), *Can a 'History of Israel' Be Written?* (JSOTSup, 245; ESHM, 1; Sheffield: Sheffield Academic Press, 1997), pp. 84-103; *idem*, 'Exile! What Exile? Deportation and the Discourses of Diaspora', in Lester L. Grabbe (ed.), *Leading Captivity Captive: 'The Exile' as History and Ideology* (JSOTSup, 278; ESHM, 2; Sheffield: Sheffield Academic Press, 1998), pp. 62-79. It could also be said to continue what I had to say in 'Textual Strategies and Ideology in the Second Temple Period', in Philip R. Davies (ed.), *Second Temple Studies 1: Persian Period* (JSOTSup, 117; Sheffield: JSOT Press, 1991), pp. 108-124; *idem*, 'So What Do We *Know* about the Temple? The Temple in the Pro-phets', in Tamara C. Eskenazi and Kent H. Richards (eds.), *Second Temple Studies 2: Temple Community in the Persian Period* (JSOTSup, 175; Sheffield: JSOT Press, 1994), pp. 34-51; cf. Robert P. Carroll, 'Clio and Canons: In Search of a Cultural Poetics of the Hebrew Bible', *BibInt* 5 (1997), pp. 300-23 (esp. 304-308).

possible information). For example, what might be constituted by 'the other books of our fathers'? Nor does the reference to his grandfather Jesus help us much with dating the possible origins and first produc- tions of 'the law, the prophets and the other books'. So this essay will not be a defence of an *a priori* position. It will be a series of exploratory reflections and, more importantly, questions on what I take to be *some* of the baseline approaches to the topic of the Hebrew Bible as a product of the Greek period, and more especially of the later Graeco-Roman period, rather than, say, a production of the Assyrian, Babylonian or Persian periods.[5] Such reflections are at best tentative, speculative and hypothetical, but they are all these three things because we do not know any better nor do we have any *concrete evidence* which would *demon- strate* the claim that the Hebrew Bible (as we now have it as a *struc- tured collection* of writings) was committed to writing and collected together in pre-Greek and pre-Graeco-Roman times.

Scrolls: Written, Collected, Canonized

To begin at the beginning: what do we *know* about the origins of the writings now contained in the Hebrew Bible? Our starting-point has to be the scrolls found at Khirbet Qumran because we have no manu- scripts earlier than whatever period is assigned to the writings from Qumran. So we must start in the third/second century BCE—that is, *in the Greek period*. We have no reliable information before that period. Of course there are many biblical scholars who like to make grandiose speculations about the imagined origins of the scrolls constituting the Bible and they are not above suggesting that many of the writings go back *centuries* before the third century. But how could they possibly *know* this? What is the hard evidence for their speculative fantasies? Such speculations tend to reflect the deformed and deforming theory that any writing is datable by reference to its contents. If we were to use this kind of approach then it would be necessary to take the view that a novel set in Stone Age times would have been written in Stone Age times, for example, William Golding's *The Inheritors*, or that Charles Dickens's *A Tale of Two Cities*, written in 1854, was in fact written in

5.   For a very interesting treatment of the Pentateuch as a Persian period pro- duction see Samuel E. Balentine, *The Torah's Vision of Worship* (OBT; Minne- apolis: Fortress Press, 1999), esp. pp. 39-57.

the 1790s because its subject matter belongs to the period following on from the French Revolution. Such confusion of content with production is all too prevalent in contemporary biblical scholarship, even though the speculative view that biblical writings may be somewhat, however little, older than their first appearance (survival) in manuscript form is an entertainable, if not a demonstrable, hypothesis. On the other hand, if we were to assume that *before Qumran* the manuscripts found there had had an existence of some decades or perhaps a half-century—I am settling for the point of view which is, of course, an assumption itself that the documents were not *first* written at Qumran, but do represent copies of earlier documents—this would place their origins nearer the cusp of the Persian-Greek periods, thereby suggesting a strong case for treating the Bible as having its origins as a written (if not collected) text in the Greek period—or close to it at the end of the Persian period in the late fourth century. If there is to be a default mode for this debate, then let it be the one here outlined—the Qumran hypothesis—and let others who wish to argue for an earlier period of origins produce the arguments, manuscripts and data to support such a radical departure from the default mode point of view. The default mode therefore must be the Hellenistic or Graeco-Roman period for the production of scrolls which would eventually go to the making of the collections of manuscripts and scrolls reflective (or anticipatory) of what came to be known as the Bible. So the origins and roots of the Bible may loosely be said to have some connections with the Qumran phenomenon (social context) and to belong to the Graeco-Roman period, with a possible link to the Hellenistic period.

I think strong distinctions have to be made between written, collected and canonized scrolls, because there is no necessary connection between the three different dispositions of scrolls. The Hebrew Bible is constituted *as* a collection of written scrolls. It is not simply the sum total of all the individual scrolls, but an integrated collection of *arranged* scrolls. Organization of separate scrolls into a coherent collection is of the essence here. Originally there was only a scattering of discrete scrolls and then perhaps a collection of them—in baskets, boxes, jars or on shelves (or whatever) in the temple (or wherever)—but the 'canons' of the Bible with which we are familiar are more than discrete lots of individual scrolls simply gathered together into one place. They are collections of *redacted* scrolls organized into patterns of collections: for example, Torah, prophets (former and latter), writings, and so on. So what any Bible consists of is *a series of stages of production*: first the written scrolls, then edited scrolls, then collected and redacted scrolls, and finally perhaps canons of Scripture.[6] All of these distinctive activities represent different time factors and stages of production. Even if the origins of some of the scrolls contained in the Hebrew Bible were to have had their imagined beginnings in the Persian period, the final stages of the production of the Hebrew Bible would have to be assigned to the Graeco-Roman periods. I see no way of avoiding such a conclusion. I must confess that I do not, at the moment anyway, see any need to dissent seriously from an opinion I published some years ago: 'that the Bible *as we know it* (i.e. the fully redacted final form of the various books constituting it) comes from the Second Temple period seems to me ungainsayable'.[7] Now perhaps I probably would want to be a little more extensive in my assessment than that observation allowed for and would view it as perhaps an overly conservative and rather optimistic point of view: I think that the period allowed for the production and collation of the Hebrew Bible probably should be extended to include the post-Second Temple period. As for matters having to do with 'the canons of Scripture' I shall say nothing further here, other than to make one point about 'canonical literature', because the matter is too complicated for an essay on historiography and the origins of the Bible and because canons have to do with authorizing communities of readers—a topic I shall consider to be outside my remit here. My one point about canon comes from something Ferdinand Deist recently wrote about the nature of canonical literature:

> Since it is readers who make canons, it is impossible to conduct a discussion on canonical literature without reference to readers. From an

---

6. I shall resist the temptation to write a massive footnote on current writings on canon and all the matters pertaining to the collection and authorization of scrolls constitutive of 'sacred Scripture'. In my judgment the centre here is too soft and fuzzy-edged to be usefully discussed in a few lines. However, for good, up-to-date discussions see John Barton, *The Spirit and the Letter: Studies in the Biblical Canon* (London: SPCK, 1997); Philip R. Davies, *Scribes and Schools: The Canonization of the Hebrew Scriptures* (Library of Ancient Israel; Louisville, KY: Westminster/John Knox Press, 1998); Moshe Halbertal, *People of the Book: Canon, Meaning, and Authority* (Cambridge, MA: Harvard University Press, 1997); cf. Carroll, 'Clio and Canons', pp. 315-21.

7. Carroll, 'Textual Strategies', p. 108.

ideology-critical point of view, the difference between canonical and
other literature lies not in the nature of the literature or its genre, but in
the context in which it is interpreted and, therefore, in the special set of
intertexts of which it forms a part. These intertexts include power relations, views of authority, specific beliefs and religious traditions, particular textual theories and methodologies with their implied interpretive
strategies, readers' expectations, and so forth. As long as such interests
exist there will be a literature that is read *as* canonical literature, that is,
literature that *functions* in a way no other literature can function.[8]

The question implicit for me in this discussion of the topic of the
European Seminar in Historical Methodology's Cracow meeting in
1998 was whether by Hebrew Bible is meant the original writing of the
material contained within it or the scrolls as edited and collected and
now constituting the Hebrew Bible. Were the original scrolls written in
the Greek period or were the scrolls collected and redacted in the
Greek? While I think the answer to the first form of the question is
possibly 'Yes', I suspect that the answer to the second form of the
question is 'No, they were collected and edited in the Roman period'.
But Graeco-Roman will serve as the designated period for the production of the Hebrew Bible. I think it would be unrealistic and purely
speculative to suggest that by the end of the Persian period the Hebrew
Bible had been written, edited and collated, so that it was in existence
in a form similar to what we now know it to be by the Greek period.
That would be to exclude Ben Sira, Daniel, Esther and other texts of a
later period from the collection. I also suspect that there is a considerable amount of equivocation contained in the way many biblical scholars talk about the Bible and that there is a great need for us to clarify
our terms by defining what is intended by any and every use of the term
'Hebrew Bible'. What do we mean by such terms as Bible or Hebrew
Bible or Christian Bible? What Bible, which Bible, whose Bible and all
the usual leading questions suggest themselves for this discussion.[9] If
we mean the complete enchilada (Genesis–Chronicles seriatim) then of
course the Graeco-Roman period has to be the time of its production
because the book of Daniel is to be dated to the second century BCE

8. Ferdinand E. Deist, 'Canonical Literature: Some Ideology-Critical Observa-
tions', *Acta Academica Supplementum* 1 (1995), pp. 66-80 (78; emphases original).
    9. I have discussed some of these matters in my chapter on 'The Book of
Books' in Robert P. Carroll, *Wolf in the Sheepfold: The Bible as Problematic for
Theology* (London: SCM Press, 1997), pp. 7-33.

(and no doubt Ben Sira, various psalms, narratives and additions to the biblical texts).

Furthermore, it should be clear from the fact that every version we have of the Bible, or its various contents (see Jeremiah in the Masoretic Text and/or the Septuagint), is different and distinct from every other version (cf. Septuagint with the Masoretic Text or the Qumran scrolls with either of these texts), so that in the period of the origins of the books of the Bible through to the period of canonization of various collections of biblical books there never was either an original or a definitive text. Perhaps the notions of a definitive text or even an orig-inal text are largely the product of post-Gutenburg-generated expec-tations and thinking when printing introduced the notion of 'same' or uniform productions of texts. Every version is different, so which should we count as the original or originating Bible? If we posit the ori-gins of the Bible as being equivalent to whenever the individual scrolls were written—all of them, that is—then we would have to date the beginnings of the origins of the Bible (as such) to whenever and what-ever is judged to have been the latest document to be written (Daniel, some psalms, intrusions into texts or whatever). Such a dating would only apply to the individual scrolls as a *totality* of individual scrolls and not to the collected and edited volume constituting the later-to-be-can-onized text. So it seems to me that there are invariably and inevitably some *equivocal* notions involved in our normal discussions about the origins of the Bible and these need to be clarified in the discussion period. The writings constituting the Hebrew Bible had their origins perhaps during a long period of time[10]—beginning in the Persian or Greek periods perhaps or may be in the Graeco-Roman period—but only came into existence *as the Bible* many centuries after their original period of writing. What period might that have been? Lots of questions here, with only speculations for answers. But the production of the Bible has to be seen as a long, drawn-out process taking place over a number of centuries and in order to describe such a process adequately it is not easy to assign the Bible's production just to one period of time or just to the Greek era.

---

10. Philip R. Davies suggests a much shorter period in his *In Search of 'Ancient Israel': A Study in Biblical Origins* (JSOTSup, 148; Sheffield: JSOT Press, 1992), p. 120.

Silence, Speculation and Hypothesis

Elsewhere in these Seminars I have drawn attention to the role that speculation about the absence of evidence tends to play as 'fact' in discussions relating to the Bible and historiography. In the Lausanne paper I referred to the oft-cited slogan of apologists 'the absence of evidence is not evidence of absence', using Röllig's form of the citation and noting that it was a much-embraced principle except whenever its application did not suit the ideologues who normally employ it.[11] While I have no wish to document such a point because it would take endless pages of examples to demonstrate how pervasive the practice is, I will provide one further example here of how it works in reverse. While reading a book with a quite foolish title, *Reclaiming the Bible for the Church*—foolish because the Bible has never ever yet been out of the possession of the churches as far as I know!—I encountered yet again another apologist working with the alternative principle 'absence of reference is proof of absence of concept or practice'. This time the principle is employed in attacking homosexual readings of the Bible.[12] Thus the ubiquitous Alister McGrath—for it is he!—writes against the American writer Bishop John Shelby Spong:

> For example, at one point Spong tentatively advances the idea that Paul might have been a homosexual. A few pages later, this seems to have become an established result of New Testament scholarship, leading Spong to the conclusion that one of the church's greatest teachers was a 'rigidly controlled gay male'. *The hard historical evidence for this dramatic assertion? Nil.*[13]

11. Carroll, 'Exile! What Exile?', p. 72; cf. W. Röllig, 'On the Origin of the Phoenicians', *Berytus* 31 (1983), pp. 79-83 (82).

12. In an example of 'life imitating art' I should say that as I revise this essay (January 2000) contemporary Scottish culture is currently ripping itself apart debating the government's proposed repeal of Section 28 (a local government act constructed by the Thatcher government of the 1980s designed to prevent 'promotion of homosexuality'—whatever that might mean—in school education). In spite of the general disappearance of most biblical cultural practices from modern culture (e.g. slavery, polygamy, concubinage, local genocide, wearing mixed clothing stuffs, etc.), there is an odd refusal to let go of the prohibition of this particular biblical abomination.

13. Alister E. McGrath, 'Reclaiming our Roots and Vision: Scripture and the Stability of the Christian Church', in Carl E. Braaten and Robert W. Jenson (eds.), *Reclaiming the Bible for the Church* (Edinburgh: T. & T. Clark, 1996), pp. 63-88

I shall call this hardnosed attitude where no evidence represents evidence of nothing, 'the sex life of Jesus paradigm'. It is a principle only invoked when its invocation can align itself with ideological positions *already* held. Whereas following Röllig's enunciated principle we already know that 'the absence of evidence is no evidence of absence', so McGrath has no case to make here. However, when it suits people to make absence of evidence an evidential claim then the absence will be the key factor in the argument, but when it suits the same people to make absence a neutral factor in the argument—or even perhaps a hint of a positive contribution to their claim in the sense that although currently absent there are no grounds for thinking that such evidence may not yet turn up—then it will be factored into the argument accordingly. This two-faced (Janus-faced) approach to evidence and its absence tends to reflect a prior ideology which determines which way the absence of anything is to be construed in any argument (i.e. pretextual eisegesis). Whatever the evidence it will always be manipulated in such a way that whether there or absent it will support the case ideologues wish to make. Just as the claim that 'the sand of Judah does not protect manuscripts' is always invoked for lack of evidence, manuscriptal or otherwise, of the biblical writings—Qumran notwithstanding!—so there being no currently acceptable, canonical details of the sex life of Jesus Christ it is assumed by those who are already committed to such a position that Jesus Christ was celibate, a model and exemplar for chaste, celibate priests, monks and religious (folk) and also that he was not interested in sexual activities except to forbid them (virtually another textual absence!).[14] Whereas, in my opinion, the opposite case may just as easily be made from the absence of evidence because absence of evidence is not evidence of absence! McGrath is no less guilty of making Scripture mean what he wants it to mean than is Bishop Spong— here the minister-theologian is calling the bishop-theologian...er, (black) er, non-pink! Logs and splinters is what the Sermon on the

(74; emphases added). It is especially Spong's book *Rescuing the Bible from Fundamentalism* (San Francisco: HarperCollins, 1991) which has attracted McGrath's outrage, but everything Spong has written seems to be a target of McGrath's sweeping invective.

14. The exception clause in Mt. 5.32 poses as many problems of interpretation, reception and application as it resolves, but it does provide ostensibly 'the authority of Jesus' for the practice of divorce, whatever the reasons for its inclusion (interpolation into?) in the text.

Mount would call this kind of practice: that is, the ability to spot a splinter in one's brother's eye while all the time ignoring the plank of wood in one's own eye (Mt. 7.1-5). Circular reasoning is what logicians would call it, and, in my judgment, 'scripture's wax nose' is what John Locke might have called it.[15] I do not find McGrath's Paul any more convincing or persuasive than I find Bishop Spong's Paul, but the key to this position does not lie in the absence or presence of textual evidence to support either of their positions. I just do not think that texts (biblical or otherwise) can be read in these daft ways to yield the information either writer wishes to extract from such texts, hence the use of the Thompson citation as my third epigraphic gloss on this essay (above).

The point about there being 'nil evidence' for a specific reading of the Bible is such a grossly inadequate hermeneutic of reading, reflecting as it were *a fundamentalism of the Spirit*, that it would not interest me at all if it were not for the fact that this kind of sloganizing is so very typical of much of what passes for argumentation in relation to biblical interpretation in the current historiography debate. If absence of evidence is not evidence of absence except when one's own dogmatic presuppositions require it to be precisely that, what are we to make of the almost entire lack of evidence for resolving the question of 'when was the Hebrew Bible produced'? One reasonable approach would be to rule the whole historiographic issue out of court on the grounds of lack of data. The lack of facts underdetermine any historical account or, as I am rather fond of citing James Joyce in this matter (the Joycean quotation itself is not a propos this particular topic), 'thus the unfacts, did we possess them, are too imprecisely few to warrant our certitude...'[16] Of silence we may make anything or nothing at all. As Wittgenstein's famous Proposition 7 has it, *Wovon man nicht sprechen kann, darüber muß man schweigen* (what we cannot speak about we must pass over in silence).[17] So should this whole historiographic dis-

---

15. See John Locke, *A Second Vindication of the Reasonableness of Christianity as Delivered in the Scriptures* in *The Works of John Locke*, VII (London: Thomas Tegg, 1823).

16. James Joyce, *Finnegans Wake* (London: Faber & Faber, 3rd edn, 1964), p. 57 (cited as epigraph to Carroll, 'So What Do We *Know* About the Temple?', pp. 34, 51).

17. Ludwig Wittgenstein, *Tractatus Logico-Philosophicus* (trans. D.F. Pears and B.F. McGuinness; International Library of Philosophy and Scientific Method;

cussion now be consigned to silence? For how are we to interpret the silences of the Bible about its own production? What *hermeneutic of silence* should we develop then in these cases? The absence of evidence about the Bible's origins, composition, collation and of reliable evidence about its subsequent canonization poses profound and fundamental problems for any historigraphical theory about biblical origins and development. It is not, of course, a case of the Bible not (never) having existed in the past—that would be an absurd conclusion—but it *is* a case of our not knowing how it came into existence: that is, when its constituent scrolls were first committed to writing, when these scrolls were first collated into collections of significant scrolls and then when they were canonized as authoritative community writings. Now that is an incredible amount of nescience for biblical scholars to have to admit to and to have to factor into their historiographical writings on the Bible.

A different but perhaps equally reasonable approach would be to maximize the number of theories we could generate from such silence. Each and every point of view produced along these lines would be both purely speculative and a highly imaginative manipulation of the data which we chose to illuminate the silence. Speculation may be entirely necessary and proper in the absence of concrete data, but it will always be open to competing speculations and will always remain what it is—speculation. Yet in the absence of data biblical scholars also have a terrible tendency to seize upon any fragment or phrase from the Bible and manipulate it into a theory of production. For example, Jeremiah 36 is frequently used as the basis for an account of the origins, writing and production of the book of Jeremiah and thereafter of the whole Bible! Or Isa. 8.16 is used to construct a theory of the production of prophetic writings in terms of constructing and positing a social context involving a prophet and his disciples. Even an allusion to 'prophet' in the Lachish Letters is sufficient to provide an underwriting of the biblical traditions about prophets! Or the 'finding' of bullae with inscribed biblical names can be used to underwrite the whole biblical tradition.[18] This clutching at

London: Routledge & Kegan Paul, 1961), §7, pp. 150-51. I am very conscious of having referred to Proposition 7 in my 'Exile! What Exile?' article (p. 72), but this historiography debate inevitably entails going around the same mulberry bushes ad infinitum!

18. See Avigad's 'discovery' of bullae relating to Jeremiah in N. Avigad, *Hebrew Bullae from the Time of Jeremiah: Remnants of a Burnt Archive* (Jerusalem: Israel

straws is an act of desperation which says more about the politics and ideologies of current scholars and/or biblical devotees than it does about ancient texts. Furthermore, each of these examples seems to me to be the product of highly defective interpretative schemes and yet they are also a constant of current biblical interpretation. It would appear to be the case that in the absence of evidence scholars choose to construct out of such absence theories based on transferred and misapplied interpretative treatments of chapters and verses from the Bible. What one scholar constructs by means of such speculation and hypothesis is then taken up by his (it usually or most frequently *is* a 'he') students and passed on down through the generations (what is now known in European circles as the Harvard-Yale fallacy) in such a way that it becomes the Guild's 'knowledge' or default mode.

The Fallacy of Origins as Meaning

As I read the standard Introductions to the Hebrew Bible I am very conscious of the tendency of such authorities/writers to work with the practice of 'hand-me-down-my-*Einleitungen*-approach' to dating documents or, the equally speculative, 'dating-by-reference-to-the-narrated-contents-of-biblical-books-approach' to fixing the *Sitz im Leben*/social context of matters to be found in the Bible. Following such approaches one would end up with a dating for the writing of the Hebrew Bible which approximated to whenever the last book was judged to have been written or, in the case of fundamentalistic readings, wherever the final book of the collection was judged to be set (e.g. sixth century for Daniel). In traditional Jewish and Christian treatments of the Hebrew Bible (Old Testament) Ezra tends to be the figure associated with the final production of the Bible. This particular viewpoint is facilitated by the tradition of Ezra as the *rewriter* of the scriptures lost or destroyed during the Babylonian captivity (cf. 2 Esd. 14). The notion of things being done twice is also reflective of the biblical topos of two productions of things: two stories of creation in Genesis 1–2; two writings of the decalogue; two writings of Jeremiah's scroll; and the two writings of the scriptures (Moses and Ezra)—the *doublement* motif. Conventional critical scholarship would not necessarily follow these approaches because it knows the book of Daniel to be much later than the

Exploration Society, 1986) and my discussion of it in 'Madonna of Silences', in Grabbe (ed.), *Can a 'History of Israel' Be Written?*, pp. 96-100.

time of Ezra (even where it does not regard Ezra as a fictional figure). But does conventional critical scholarship date the origins of the Hebrew Bible (book as collection) to the second century BCE? The logic of setting the book of Daniel in the Maccabaean period suggests that it ought so to assign the origins of the Hebrew Bible to at least not being earlier than the second century, but does it in practice do so?

I am very conscious of this essay doing nothing more than raise question after question, but then I never ever find the discussion period addresses the questions I have raised in my work. Never mind, as the Beckett character has it, 'Ever tried. Ever failed. No matter. Try again. Fail again. Fail better.'[19] Essential to my project of 'failing better' is the formulating of questions and that is what I now choose to do when it comes to speculating about the origins of the Bible. Attempting to formulate them as correctly or as sophisticatedly as I can is about the best I can do by way of contributing to this debate about historiography and the origins of the Hebrew Bible. While I read what other scholars write and while I can in parrot-fashion repeat their opinions, I seldom ever find their proposed solutions or theories interesting, adequate or convincing! So I go on asking my own questions, even if only for *my own benefit*. It is very much a 'reinventing the wheel' approach to speculating about the Bible. I can do no other (*Ich kann nicht anders* as a late mediaeval biblical commentator once expressed a rather different matter!) because I am very conscious of how any chosen fragment of the text may be so easily manipulated into a number of theories without any foundation *outside of the text*. These questions are the ruins I shore up against my future, in the hope that after my time other readers may find them worth working with, even exploring them to better point than I have or formulating better questions in order to fail better than I have failed.

The myths of origins of the Hebrew Bible seem to focus on Moses and Ezra, but these I regard as part of the myth of the Bible itself and therefore as not affording real information (or knowledge) about the 'true' origins of the Bible. Nor would I regard such myths of origins as binding on scholars. The fallacy of the myth of origins may be exposed by the simple observation that 'a mouse born in a biscuit tin is not a biscuit'! I know that that is a very simplistic observation, but it is a start in the right direction. We do not know how or when the Hebrew Bible

19. Samuel Beckett, *Worstward Ho* (London: John Calder, 1999 [1983]), p. 7.

as a bible—that is, as a collection of ordered texts or an orderly collection of texts—came into existence, even though we may offer a 1001
speculations and hypotheses or give intellectual allegiance to many legends and myths, *believing* as much as we can, about the possible origins
and collections of the writings we know as the Hebrew Bible. The
claim that the Bible came into being during the Hellenistic period looks
to me like the beginning of wisdom and we should go with such a claim
in order to see how far it will take us.[20] It is a start, but it will require
considerably more speculation and hypothesizing than this essay currently has to offer to flesh out such a sensible suggestion. In answer to
the question about the origins of the Hebrew Bible (*as bible*) I think I
would want to say that 'It's all Greek to me'. Perhaps I could go a little
further and say that such an account of the Bible's origins is a nice
example of the Joycean notion of 'jewgreek is greekjew', whereby the
two become interchangeable in some sense. Out of the Hellenistic and
Graeco-Roman periods came the quintessence of Hebrew-Jewish origins, as it were. But I do not think that I would necessarily want to stop
there. I think the claim is a safe claim, but I suspect that the implica-
tures of such a claim would require a book-length treatment. I shall not
produce that book-length treatment here, but others have already begun
the book writing which will help to transform our understanding of
these matters.

Since the Seminar in Cracow in 1998 both Niels Peter Lemche and
Thomas L. Thompson have published books on the subject of biblical
historiography and the production of the biblical story (meganarrative
of Israel's past) and the appearance of these books has strengthened
considerably the radical rethinking of these historiographical issues.[21] I
shall not—nor could I—add to these fine works here, but there are
aspects of these historiographical approaches to reading the Bible which
do intrigue me. I am concerned to understand the ways in which the
biblical writers appear to provide such misdirection and misinformation
about the origins of the nation, while at the same time concealing the
scaffolding used to produce the stories in the first place. For example,
according to the conventional view of the matter the Chronicler writes

20. I have in mind here as a starting-point Niels Peter Lemche, 'The Old Testament—A Hellenistic Book?', *SJOT* 7 (1993), pp. 163-93.

21. See Niels Peter Lemche, *The Israelites in History and Tradition* (Library of
Ancient Israel; Louisville, KY: Westminster/John Knox Press, 1998); Thompson,
Bible in History.

at a time when the second temple has been built, yet he deliberately ignores that building in order to produce yet another account of the building of David's—well, technically Solomon's—temple. Just how much false consciousness can be tolerated in a text? The textualities of his work seen to be pitted against his ostensible writing of times past in order to blanket out times present—here the current work of Graeme Auld on the Chronicler should be brought into the debate. The point I wish to make is a very simple one: why would anyone writing about the past existence of an institution which had been reconstructed in their own times not refer, even if only in the time-honoured fashion of an 'as at this day' phrase or allusion, to such a wonderful eventuality which in itself would have sealed and cemented the continuity of his own age with the glorious past of the nation? I find that most peculiarly odd, just as in the case in which Sherlock Holmes made so much of the fact that 'the dog did nothing in the nighttime—that was the curious incident'.[22] I really do find the Chronicler's reticence here most peculiarly odd and worthy of note too. Was there a deliberate misdirection in his scheme of writing or a pretence at antiquity which required his ignoring the obvious or even a deliberate omission of information which could be interpreted as designed to mislead or decieve his readers? How can we answer these questions, suspicions or doubts about the historiographical reliability of the Chronicler? There are lots of questions here which really need to be raised and thrashed out rather than ignored. For my money the Chronicler's work really does make for very strange reading, as if a world of the past is being created deliberately in opposition to or even to replace a world of the present where reality was other than pleasing to the Chronicler's mind and work.

The point I want to draw attention to here by way of concluding this essay is a very simple one: why would anyone writing about the past existence of an institution which had been reconstructed in their own time not refer, even if only in terms of the normal biblical conventional indicator of 'as at this day', to such an eventuality? Why the obfuscation, reticence or silence of the Chronicler? Leaving aside the most obvious point that the second temple had not yet been constructed or

---

22. See 'The Adventure of Silver Blaze', in *The Memoirs of Sherlock Holmes* in Sir Arthur Conan Doyle, *Sherlock Holmes: The Complete Illustrated Short Stories* (London: Chancellor Press, 1985), p. 250. I used this example as one of the epigraphs to my article 'So What Do We *Know* About the Temple?', but it will survive a further citational usage here.

rebuilt—the appropriate verb to use here would require a considerable amount of justificatory discussion but I shall leave that discussion for another essay—a claim which many conventional biblical scholars would probably wish to argue hotly against whatever justifications I might offer for it, various questions are prompted by this the most curious of the Chronicler's omissions. Was there a deliberate misdirection or pretence at antiquity or absenting of information designed to mislead on the Chronicler's part? Lots of questions here which really need to be raised rather than ignored. It does make for a very strange reading as if a world of the past is being created deliberately in order to represent a reality other than the one obtaining at present. That is, a mediocre present has been displaced by an account of a wonderful past. To the obvious question of 'Why?' one can only speculate and wonder. But given this kind of *deep unreliability* of a biblical writer, what shall we make of the historiographical foundations of the Bible as a guide to modern historians attempting to make historiographical sense of the Bible? These questions all lead in the direction outlined for us at the very beginning of this essay when I cited as my second epigraph Edward Said's remark about how it is the nature of interpretation to send us back to the primary problems of interpretation. Furthermore, I would want to emphasize the point Said makes, referring to Matthew Arnold's position on culture, about 'interpretation, knowledge and...culture itself are always the result of contests and not simply a gift from heaven'. The writings constitutive of the Bible *do not come to us from heaven*— whatever the dogmatic theologians may have said in the past—but from contested practices, debates and issues in the past. We may not have access to such vexed contests, but we should not imagined that they did not exist—absence of evidence is not evidence of absence! All the fundamental questions of 'who?', 'why?', 'for what purpose?' and 'for whose benefit?' are raised for us in this Seminar both by the Chronicler's writings (for example) and by all the concealments, displacements, misdirections, nesciences and silences embedded in or reflected by the productions of the biblical writers in their historiographical representations and constructions of the nation's stories of its past and in the lack of reliable accounts of the origins of the biblical narratives.

From the point of view embodied in contemporary usage of the terms 'history' and 'historiography' the biblical writers seem *at best* only to be interested in producing stories of the past. Their constructions can hardly be said to be interested in any sense in what we today would understand by the category 'history'. Nor do they seem to have any interest whatsoever in providing detailed, accurate or even informative accounts of the hows and whens of the production of their writings. In my judgment there is therefore much to be said for abandoning the use of the term 'history' when writing about the past which the biblical writers were writing about or constructing in the first place. So I shall conclude this essay with a quotation from a recent work by the cultural historian Lutz Niethammer writing in passing on the topic of the biblical focus on the past rather than on history (as we know it):

> First, let us confess our surprise at the peculiar image of an *angel* of history. Usually historians have chosen a muse as their higher being; the various angels who appear in the Bible and the Jewish tradition act as divine messengers, protectors, awakeners or avengers, or as ephemeral beings who exist only to sing their hymn in praise of God and then fade away. Each time the angel relates to God or humanity or both, but not to history. Besides, history in the singular—as in the modern philosophy of history which joins together past and future as a social process—is foreign to the Hebrew Bible. What the Bible knows is the past: in Hebrew this is typically denoted by the same word that refers to what the face is turned towards in attention; while the word for the future also signifies what is hidden behind one's back.[23]

23. Lutz Niethammer, *Posthistoire: Has History Come to an End?* (London: Verso, 1992 [ET of German original 1989]), p. 111. The 'angel of history' discussed by Niethammer is, of course, a reference to Walter Benjamin's famous discussion of the Paul Klee painting in his seminal essay 'Theses on the Philosophy of History' (in Walter Benjamin, *Illuminations* (ed. Hannah Arendt; trans. Harry Zohn; London: Fontana Press, 1992 [1970]), pp. 245-55 (249).

Philip R. Davies

The Problem

> Now you shall see what I will do to Pharaoh; for with a strong hand he will send them out; indeed, with a strong hand he will expel them from his land (Exod. 6.1).

> When [Pharaoh] lets you go, he will drive you out completely. Speak now to all the people, and tell each one to ask, man and woman, of their neighbour, for gold and silver jewellery. And Yahweh caused the Egyptians to look favourably on the people (Exod. 11.2-3).

> And a mixed crowd also went up also with them; and flocks, and herds, indeed, a lot of livestock (Exod. 12.38).

The narrative in the book of Exodus about the enslavement and subsequent departure of the descendants of Jacob incorporates several strands. Some of these are contradictory. For instance, the main theme of the narrative of departure itself has a reluctant Pharaoh permitting the Israelites to leave only after a series of plagues, and even then being pursued by an army. However, as the passages quoted at the beginning of this essay show, there are also present statements about the Pharaoh 'driving out' these descendants of Jacob; others about the Israelites leaving with goodwill, and even gifts, from their Egyptian neighbours,[1] and a suggestion that accompanying the Israelites were others.[2] The presence of different conceptions about the departure suggest, to most commentators, a combination of different source-materials, and a complicated history of redaction, within a broadly coherent narrative line.

Though the nature and history of the 'Exodus' story are matters of

---

1. The 'neighbours' of Exod. 11.2 must be Egyptians, as the great majority of interpreters understand, and not fellow Israelites. The following sentence makes this clear, as does 12.36.

2. Exodus 12.38: ‏ערב רב‎.

wide disagreement, it is difficult not to recognize the essential literary, if not mythical quality of the narrative: the child miraculously saved from death; the bush on fire but not being consumed; the dramatic plagues; the historicizing of the agricultural festivals of Unleavened Bread and 'Passover'; the miraculous drying of the sea; the huge numbers of emigrants (2-3 million); stylized lawgiving(s) on the holy mount. The literary composition has been explained in various ways: as a product of the weaving of different documents (such as the classical four-source hypothesis),[3] or as part of an ancient historiographical narrative in which a series of themes coagulated, under the influence of the cultic activity of a union of tribes, into a national epic;[4] or even as a sixth-century biography of Moses.[5] No review of the range is particularly useful, for no secure conclusions are achievable. But the arguments in favour of an elaborated narrative incorporating several distinct motifs, with an uncertain level of historical precision, seem strong.[6]

3.   T.N. Sarna, 'Exodus, Book of', in *ABD*, II, pp. 689-700, rightly speaks of a 'veritable kaleidoscope of topics and literary genres' and 'apparent doublets, inconsistencies, redundancies and interpolations (p. 693), as well as 'seeming differences in ideological and theological outlook' (p. 694). The fullest account of such inconsistencies, and an explanation on source-critical grounds, following the New Documentary Hypothesis of Graf and Wellhausen, can be found in S.R. Driver, *Exodus* (Cambridge: Cambridge University Press, 1911), (see also his *Introduction to the Literature of the Old Testament* [Edinburgh: T. & T. Clark, 1909], pp. 22-42). The commentary by J.P. Hyatt (*The Book of Exodus* [NCB; London: Oliphants, 1971]) follows this line of explanation, and B.S. Childs also incorporates it in his *Exodus: A Commentary* (OTL; London: SCM Press; Philadelphia: Westminster Press, 1974). For a revised source-critical approach, see Joseph Blenkinsopp, *The Pentateuch* (ABRL; New York: Doubleday, 1992) especially pp. 141-60. The view taken in this essay is that the literary process is largely irrecoverable, though not undetectable.

4.   This is the thesis of M. Noth, *A History of Pentateuchal Traditions* (Englewood Cliffs, NJ: Prentice–Hall, 1972 [German 1948]), and applied in detail in his *Exodus: A Commentary* (London: SCM Press; Philadelphia: Westminster Press, 1962 [German 1959]).

5.   J. Van Seters (*The Life of Moses: The Yahwist as Historian in Exodus-Numbers* [Louisville, KY: Westminster/John Knox Press; Kampen: Kok Pharos, 1994]). See also his *The Pentateuch: A Social-Science Commentary* (Trajectories: A Social Science Commentary, 1; Sheffield: Sheffield Academic Press, 1999).

6.   The historicity of the events as the basis for the biblical narrative, which has always had its firm supporters, is most recently defended by James K. Hoffmeier, *Israel in Egypt* (Oxford: Oxford University Press, 1996). However, these accounts

However, despite the widespread recognition that the narrative of Exodus is the probable result of a literary combination of themes and episodes, the idea has persisted that this account of a departure from Egypt was initially prompted by, or at least continues to reflect, an event. It remains a widely held view that this story came into Israelite-Judaean tradition as the result of experiences of, if not all, then at least some population elements, and hence developed into a central feature of the national 'historical memory', or even an early oral or written national historiography. Between the literary history and the assumed event, however, lies a gap, and since there is no consensus over the date of the supposed event or the earliest level of the Exodus story, that gap cannot be measured; nor can it be bridged. It is better described as a chasm. Yet, for most scholars, in that chasm lies the reason why there is an Exodus story at all. 'Fiction' remains too close to 'forgery' and 'fraud' to comfort many biblical scholars, for whom 'tradition' is a more congenial euphemism. Yet a tradition with a chasm in it is not a tradition. Traditions are supposed to be continuous, and there is no demonstrable continuity between supposed event and story.

The reason for the belief that a historical event underlies the narrative is hard to express in terms of historical methodology. Three reasons can be identified, though neither is particularly sound. First, why else would such a story have been invented? It is thought that slavery and escape are not the kinds of events that a national historiography simply invents: it is too unflattering. Second is the wide range of allusion to the story (or at least to an original 'being brought out of Egypt') throughout the canonized literature. A third reason is the realization that Semites regularly *did* visit (and leave) Egypt during the Middle and Late Bronze Ages (though no more so than in earlier or later times). These factors are often rehearsed as if they inevitably pointed towards a historical kernel.

---

rarely bother to deal directly with the evidence of literary complexity and its implications (e.g. Hoffmeier, *Israel in Egypt*, pp. 7-10). Critiques of the source-critical and traditio-historical solutions to the composition of the Pentateuchal are nevertheless available in R. Rendtorff, *The Problem of the Process of Transmission in the Pentateuch* (JSOTSup, 89; Sheffield: JSOT Press, 1990 [German 1977])— though focused on Genesis, not Exodus; R.N. Whybray, *The Making of the Penta-teuch: A Methodological Study* (JSOTSup, 53; Sheffield: JSOT Press, 1987); T.L. Thompson, *The Origin Tradition of Ancient Israel: The Literary Formation of Genesis and Exodus 1–23* (JSOTSup, 55; Sheffield: JSOT Press, 1987).

William Johnstone has conveniently summarized the literary evidence for second millennium contacts between Semites and Egyptians:[7]

For the descent of Semites into Egypt:

the Beni Hasan mural (c. 1890)
the Hyksos invasion (c. 1720–1570)
the captive lists of Amenophis II (mid-sixteenth century)

For the sojourn of Semites in Egypt

a text naming Asiatics with Asiatics receiving Egyptian names
(mid-eighteenth century)
a text of Rameses II mentioning the *'apiru* in building operations
(thirteenth century)
a text of Rameses IV mentioning *'apiru* in the army (twelfth
century)

For attainments by Asiatics in Egypt

Dod (David?) as chamberlain at the court of Amenophis IV (early
fourteenth century)
the rule by a Syrian between XIX and XX dynasties (end of
thirteenth century)

For the departure of Semites from Egypt

the tale of Sinuhe (twentieth century)
the expulsion of the Hyksos (sixteenth century)
the pursuit of two runaway slaves (copy of text from the end of
thirteenth century)

Johnstone also provides a succinct but cogent critique of any attempts to fit the Exodus story into a historical framework:[8] numbers (2-3 million people); locations (Pithom, Sinai, Sea of Reeds); absence of Egyptian power from Palestine; the absence of any named Pharaoh; the two midwives; the plagues. Johnstone's conclusion is that the story reflects, in a broad way, the collapse of Egyptian power in the Levant from the end of the Late Bronze Age and the emergence of small kingdoms in Syria-Palestine. The story is a mythic account of Israelite origins:

7.   W. Johnstone, *Exodus* (OTG, 3; Sheffield: JSOT Press, 1990), pp. 19-20.
8.   Johnstone, *Exodus*, pp. 20-38.

> Israel's religion is not founded on historical events; rather, Israel's religious writers are using a narrative form of presentation in which history provides the general framework: for the filling in of the detail, historical circumstances are only one source among many. The complex narrative is the medium for expressing a prior religious tradition: the historical events in Exodus are not the source, but the vehicle, not the basis but the confirmation, not the proof but the proving-ground.[9]

To these observations one could add Sarna's list[10] of 17 items of 'undeniable Egyptian coloration', including the title 'pharaoh', the making of bricks, the 'birth stool' (Exod. 1.16), and some of the plagues. Indeed, one has to add the very name of Moses (plus Aaron [?] and probably Hophni and Phinehas) to the list of arguments for strong Egyptian influence on the story.

But is a singular event the most reasonable explanation for such features, as many scholars are tempted to suppose? Or even a narrative that, whatever its historicity or lack of it, is the exclusive creation of Judaean scribes giving a basic religious belief a narrative expression? For even Johnstone's comments just quoted leave some murky areas: what do we know of 'Israel's religion' that would generate such a narrative as an immediate vehicle? What, if any, *are* the 'historical details'? Why do we now have an undeniably 'complex narrative', and what (and from where) the 'tradition'? What, in fact, lies behind the story as its cause? And indeed, if we acknowledge the complexities, including the contradictions and tensions within the present account, do we not need to confront the possibility of a single storyline expressed or developing in various forms? If so, why the particular variations?

For it is surely necessary to ask why, given the overwhelming affirmation of the Exodus as a divine defeat of the Egyptians and as a liberation, echoes of a *fundamentally contradictory account* (expulsion, gift-laden departure) should either have been preserved or introduced into it. For these are not exactly *incidental* features, even if they are not prominent. They hint at different *conceptions* of the circumstances, ones that directly challenge the dominant theme of a conflict between Yahweh and the Pharaoh, in which the deity makes the Pharaoh resist the Israelite departure so as to prove his superiority. Deploying the argument that a story such as slavery in Egypt would not have been

---

9.   Johnstone, *Exodus*, p. 36.
10.   Sarna, 'Exodus, Book of', pp. 697-98.

'invented', one may equally well ask whether such details as *these* would have been 'invented', either. The suggestion of a single account fares no better against this objection: even creative biographies try not to contradict themselves in this way. No: contradictions of the sort mentioned earlier are not accounted for by historical events, nor by authorial intent. They exist *despite* such 'solutions'. They belong to the life of a story itself, to the biography of a tale that develops over time, told by different persons for different purposes and with different configurations.

A Comparative 'Solution'

This paper is an attempt to apply the perspective of the history of a story without appealing either to a unique historical episode or a unique religious tradition. It deals with the history of a story, not an event. Insofar as it is methodologically informed, it draws upon the study of folklore,[11] from which we know about the fluidity of stories often told, and the impossibility of reconstructing 'original' accounts, of the irrelevance of historical fact to the life of the story and toleration (perhaps even celebration) of the fact that variants exist. But the history of the 'Exodus' story (to give it its canonized name) cannot be confined to an exegesis of the canonized narrative, *because it also belongs elsewhere.* The same story, or at least some version of it, appears in Egyptian writings at the beginning of the third century BCE, and looks to be already somewhat older than this period. It is disappointing that both commentators on the book of Exodus and biblical historians generally ignore these accounts as being irrelevant to the development of the biblical narrative. The reason, so far as one can deduce it, is that since they hold the Exodus story to be the primary witness to an ancient event, non-Jewish versions from the Ptolemaic period can only be derivative of the Judaean version(s), and thus of no primary historical value in themselves. But in fact it cannot be proven that the canonized Jewish story is more ancient, or more true. Its primacy in the eyes of

11. The literature on folklore is simply too vast to document. The most frequently cited authority among biblical scholars is the work of Parry and Lord, which will certainly suffice for the present purpose. See A.B. Lord, *The Singer of Tales* (New York: Athenaeum, 1960); and for the influence of folklore studies on Old Testament/Hebrew Bible research, see Patricia G. Kirkpatrick, *The Old Testament and Folklore Study* (JSOTSup, 62; Sheffield: JSOT Press, 1988).

scholarship rests on its canonical status, not on literary or historical analysis. We have to start by recognizing that the story is *also an Egyptian one* and to ask, with an open mind, about the relationship between the Egyptian and Judaean forms, and about their joint and separate history.

What distinguishes my approach from virtually all others, then, is a recognition that we do not *know* the date and origin of the canonized story (or its sources), and thus we cannot *assume* either that it constitutes the 'standard' version by which to judge the conformity or deviation of other accounts. My agenda is to explore what I take to be versions of a single narrative in both Judaean and Egyptian sources, fully aware that I know at the outset nothing about the origins of either version, or of the story itself.

The Egyptian Sources

Manetho[12]

Although Manetho is not the earliest witness to the story, his account is the fullest and the best known. In his treatise *Against Apion* (1.73-105) Josephus Flavius quotes from Manetho, the early third-century Graeco-Egyptian historian, about an ancient invasion of Egypt by a people called 'Hyksos' (understood to mean 'shepherds' in Egyptian), who occupied Egypt for 511 years, and who were finally driven from most of the land, but confined to an area called Avaris which they fortified. Unsuccessful in capturing this stronghold, the Egyptian king Thummosis came to an agreement with them by means of which they left; and 240,000 consequently left and travelled to Syria. They built a city 'in that country that is now called Judea...and called it Jerusalem'.

A second excerpt (*Apion* 1.228-52) concerns a king Amenophis (erroneously, as it has turned out, dismissed by Josephus as a 'fictitious' ruler) who, 518 years (as Josephus reckons it after Manetho's data) after the 'shepherds' had been driven out by Tethmosis (*sic*), wished to rid his country of lepers and other diseased persons, 80,000 of whom were sent east of the Nile to work in quarries. Some leprous priests were sent to the old Hyksos capital of Avaris, and these appointed a

---

12. For a collection of the relevant sources and discussion, see M. Stern (ed.), *Greek and Latin Authors on Jews and Judaism* (2 vols.; Jerusalem: Israel Academy of Sciences and Humanities, 1976; Carl R. Holladay, *Fragments from Hellenistic Jewish Authors*. I. *Historians* (SBLTT, 20; Chico, CA: Scholars Press, 1983).

ruler among them called Osarsiph, a priest of Heliopolis, who made them forswear the Egyptian gods and follow new laws. Osarsiph then wrote to the 'shepherds' in Jerusalem (whose ancestors had been expelled in the earlier episode) and invited them to assist him in a war against Amenophis. Subsequently the Jerusalemites did invade Egypt, and behaved cruelly. Osarsiph, once he had joined the Jerusalemites, came to be known as Moses. Amenophis, having returned from Ethiopia, then drove the shepherds and the lepers back to Syria.

As is well known, Josephus calls Manetho to witness as to the antiquity of the Jews: in respect of the first of Manetho's stories, he accepts that Manetho is accurately conveying ancient sources, and says: 'these shepherds...were none other than our ancestors'. But he rejects the second story, arguing that Manetho has abandoned his ancient chronicles and proceeds at some length to discredit it as 'rumour' and 'incredible stories'. He does not in fact deny the story outright, but says that the diseased persons in question were Egyptians.

The importance of Manetho's accounts (assuming Josephus to have preserved them correctly) has been somewhat overshadowed by the polemic use to which they were subsequently put and perhaps also by scholarly attention to the anti-Jewish nature of a good deal of non-Jewish writing in the classical period.[13] It is thus tempting, in implying the primacy of the Jewish scriptural account, to explain many deviations in non-Jewish writing as the result of deliberate distortion. Given the hatred between Egyptians and Jews in Alexandria documented in the first centuries BCE and CE, it is probable that each side used a version of the same story against the other, Egyptians accusing the Jews of having been oppressors who were once driven out (and had now insidiously made their way back?), Jews arguing (as for example, the author of the Wisdom of Solomon will have believed) that their god, as their canonized scriptures said, had once defeated the oppressing Egyptians and liberated his chosen people from them. The Egyptian version was also used against Jews by later anti-Jewish authors (as, of course, the Jewish version was used by Jewish and Christian authors). Beyond the Exodus story itself, there is evidence in Isaiah, Jeremiah and Ezekiel of

---

13. E.g. Mnaseas, Lysimachus, Cheraemon, Apion; later Tacitus (*Histories* 5.3-4), one of several explanations given by him of the origins of the Jews (see, e.g., L.H. Feldman, *Jew and Gentile in the Ancient World* [Princeton, NJ: Princeton University Press, 1993], pp. 184-96), though not Strabo (see, e.g., John G. Gager, *The Origins of Anti-Semitism* [New York: Oxford University Press, 1985], pp. 72-75).

contemporary hostility to Egypt itself, presumably reflecting the Persian or early Hellenistic period. Thus it is quite probable that the story of a departure of Judeans, or Palestinians, from Egypt in antiquity could have been told in a polemical fashion by both Judaeans and Egyptians well before the Ptolemaic period when they surface in the preserved literary record.

Manetho's account contains two episodes of departure from Egypt: first the shepherds to Jerusalem, and then the lepers 'to the borders of Syria'. But it is only with the second that he explicitly associates the name of Moses.[14] The story about the Hyksos shepherds, which is set somewhat earlier, has, in the work of some previous scholars, been linked with the career of Joseph, and this, of course, is how Josephus understands it. But at first sight it is the invasion of people from Jerusalem into Egypt and, indeed the name 'Osarsiph'—in other words the second episode—that suggest connections with the Jewish Joseph story and the departure under Moses. It is not impossible to reduce the two episodes in Manetho's account to accidentally or deliberately garbled versions of an earlier Jewish scriptural account of respectively Joseph and then Moses, despite Josephus. But that is not by any means a necessary conclusion.

It is important first of all not to read Manetho in the light of the Judaean version, but on its own terms. Undoubtedly an important element in his presentation is the Greek-Hellenistic ethnographic tradition and the chauvinistic programmes of native historians to assert the supreme antiquity of their own nation. In support of this, Manetho offered an account, also cited by Josephus (*Apion*, 1.93-105) of how Danaos, the ancestor of the Greeks, was Egyptian. It has been suggested[15] furthermore that the nature of Manetho's account may belong with native Egyptian anti-Semitic stories, generated by the Assyrian and then Persian invasions of the country, and in both cases Judaean soldiers were among the invaders and/or the garrison troops (as the Elephantine papyri, for example, show).

But the Egyptian story about the expulsion of Judaeans from Egypt is clearly older than the third century BCE, and some information is very much older. In at least part of his account of the 'Hyksos', Manetho

14. A version of the same story is related by Strabo (16.2.35.760) who describes Moses as a Jewish priest who left because of a dislike of Egyptian worship of animals

15. T. Säve-Söderbergh, 'The Hyksos Rule in Egypt', *JEA* 37 (1951), pp. 53-71.

was drawing upon a Demotic source, and thus a story older than himself. How much older is impossible to say, but his information about the Hyksos is accurate to a considerable degree, including names of Egyptian kings and the name of the capital city. It is improbable that Manetho's story is a Ptolemaic invention, and the fact that it has earlier origins (how much earlier cannot be said) alone make a comparison with the Judaean version of the story even more intriguing.

Hecataeus of Abdera

The idea that Manetho, or his sources, is manifesting a deliberate anti-Semitic or anti-Judaean bias, even if correct, does not mean that the Egyptian story of the expulsion of Judaeans, as told in the Ptolemaic era, is itself necessarily the product of anti-Judaean ideology, because we find elements of that story contained in a nearly contemporary (perhaps slightly older?) writer, Hecataeus of Abdera, who is generally conceded to have exhibited a good knowledge of contemporary Judaean culture, without any evidence of anti-Judaean bias.

For Hecataeus,[16] we have, as for Manetho, the element of insecurity afforded by the loss of any original documents: his writings have been preserved by others. Thus, a summary of his accounts of Judaean history and constitution is preserved in the work of Diodorus Siculus (40.3);[17] and a further excerpt from his book 'written entirely about the Jews', in Josephus,[18] but the extent of its authenticity remains disputed, and it will not be considered here. It is widely recognized that some writings ascribed to Hecataeus are probably not from him at all.[19]

16. There is a convenient summary of the literature and issues in L.L. Grabbe, *The Jews from Cyrus to Hadrian* (2 vols.; Minneapolis: Fortress Press, 1991), I, 173; for this particular account see pp. 216-18. Text, translation and discussion are in Stern (ed.), *Greek and Latin Authors*, I, pp. 20-35; further discussion in M. Hengel, *Judaism and Hellenism* (ET London: SCM Press, 1974), I, pp. 255-56; II, p. 169, and E. Schürer, *The History of the Jewish People in the Age of Jesus Christ*, III.1 (rev. and ed. G. Vermes, F. Millar and M. Goodman; Edinburgh: T. & T. Clark, 1986), pp. 671-77.

17. The ascription by Diodorus (or by Photius? Diodorus's text is preserved in Photius's *Bibliotheca*) of these comments to Hecataeus of Miletus (c. 500 BCE) is generally taken as an error.

18. *Apion* 1.183-204; see Stern (ed.), *Greek and Latin Authors*, I, pp. 35-44, who takes it as basically authentic, as does the revised edition of Schürer.

19. For a detailed recent discussion, see B. Bar-Kochva, *Pseudo-Hecataeus,*

However, there is reasonable confidence in the sections of his writings to be considered presently, and thus we may date them more or less precisely to the early Ptolemaic period (c. 300 BCE).

Hecataeus, like the canonized Jewish narrative, knows of only one story of Judaeans leaving Egypt.[20] According to the preserved material, a pestilence in Egypt at some time (Hecataeus gives no chronological clues) prompted the inhabitants to expel certain strangers who practised alien rites; of these deportees some landed in Greece, but the larger number landed in Judaea, which was then uninhabited. They settled under the leadership of Moses, who founded several cities, including Jerusalem, where he established a temple. He also set up 'forms of worship and ritual', laws and political institutions. He divided the people into 12 tribes, forbade images to be made of their sole deity, and appointed priests, who were to be not only in charge of the cult but also political leaders and judges. (Thus, he says, 'the Jews have never had a king' but are ruled by a high priest, who enjoys great power and prestige.) Moses, continues the account, also instituted a military education and led the people to many conquests against neighbouring tribes, after which he apportioned the land equally, but reserving larger portions for the priests. The sale of land was forbidden, specifically so as to avoid oppression of the poor by the rich through accumulation of land. The people were also enjoined to reproduce. In marriage and burial their customs differed from those of others, though their traditional practices were disturbed under the Persians and Macedonians. The Judaeans' laws claim to have been words heard by Moses from God.

Now, it is again clear that, at least superficially, Hecataeus's narrative demonstrates some Hellenistic features. Moses appears as a typical colony founder, city-builder and law-giver. It is also evident that Hecataeus is well informed about the main features of Judaean society in his own day. It has for this reason been widely surmised that he must have had some Judaean information, whether from Judaeans living in Egypt or from those in Judaea itself. Mendels, suggesting that Hecataeus's account emanates from priestly circles from his own time,[21]

'On the Jews': Legitimizing the Jewish Diaspora (Berkeley: University of California Press, 1996).

20. I have already discussed this account in 'Scenes from the Early History of Judaism', in D.V. Edelman (ed.), *The Triumph of Elohim* (CBET; Kampen: Kok Pharos, 1995), pp. 145-82.

21. D. Mendels, 'Hecataeus of Abdera and a Jewish "patrios politeia",' *ZAW* 95

draws attention to correspondences between Hecataeus's account and the situation described in Ezra and Nehemiah. For reasons that I cannot elaborate here,[22] I cannot be as confident as Mendels that Ezra and Nehemiah offer a reliable portrait of Yehud in the Persian period, though it hardly matters, since a later date for these books could perhaps even strengthen Mendels's argument. Indeed, many of Mendels's observations and arguments do suggest that Hecataeus was fairly closely reflecting the state of affairs in Judaea during his own time. Thus, he notes that the Judaeans are said to have occupied a land that was 'utterly uninhabited' after leaving Egypt. This, as he observes, conflicts with the Pentateuchal tradition, but is in accordance with the ideology represented in Nehemiah, Ezra (and Chronicles) that maintains that the returnees from exile had come to an empty land 'enjoying its sabbaths'.[23] Hecataeus's view, then, is reflected in some biblical texts, giving support to Mendels's contention that Hecataeus reports a perspective of the land as having been 'empty' from the point of view of the immigrants who would have been the ancestors of his informants.[24] This view persisted.

There are, however, details that diverge from the canonized Judaean version. Jerusalem (and other cities) is said to have been founded by Moses, who is credited also with having conquered the land. He is also said to have been responsible for the creation of 12 tribes and for the

(1983), 96-110 (= *Identity, Religion and Historiography: Studies in Hellenistic History* [JSPS, 24; Sheffield: Sheffield Academic Press, 1998], pp. 334-51).

22. An outline of the main reasons will be found in my 'Scenes from the the Early History of Judaism'.

23. Mendels cites Neh. 2–4 and Jud. 5.19 as evidence of this ideology ('Hecataeus of Abdera', p. 99 [= p. 338]); but as noted by R.P. Carroll the 'empty land' appears even more emphatically in Jer. 32 and Lev. 25–27 and so can be seen as a perception outside the books of Ezra and Nehemiah. See R.P. Carroll, 'Textual Strategies and Ideology', in Philip R. Davies (ed.), *Second Temple Studies*. I. *Persian Period* (JSOTSup, 117; Sheffield: Sheffield Academic Press 1991), pp. 108-24.

24. The argument could be pressed further: such an attitude points to a strongly imperialistic or at least colonial mentality on the part of the immigrants and strengthens the suspicion that they were not conscious of being (and perhaps were not in reality) of the same stock and nationality as those who lived in the land being colonized. The strenuous efforts of the writer of Isa. 40–55 to persuade the Judaeans that the newcomers really were 'daughters of Zion' suggests that the indigenous inhabitants (specifically, their hitherto ruling classes) were not convinced of shared roots with the new immigrants, either.

division of land. In the Judaean version of the story, the conquest and division of the land are assigned to Joshua. Hecataeus's statement that the Judaeans had always been ruled by priests and never by a king is also strongly opposed to the contents of the books of Samuel and Kings. Thus, Hecataeus's sources do not seem to have known of the contents of the books of Joshua–Kings, or Chronicles, or his researches did not extend as far as these books, if they already existed. However, in assigning the laws governing cult and ritual to Moses; in stating that Moses is claimed to have heard them from God; in calling this cult monotheistic and aniconic; and in recognizing the Judaean system of land tenure as unusual, Hecataeus is in agreement with the Judaean descriptions. He even knows that Moses appointed judges, as reported in Numbers 11. He is correct, too, as far as is known, about the high priest being the ruler of the Judaeans.

Then there is the matter of military education. The widespread use of Jews as mercenaries is well known from the Assyrian period (when the Elephantine colony was set up) to the Hellenistic and Graeco-Roman periods. There were Jewish military colonies not only in Egypt, but in North Africa, Syria and no doubt elsewhere. The likelihood that Judaeans were trained in the military arts is quite high, in view of this and of their initial success during the Maccabaean wars, when a quite effective militia seems to have been organized. In any case a military aspect of Judaean culture is betrayed in the elaboration not only of the military victories in Joshua and the 'holy war' ideology of Deuter-onomy and Deuteronomistic writings, but also in the depiction of the Israelites in the wilderness as a nation-army. That material strongly suggests a self-image of Judaeans as a nation of warriors. Indeed, one title given to their deity, *Yhwh Sebaoth*, probably means 'Yahweh of armies' (whether astral or earthly is not very important: probably both).

Hecataeus appears to understand Judaeans as an ancient race, founded by Moses and ruled by high priests, devoted to their laws and of military renown. But here the focus is on the story of the departure of Moses and his followers from Egypt. Here a pestilence (*loimikē*) was ascribed by the populace to a divine (*daimōnion*) cause, namely that traditional observances has fallen into disuse, and aliens were practising different rites; upon which aliens were driven from the country. Of these, some settle in Greece, but the majority into Judaea. Their leader was Moses and he founded Jerusalem, and created the Judaean con-stitution.

Reflected here are several of the features observable in Manetho. First is an aetiology of ancient peoples, Judaean and Greek, whose origin is attributed to Egypt (which is hence the oldest of the civilizations). In a passage almost certainly reproduced from Hecataeus, Diodorus elsewhere (1.28.1-3) reproduces an Egyptian legend or myth that most of the civilized world came about through colonization from Egypt: Belus led colonists to Babylon, Danaos to Greece, and others to Colchis and Judaea.[25]

But some other elements of Hecataeus's account are also traceable in Manetho's stories. Among these is the idea of a plague (or leprosy), the name 'Moses' and the immediate connection between the departure from Egypt and the foundation of Jerusalem. These features suggest that Manetho's story is fundamentally Hecataeus's, whether or not he used Hecataeus as a source. The outlines of the story are close enough, and the crucial elements are plague/disease; expulsion; Moses; and Jerusalem. In Manetho's case we also have the theme of religious nonconformity. The curious feature is that this version exists in both pro-Judaean and anti-Judaean forms: anti-Judaism is not likely to have played any role in creating the version, though the version was exploited for such purposes.

The History of the Story

It remains possible that the narratives of Hecataeus and Manetho are a garbled form of a Judaean story of an 'exodus', in which the plagues, the name of Moses and the departure of a group of people to(wards) Judah have been transformed. But it is equally possible (since we do not know the date of the Judaean or of the Egyptian story) that the opposite is true, and that the story of the plagues, and the transformation of an expulsion into a miraculous escape, is a Judaean revision of an older, Egyptian story known to Hecataeus and Manetho. However, it is probably simplistic to think in these terms, for the nature and longevity of contacts between Judaeans and Egyptians makes it very likely that the story developed to some extent through interaction.

It must be conceded that Hecataeus reports reliably on a number of matters, and that he may have acquired information from Judeans

25. For the text and translation, see Stern (ed.), *Greek and Latin Authors*, I, p. 169.

themselves[26]; if so, he has cleverly exploited the Exodus story as one about the greater antiquity of the Egyptian race, a fairly standard device of Hellenistic historians, especially from one known to have been attached to Egyptian antiquity, since he wrote a treatise about it. But such an explanation does not easily explain the divergence of Hecataeus (or Manetho) from the Judaean version. Manetho, after all, seems to have got his information about the Hyksos from Egyptian sources; why could not Hecataeus have taken his story from Egypt also?

It seems to me probable that we are dealing with a story that has two versions, and thus we must also recognize that both versions have undergone some development of their own. Indeed, between Hecataeus and Manetho there are differences as well as similarities; for example, in the role played by the plague. In the same way, documentary critics have pointed out differences in the story between either J and P or D and P: for example, in the manner of description of the waters of *yam suph* receding. It is, then, the case that the canonized Judaean story is the result of a process of expansion and elaboration: the tensions referred to at the beginning of this essay illustrate this further. We are therefore considering a story that in both versions has enjoyed a certain amount of development. This development should be seen against the background of Egyptian as well as Judaean history, and especially the history of interaction of the two.

From at least as early as the second millennium, Egypt regarded Palestine as part of its own sphere of influence, an influence that is most clearly documented for us in the Amarna letters, as a weak Pharaoh was losing control over his nominal vassals in the cities of the region. Egyptian claims on Palestine were continually exerted before and afterwards, and documented in the Merneptah stela, the campaign reports of Shoshenq, the ambitions of Necho, and the annexation of Palestine by Ptolemy I. The idea that the people who lived there were in some sense the offspring of Egyptian civilization (as, even more ambitiously, Hecataeus suggests of the Greeks too!) and yet of a quite different religion and culture could give rise to the explanation that they were originally from Egypt. This is perhaps a counterpart to Johnstone's suggestion (see above) that the Exodus story may have developed as a reflection of the wane of Egyptian power over Palestine.

---

26. V. Tcherikover, *Hellenistic Civilization and the Jews* (Philadelphia: Jewish Publication Society of America, 1915), pp. 92-95; Mendels, 'Hecataeus of Abdera'.

From the Judaean point of view, Egypt is viewed, at least in the canonized literature, in both friendly and hostile terms; as a refuge in time of war or famine, but also as a potentially hostile neighbour. The growing number of Judaeans in Egypt during the Second Temple period and the virtual integration of Judah into the Ptolemaic economy in the third and second centuries BCE probably reinforced both sentiments. The story of the 'Israelites' having been enslaved there and having escaped underlined the feeling that Egypt was always a potential master regarding the inhabitants of Palestine as his property, and the story asserted that independence from Egypt had been won (once and for all) through a divine victory.

But these contexts are not isolated from one another. Without prejudging the antiquity of the story, let us begin in the middle of the seventh century BCE, when the Egyptian king Psammetichus I, as part of his strategy to gain control of the country, stationed garrisons in various places within his country: Elephantine, Naukratis and Daphne (Tahpanes). These troops comprised mercenaries from areas such as Greece and Libya and also Syria (Phoenicia, Samaria) as well as Judah.[27] Later, Judaean troops were said to have been in the Egyptian army at the battle of Carchemish,[28] for it seems that at this time Judah was both subject to Assyria and under the control of Egypt.

At the time of the capture of Jerusalem by Nebuchadrezzar in 586 BCE (according to 2 Kgs 25.26 after the assassination of Gedaliah) many Judaeans went to Egypt. Jeremiah 43–44 expresses hatred both of these Judaean immigrants and of Egypt, threatening destruction at the hand of the Babylonians. In 44.1 and 15 the locations of Judaean communities are names as Migdol, Tahpanes, Memphis and Pathros (Pathros denotes Upper Egypt, where Elephantine–Syene lay). According to the *Letter of Aristeas* 12–14, Ptolemy III (246–221) later transported thousands of Judeans to Egypt as military colonists and slaves. In the early second century BCE a high priest from Jerusalem, Onias IV, fled with his supporters to Leontopolis and built a temple there. The large Jewish population of Alexandria was one of the consequences of this history of Judaean immigration to Egypt, and the conflicts between Jews and Egyptians in this city are well documented.

27. The *Letter of Aristeas* 13 speaks of Jews sent to Egypt to help Psammetichus.

28. According to Berossus, quoted by Josephus (*Apion* 1.136-37).

There is, accordingly, an almost continuous process of Judean settlement in Egypt over the entire Second Temple period. Moreover, the increasing use of Aramaic, then Greek, in Egypt probably facilitated the interchange of stories. A degree of knowledge among Egyptians and immigrated Judaeans of each other's stories is to be expected; and among such stories may have been one about the origin of the Judaean race in Egypt.

There was certainly a lively interest within Judah itself towards émigrés to Egypt. The comments in Jeremiah are hostile. But Isa. 19.16-22 addresses Jewish settlements in Egypt, combining threats against Egypt itself with positive references to such groups, concluding with the hope of conversion:

> In that day Egypt shall be like women: afraid and fearful of the shaking of the hand of Yahweh of armies. The land of Judah shall be a terror to Egypt, everyone mentioning it shall be afraid in themselves, because of the plan that Yahweh of armies has devised against it. In that day five cities in the land of Egypt will speak the language of Canaan, and swear to Yahweh of armies; one shall be called the City of Destruction [MT 'City of the Sun', with some mss and Vulgate; or: 'City of Righteousness', LXX]. In that day there will be an altar to Yahweh in the middle of the land of Egypt, and a pillar to Yahweh at its border. It shall be a sign and a monument to Yahweh of armies in the land of Egypt: for they shall call to Yahweh because of the oppressors, and he will send them a saviour, a hero, who will deliver them. Yahweh will be known to Egypt, and the Egyptians will know Yahweh in that day, and will perform sacrifice and oblation; yes, they will make a vow to Yahweh and fulfil it. Yahweh will strike Egypt: strike it then heal it: and they shall return to Yahweh, and plead with him, and he shall heal them.

The 'City of Destruction' (*'ir haheres*, MT) of 'of the Sun' (*'ir haheres*) in v. 18 are generally identified as respectively Leontopolis and Heliopolis; in the former a Judaean colony certainly existed at the site later known as *tell el-yahudiyah* (whose cult would, according to Jer. 43.13, be dismantled). The date and the unity of the contents of Isaiah 19 is disputed, of course, and opinions range between the seventh century and the Seleucid period (a possibility entertained by Kaiser, who thinks of the fourth century as the earliest possible date, identifying 'Assyria' with the Seleucid kingdom).[29] I have cited this passage

---

29. O. Kaiser, *Isaiah 13–39* (OTL; London: SCM Press, 2nd edn, 1980), pp. 108-109; see also J. Vermeylen, *Du prophète Isaïe à l'Apocalyptique*, I (Paris: J. Gabalda, 1977), p. 324.

in full, without the space to analyse it, because it bears a curious relationship to the 'Exodus' story. It speaks of *future* settlements in Egypt, and of future deliverance from Egypt: and without any overt reference to an Exodus story. That the future deliverer is a *second Moses* (as Kaiser, for example, suggests) is to miss the point. There is no hint of a first Moses. Has this passage any connection with an 'Exodus' story? What of Isa. 52.4, 'For thus says Lord Yahweh, "My people went down previously into Egypt to settle there; and the Assyrians oppressed them without cause"'?

The well-known fifth-century papyri from Elephantine[30] (situated in the middle of the 'land of Pathros') illustrate some of the features of Judaean military colonies in Egypt. The Elephantine colony, which included women and children, observed its own customs, and, to judge from the onomastic evidence, there is little evidence of assimilation, although oaths in the name of foreign gods were taken and some syncretism is evident. It had its own sanctuary, where sacrifices were offered to Yahu, though other deities are also mentioned.

In 410 BCE, according to one document,[31] the local priests of the god Khnum (represented by a ram) were upset by the colony and built a wall inside it. They stopped up a well, prevented meal-offerings being offered, and dismantled the sanctuary, plundering its treasurers, and prompting an appeal to the Persian authorities, and subsequently letters to Jerusalem and Samaria.[32] Permission was subsequently granted from Jerusalem and by the satrap.[33]

However, in 399 Persian sovereignty over Egypt ended for over half a century, and the consequences for the colony and its sanctuary were no doubt serious. The sequence of documents ends in 399/398, and although Persian hegemony was restored in 343, it lasted only 12 years. Presumably the colonists were driven out; it is hard to imagine that they remained, or wished to.

---

30. On the Elephantine texts, see A.E. Cowley, *Aramaic Papyri of the Fifth Century B.C.* (Oxford: Clarendon Press, 1923); E.G. Kraeling, *The Brooklyn Museum Aramaic Papyri* (New Haven: Yale University Press, 1953); B. Porten and A. Yardeni, *Textbook of Aramaic Documents from Ancient Egypt*. I. *Letters* (Jerusalem: Hebrew University, 1986). Subsequent references to individual texts in the Cowley and Porten-Yardeni editions are given by number only.

31. Cowley no. 27; Porten-Yardeni 1 A4.5.

32. Cowley nos. 30-31; Porten-Yardeni 1 A4.7-8.

33. Cowley nos. 32-33; Porten-Yardeni 1 A4.9-10.

To sum up the thrust of the preceding remarks: the arrival and settlement of Judaeans (among other 'Asiatics', Nubians and Greeks) in Egypt during the Persian and Ptolemaic periods, which has been sketched here; the evidence of a lively interest in such settlements in the books of Isaiah and Jeremiah and the evidence of tension between Egyptians and Judaeans forms a background to the development of stories about the arrival and departure of Judaeans among both Egyptians and Judaeans. Many of these immigrants were military, and thus could be seen as invaders. The case of Elephantine suggests antagonism towards Judaean practices on the part of certain cults, and it is likely that the members of the colony were forcibly driven out by the Egyptians.

None of this is to suggest that the 'historical Exodus' is to be seen in any one of these events. But just as a *pattern* of events involving Asiatics in Egypt in the second millennium has been posited as a general context for an 'Exodus', so an even better documented pattern of Judaean colonies and settlements in Egypt during the Second Temple period may provide a context for the development of the story—by both Egyptians and Judaeans.

Reflections

What cannot be done, here or elsewhere, now or in the future, is to reconstruct the development of the story I have been investigating. However, certain outlines can perhaps be drawn.

The name Moses is Egyptian, despite his Semitic etymology and the story of his birth. Even on the basis of an exegesis of Exodus, it has been surmised that Moses has been converted from an Egyptian into an Israelite. According to the Egyptian versions, however, the people expelled were in fact aliens, either invaders (Manetho on the Hyksos) or foreign 'learned priests' (Hecataeus). However, Manetho's Moses story refers to his followers as lepers, not necessarily foreigners.

The Egyptian story features the practice of 'different religious rites' (Hecataeus) by those to be banished, or characterizes them (Manetho) as developing a religion in which the Egyptian gods were rejected and sacred animals sacrificed. In both cases this seems a natural reflection of a characteristic for which the Jews were widely known among the Greeks. But the Judaean story itself makes as a pretext for departure from Egypt a celebration of an Israelite feast (Exod. 5.1). There is also the theme of the plagues on Egypt in Exodus, which is echoed also in the Egyptian version as either a cause of the country's misfortunes (Hecataeus) or as the condition of those to be driven out. Manetho has the lepers working in stone quarries: the Judaean version has them working on store-cities (is that such a difference?).

Finally, we should not forget the problem with which I started: the hints in the Exodus story that the escape was really an expulsion, as in the Egyptian version. From where did this notion come? Does the theme of 'hardening the heart of Pharaoh' also have some origin in the transformation of this Pharaoh from one who wished to be rid of these people to one who wished to keep them enslaved? And is the fact that Moses has two foreign wives (Midianite in Exodus, Cushite in Numbers) at all connected with the importance of the theme of 'foreignness' in the Egyptian story; or Miriam's leprosy with Manetho's lepers? Of course one cannot determine in individual cases such as these; but the capacity to generate explanations for such incidental details strengthens the approach being advocated in this paper.

As an illustration of the way in which Judaean and Egyptian versions of the story may have continued to be combined, Artapanus, the second-century BCE Alexandrian Jew,[34] relates an expedition by Moses to Cush (Ethiopia). Manetho's 'Osarsiph' account has the Egyptian king Amenophis leading an expedition to Ethiopia during the belligerence of the 'lepers' and their Jerusalem allies, before returning to expel them. Expeditions to Ethiopia are, of course, a stock item of Egyptian historiography, but the parallel is suggestive.

Let me end with Moses's other name. The hint in the Judaean story of a non-Israelite element included in the departing horde (Exod. 12.38) seems to recur in Num. 11.4,[35] where a separate entity from the 'people of Israel' is named *ha'ssaphsuph*. The term is a *hapax* in biblical Hebrew, although its derivation from אסף or סוף is generally accepted. Given the abrupt manner in which this unique term is introduced into the narrative, however, it is not unreasonable to wonder whether it represents an originally extraneous element; and if so, whether its close similarity with Manetho's other name for Moses, Osarsiph, is entirely coincidental. A direct borrowing from one source to the other is unlikely, however: the original word (Egyptian?) perhaps belongs to the

34. Preserved in Eusebius, *Praep. ev.* 9.27, from Alexander Polyhistor.

35. Noted by M. Noth, *Exodus* (London: SCM Press, 1962) and B. Levine, *Numbers 1–20* (AB; New York: Doubleday, 1993), pp. 320-21.

common story and has been deployed differently by the extant literary sources.

The pattern of differences between the two versions of the one story, and the fluctuations *within* the two versions, suggest to me that we have here not a case of one version distorting another, nor indeed of a stable autonomous version among either Judaeans or Egyptians. While we have not been able to show, in the best manner of biblical tradition historians, exactly how each historical circumstance effected a change in the text, I have tried to cast the Exodus story into a different perspective, one in which questions of originality and historicity give way to a realization that people tell stories to each other, even Judaeans and Egyptians, and that in the process stories are borrowed (Ahiqar, after all, joins Tobit's family!) and change their nationality. But they continue to develop. My suggestion is that the Exodus story has grown in much the same way. I would not want to assert that it originated as an account of the Hyksos; nor with an escape of Judaean mercenaries from a military colony; nor that it began as an Egyptian story with an Egyptian hero driven out in order to avert a plague. But all these, of course, remain possibilities with which we can play.[36]

---

36. Since this paper was originally presented, my attention was drawn by Lester Grabbe to Chapter 2 of Erich S. Gruen, *Heritage and Hellenism: The Reinvention of Jewish Tradition* (Berkeley: University of California Press, 1998), 'The Use and Abuse of the Exodus Story', pp. 41-72, which brilliantly illuminates the creative impulses and contexts that shaped the various tellings of the Exodus story in the Hellenistic literature.

JEWISH HISTORIOGRAPHY AND SCRIPTURE
IN THE HELLENISTIC PERIOD

Lester L. Grabbe

The approach in this article is to look at the sources for the Hellenistic period and what we can know about Jewish history and religion in that period.[1] One question always in view is to what extent the Jews had authoritative writings or 'scriptures' at that time.[2] I make several assumptions in this investigation:

1. Historical knowledge is possible. We all believe that. None of us rejects our own past. Knowledge of antiquity is generally more difficult of access than knowledge of the recent past, but in principle there is no distinction between the two.

2. All sources of information are legitimate; that is, no source or class of source should be excluded a priori. Although each source has its own difficulties and provides its own sort of information, there is no intrinsic principle against using literary sources alongside archaeological ones. Literary sources may present particular complexities in interpretation, but every source requires interpretation by the historian. There is no such thing as uninterpreted data. Investigation may also show

---

1.   To some extent this parallels the treatment in chapter 4 of Lester L. Grabbe, *Judaism from Cyrus to Hadrian*. I. *Persian and Greek Periods*. II. *Roman Period* (Minneapolis: Fortress Press, 1992; British edition in one volume, London: SCM Press, 1994), pagination continuous in both editions. Whereas in the book I was attempting to reconstruct a probable picture to the extent that our sources allow, in this article I focus more on the limits of our knowledge and also the specific question of Scripture.

2.   One thesis to be investigated in particular is that of Niels Peter Lemche, 'The Old Testament—A Hellenistic Book?', *SJOT* 7 (1993), pp. 163-93; reprinted pp. 287-318 below.

that some sources are too questionable or problematic to use, but this is a decision which must be made a posteriori.

3. Writing history is an exercise in weighing probabilities. We can never be 100 per cent certain about our data; there is no such thing as unproblematic data. We argue the pros and cons of each source, recognizing the uncertainties that always exist with any source, and make a judgment. Someone else may make a different judgment from the same data, but any reconstruction is only as good as the arguments given in support of it.

Analysis

Beginning of the Greek Period

For the period of Alexander's conquest and the Diadochi—in short the first 75 years of Greek rule (c. 334–260 BCE)—we have almost no information about the Jews. The extant Greek sources do not mention them specifically, and all we have are some brief references in Josephus. One is the account of Alexander's coming to Jerusalem and bowing to the high priest, but this must be rejected as legendary with no historical substance behind it.[3] Josephus also quotes Hecataeus of Abdera, but Josephus's quotes from Hecataeus have long been disputed. The latest treatment of the issue argues that they are not from Hecataeus but the creation of a Jewish writer around 100 BCE.[4] What seems to be the one authentic reference to the Jews does not, unfortunately, tell us a great deal. Agathachides of Cnidus states:

> The people known as Jews, who inhabit the most strongly fortified of cities, called by the natives Jerusalem, have a custom of abstaining from work every seventh day; on those occasions they neither bear arms nor take any agricultural operations in hand, nor engage in any other form of public service, but pray with outstretched hands in the temples until the evening. Consequently, because the inhabitants, instead of protecting their city, persevered in their folly, Ptolemy, son of Lagus, was allowed to enter with his army; the country was thus given over to a cruel master, and the defect of a practice enjoined by law was exposed. That expe-

3. See Grabbe (*Judaism from Cyrus to Hadrian*, pp. 181-83) for discussion and bibliography.

4. Bezalel Bar-Kochva, *Pseudo-Hecataeus, On the Jews: Legitimizing the Jewish Diaspora* (Hellenistic Culture and Society, 21; Berkeley: University of California Press, 1996), especially p. 249.

rience has taught the whole world, except that nation, the lesson not to resort to dreams and traditional fancies about the law, until its difficulties are such as to baffle human reason.[5]

This tells us little, other than that Ptolemy I at some point captured Jerusalem, perhaps about 312 BCE but certainly no later than 301. The other quotations in the same context, which might help to fill out this reference to the Jews, now appear to be fabricated.[6]

Hecataeus of Abdera

Writing about 300 BCE, Hecataeus had one of the few descriptions of the Jewish people in Palestine and one of the earliest in Greek:

(1) When in ancient times a pestilence arose in Egypt, the common people ascribed their troubles to the workings of a divine agency... (2) Hence the natives of the land surmised that unless they removed the foreigners, their troubles would never be resolved. At once, therefore, the aliens were driven from the country, and the most outstanding and active among them banded together and, as some say, were cast ashore in Greece... But the greater number were driven into what is now called Judaea, which is not far distant from Egypt and was at that time utterly uninhabited. (3) The colony was headed by a man called Moses, outstanding both for his wisdom and for his courage. On taking possession of the land he founded, besides other cities, one that is now the most renowned of all, called Jerusalem. In addition he established the temple that they hold in chief veneration, instituted their forms of worship and ritual, drew up their laws and ordered their political institutions. He also divided them into twelve tribes, since this is regarded as the most perfect number and corresponds to the number of months that make up a year. (4) But he had no images whatsoever of the gods made for them, being of the opinion that God is not in human form; rather the Heaven that surrounds the earth is alone divine, and rules the universe. The sacrifices that he established differ from those of other nations, as does their way of living, for as a result of their own expulsion from Egypt he introduced an unsocial and intolerant mode of life. He picked out the men of most refinement and with the greatest ability to head the entire nation, and appointed them priests; and he ordained that they should occupy

5.   His work has not been preserved but is quoted in Josephus, *Ant.* 12.1.1 §§3-10; *Apion* 1.22 §§209-212 (the quotation here is from the latter work). On the authenticity of these quotations, see Bar-Kochva, *Pseudo-Hecataeus*, pp. 74-75; Menahem Stern, *Jews and Judaism in Greek and Latin Literature* (3 vols.; Jerusalem: Israel Academy of Arts and Sciences, 1974–84), I, pp. 104-109.

6.   See Bar-Kochva, *Pseudo-Hecataeus*.

themselves with the temple and the honours and sacrifices offered to their god. (5) These same men he appointed to be judges in all major disputes, and entrusted to them the guardianship of the laws and customs. For this reason the Jews never have a king, and authority over the people is regularly vested in whichever priest is regarded as superior to his colleagues in wisdom and virtue. They call this man the high priest [*archierea*], and believe that he acts as a messenger to them of God's commandments. (6) It is he, we are told, who in their assemblies and other gatherings announces what is ordained, and the Jews are so docile in such matters that straightway they fall to the ground and do reverence to the high priest when he expounds the commandments to them. And at the end of their laws there is even appended the statement: 'These are the words that Moses heard from God and declares unto the Jews'. (7) He [Moses] led out military expeditions against the neighbouring tribes, and after annexing much land apportioned it out, assigning equal allotments to private citizens and greater ones to the priests, in order that they, by virtue of receiving more ample revenues, might be undistracted and apply themselves continually to the worship of God.[7]

In addition to discussing the supposed origin of the Jews (expelled from Egypt under the leadership of Moses), Hecataeus describes a Jewish ethnic and national community centring on Jerusalem. The priests provide leadership and act as judges, as well as running the cult and teaching the law. Chief authority is invested in the high priest who is chosen for his wisdom. One rather interesting statement is that the priests possess land, at least collectively, which differs from the explicit statements of the Old Testament (Num. 18.24; Deut. 10.9; 12.12; 28.1). As for religion, he presents an aniconic and most likely a monotheistic temple-based religion. Finally, he states that they have a law and gives a quotation which closely parallels Lev. 27.34 and Num. 36.13.

It can be argued that the ultimate source of this picture is priestly teaching.[8] For example, the period of the monarchy is completely un-

7.   *Apud* Diodorus Siculus, 40.3.1-8. For text, translation and commentary, see Stern, *Jews and Judaism*, I, pp. 26-35. For a survey of the most recent scholarship on the work, see Bar-Kochva, *Pseudo-Hecataeus,* pp. 7-43. Unfortunately, the quotations in Josephus are not likely to be authentic, as Bar-Kochva has now demonstrated.

8.   O. Murray (in Menahem Stern and O. Murray, 'Hecataeus of Abdera and Theophrastus on Jews and Egyptians', *JEA* 59 [1973], pp. 159-68) suggests that Hecataeus consulted Jews, even priests; Doran Mendels ('Hecataeus of Abdera and a Jewish "patrios politeia" of the Persian Period (Diodorus Siculus XL, 3', *ZAW* 95

known, and the priestly class is pictured as being in charge from the beginning. However, our concern is not with the accuracy of Hecataeus with regard to the past but with the Jews of Palestine of his own time. Whether he used a written Jewish source or consulted Jews verbally, the source of the information is not the biblical tradition (or at least not primarily). Hecataeus seems to be describing the Jews as they existed in approximately his own time. This picture has been idealized in certain ways, probably by Hecataeus himself,[9] but that does not negate the value of the basic information. The statement that the priests owned property is more likely to match the reality of the Hellenistic period than the idealized portrait of the Pentateuch.

Zenon Papyri

Probably the most important source for the Jews in this period is the Zenon papyri.[10] They are contemporary evidence and were written with no ideological motive (at least, as far as it concerns Jewish history). Regretably, they give little information about the structure of Jewish society or specific historical events, but what they do give can be linked with other sources to help develop a framework. They originated in a private archive of the Zenon who was an agent of the Ptolemaic financial minister Apollonius. This Zenon went on a lengthy journey through Palestine and southern Syria about 259 BCE in the service of Apollonius (a number of the documents arising from that tour found their way into his archives). After returning home, he continued to correspond with some of those he met in Syria-Palestine, and their letters were also added to the archive.

The first document to be considered is a bill of sale for a slave:

> In the 27th year of the reign of Ptolemy, son of Ptolemy, and his son Ptolemy, the priest of Alexander and of the gods Adelphoi and the kanephoros of Arsinoe Philadelphos being those in office in Alexandria, in the month Xandikos, at Birta of the Ammanitis. Nikanor son of Xenokles, Kaunian, in the service of Toubias, sold to Zenon son of Agreophon, Kaunian, in the service of Apollonios the dioiketes, a Sidonian girl

[1983], pp. 96-110) argues that Hecataeus made use of a Jewish source which gave a priestly interpretation of the the Jewish past.

9.   E.g. Mendels, 'Hecataeus of Abdera', argues that he has assimilated his description to the Greek model of the *patrios politeia* or native constitution.

10.   For the main study of those relating to the Jews, see Victor A. Tcherikover, A. Fuks and M. Stern (eds.), *Corpus Papyrorum Judaicarum* (3 vols.; Cambridge, MA: Harvard University Press; Jerusalem: Magnes Press, 1957–64), I (= *CPJ*).

named Sphragis, about seven years of age, for fifty drachmai. Guar-
antor...son of Ananias, Persian, of the troop of Toubias, kleruch...[11]

This mentions a location in the *birta* (Aramaic 'fortress') in the Ammonite region. The seller is in the service of a Tobias (the Greek form
of Tobiah, a Jewish name) who seems to be in command of a troop of
cleruchs which includes soldiers of a variety of ethnic origins. This
Tobias seems to have provided hospitality to Zenon and his entourage
at some point. Later, after Zenon returned to Egypt, Tobias wrote to
Apollonius several times and once dispatched a gift of rare wild animals to Ptolemy II, via Apollonius. On another occasion he sent a gift
of slaves to Apollonius, with the following letter:

> Toubias to Apollonios, greeting. If you and all your affairs are flour-
> ishing, and everything else is as you wish it, many thanks to the gods! I
> too have been well, and have thought of you at all times, as was right. I
> have sent to you Aineias bringing a eunuch and four boys, house-slaves
> and of good stock, two of whom are uncircumcised. I append descrip-
> tions of the boys for your information.
>
> Goodbye. Year 29, Xandikos 10[12]

Tobias's Greek scribe has used a standard greeting in the statement,
'thanks to the gods', but it unlikely that Tobias was ignorant of it. To
what extent Tobias could read or understand Greek is not certain, but as
will be noted below, other sources suggest that the family came to be at
home in the wider Hellenistic world.

Another letter is enlightening about the general situation in society:[13]

> [Alexan]dros to Oryas, greeting. I have received your letter, to which
> you added a copy of the letter written by Zenon to Jeddous saying that
> unless he gave the money to Straton, Zenon's man, we were to hand over
> his pledge to him (Straton). I happened to be unwell as a result of taking
> some medicine, so I sent a lad, a servant of mine, with Straton, and wrote
> a letter to Jeddous. When they returned they said that he had taken no
> notice of my letter, but had attacked them and thrown them out of the
> village. So I am writing to you (for your information).
>
> Goodbye. Year 27, Peritios intercalary 20
> (Addressed) To Oryas

Jeddous (Jaddua) seems to be a local Jewish man, prominent in his
village or perhaps even headman of it. He is not afraid of Zenon's man

11. *CPJ*, I, p. 120, text no. 1.
12. *CPJ*, I, p. 126, text no. 4.
13. *CPJ*, I, p. 130, text no. 6.

(who suddenly developed a convenient illness and sent his servant instead of dealing with it himself). Although probably not so powerful as Tobias, Jeddous is another example of a native Jew who seems to be doing all right under Ptolemaic rule, has a great deal of autonomy, and is not afraid to throw his weight around.

Decree of Ptolemy II

Among the Rainer papyri in Vienna is one with parts of two decrees by Ptolemy II Philadelphus issued around his twenty-fourth year (260 BCE).[14] The legible parts read as follows:[15]

> [Col. 1 = left col., ll. 1-10]—to the *oikonomos* assigned in each hyparchy [*huparcheia*], within 60 days from the day on which the [ordinance] was proclaimed, the taxable and tax-free [livestock]…and take a receipt. And if any [do not do as] has been written above, [they shall be deprived of] the livestock and shall be [subject to the penalties] in the schedule. [Whatever] of the livestock was unregistered up to the proclamation of [the ordinance shall be free of taxes] for former years, of the pasture tax and crown tax and the other penalties, but from the 2[5]th year they shall pay the sum owing by villages…As for those…who make a registration in the name of another, the king will judge concerning them and their belongings shall be confiscated. Likewise,

> [Col. 1, ll. 17-21] Those holding the tax contracts for the villages and the komarchs [*komarchas*] shall register at the same time the taxable and tax-free livestock in the villages, and their owners with fathers' names and place of origin, and by whom the livestock are managed. Likewise they shall declare whatever unregistered livestock they see up to Dystros of the 25th year in statements on royal oath.

> [Col. 1, ll. 23-28] And they shall make each year at the same time declarations and shall pay the sums due as it is set out in the letter from the king, in the proper months according to the schedule. If any do not carry out something of the aforesaid, they shall be liable to the same penalties as those registering their own cattle under other names.

---

14. Now SB 8008 = M.-T. Lenger, *Corpus des ordonnances des Ptolémées* (Académie Royale de Belgique, Classe des Lettres, Mémoires, t. 56.5; Brussels: Palais des Académies, 1964), pp. 21-22; see also H. Liebesny, 'Ein Erlass des Königs Ptolemaios II Philadelphos über die Deklaration von Vieh und Sklaven in Syrien und Phonikien (PER Inv. Nr. 24.552 gr.)', *Aegyptus* 16 (1936), pp. 257-91.

15. Translation from R.S. Bagnall and P. Derow, *Greek Historical Documents: The Hellenistic Period* (SBLSBS, 16; Atlanta: Scholars Press, 1981), pp. 95-96.

[Col. 1, ll. 29-32] Anyone who wishes may inform (on violations), in which case he shall receive a portion of the penalties exacted according to the schedule, as is announced in the schedule, and of the goods confiscated to the crown he shall take a third part.

[Col. 1, l. 33—col. 2 = right col., l. 11] By order of the king: If anyone in Syria and Phoenicia has bought a free native person or has seized and held one or acquired one in any other manner—to the *oikonomos* in charge in each hyparchy within 20 days from the day of the proclamation of the ordinance. If anyone does not register or present him he shall be deprived of the slave and there shall in addition be exacted for the crown 6000 drachmas per head, and the king shall judge about him. To the informer shall be given...drachmas per head. If they show that any of the registered and presented persons were already slaves when bought, they shall be returned to them. As for those persons purchased in royal auctions, even if one of them claims to be free, the sales shall be valid for the purchasers.

[Col.2, ll. 12-15] Whoever of the soldiers on active duty and the other military settlers in Syria and Phoenicia are living with native wives whom they have captured need not declare them.

[Col. 2, ll. 16-26] And for the future no one shall be allowed to buy or accept as security native free persons on any pretext, except for those handed over by the superintendent of the revenues in Syria and Phoenicia for execution, for whom the execution is properly on the person, as it is written in the law governing farming contracts. If this is not done, (the guilty party) shall be liable to the same penalties, both those giving (security) and those receiving it. Informers shall be given 300 drachmas per head from the sums exacted.

This document says nothing directly about the Jews, and its value falls mainly in the economic, social and legal spheres.[16] Nevertheless, it is extremely important in helping to make a judgment about the authenticity of Antiochus III's decree on behalf of the Jews (see below).

The Story of the Tobiads
A significant section of Josephus's treatment of the Ptolematic period is taken up with the story of Joseph Tobiad and his sons (*Ant.* 12.4.1-11

---

16. For an indication of its importance, see R.S. Bagnall, *The Administration of the Ptolemaic Possessions outside Egypt* (Columbia Studies in Classical Texts, 4; Leiden: E.J. Brill, 1976), pp. 11-24; M. Rostovtzeff, *The Social and Economic History of the Hellenistic World* (3 vols.; Oxford: Clarendon Press, 1941), I, pp. 340-51.

§§154-236). It describes how Joseph son of one Tobias intervened when his uncle the high priest Onias refused to pay a tribute of 20 talents to Ptolemy. Joseph gained Ptolemy's favour and obtained the tax farming rights for Syria and Palestine. After 22 years of building up wealth and influence in the region, his youngest son Hyrcanus displaced him by subterfuge. This caused a breach between Joseph and his other sons on the one side and Hyrcanus on the other. The result was that Hyrcanus established a fortress in the Transjordanean region where he lived until Antiochus IV came to the throne, at which point he committed suicide.

This story has often been called a 'romance' because it clearly contains novelistic elements. Joseph ends up marrying his niece because his brother substitutes his daughter for a non-Jewish actress with whom Joseph had fallen in love. Joseph tests his son Hyrcanus by sending him to plough with oxen but without including any yokes. Hyrcanus makes a clever reply to the king when rivals play a joke on him at a banquet. In addition, the perspective of the story is that of the Tobiad family rather than of Judah as such and thus looks like some sort of family chronicle rather than the account of a general historian.[17] Family chronicles can still contain valuable information, but the genre of the story adds another difficulty in evaluating it as a historical source. Is this just a novel or romance with some historical elements within it, much as some of the other Jewish writings of this period (e.g. Judith)?

There are some errors in Josephus's account. He states that Antiochus III held Syria and Palestine but gave them to Ptolemy as a dowry for his daughter Cleopatra when Ptolemy married her. This Ptolemy is identified as Ptolemy V Epiphanes (c. 204–180 BCE), which is impossible. The general dating of the events in Josephus does not make sense.[18]

However, these errors show only that Josephus has made mistakes in placing his source into an overall framework, not that the errors were a part of the original story. The story itself fits well into the period of Ptolemaic rule in Palestine, and parts of it match with independent data from sources not known (or at least unlikely to be known) by Josephus:

---

17. Jonathan A. Goldstein argues that the account was written by Onias IV, the Jerusalem high priest who built the temple in Leontopolis ('The Tales of the Tobiads', in Jacob Neusner [ed.], *Christianity, Judaism and Other Greco-Roman Cults*, III [SJLA, 12; Leiden: E.J. Brill, 1975], pp. 85-123).

18. For a further discussion, see Grabbe, *Judaism from Cyrus to Hadrian*, p. 196.

1. Joseph is son of Tobias. The Tobias known from the Zenon papyri matches well as a father.

2. Onias the high priest also acts as the representative of the people to the Ptolemaic court. This coincides with other information we have that the high priest was also the main leader of the nation.

3. The son of Onias is the high priest Simon. According to Ben Sira 50, a Simon son of Onias was high priest shortly after Antiochus III took Palestine in 200 BCE.

4. A Hyrcanus 'son of Tobias' or possibly 'the Tobiad' (*tou Tōbiou*) had some money deposit at the Jerusalem temple during the reign of Seleucus IV, according to 2 Macc. 3.11-12.[19]

5. The archaeological site of Araq el-Emir in Jordan matches the 'Tyre' of Hyrcanus as described by Josephus.[20] The 'fortress' (*birta*, presumably a transliteration of the Aramaic word) of the Tobias in the Zenon papyri is not described with any precision but could also fit this site. The name Tobiah is twice carved in the rock in the square Hebrew script (טביה), though the dating is disputed. One building phase in the late third or early second centuries BCE seems to fit well the construction of Hyrcanus; unfortunately, that construction removed some of the earlier layers, and it in turn was greatly damaged by Byzantine construction.

The detail of the story is by no means confirmed; even the main character of Joseph Tobiad is nowhere else attested so far. Yet the existence of Hyrcanus is apparently attested directly by 2 Macc. 3.11-12

---

19. According to the new Schürer, this is not a reference to the Tobias of the Zenon papyri (Emil Schürer, *The Jewish People in the Age of Jesus Christ* [rev. and ed. G. Vermes; 3 vols. in 4 parts; Edinburgh: T. & T. Clark, 1973–87], I, pp. 149-50 n. 30) but rather to a son of Joseph, which would make the Hyrcanus of 2 Maccabees a nephew of the Hyrcanus in the Tobiad romance. The explanation is ingenious but only speculation.

20. See the summary of Paul Lapp and Nancy Lapp, with bibliography, in E. Stern (ed.), *The New Encyclopedia of Archaeological Excavations in the Holy Land* (4 vols.; New York: Simon & Schuster; Jerusalem: Israel Exploration Society, 1992), II, pp. 646-49; see more briefly in Grabbe (*Judaism from Cyrus to Hadrian*, pp. 188-89). The most recent excavations are published in Ernest Will, *'Iraq el-Amir: Le chateau du Tobiade Hyrcan* (Texte et Album; Paris: P. Geuthner, 1991).

and indirectly by the archaeological finds at Araq el-Emir. This suggests that the outlines of the story should be given some credence, especially the part about the power and influence of the Tobiad family.[21]

The Edicts of Antiochus III

Antiochus III defeated Scopas, the general of Ptolemy V, about 200 BCE. We have two decrees from him. One has been found on a stela near Hefzibah and contains the contents of several letters written between 202 and 195 BCE relating to protecting local people from Seleucid soldiers. For ease of reading, the following excerpt does not have minor restorations indicated:

> [IVa 20-26] To the great King Antiochos, memorandum by Ptolemaios, *strategos* and chief-priest. I propose, if you approve, King,—to [Kle(?)]on and Heliodoros the *dioiketai* respecting the villages belonging to me as property and hereditary tenure and respecting those which you ordered to be assigned (to me), that nobody should be allowed to quarter under any pretence, or to bring in others or to commandeer the draught animals or to eject the villagers. The same (letter) to Heliodoros. [V 27-33] King Antiochos to Marsyas greetings. There announced to us Ptolemaios the *strategos* and chief-priest, that man[y of those] travelling through lodge by violence in his villages and do many other acts of injustice, not caring for the qua[rters(?) (prepared) by] us. Relating to this now take care that they not only be restrained but also punished tenfold if damages are done. The same (letter) to Lysanias, Leon, Dionikos.[22]

This is an important original document for comparison with the other alleged decree of Antiochus III, which follows.

According to Josephus, Antiochus III issued a decree which lists the temple personnel and relieves some of their taxes temporarily so the temple can be repaired of war damage. The decree is as follows (the sections in square brackets being further discussed below):

> King Antiochus to Ptolemy, greeting. Inasmuch as the Jews, from the very moment when we entered their country, showed their eagerness to

21. See most recently Dov Gera, *Judaea and Mediterranean Politics 219 to 161 B.C.E.* (Brill's Series in Jewish Studies, 8; Leiden: E.J. Brill, 1998), pp. 36-58. Although sceptical of many details, he seems to accept that figures such as Joseph and Hyrcanus Tobiad existed and had a good deal of influence in the region.

22. Y.H. Landau, 'A Greek Inscription Found near Hefzibah', *IEJ* 16 (1966), pp. 54-70 (61) (trans. modified in the light of Fischer [see below]); T. Fischer, 'Zur Seleukideninschrift von Hefzibah', *ZPE* 33 (1979), pp. 131-38; J.M. Bertrand, 'Sur l'inscription d'Hefzibah', *ZPE* 46 (1982), pp. 167-74.

serve us and, when we came to their city, gave us a splendid reception
and met us with their senate and furnished an abundance of provisions to
our soldiers and elephants, and also helped us to expel the Egyptian garrison in the citadel, we have seen fit on our part to requite them for these
acts and to restore their city which has been destroyed by the hazards of
war, and to repeople it by bringing back to it those who have been
dispersed abroad. In the first place we have decided, on account of their
piety, to furnish them for their sacrifices an allowance of sacrificial
animals, wine, oil and frankincense to the value of twenty thousand pieces
of silver, and sacred *artabae* of fine flour in accordance with their native
law, and one thousand four hundred and sixty *medimni* of wheat and
three hundred and seventy-five *medimni* of salt.

[And it is my will that these things be made over to them as I have
ordered, and that the work on the temple be completed, including the
porticoes and any other part that it may be necessary to build.]

The timber, moreover, shall be brought from Judea itself and from
other nations and Lebanon without the imposition of a toll-charge. The
like shall be done with the other materials needed for making the
restoration of the temple more splendid. And all the members of the
nation shall have a form of government in accordance with the laws of
their country, and the senate, the priests, the scribes of the temple and the
temple-singers shall be relieved from the poll-tax and the crown-tax and
the salt-tax which they pay.

[And, in order that the city may the more quickly be inhabited, I grant
both to the present inhabitants and to those who may return before the
month of Hyperberetaios exemption from taxes for three years.]

We shall also relieve them in future from the third part of their tribute,
so that their losses may be made good. And as for those who were carried off from the city and are slaves, we herewith set them free, both
them and the children born to them, and order their property to be
restored to them.[23]

This document has generally been taken as authentic, even if those in
§§145-46 and §§148-53 are rejected.[24] We should expect such a decree

23. Quoted in Josephus, *Ant.* 12.3.3-4 §§138-46 (translation from H.St.J. Thackeray *et al.* [eds.], *Josephus*, VII [LCL; London: Heinemann; Cambridge, MA:
Harvard University Press, 1926–65], pp. 71-75).

24. See most recently Jörg-Dieter Gauger, *Beiträge zur jüdischen Apologetik:
Untersuchungen zur Authentizität von Urkunden bei Flavius Josephus und im I.
Makkabäerbuch* (BBB, 49; Cologne: Peter Hanstein, 1977), especially pp. 19, 23-
24, 61-63, 136-39. Although he argues against the other two documents in the context (*Ant.* 12.3.3-4 §§138-53), he thinks the Antiochus edict to Ptolemy is authentic,
though adapted for its context by Josephus. The main linguistic study of the text is
E.J. Bickerman, 'Une question d'authenticité: les privilèges juifs', in *Studies in*

from a conqueror, and a number of considerations argue for its existence. First, there is the statement in 2 Maccabees about 'the royal concessions to the Jews, secured through John the father of Eupolemus' (4.11), the only logical context being the time of Antiochus III's conquest. Secondly, it fits the general situation in Syro-Palestine at the time. A subordinate people is often ready for a change, in hopes of a bettering of their condition, if ruled by a particular power for a long period of time. Thirdly, the last section of the decree fits the general approach of Ptolemy II's decree in the Rainer papyrus, suggesting not only a common administrative approach and style but also a common administrative policy towards those being governed. The basic agreement in style and content with other Seleucid documents (even by one so exacting as Gauger), has been well demonstrated, and the contents are not intrinsically unlikely.[25] Antiochus also interacts with his minister Ptolemy, just as he does in the Hefzibah stela quoted above. Fourthly, there is little that looks like Jewish propaganda here. Antiochus remits certain taxes temporarily to help in rebuilding the damaged city, as one might expect. He does not deliver fantastic sums of money nor treat the Jews in any special way, as one might expect in falsified letters.

These positive points do not remove all the problems. Establishing authenticity in a document preserved by later scribal tradition is never

Jewish and Christian History, II (AGJU, 9; Leiden: E.J. Brill, 1980), pp. 24-43; *idem*, 'La charte séleucide de Jérusalem', in *Studies in Jewish and Christian History*, II, pp. 44-85 (orig. in *REJ* 100 [1935]); 'Une proclamation séleucide relative au temple de Jérusalem', in *idem*, *Studies in Jewish and Christian History*, II, pp. 86-104 (orig. in *Syria* 25 [1946–48], pp. 67-85). For other studies, see Martin Hengel, *Judaism and Hellenism* (2 vols.; London: SCM Press; Philadelphia: Fortress Press, 1974), I, pp. 271-72 (and notes); Ralph Marcus, 'Appendix D: Antiochus III and the Jews (*Ant.* xii. 129-153)', in Thackeray (ed.), *Josephus*, VII, pp. 743-66.

25. On the style, see Gauger, *Beiträge zur jüdischen Apologetik* and Bickerman's essays in the previous note, and also compare the original decrees of Ptolemy II and Antiochus III quoted in this essay. Although some tax concessions are made to the Jews, they are only temporary, to allow repair of the temple and city. There is nothing of the wholesale exemption of temple personnel from tax or special privileges bestowed on the Jews as found in other royal decrees which are likely to be examples of Jewish propaganda (e.g. some of the decrees in Ezra; on them see Lester L. Grabbe, *Ezra and Nehemiah* [Readings; London: Routledge, 1998], pp. 128-32).

easy. Some alteration is inevitable simply through scribal error. It takes only a small number of changes to completely alter the tenor of a document.[26] There are two problems that remain, despite the positive arguments: the first is that in contrast to the normal style of royal Seleucid documents, two sections (§§141 and 143) are in the first person singular, making them the most suspect.[27] These are marked in square brackets above. The second is the failure to mention the high priest. There are several possible explanations for this: Antiochus may have wanted to concentrate on the institutions (the 'senate') or groups rather than individuals; Simon may have opposed Antiochus (but then why was he allowed to continue in office?); there was no high priest at the time of the invasion, or perhaps the high priest was killed in the fighting over Jerusalem, and Simon came to the office only after Antiochus had entered the city. These are only suggestions, but lack of mention of Simon, while a puzzle, is not fatal to the decree's authenticity.

Ben Sira

The book of Jesus ben Sira was written shortly after 200 BCE.[28] The book is extant in the Greek translation, with about two-thirds of the text

---

26. This is well demonstrated in the debate over Jewish citizenship in Alexandria in the first century. Josephus quotes an alleged document of the emperor Claudius showing that the Jews had equal citizenship rights with the Greeks (*Ant.* 19.5.2 §§280-85). We now have an authentic document of Claudius's which may well be the original on which Josephus's document is based (see *CPJ*, II, pp. 36-55 [text no. 153]). Only a few minor changes have completely altered the message of the decree from one denying citizenship to the Jews to one affirming it. Miriam Pucci ben Zeev, *Jewish Rights in the Roman World: The Greek and Roman Documents Quoted by Josephus Flavius* (Texte und Studien zum Antiken Judentum, 74, Tübingen: Mohr Siebeck, 1998), pp. 295-326, thinks that there are two different decrees here, which remains a possibility.

27. Gauger, *Beiträge zur jüdischen Apologetik*, pp. 19, 23-24, 61-63, 136-39. Despite Bickerman's able defence of the document, his attempt to salvage the text at this point is ingenious but unconvincing. It is better simply to recognize that two passages have probably been subject to scribal reworking at some point.

28. The book shows no knowledge of the 'abomination of desolation' set up in the temple about 168 BCE nor of the Maccabaean revolt that followed, suggesting it was written before then. But it mentions Simon son of Onias and also war damage to the city, likely to have been caused by Antiochus III's taking of the city in 200 BCE. Finally, his grandson went to Egypt in 132 BCE where he translated the book into Greek. The evidence of this colophon in the Greek text is confirmed by the presence of the Hebrew text which does not contain it. The two different versions,

available in the original Hebrew.[29] The question of how faithful the Greek is to the Hebrew is an important one since large sections of the text are extant only in Greek. The most recent studies suggest that the translation is faithful in conveying the thought but is not a slavishly literal one.[30] The most important section for our purposes is the 'Praise of the Fathers' (44–50) which goes through the heroes (no heroines) of Israel, extending from Adam to Ben Sira's own time. Only some of ch. 44 is available in the earliest witness to the Hebrew text from Masada.[31] For the rest one must depend on the Hebrew text from the Cairo Genizah (Manuscript B) and the Greek text. However, the Masada manuscript seldom differs from the Cairo manuscript in anything more than orthography or minor textual variations. This suggests that Cairo Manuscript B is a reasonable witness to the original text written by Ben Sira himself, and the Hebrew text is by and large extant for this section.

in the original Hebrew and a Greek translation claiming to be by the grandson, are most easily explained by accepting the testimony of the Greek text. These data together indicate a writing in the first quarter of the second century BCE.

29. The textual history of the book is somewhat complicated, but there is a considerable consensus on how it should be evaluated. See especially A.A. Di Lella, *The Hebrew Texts of Sirach: A Text-Critical and Historical Study* (Studies in Classical Literature; The Hague: Mouton, 1966); also the summary in P.W. Skehan and A.A. Di Lella (*The Wisdom of Ben Sira* [AB, 39; Garden City, NY: Doubleday, 1987], pp. 51-62) and Benjamin G. Wright (*No Small Difference: Sirach's Relationship to its Hebrew Parent Text* [SBLSCS, 26; Atlanta: Scholars Press, 1989], pp. 2-10). For the Hebrew text, I have used the Academy of the Hebrew Language's *The Book of Ben Sira: Text, Concordance and an Analysis of the Vocabulary* (The Historical Dictionary of the Hebrew Language; Jerusalem: Academy of the Hebrew Language, 1973) and Pancratius C. Beentjes (*The Book of Ben Sira in Hebrew: A Text Edition of All Extant Hebrew Manuscrits and a Synopsis of All Parallel Hebrew Ben Sira Texts* [VTSup, 68; Leiden: E.J. Brill, 1997]); for the Greek text, Joseph Ziegler (*Sapientia Iesu Filii Sirach* [Septuaginta, Vetus Testamentum Graecum 12.2; Göttingen: Vandenhoeck & Ruprecht, 2nd edn, 1980]).

30. Wright (*No Small Difference*, p. 249) concludes: 'These outlines, however, do suggest that the grandson was not usually concerned to give a word-for-word translation of the Hebrew.... Here was a translator concerned to give a *translation* of his grandfather's wisdom, not a mechanical *reproduction* of his grandfather's Hebrew' (italics in the original).

31. For the official publication of this text, see Shemaryahu Talmon and Yigael Yadin (eds.), *Masada VI: Yigael Yadin Excavations 1963–1965, Final Reports* (Jerusalem: Israel Exploration Society, 1999).

Ben Sira	*Hebrew Bible*
(49.16: Adam)	
44.16: Enoch: והתהלך עם ייי ונלכח	Gen. 5.24: ...את־האלהים...ויתהלך
(49.14: Enoch taken away: נלקח פנים)	כי־לכח אתו אלהים
(49.16: Seth)	Gen. 4.25
(49.16 Enoch)	Gen. 4.26
44.17-18: Noah: צדייק במצא תמים	Gen. 6.9: צדיק תמים...בדרתיו
(49.16: Shem)	Gen. 6.10, etc.
44.19-21: Abraham: אב המון גוים	Gen. 17.5: אב־המון גוים
Covenant in his flesh	Gen. 22.18
Promise to bless the nations through his descendants	Gen. 15.18
Inheritance from Euphrates to ends of earth	
44.22: Isaac	
44.23-24: Israel (Greek Jacob)	Gen. 37, 39–50
(49.15: Joseph)	
(Dead body provided for)	Gen. 50.25
45.1-5: Moses	
Performed miracles	
In king's presence	
His meekness	Num. 12.3, 7
Given commandments for his people	
45.6-22: Aaron	
Description of priestly garments	Exod. 39.1-31
Dathan, Abiram, Korah	Numbers 16
Priests have no inheritance	Numbers 18
45.23-24: Phineas, son of Eleazar	Numbers 25
45.25-26: Covenant of priesthood forever	Num. 25.13
46.1-6: Joshua, son of Nun	
Sun stood still	Josh. 10.12-14
Hail sent down on the enemy	Josh. 10.11
46.7-8: Joshua and Caleb opposed rebels and allowed to go into inheritance	Num. 14.6-38
46.9-10: Caleb	Judg. 1.10-15
46.11-12: Judges	
46.13-20: Samuel	
Prophet	1 Sam. 9.9
Pledged from mother's womb	1 Sam. 1.11
Established the kingship/anointed princes	1 Sam. 8-10, 16
Visited the settlements of Jacob	1 Sam. 7.16-17
When pressed by enemies, offering sucking lamb	1 Sam. 7.9-11
God thundered from heaven against Philistines	1 Sam. 7.10

Ben Sira (cont.)	*Hebrew Bible* (cont.)
Had taken no bribe	1 Sam. 12.3-5
Pronounced king's fate from the grave	1 Samuel 28
47.1: Nathan successor to Samuel	2 Samuel 7
47.2-11: David	
Killed lions and bears	1 Sam. 17.34-37
Slew the giant with a slingstone	1 Sam. 17.49-50
Women ascribed 10,000s defeated by him	1 Sam. 18.7
Defeated the Philistines and other enemies	
Added string music to altar celebration of festivals	1 Chron. 16; 23.5; 2 Chron. 7.6
47.12-22: Solomon	
Built house in God's name	1 Kings 6
Wise when he was young	1 Kgs 5.9-14
Fame reached wide	1 Kgs 5.14; 10.1, 23-24
Astonished by wisdom and proverbs	1 Kgs 5.9-14
Heaped up gold like iron, silver like lead	1 Kgs 10.21, 27
But gave himself over to women	1 Kgs 11.1-5
Division of kingdom but something left to David	1 Kgs 12.20
47.23-25: Rehoboam and Jeroboam	
Rehoboam lacked sense and caused the people to rebel	1 Kgs 12.1-19
Sinner (Jeroboam) who caused Israel to sin and, eventually, to go into captivity	1 Kgs 12.25–13.5; 2 Kgs 17.21-23
48.1-11: Elijah	
Shattered their staff of bread and shut the heavens	1 Kgs 17–18
Brought down fire three times	1 Kgs 18.38; 2 Kgs 1.10, 12
Brought dead child to life	1 Kgs 17.17-24
Heard threats/punishment at Sinai/Horeb	1 Kgs 19.5-18
Anointed prophet in his place	1 Kgs 19.19-21
Taken up in whirlwind	2 Kgs 2.11-12
Destined to come before day of Lord, to turn hearts of parents to children	Mal. 3.23-24
48.12-14: Elisha	
Did twice as many miracles	2 Kings 2.9
Performed miracles after death	2 Kgs 13.20-21
48.17-25: Hezekiah	
Cut through rocks to bring water	2 Kgs 20.20; 2 Chron. 32.30; Isa. 22.9-11
Sennacherib's invasion	2 Kgs 18–19; Isa. 36–37
Saved by prayer through Isaiah	2 Kgs 19.5-7, 14-34; Isa. 37.5-7, 14-34

Ben Sira (cont.)	*Hebrew Bible* (cont.)
Angel struck down Assyrian army	2 Kgs 19.35-36; Isa. 37.35-36
Isaiah turned back the sun and saved life of king	2 Kgs 20.1-11; Isa. 38.1-8
(Isaiah) foretold what would happen in future	
49.1-3: Josiah	
Destroyed the idols and practised virtue	2 Kgs 22–23
49.6: Jeremiah	
Made prophet in womb	Jer. 1.5
Sent to root out, pull down, destroy, and to build and plant	Jer. 1.10
49.8: Ezekiel	
Vision of creatures with chariot throne	Ezekiel 1, 10
49.9: Job	
49.10: Book of Twelve	
49.11: Zerubbabel	
Like signet ring on God's hand	Hag. 2.23
49.12: Jeshua b. Jozadak	
Rebuilt the altar and erected the temple	Haggai 1–2; Ezra 3–6
49.13: Nehemiah	
Rebuilt Jerusalem's walls and defences	Nehemiah 3–4

The table above shows the extent to which Ben Sira's account follows the text of the Hebrew Bible, often in some interesting details. He begins his survey with Enoch (44.16), followed by Noah (44.17-18), Abraham (44.19-21), Isaac (44.22), and Jacob (44.23-24). A section is devoted to Moses (45.1-5), but particular emphasis is placed on Aaron (45.6-22), including a reference to Phinehas son of Eleazar (45.23-24). The description of the high priestly garments closely follows the account in Exod. 39.1-31. What is surpising is that Ben Sira follows the biblical text in saying that the priesthood had no inheritance among the tribes, even though it is likely that by his own time the priests owned land, collectively and possibly individually.[32] Then come Joshua son of Nun who made the sun stand still (46.1-6), Caleb son of Jephunneh who was his companion as they spied out the land (46.7-10), the judges (46.11-12), Samuel the prophet, with a close paraphrase from 1 Sam. 12.3-4 (46.13-20), followed by David son of Jesse who slew the giant, crushed the Philistines and had a covenant with God (45.25; 47.2-11)

---

32. See also my discussion in *Judaic Religion in the Second Temple Period: Belief and Practice from the Exile to Yavneh* (London: Routledge, 2000), pp. 38-39.

with Nathan the prophet (47.1). The reign of Solomon, who was wealthy and wise but had too many women (47.12-22), was followed by Rehoboam and Jeroboam under whom the kingdom split (47.23-25). Space is then given to Elijah (48.1-11) and Elisha (48.12-14), but the people did not repent (48.15-16). Next are Hezekiah (48.17-25), under whom was Isaiah, followed by Josiah (49.1-3). Except for David, Hezekiah and Josiah the other kings were guilty of forsaking God's law (49.4-5). The prophets Jeremiah, Ezekiel and the Twelve are mentioned (49.6-10), then Zerubbabel and Jeshua son of Jozadak and Nehemiah (49.11-13). The survey is rounded off (49.14-16), including a reference to Adam, Shem and Seth who had not been mentioned earlier. But then Ben Sira moves on to speak of a contemporary hero, Simon the high priest (50.1-29):

> [1] Greatest among his brothers and the glory of his people was the high priest Simon son of Onias in whose lifetime the house was repaired, in whose days the temple was fortified. [2] He laid the foundation for the high double wall, the high retaining wall of the temple precinct. [3] In his day a reservoir was dug a cistern broad as the sea. [4] He was concerned to ward off disaster from his people and made the city strong against siege. [5] How glorious he was as he processed through the temple, emerging from behind the veil of the sanctuary!

What is obvious to a careful reader of the details is that Ben Sira has summarized in outline form much of the contents of the present Torah and Prophets sections of the Hebrew Bible. Even the table above cannot include all the various details included by him, but in almost all cases they coincide with information in the present biblical text. This is more than just a collection of oral traditions or material derived from several sources. The Minor Prophets are already a unit, for example. He gives a close paraphrase—almost a quote—from a number of passages (e.g. Gen. 5.24; 6.9; 15.18; 1 Sam. 7.10; 12.3-5; Hag. 2.23; and Mal. 3.23-24). The most reasonable conclusion is that Ben Sira had essentially the present biblical text of the Pentateuch, Joshua to 2 Kings, 1–2 Chronicles, and the Prophets in front of him.[33]

33. I say 'essentially the present biblical text' advisedly since it is clear that slightly different versions of some parts of the Old Testament circulated in Hebrew until at least the first century CE, and translations of variant Hebrew texts are still extant. In some cases, the differences between the various forms of the text are not usually very significant (e.g. the MT, LXX, and Samaritan Pentateuch of the Torah), but in other cases there are rather more substantial differences (e.g. the book of

On the period of the kings, it looks as if he had 1 and 2 Samuel available. But when he describes David, some aspects of his description appear to be taken from 1 Chronicles. For example, his emphasis on David's establishment of the cult and the various singers (Sir. 47.9-10//1 Chron. 15.16; 16.4-6; 23.5, 31-32). This suggests that Ben Sira's Bible had not only 1 and 2 Samuel and 1 and 2 Kings but also 1 and 2 Chronicles. Why must it have had 1 and 2 Kings, since his information on David could all have been taken from Chronicles? It just seems rather unlikely that he had an edition with Samuel and Chronicles, but not Kings.

Synthesis

The century and a half of Jewish history between Alexander's conquest and Antiochus IV is an obscure period, but it is not a complete blank. The sources for it are diverse and varied in quality, and they hardly give us a complete history of the Jews; nevertheless, they give us some valuable information about the structure of the province, the style of government and some details about the Jewish religion. What is more, these sources do not differ in general kind or quality from those for the wider history of the Mediterranean world and the ancient Near East. The sources for Jewish history are fewer than for the Seleucid or Ptolemaic empires as a whole, but the problems encountered are of the same order, and the results of a similar probability.

The most straightforward source is the Zenon papyri, representing genuine documents from the third century BCE. What they tell us is extremely valuable, but because of their nature as legal documents, lists,

Jeremiah). Various theories about how various texts developed and were revised have been advanced, but most of these are more or less speculative (see the summary in Emanuel Tov, *Der Text der Hebräischen Bibel: Handbuch der Textkritik* [Stuttgart: W. Kohlhammer, 1997]). For example, it is widely held that the Greek Minor Versions represent revisions of the LXX; I accept this with regard to the *kaige*/Theodotion version but argue that Aquila and Symmachus are original translations; see Lester L. Grabbe, 'Aquila's Translation and Rabbinic Exegesis', *Essays in Honour of Yigael Yadin* (=*JJS* 33 [1982]), pp. 527-36); *idem*, 'The Translation Technique of the Greek Minor Versions: Translations or Revisions?', in George J. Brooke (ed.), *Septuagint, Scrolls and Cognate Writings: Papers Presented to the International Symposium on the Septuagint and its Relations to the Dead Sea Scrolls and Other Writings (Manchester, 1990)* (SBLSCS, 33; Atlanta: Scholars Press, 1992), pp. 505-56.

official letters, and the like, they are more important for economic and legal matters than for Jewish society or historical events. After this comes Hecataeus of Abdera whose account in Diodorus Siculus is unlikely to be a forgery of any sort (unlike the quotations in Josephus). The question is not one of authenticity but of the source of his knowledge. Although his information is likely to come from a Jewish source rather than direct observation of the Jews living in Palestine, the picture he gives does not look like one based primarily on the biblical tradition. There is a good chance that when he describes the Jews as such (rather than their origins), he is giving an outline of their administrative structure and society in his own time. Allowance must of course be made for Hecataeus's own interpretation of the information he received and whatever conscious or unconscious models he may have followed.

Of great potential value is the decree of Antiochus III, but to establish its authenticity is complicated. Bickerman's defence is very well done by one at home in the Seleucid sources, but Gauger's arguments that the first-person sections must represent some sort of rewriting are convincing. On the other hand, one so sceptical as Gauger still thinks the basic document is authentic, and in this he is supported by most classical scholars who have examined the writing. Finally, there is the Tobiad story. There is no doubt that it contains novelistic elements, and it would be foolish to take it completely at face value. Yet there is a surprising amount of circumstancial evidence for the essentials of the story: the existence of two powerful families, the Tobiads and Oniads; the important part played by some members of the Tobiad family in the region; the existence of such indivduals as Joseph and Hyrcanus. There are thus two strong arguments for accepting the basic outline that it gives: first, it fits so well the society and Ptolemaic rule in third-century Syria-Palestine; secondly, some individual details within the story are confirmed by other independent sources or intersect seamlessly with other sources such as the Zenon papyri.

Any one source (apart from the Zenon papyri, which still must be interpreted) has problems, and almost any particular detail can be questioned. Yet the sources as a whole have to be accepted as being more or less probable *in toto*, and any wholesale rejection unsupportable without careful argument. My view is that they mutually re-enforce certain points, independently, which means that the picture emerging from them is likely to be authentic. Here is a list, with the particular sources indicated:

1. The Jews in Judah had a form of internal government analogous to a temple state (Hecataeus of Abdera, decree of Antiochus III, Sir. 50, Tobiad romance [*Ant.* 12.4.1 §§157-59]). There are some objections to the designation 'temple state' since the classic temple state owned lands from which it derived income, whereas the Jerusalem temple may not have been so structured. The matter is somewhat uncertain since Hecataeus seems to suggest that the priests did own property, contrary to the law of Moses.

2. The sources listed at (1) further indicate that the head of the community (we do not know that the Ptolemies had a province of Judah) was the high priest, assisted by other senior priests and lay aristocrats who made up a sort of 'senate' (*gerousia*). The priesthood had an important role not only in the cult but also in the administration of justice and government of the people. This fits with the picture given in the Elephantine papyri, suggesting that the internal structure of the community passed basically unchanged from Persian to Greek rule.[34]

3. Two family names come to prominence in the sources: the Todiads with a family possession in Transjordan in the old Ammonite area, and the high priestly Oniad family. As two powerful families, they were rivals to a lesser or greater extent, but they were also intermarried, indicating the compli-

34. See especially the letter from Jedaniah to Bagohi the governor of Judah, written in 410 BCE. The letters nos. 30 and 31 in A. Cowley, *Aramaic Papyri of the Fifth Century B.C.* (Oxford: Clarendon Press, 1923) (= A4.7 and A4.8 in Bezalel Porten and Ada Yardeni, *Textbook of Aramaic Documents from Ancient Egypt*, I [Hebrew University, Department of the History of the Jewish People, Texts and Studies for Students; Jerusalem: Hebrew University, 1986]) are two copies of the same document with only slight differences. Within the letter is the following statement:

We sent a letter to our lord [Bagohi the governor] and to Yehohanan the high priest and his companions the priests who are in Jerusalem and to Ostan the brother of Anan and the nobles of the Jews. They did not send a single letter to us.

These brief lines indicate that within the Persian province of Yehud (or perhaps co-extensive with it) is a Jewish community with a temple located at or centred on Jerusalem, having a leadership (in addition to the officially appointed governor) composed of the high priest and his fellow priests and the local nobility.

cated interrelationship which affected the local politics. The Zenon papyri indicate the importance of an individual named Tobias about 260 BCE. If the Tobiad romance has any basis in reality, a son (grandson?) Joseph rose to even higher prominence in the late third century, possibly obtaining a formal Ptolemaic office. But the story that Joseph's sons became rivals is plausible in the wider political opposition between the Ptolemaic and Seleucid courts.

4.   Hecataeus of Abdera hints that there was a written word called the 'law of Moses', and he makes a statement very similar to the endings of both Numbers and Leviticus, but his comment by itself is too ambiguous to be certain. However, when we find that Ben Sira, writing about 200 BCE, has something that looks very much like our present Genesis to 2 Kings, 1–2 Chronicles and the Latter Prophets, it makes Hecataeus's statement rather more likely to be significant. It seems improbable that the collection possessed by Ben Sira had attained divine authority in a few decades. These sections of what became the Hebrew Bible were probably already in much their present form by the time of Alexander, though they continued to develop on the textual level and—in the case of a few books—on the literary level.

These are not a lot of data for almost a century and a half, but they are better than nothing. What we have here is sufficiently substantial to give a basis for further work. Skimpy as it is, we still possess a precious critical minimum, and we can be grateful for that. One can take the bare bones and flesh them out with educated guesses, even speculation as long as it is clearly so labelled.

Is the Bible a Hellenistic Book?
The last point above (4) brings us to a very important topic which needs more lengthy discussion. It is the critical question, 'is the Bible a Hellenistic book?' This provocative and stark question cannot be answered with a categorical and unequivocal reply, at least without specifying exactly what is meant by 'Hellenistic book'.[35] Critical scholarship has

---

35. The question, of course, arises from what is rapidly becoming a classic article by Niels Peter Lemche ('The Old Testament'). My comments here are by no means a full response to Lemche's article, a good portion of which really relates

long held that a significant part of the Hebrew Bible is Hellenistic. Daniel 7–12 can be dated within a few years of 165 BCE; although Daniel 1–6 is harder to place, it looks to be from the third century.[36] Qohelet is also normally dated to the Ptolemaic period, though a case has recently been made for a Persian dating.[37] The argument is not convincing in the sense that the Persian period is demonstrated for the book; on the contrary, the case is far from conclusive, but what it does demonstrate is that the Ptolemaic case is also difficult to prove.[38] Nevertheless, if I had to put money on it, I would opt for the Ptolemaic period. Some recent works put the completion of the books of Chronicles after the time of Alexander.[39] Other books which may be either from the Persian or the Hellenistic period are Ezra and Nehemiah, Esther, Ruth and the Song of Songs. If one includes Jewish writings which entered other canons (albeit in Greek or other translations), we could perhaps add 1 Esdras, Ben Sira, Tobit, *Jubilees*, Judith, 1 and 2 Maccabees, and *1 Enoch* (except 37–71) to the list of Hellenistic compositions. In that sense, a substantial percentage of the Old Testament text is Hellenistic in origin.

If, on the other hand, by 'Hellenistic book' is meant that the bulk of the text was edited post Alexander, then I have to dispute the designation. There are a number of reasons for this:

1. The Judaean deportations in the early sixth century and the destruction of Jerusalem about 587 BCE were traumatic events. People

more to pre-exilic versus postexilic than Hellenistic specifically. His article is also very wide ranging and, additionally, programmatic; it would require considerable space to deal with in any detail and to do it justice.

36. See the discussion in John J. Collins, *Daniel* (Hermeneia; Minneapolis: Fortress Press, 1993).

37. Choon-Leong Seow, *Ecclesiastes: A New Translation with Introduction and Commentary* (AB, 18C; New York: Doubleday, 1997).

38. A lot depends on the extent to which one finds Greek influence on the book, but this is very difficult to prove conclusively.

39. For example, Sara Japhet (*I and II Chronicles: A Commentary* [OTL; London: SCM Press; Louisville, KY: Westminster/John Knox Press, 1993], pp. 27-28) states that it is 'more probably' the fourth century, while Georg Steins (*Die Chronik als kanonisches Abschlussphänomen: Studien zur Entstehung und Theologie von 1/2 Chronik* [BBB, 93; Weinheim: Beltz Athenäum, 1995], pp. 491-99) argues for the Maccabaean period. However, if Ben Sira is indeed using Chronicles for part of his information, that rather argues against so late a dating as that of Steins's. See further Peltonen's lengthy article in this volume (pp. 225-71 below).

often become aware of their traditions when there are major disruptions, when their heritage and even their identity might be lost. It seems unlikely, prima facie, that no attempt to gather the traditions or create a national or ethnic 'history' would have been made.[40] Given the fact that such a literature was created and we therefore need to find a context for it, the Persian period is a better candidate on the face of it than the Hellenistic.

2. The testimony of Ben Sira indicates that a considerable portion of the present Hebrew Bible had not only come together but had become authoritative by about 200 BCE. To see that process from creation to authoritative status for the Pentateuch, Deuteronomistic History, Chronicles and the Latter Prophets between Alexander and Ben Sira stretches the imagination considerably. Rather, this collection in a form close to its present form is probably pre-Alexander.[41]

3. Some sections of the Deuteronomistic History show a rather accurate outline of the kings of Israel and Judah as attested by external sources;[42] 2 Kings 25 in particular gives a very detailed catalogue of

40. Cf. Lemche, 'The Old Testament', pp. 163-64.

41. I must take exception to a statement made at least twice by Lemche, that the present Hebrew Bible is 'a Jewish-Rabbinic collection of writings no earlier than the 2nd century CE' ('The Old Testament', pp. 163, 190). First, we have no evidence that 'the rabbis' had anything to do with forming a canon (cf. Jack Lewis, 'What Do We Mean by Jamnia?', *Bible and Religion* 32 [1958], pp. 125-32). Considering that rabbinic Judaism is a post-70 development, much that is credited to 'the rabbis' is an invention of modern scholarship (cf. Jacob Neusner, 'The Formation of Rabbinic Judaism: Yavneh (Jamnia) from A.D. 70 to 100', *ANRW II* [1979], XIX.2, pp. 3-42). Secondly, in the late first century two sources suggest a canon similar to the present Hebrew canon. Josephus refers to 22 books and lists a number of them (*Apion* 1.8 §§37-43). It is often asserted that his 22 books can be reconciled with the 24 books of the Hebrew canon; perhaps, but I am not so sanguine. Nevertheless, it is very close to the 24 of the known Hebrew canon. On the other hand, *4 Ezra* 14.44-46 lists 24 books, and these are unlikely to be different from the present Hebrew canon. Thus, there is an argument that the Hebrew canon was fixed by 70 CE, at least in priestly circles. If so, that may not settle the issue, but it leaves less room for speculation than might be suggested by Lemche's statements. See further chapter 8 in my book, *Judaic Religion in the Second Temple Period*.

42. Sketched out in my earlier article ('Are Historians of Ancient Palestine Fellow Creatures—Or Different Animals?', in Lester L. Grabbe [ed.], *Can a 'History of Israel' Be Written?* [JSOTSup, 245; ESHM, 1; Sheffield: Sheffield Academic Press, 1997], pp. 19-36), though a full detailed study has yet to be undertaken.

events leading up to the capture of Jerusalem in 597 BCE.[43] Whatever his source(s), the writer had access to a rather impressive amount of historical data to draw on, but this is more easily explained by a writer in the Persian period (or even earlier) than by one in the Hellenistic period which was much further removed from the actual events.

4. Apart from the book of Daniel—which is definitely Hellenistic—there is little in the prophetic literature which relates to Greece or the Hellenistic kingdoms. The Assyrians, the Neo-Babylonians, and the Medes and Persians are mentioned in various prophecies. Why should the Greeks be absent, if large chunks of the Prophets were written when the Greeks ruled the ancient Near East? It is possible that the Greek overlords could be prophesied about under a cipher of some sort, but ciphers are not usually used completely consistently or completedly without any attempt to indicate their true meaning.

5. There are indications that the Greek version of at least the Pentateuch was translated about the middle of the third century BCE, which is unlikely to have happened for a collection only assembled at most a few decades before.[44] Only portions of the work of Demetrius the Chronographer have been preserved,[45] but it is very clear that he depended on the Pentateuch in Greek.

6. The general situation in Judah with regard to government and society seems, as far as we can determine, to have been fairly similar for both the Persian and the Greek periods, with a small ethnic/religious community around a single city with a temple at its centre. However, there was one major distinction, and this was a governor over the province. So far, we have no evidence that there was a province of Judah

43. See the table in my article ('"The Exile" under the Theodolite: Historiography as Triangulation', in Lester L. Grabbe [ed.], *Leading Captivity Captive: 'The Exile' as History and Ideology* [JSOTSup, 278; ESHM, 2; Sheffield: Sheffield Academic Press, 1998], pp. 80-100).

44. The *Letter of (Pseudo-)Aristeas* puts the translation under Ptolemy II (282–246 BCE). Although its story of how the Septuagint was translated is now generally rejected by modern scholarship, a translation of the Pentateuch about the middle of the third century is still widely accepted among Septuagint scholars. See Harry M. Orlinsky ('The Septuagint as Holy Writ and the Philosophy of the Translators', *HUCA* 46 [1975], pp. 89-114) and in general Sidney Jellicoe (*The Septuagint and Modern Study* [Oxford: Clarendon Press, 1968]).

45. For an edition, translation and commentary, see Carl R. Holladay, *Fragments from Hellenistic Jewish Authors*. I. *Historians* (SBLTT, 20; Pseudepigrapha Series, 10; Atlanta: Scholars Press, 1983), pp. 51-91.

under either Ptolemaic or Seleucid rule. (It has been suggested that there was a governor over the entirety of Palestine and southern Syria, but this is disputed.[46]) Much of any literary activity was likely to have been carried out under the priests as the ones who had the leisure and training to undertake such work.[47] Thus, the difficulties and opportunities of writing and/or editing a large quantity of traditions would have been the same in either period. The question is what would have happened in the Greek period for the priests suddenly to feel the need for a collection of written religious texts? It seems more likely that the need would have been felt already in the two centuries of the Persian period.

Thus, in my opinion the evidence favours the view that a large section of the Hebrew Bible was in substantial shape by the end of the Persian period. By this I mean that the Penteteuch, the Deuteronomistic History, Chronicles and the Latter Prophets would have been recognizable to one who knows the Hebrew Bible today. The text continued to develop, circulating in different text-types for centuries. Some books also continued to develop literarily, with different versions of certain books (e.g. Jeremiah and Esther) existing side by side for a long time. Some concept of 'Scripture' in the sense of a collection of books with certain religious authority had also developed by the end of the Persian period. But there was no concept of a closed canon. Exactly when and how the canon was finally complete is a matter of speculation. Our present Hebrew canon seems to be attested for certain circles no later than the first century CE, but when it became widely accepted by most or all Jewish communities could be later than this. The Masoretic Text—the best representative of the Hebrew Bible—is a product of the mediaeval period, though it represents an old tradition.[48]

46. Bagnall, *The Administration of the Ptolemaic Possessions*, pp. 15, 219; on the administration under the Ptolemies in general, see the discussion in Grabbe, *Judaism from Cyrus to Hadrian*, pp. 189-91.

47. Cf. Lester L. Grabbe, *Priests, Prophets, Diviners, Sages: A Socio-historical Study of Religious Specialists in Ancient Israel* (Valley Forge, PA: Trinity Press International, 1995), pp. 65, 170, 198-99, 219-20.

48. On the development of the text and canon, see n. 33 above and chapter 8 of my book, *Judaic Religion in the Second Temple Period*. On the antiquity of the Masoretic tradition, see Lester L. Grabbe, *Comparative Philology and the Text of Job: A Study in Methodology* (SBLDS, 34; Missoula, MT: Scholars Press 1977), pp. 179-97.

WHO WERE THE FIRST REAL HISTORIANS?
ON THE ORIGINS OF CRITICAL HISTORIOGRAPHY

Lester L. Grabbe

The question of who the 'first historians' were has been exercising biblical scholars for some time. Part of this interest arises out of the old Biblical Theology Movement in which 'taking history seriously' was an important feature of theology itself.[1] But the demise of the Biblical Theology Movement did not bring an end to the question, and the matter is still debated from a variety of points of view, whether theology[2] or the history of Israel. However, there are a number of hints that theological concerns are subtly underpinning a number of the studies which are ostensibly about the history of Israel; even those who take a very sceptical view of the biblical text at times seem to be intent on undermining any theological authority the text might appear to have.[3]

The question of the 'first historians' is partly determined by definition, as I point out in the first section of this paper, and I am not really

---

1. For the main characterization of the Biblical Theology Movement, see Brevard S. Childs, *Biblical Theology in Crisis* (Philadelphia: Westminster Press, 1970); on the question of 'history' as a part of the movement, see James Barr, *Old and New in Interpretation: A Study of the Two Testaments* (London: SCM Press, 1966), pp. 65-102; *idem*, 'Story and History in Biblical Theology', *JR* 56 (1976), pp. 1-17. See also John J. Collins, 'The "Historical" Character of the Old Testament in Recent Biblical Theology', *CBQ* 41 (1979), pp. 185-204.

2. In addition to works in the previous note, see Bertil Albrektson, *History and the Gods: An Essay on the Idea of Historical Events as Divine Manifestations in the Ancient Near East and in Israel* (ConBOT, 1; Lund: C.W.K. Gleerup, 1967); J.J.M. Roberts, 'Myth Versus History: Relaying the Comparative Foundations', *CBQ* 38 (1976), pp. 1-13.

3. Cf. the perceptive comments of Hans M. Barstad, 'The Strange Fear of the Bible: Some Reflections on the "Bibliophobia" in Recent Ancient Israelite Historiography', in Lester L. Grabbe (ed.), *Leading Captivity Captive: 'The Exile' as History and Ideology* (JSOTSup, 278; ESHM, 2; Sheffield: Sheffield Academic Press, 1998), pp. 120-27.

interested in wrangles about who might claim the label 'first historian' in a general sense. However, some aspects of the debate have implications for how one approaches the history of Israel. My focus in this essay is the question of *critical* historical writing, and other aspects of the controversy will be taken up only as they impact on my central purpose.

The Question of Definitions

Unfortunately, much of the debate about the 'first historians' revolves around—or even depends upon—the particular definition one uses for 'history'. This can easily lead to 'disputes about words' and quickly bypasses any useful debate on the essential issues. Because so much depends on definitions, however, it is important here to clarify the basis on which I am working and why I differ from others (in those cases where I differ). There is no doubt that the most influential recent work on the question is John Van Seters's *In Search of History*.[4] He draws heavily on Johan Huizinga's now classical statement, 'History is the intellectual form in which a civilization renders account to itself of its past'.[5] Van Seters isolates the following characteristics of history writing:

1. A specific form of tradition in its own right.
2. Not primarily the accurate reporting of past events but also the reason for recalling the past and the significance given to past events.
3. Examination of the causes of present conditions and circumstances.
4. National or corporate in character. The reporting of the deeds of the king may be only biographical unless these are viewed as part of the national history. Towards the end of the book, he states that 'to communicate through this story of the people's past a sense of their identity…is the *sine qua non* of history writing'.[6]

4. John Van Seters, *In Search of History: Historiography in the Ancient World and the Origins of Biblical History* (New Haven: Yale University Press, 1983).

5. Johan Huizinga, 'A Definition of the Concept of History', in Raymond Klibansky and H.J. Paton (eds.), *Philosophy and History: Essays Presented to Ernst Cassirer* (Oxford: Clarendon Press, 1936), pp. 1-10.

6. Van Seters, *In Search of History*, p. 359.

5. Part of the literary tradition and plays a significant role in the corporate tradition of the people.[7]

Although Van Seters specifically draws on Huizinga's definition and claims that his criteria are in keeping with Huizinga's definition, it seems to me that his own formulation actually goes against Huizinga at various points. For one thing, Van Seters seems to see history writing as a single genre, whereas Huizinga is referring to history as a total enterprise. Huizinga also clearly includes writings as history that Van Seters would exclude:

> It comprises every form of historical record; that of the annalist, the writer of memoirs, the historical philosopher, and the scholarly researcher. It comprehends the smallest antiquarian monograph in the same sense as the vastest conception of world history.[8]

Huizinga's definition is not primarily an attempt to tell whether to categorize a particular work as history, but that is precisely what Van Seters is seeking. Contrary to Huizinga, Van Seters wants to exclude annalists as historians. He also wants to exclude descriptions of the king's deeds; indeed, he strangely excludes biography as a historical work, whereas most historians would include biography as a form of history-writing. Especially problematic to me is that Van Seters wants to exclude anything that is not national or corporate in character. But few modern historians would see their work as national or corporate, nor do most modern historians of ancient history feel that they must of necessity examine the causes of present conditions and circumstances.

The problem with this definition and these characteristics is that they do not always characterize what contemporary historians do, and any definition that excludes the work of modern historians cannot be acceptable in the debate. Few historians in the modern academic world see themselves as furthering national goals, and most would argue that although their historical writing represents an interpretation, that interpretation is still based on certain methodological principles of critical argument, evidence and falsifiable hypotheses.

Another example is Van Seters's statement that tradition does not become history until it deals with the people as a whole. Thus, a catalogue of the king's deeds is not history.[9] Once again I find this

7. Van Seters, *In Search of History*, pp. 4-5.
8. Huizinga, 'A Definition', p. 10.
9. Van Seters, *In Search of History*, p. 2.

rather difficult: by this criterion we would have to exclude Arrian's history of Alexander's conquests because it is by and large about Alexander. Any criterion which excluded a work like Arrian's or Caesar's *Gallic War* must be seen as absurd *ab initio*.

The more recent work of Baruch Halpern, *The First Historians*, appears on the surface to take a rather different approach from Van Seters whom he indeed critiques at various points.[10] Yet despite the differences—or rather because of these differences—one is surpised to find how much the two writers have in common. Both see the Deuteronomistic Historian as the first historian, a remarkable agreement considering that they date the work to quite different periods of time. They also both want to exclude annals from their definition of history. Unfortunately, Halpern does not give a clear definition of what he means by 'history-writing', though it appears to be interchangeable with 'historiography'.[11] Indeed, his whole discussion on the difference between history and fiction is ultimately only confusing even if some of the examples and comments seem to be relevant.[12]

Thomas L. Thompson has produced a definition that is very much in keeping with modern sensibilities:

> …the ancient and particularly the classical Greek genre of historiography used the term in a much narrower, more restrictive sense. This more distinctive meaning has been maintained also in its present usage, namely, as a specific literary genre relating to critical descriptions and evaluations of past reality and events, in contrast to more fictional varieties of prose.[13]

For Thompson to call this 'historiography' and not 'history-writing' is confusing but, in fact, his definition is really a definition of *critical* historical writing.

Diana Edelman has contributed a useful summary and given a helpful

---

10. Baruch Halpern, *The First Historians: The Hebrew Bible and History* (San Francisco: Harper & Row, 1988).

11. Halpern, *The First Historians*, p. 6; cf. D. Edelman, 'Clio's Dilemma: The Changing Face of Historiography', in André Lemaire and Magna Sæbo (eds.), *Congress Volume: Oslo 1998* (VTSup, 80; Leiden: E.J. Brill, 2000), pp. 247-55.

12. Halpern, *The First Historians*, pp. 3-15.

13. Thomas L. Thompson, 'Historiography, Israelite Historiography', in *ABD*, III, pp. 206-212; *idem, Early History of the Israelite People: From the Written and Archaeological Sources* (SHANE, 4; Leiden: E.J. Brill, 1992), pp. 372-83, especially pp. 372-73.

evaluation of four different definitions.[14] However, her major contribution to the debate is to make a distinction between ancient and modern
historiography. She ultimately concludes that history-writing in Greece
and Israel were of the same general type, and the real distinction to be
made is between ancient history-writing and modern history-writing:

> It is clear that modern standards of critical evaluations of past reality and
> events were not part of standard practice for ancient Greek history-writ-
> ers like Herodotus and Thucydides. Herodotus uses folktales, genealogies,
> hearsay, eyewitness reports and official records as sources for his work
> and does not challenge their validity as accurate reports about the past, as
> a modern historian would. Modern historians do not show that truth is
> complex by posing an antithesis between dull fact and colorful falsehood
> by telling two stories about the same matter, one factual and one anec-
> dotal. They do not invent long speeches and put them into the the mouths
> of important individuals, trying thereby to convey a sense of what would
> have been appropriate or in character. They do not include the divine
> realm as agents of causation in the human realm and do not presuppose a
> world view in which the universe and the earth are affected by the
> coexistence of opposites and in which the history of nations or individ-
> uals is understood to be part of larger cycles of greatness or prosperity
> and decay. Finally, modern historians do not feel compelled to restrict
> their subject matter to war, politics and great leaders and the accompa-
> nying motivation to use history as object lessons to determine present
> and future political behavior and policy, to illustrate morality, to explain
> or justify the present, to predict or control the future, to justify disaster,
> or to entertain.[15]

Edelman thus finds many resemblances between, for example, the
story of Saul and the work of Herodotus. From that perspective, although she does not discuss the question explicitly, the first to write
critical history would not have been any of the ancients, but critical history would be entirely a modern phenomenon. However, Edelman does
make a distinction between Greek history-writers such as Herodotus
and Thucydides and other ancient writers, finally suggesting that such
writers might form a 'third category' between ancient and modern history-writers. As will be clear in the next section, I find that conclusion
problematic in certain respects.[16]

---

14. Edelman, 'Clio's Dilemma'. The four scholars she discusses are Van Seters,
Thompson, Halpern and M.Z. Brettler.
15. Edelman, 'Clio's Dilemma', p. 249.
16. Amélie Kuhrt also disagreed with this approach in comments made publicly

I would like to summarize this section with the following observations:

1. A variety of valid definitions can be advanced, depending on the perspective from which one approaches the subject. I would simply argue that whatever definition is used, it must not exclude any of the writers of antiquity called 'historians' by common consent, and it certainly must not exclude the work of modern historians.

2. The question of definition is important because one's conclusions can often be anticipated in the definition one uses of 'history' or 'history-writing'. Some of the present debate unfortunately turns on definition. On the one hand, if someone wishes to define 'history' as anything showing 'antiquarian interest', they should not object if someone else wishes to be more rigorous; on the other hand, the use of a definition that takes in a writing which is not truly critical from a modern point of view can still be legitimate and fully justifiable.

3. For purposes of this essay, I am asking when *critical* historical writing first developed. The rest of this essay will be addressing that particular question. Thompson's definition above seems to approximate what I have in mind. By 'critical historical writing' I do not mean a particular 'positivistic' form of writing. I have reference to the term 'critical' as used in a wide sense in modern scholarship to refer to an attitude or approach which does not take things at face value but shows a certain scepticism, asks questions about epistomology and rational explanation, is most concerned about human causation, and wants to test the evidence. My definition does not rule out approaches which attempt to apply a grand scheme to history (e.g. an evolutionary model), for this has been characteristic of a number of modern historians (e.g. Marxist interpretation).

Greek Historical Writing

The development of historical writing among the Greeks is well documented. What might be called the beginnings of historiography can be traced in the myths of origin found in such writers as Hesiod who attempted to synthesize traditional myths into some sort of coherent

during the panel discussion at the meeting of the International Organization for the Study of the Old Testament in Oslo, August 1998; for publication, see A. Kuhrt, 'Constructions of the Past in the Ancient Near East', in Lemaire and Sæbo (eds.), *Congress Volume*, pp. 257-79.

system. Epic poetry was also a factor in that it consolidated certain traditions that had some elements of actual history into a narrative sequence of events, which might make Homer in some sense 'the father of history'.[17] The dramatic tradition also seems to be important to the development of historical writing and has left its marks even on some of the more scientific writers such as Polybius.[18] However, the real impetus for writing history arose out of the 'Ionian enlightenment', the same movement from which sprang philosophy and science as exemplified in the pre-Socratic philosophers. It was here that we first have attested the important critical attitudes that led to scientific inquiry: 'The will toward critical examination and comprehension of truth and actuality embodies itself in a way of approach to certainty through the testing and rejection of hypotheses—an entirely new form of intellectual procedure which has been the basis of all subsequent advance in the sciences'.[19] The same attitudes were essential to the development of the true historical method.

In the fifth century BCE a writer such as Hellanicus of Lesbos used the traditional mythological genealogies to develop a historical chronological system.[20] Unfortunately, the links between the old literary traditions containing much myth and legend and the rise of history-writing is not well documented. The result is that Hecataeus of Miletus is one of the first about whom we know anything extensive, even if his work has not been preserved intact, and some have even suggested that he is the true 'father of history'. This last designation can probably now be rejected since it seems unlikely that he wrote an actual historical narrative as such.[21] However, we do have indications that he championed the principle so important to subsequent Greek historians, that of *autopsy*. Not having his work intact creates problems of interpretation, but some of his comments show a critical spirit of mind:

17. See the brief but incisive summary in Albin Lesky, *A History of Greek Literature* (trans. J. Willis and C. de Heer; New York: Thomas Crowell, 1966), pp. 216-19; ET of *Geschichte der griechischen Literatur* (Bern: Francke, 1957–58).

18. Charles William Fornara, *The Nature of History in Ancient Greece and Rome* (Eidos; Berkeley: University of California Press, 1983), pp. 171-72.

19. Lesky, *History of Greek Literature*, p. 217.

20. Truesdell S. Brown, *The Greek Historians* (Civilization and Society; Lexington, KY: D.C. Heath, 1973), pp. 14-18.

21. For a discussion of the issue, see Robert Drews, *The Greek Accounts of Eastern History* (Publications of the Center for Hellenic Studies; Cambridge, MA: Harvard University Press, 1973), pp. 11-15.

> Hecataeus the Milesian speaks so: I write the things that follow as they seem to me to be true. For the stories of the Greeks are both many and, as they appear to me, ridiculous.

> Aegyptus did not himself go to Argos, but his sons did—fifty of them in Hesiod's story, but as I reckon not even twenty.[22]

With all the excavations and new finds, Herodotus remains the 'father of history'. In his writing we can see the historian at work and are able to make explicit deductions about the process of critical historiography. Herodotus contains all sorts of material, to the point that some would see him as more of a travel writer than a historian. But a number of points arise from study of his work, some explicit and some implicit:

1. Herodotus accepts reports of events and forms of causation that would not be entertained by modern historians. For example, 'prodigies' such as a cow giving birth to a lamb are seen as signs presaging certain significant events. Divine causation is also taken for granted. On the other hand, we should not be too patronizing about this. Acceptance of divine causation is not all that different from metaphysical causes that some modern historians have adumbrated with great seriousness. Some modern historians have seen such intangible drivers of history as an organistic development of nations (birth, youth, maturity, senility, death).[23]

2. Herodotus himself shows a critical spirit in a number of explicit examples. For example, he critiques the standard story of the Trojan war and gives reasons why another version is more likely to be correct.[24] He also questions stories that he has heard but records them

22. The translations here are taken from Peter Derow, 'Historical Explanation: Polybius and his Predecessors', in Simon Hornblower (ed.), *Greek Historiography* (Oxford: Clarendon Press, 1994), pp. 73-90 (74).

23. See, e.g., Oswald Spengler, *Der Untergang des Abendlandes: Umrisse einer Morphologie der Weltgeschichte* (2 vols.; Vienna: Braumüller, 1918–22); ET *The Decline of the West* (authorised translation with notes, Charles Francis Atkinson; 2 vols.; London: G. Allen, 1922).

24. 2.118-20. He points to a tradition (obtained from the Egyptian priests) at some variance with that found in the Homeric poems, a rather bold criticism since the Homeric poems had a quasi-canonical status in the Greek world. This version says that when the Greeks came, the Trojans swore to them that Helen was no longer there but had already absconded to North Africa. With wonderful critical acumen Herodotus notes that this was likely to be true since no nation would allow itself to be besieged for ten years for the sake of a mere woman, queen though she might be.

nevertheless, such as the position of the sun in the circumnavigation of Africa.[25] In this he does not differ in kind from a modern historian who collects data and then attempts to evaluate it critically. The fact that Herodotus happened to have been wrong about the incident of the sun is irrelevant; after all, complete accuracy in judgment is also hardly a trait of modern historical study.

3. We have a fair amount of indirect evidence that Herodotus used good sources for important aspects of his history. His account of Darius I's taking of the throne is consonant with and complementary to the information we have from Darius's own inscription at Behistun.[26] Although he does not name his informants in this particular case, he has evidently consulted members of the Persian aristocracy. The ability to choose and interrogate good sources is part of the critical historical work.

4. Herodotus's qualitative advance over his predecessors can be seen by comparing him with Hellanicus of Lesbos whose attempts to bring some chronological order into the heroic traditions look primitive beside Herodotus, yet Hellanicus is a contemporary of Herodutus and actually wrote some of his works after the great historian.

Herodotus was quickly followed by Thucydides whose methodological innovations still meet the standards of modern historical research.[27] Thucydides tells us about some of the criteria he applied in his work (*Hist. Pel.* 1.20-22):

> In investigating past history, and in forming the conclusions which I
> have formed, it must be admitted that one cannot rely on every detail

---

25. 4.42. The story is related to a canal dug from the Nile to the Red Sea by Necho II. He sent out a Phoenician ship to sail round Africa and come back to Egypt through the Pillars of Hercules. The description, which Herodotus himself doubts, shows that they had sailed south of the equator.

26. 3.61-87. See especially the study of Jack Martin Balcer, *Herodotus and Bisitun: Problems in Ancient Persian Historiography* (Historia-Einzelschriften, 49; Stuttgart: Steiner, 1987). Of course, this is not the only side of the story, only the pro-Darius version. The fact that Herodotus agrees with the Behistun inscription shows only that they both reflect the same perspective, not that one confirms the other. A properly critical approach would recognize the ideological bias and attempt to consider the missing aspects of the story suppressed by the official version propagated by Darius. Nevertheless, to have searched out a reliable version of the official version is to Herodotus's credit and should not be denigrated.

27. A convenient introduction by a well-known specialist is Simon Hornblower, *Thucydides* (Baltimore: The Johns Hopkins University Press, 1987).

which has come down to us by way of tradition. People are inclined to accept all stories of ancient times in an uncritical way—even when these stories concern their own native countries...(1.20.1)

However, I do not think that one will be far wrong in accepting the conclusions I have reached from the evidence which I have put forward. It is better evidence than that of the poets, who exaggerate the importance of their themes, or of the prose chroniclers, who are less interested in telling the truth than in catching the attention of their public, whose authorities cannot be checked, and whose subject-matter, owing to the passage of time, is mostly lost in the unreliable streams of mythology. We may claim instead to have used only the plainest evidence and to have reached conclusions which are reasonably accurate, considering that we have been dealing with ancient history...(1.21.1)

And with regard to my factual reporting of the events of the war I have made it a principle not to write down the first story that came my way, and not even to be guided by my own general impressions; either I was present myself at the events which I have described or else I heard of them from eye-witnesses whose reports I have checked with as much thoroughness as possible. Not that even so the truth was easy to discover: different eye-witnesses give different accounts of the same events, speaking out of partiality for one side or the other or else from imperfect memories. And it may well be that my history will seem less easy to read because of the absence in it of a romantic element. (1.22.2-4)[28]

Thucydides 'pursued an indubitably "scientific" purpose. No other historian of antiquity treasured *akribeia*, strict accuracy, so much as he, and he is unique in estimating the factual detail as important for its own sake.'[29] Some of the principles used by Thucydides include the following (though some of these are already to be found among his predecessors):

1. The traditions about the early history of Greece are untrustworthy and to be given no credence.
2. The interrogation of eye-witnesses and the collection of a variety of eye-witness and other accounts. Although Thucydides unfortunately tells only of the account that he finds most trustworthy, from all we can tell he does appear to have followed his own rule.

28. Translation from Rex Warner (trans.), *Thucydides, History of the Peloponnesian War* (Penguin Classics; Harmondsworth: Penguin Books, 1954), pp. 46-48.
29. Fornara, *The Nature of History*, p. 105.

3.   A critical judgment made on the various accounts to select the
     one that appears to be most credible according to common-
     sense criteria.
4.   The establishment of a chronological framework which dates
     all events to within six months.

These are important rules and are still applied in some form or other
by most modern historians. Thucydides was by common consent the
pinnacle of history-writers in antiquity, and his successors did not rise
to quite the same heights. Xenophon, who continued his history of the
Peloponnesian War, was not of the same calibre. Yet Xenophon wrote
an important account of his own adventures in Persia during the 401
attempt to take the throne by Cyrus the Younger (the *Anabasis*). On the
other hand, most modern scholars consider the *Cyropaedia*, which
ostensibly gives a life of Cyrus the founder of the Persian empire, as
unreliable on the whole and to be used only cautiously and critically for
information about Persian history.[30] The anonymous writer known as
the Oxyrhynchus Historian is thought to give a quite accurate protrayal
of a few years of the Peloponnesian War; unfortunately, the author of
this work is unidentified, and the principles on which it was written
have yet to be determined.[31]

Probably the second place in the ranks of ancient historians is held by
Polybius. He was an important historian who wrote not only about
contemporary events that he witnessed himself but also about Roman
history from the First Punic War, more than a century before his own
time. Perhaps more than any other ancient historian Polybius discusses
the principles guiding him in the writing of his history. Some of the
points he makes are the following:

1. The historian cannot show favouritism. He points out that
one expects to favour one's friends and country, but

---

30. Some recent studies include Deborah Levine Gera, *Xenophon's Cyropaedia:
Style, Genre, and Literary Technique* (Oxford Classical Monographs; Oxford: Clarendon Press, 1993); James Tatum, *Xenophon's Imperial Fiction: On The Education
of Cyrus* (Princeton, NJ: Princeton University Press, 1989); B. Due, *The Cyropaedia: Xenophon's Aims and Methods* (Aarhus: Aarhus University Press, 1989).

31. For studies on this important work, see I.A.F. Bruce, *An Historical Commentary on the 'Hellenica Oxyrhynchia'* (Cambridge Classical Studies; Cambridge:
Cambridge University Press, 1967).

he who assumes the character of a historian must ignore everything of the sort, and often, if their actions demand this, speak good of his enemies and honour them with the highest praises while criticizing and even reproaching roundly his closest friends, should the errors of their conduct impose this duty on him. For just as a livng creature which has lost its eyesight is wholly incapacitated, so if History is stripped of her truth all that is left is but an idle tale.[32]

2. It is the duty of the historian not just to narrate or assemble 'facts' but to explain the cause (*aitia*) of and connections between events. The historian must explain the 'how, why, and whence' (*pōs, dia ti, pothen*) or the 'when, how, and for what reason' (*pote, pōs, di' has aitias*) with regard to events (3.7; 4.28.4).

3. Although it had become conventional from Thucydides on to include speeches in historical works, many of his successors ignored his principles and concentrated on exercising rhetorical skills. Polybius insists that speeches must reflect what was actually said: 'nor is it the proper part of a historian to practise on his readers and make a display of his ability to them, but rather to find out by the most diligent inquiry and report to them what was actually said' (36.1.7). The duty of the historian is not to create great speeches but to be faithful to the words uttered at the time (2.56.10):

A historical author should not…, like a tragic poet, try to imagine the probable utterances of his characters or reckon up all the consequences probably incidental to the occurrences with which he deals, but simply record what really happened and what really was said, however commonplace.

He notes, 'The peculiar function of history is to discover, in the first place, the words actually spoken, whatever they were, and next to ascertain the reason why what was done or spoken led to failure or success' (12.25b.1).

4. He emphasizes his own efforts to travel and question witnesses (3.57-59; 12.25g-25i; 12.26d-28a). Polybius is scathing

---

32. 1.14 (LCL I, pp. 35, 37). Unless otherwise indicated, quotations from classical texts are from the Loeb Classical Edition (LCL); for Polybius see W.R. Paton, *Polybius, The Histories* (Cambridge, MA: Harvard University Press; London: Heinemann, 1922–27).

of the 'armchair historians', among whom he especially identi-
· fies Timaeus of Tauromenium (12).

There are several questions to be answered about the Greek and
Roman historians: was history only a branch of rhetoric? Was their
concern more in teaching moral lessons or offering examples to emulate
or even in entertainment than in accuracy? Did their historiographic
methods different essentially from those of modern historians? In other
words, do the Greek and Roman historians have more in common with
the Israelite narrative writers than they do with modern historians, as
suggested above?

Let us begin by asking whether the ancient historians intended to be
accurate. A recent study has explored the various devices used by
historians in support of their work, and these devices show a great concern to give the impression of care with the facts and evidence of accuracy.[33] Whether the historians rose to the standards alleged can be
discussed for particular writers, but as a genre historical works make a
point of drawing the reader's attention to the reasons why their author
was well qualified to write the work in question. It was a commonplace
expectation that the historian's first concern was faithfulness to the data
and accuracy in presenting them, even if it was generally anticipated
that he would also write an interesting and elevating account. As
Fornara expresses it:

> At his most ambitious, the historian was an artist seeking by means of
> his art, but in fidelity to the truth, to be the teacher or the conscience of
> his people, or both...Of the various principles laid down by the ancients,
> none is more fundamental than the honest and impartial presentation of
> the facts, and it is entirely consistent with their clarity of vision and intel-
> lectual emancipation that the Greeks gave it to the world. The principle
> was a natural, indeed, reflexive inheritance from the ethnographic-scien-
> tific Ionian school: *historia*, unless accurate, is a contradiction in terms.[34]

There were dangers to the impartiality of the historian, especially
considering that many of them, the Roman historians in particular, were
politicians or were writing about matters in which they themselves had

---

33. John Marincola, *Authority and Tradition in Ancient Historiography* (Cambridge: Cambridge University Press, 1997). One important theme found widely
through historical works is that of 'autopsy' and 'inquiry', either that the writer
himself had witnessed the things described (autopsy) or had searched out persons
who witnessed the events or used sources that had direct evidence of them (inquiry).

34. Fornara, *The Nature of History*, p. 99.

some sort of direct interest. Some of the ancients accuse their fellow writers of succumbing to the temptation to be partial or praise them for not doing so. Fornara comments:

> Now although it is reasonable to doubt that Asellio, Sallust, Livy, Pollio, Tacitus, Ammianus, and others succeeded in transcending their enmities and loyalties, no evidence whatever suggests that they or their fellows intended to write propaganda; on the contrary, we have every reason to believe that the dictates of convention and the assumption of the *persona* of the historian made the contemporary writers strive to be the impartial analysts of their recent past.[35]

We come to the important question of the judgment sometimes made that for the Greeks and Romans, history was only a branch of rhetoric. There is truth in this assertion in that history was often treated alongside rhetoric, but one must be careful about drawing the conclusion that only oratory and rhetoric counted in history-writing. Cicero is alleged to have taken this view, for example, but this seems not to be the case.[36] For the orator and politician, historical examples were used primarily for their rhetorical effect, and the important thing was plausibility rather than actual historical truth.[37] We can also find examples of historians and writers who concentrated on the rhetorical at the expense of accuracy.[38] Nevertheless, neither the main historians themselves nor Cicero took this view. For them the real essence of history is its truth, voiced by 'Antonius' in the dialogue in *De Oratore* (2.15.62):

35. Fornara, *The Nature of History*, p. 101.

36. See P.A. Brunt, 'Cicero and Historiography', *Miscellanea Manni* (1980), pp. 311-40 (reprinted in his *Studies in Greek History and Thought* [Oxford: Clarendon Press, 1993], pp. 181-209); Karl-Ernst Petzold, 'Cicero und Historie', *Chiron* 2 (1972), pp. 253-76 (reprinted in his *Geschichtsdenken und Geschichtsschreibung: Kleine Schriften zur griechischen und römischen Geschichte* [Historia-Einzelschriften, 126; Stuttgart: Steiner, 1999], pp. 86-108). Neither author indicates knowledge of the other's work.

37. Cf. Cicero, *Orator* 120; *De or.* 1.5.17-18; 1.14.60; 2.82.337; *Part. or.* 9.32; 25.90; *Inv.* 1.21.29. See also the *Rhet. ad Her.* 1.16; although this work comes down to us in Cicero's corpus, modern scholarship has generally been sceptical that it is really his.

38. Polybius complains about those whose concern was to create sensational images and invent details for dramatic purposes, e.g. 2.56; 3.20.3-5; 3.47.6–48.9. In Cicero's dialogue *Brutus* the example is cited in which the historian Clitarchus and the orator Stratocles invented a spectacular death for Themistocles, contrary to the testimony of Thucydides (11.42-43).

> For who does not know history's first law to be that an author must not
> dare to tell anything but the truth? And its second that he must make bold
> to tell the whole truth? That there must be no suggestion of partiality any-
> where in his writings? Nor of malice?

This is not to suggest that all Greek 'historians' from Herodotus on
are examples of critical historians. On the contrary, many of them fall
well short of even minimum standards as exemplified in Herodotus and
Thucydides. Perhaps the nadir to Thucydides's zenith is Ctesias of
Cnidus.[39] He wrote about the same time as Xenophon and is thus a
successor of the great historians. After being captured by the Persians
and serving for 17 years as the personal physician of Artaxerxes II, he
should have been in a good position to report on many aspects of the
Persian court and Persian history at first hand. Instead, he compiled a
farrago of legends, inventions and gossip that was already denounced in
antiquity.[40] This is not to say that genuine historical data cannot be
found in his account, but he shows little interest in distinguishing the
historical from the romantic. His account is the main source of the
Ninus and Semiramus legend that continued to be so influential up to
early modern times.[41]

To summarize, the quality of historical writing in Graeco-Roman antiquity varied enormously (though this statement would apply equally
to today), and there was an inevitable division between theory and

39. The main study remains Friedrich Wilhelm König, *Die Persika des Ktesias
von Knidos* (AfO Beiheft, 18; Graz: Archiv für Orientforschung, 1972). See also
F. Jacoby, 'Ktesias', in *idem, Griechische Historiker* (Stuttgart: Alfred Drucken-
muller, 1956), pp. 311-32 (reprinted from PW 11.2032-73); J.M. Bigwood, 'Ctesias
as Historian of the Persian Wars', *Phoenix* 32 (1978), pp. 19-41; *idem,* 'Diodorus
and Ctesias', *Phoenix* 34 (1980), pp. 195-207; Arnaldo Momigliano, 'Tradizione e
invenzione in Ctesia', in *idem, Quarto contributo alla storia degli studi classici e
del Mondo Antico* (Storia e Letteratura, 115; Rome: Edizioni di Storia e Letteratura,
1969), pp. 181-212.

40. Those who criticized him include Plutarch, *Art.* 1.4.

41. The stories as they stand are completely fantastic; however, it is now believed that behind the figures of the Greek account lie the Assyrian king Šarrukīnu
II and his wife Sammuramat. See König, *Die Persika des Ktesias von Knidos*, pp.
34-40; Wilhelm Eilers, *Semiramis: Entstehung und Nachhall einer altorientalischen Sage* (Sitzungsberichte der Österreichische Akademie der Wissenschaften,
Phil.-hist. Klasse, 274; Vienna: Kommissionsverlag der Österreichischen Akademie
der Wissenschaften, 1971); Wolfgang Schramm, 'War Semiramis assyrische Reg-
entin?', *Historia* 21 (1972), pp. 513-21.

practice. Yet the best historical work rose to modern standards, including such writers as Thucydides and Polybius and perhaps even other writers such as Hieronymus of Cardia[42] and the Alexander history of Ptolemy I (which was used centuries later as the basis of Arrian's history of Alexander's conquests). Most scholars of classical historiography would be in no doubt that critical historiography had developed in the Graeco-Roman historical tradition.

The Babylonian Chronicles

If there are any ancient Near Eastern writings that we might call history by any definition of the word, the Babylonian Chronicles are they.[43] These record the period from the reign of Nabu-nasir beginning in 747 BCE and continue to the Seleucid period in two series: the Neo-Babylonian Chronicles (Chronicles 1–7) and the Late Babylonian Chronicles (Chronicles 8–13a). The compilers apparently used trustworthy sources such as the astronomical diaries. The astronomical diaries record all sorts of information on a month-by-month basis, including not only astronomical and atmospheric observations but also at the end of each year a variety of economic information and political and military activities.[44] The importance of the Chronicles is indicated by their most recent editor:

> Within the boundaries of their interest, the writers are quite objective and impartial. This is evident from the numerous times they mention defeats of the Babylonians at the hands of their enemies... Further, the authors have included all Babylonian kings known to have ruled in this period and there is no evidence that they have omitted any important events

42. See the major study by Jane Hornblower, *Hieronymus of Cardia* (Oxford Classical and Philosophical Monographs; Oxford: Clarendon Press, 1981).

43. The standard treatment of the Chronicles is A.K. Grayson, *Assyrian and Babylonian Chronicles* (Texts from Cuneiform Sources, 5; Locust Valley, NY: J.J. Augustin, 1975). See also his article, 'Assyria and Babylonia', *Or* 49 (1980), pp. 140-94. I am also grateful to Professor Amélie Kuhrt who made available to me her article, 'Constructions of the Past in the Ancient Near East'.

44. An important publication of diary material is now found in Abraham J. Sachs, *Astronomical Diaries and Related Texts from Babylonia*. I. *Diaries from 652 B.C. to 262 B.C.*; II. *Diaries from 261 B.C. to 165 B.C.*; III. *Diaries from 164 B.C. to 61 B.C.* (ed. Herbert Hunger; Österreichische Akademie der Wissenschaften, Phil.-hist. Klasse, 195, 210, 246; Vienna: Österreichische Akademie der Wissenschaften, 1988–96).

which have a bearing on Babylonia during their reigns. Every significant event known in this period from sources other than the chronicles (eponym canons, royal inscriptions, letters, business documents, foreign documents) which affects Babylonia is referred to in the chronicle... Thus one is tempted to conclude that the documents were compiled from a genuine interest in writing history. It appears that the scribes simply wished to record what had happened in and around their land. We have, therefore, what seems to be history being written for history's sake as early as the eighth century B.C.[45]

The problem with the Babylonian Chronicles is that no principles of historical enquiry are presented, and no explicit discussion is given of broader themes or how the history as a whole is to be interpreted. Yet when we find a work as accurate as they are, it is surely bizarre to argue that this is sheer accident. The authors of the Babylonian Chronicles have used good sources, but there is also indirect evidence that they also represent genuine critical historical writing and thus are an example of the critical spirit about the same time as this is attested in Greece.

Yet the Babylonian Chronicles have strangely been downplayed by writers such as Van Seters and Halpern who suggest that these do not show the true historical spirit and are thus only historiographical texts and not examples of history-writing.[46] Van Seters concludes as follows about the Chronicles in general:

> But what is most impressive about Babylonian historiography is the evidence of a kind of academic 'research'—a gleaning of materials about the past from various sources. This belongs to the very basis of the meaning of history in its classical sense, even if the ability to make critical judgments about the sources is not as yet in evidence.[47]

I find this out of line with Van Seters's own discussion. He admits that the Babylonian Chronicles are systematic and deliberate compilations from sources and that they are accurate, an admission made in a strangely offhand statement that the creation of the Chronicles 'seems to have no other function than to present a careful record of the past'. Would that more ancient historical narratives had such a function and no other! But this accuracy implies critical judgment; the fact that the Chronicles do not tell us how this was exercised is unfortunate, but it

45. Grayson, *Assyrian and Babylonian Chronicles*, pp. 10-11.

46. Van Seters, *In Search of History*, pp. 79-92; Halpern, *The First Historians*, p. 6.

47. Van Seters, *In Search of History*, p. 92.

should not blind us to the obvious. If there is an example of critical historical writing in the ancient Near East, the Babylonian Chronicles must be it.

The Hebrew Bible

At first blush, books such as 1 and 2 Kings have much in common with some of the Greek historians. One important resemblance is the system of chronological indications found at various points in the text.[48] As noted above, Thucydides's development of precise chronological placement of various events was an important development in history writing. The biblical narratives do not have such precise dating for the most part,[49] but they are not that different from writers such as Herodotus who write about past history rather than contemporary events.

Writers such as Herodotus made use of a good deal of traditional lore from Egypt, Mesopotamia, Persia and Greece itself. This material was of uneven quality from a modern perspective. Sometimes it was clearly good quality from a historical point of view;[50] at other times we would want to put it in the category of legend. We could probably make the same statement about material in the Deuteronomistic History. Some of it may contain examples of reliable traditions,[51] but other parts of it are clearly legendary and would not be accepted as having much to do with history by most critical scholars.[52]

Halpern makes the point that the Deuteronomistic Historian has used sources. He admits that there is invention of data or non-historical material but insists on the essential source basis of the work: 'DtrH bases itself, if partly on historical imagination, heavily on antiquarian research'.[53] There seems no question that for 1 and 2 Kings the com-

---

48. Van Seters makes a special point of the chronological synchronism between the two kingdoms of Israel and Judah (*In Search of History*, pp. 294-99).

49. Interestingly, some of the most precise dating is found in some of the prophetic writings such as Hag. 1.1; 1.15–2.1; 2.10 and Zech. 1.1, 7; 7.1.

50. See n. 25 above.

51. Any examples I might choose to give would be disputed by someone, but I think most would concede that such is probable, possible or would at least allow the theoretical possiblity—which is all that is necessary to continue the argument.

52. One can pick at random such examples as the story of Samson or the tales of Elisha.

53. Halpern, *The First Historians*, p. 216.

piler had some sort of source which contained reliable information on the kings of Israel and Judah. A comparison of information known from external sources with the biblical data shows that some sort of source must have been used. The suggestion that the compiler has gone around copying the data from monuments is not very credible,[54] if for no other reason than that the number of monumental inscriptions is not likely to have been high nor are the data likely to have been extensive. The last couple of centuries of archaeological exploration have turned up only a handful of inscriptions in Palestine, and this fact does not encourage us to think that they were all that numerous in antiquity. Also, it was not the custom of ancient historians to collect such data; if the Deuteronomistic Historian did, he would have been unusual.[55]

More credible is the suggestion that a court or temple chronicle was used. Such a chronicle preserved in Jerusalem, for example, would probably give the main accomplishments of a particular ruler, significant invasions or domination by a foreign king, and some events relating to the neighbouring kingdom of Israel. (Halpern is convinced that the compiler had at least two chronicles.)[56] That the writer had other sources is also credible, but whether they were as numerous or as of good quality as Halpern assumes is a question.[57]

Whether the compiler used sources is not the main issue, however. Unless the writer completely invented everything, he must have used

54. Halpern, *The First Historians*, pp. 208-209, 215; Van Seters, *In Search of History*, pp. 298, 301, 357.

55. Arnaldo D. Momigliano, 'Historiography on Written Tradition and Historiography on Oral Tradition', in *idem, Studies in Historiography* (London: Weidenfeld; New York: Harper & Row, 1966), pp. 211-20; Paul Veyne, *Did the Greeks Believe in their Myths? An Essay on the Constitutive Imagination* (trans. Paula Wissing; Chicago: University of Chicago Press, 1988), p. 8; cf. Van Seters, *In Search of History*, p. 299. E. Axel Knauf recently suggested a portion of the Solomonic tradition was based on a royal building inscription ('Le roi est mort, vive le roi! A Biblical Argument for the Historicity of Solomon', in Lowell K. Handy [ed.], *The Age of Solomon: Scholarship at the Turn of the Millennium* [SHANE, 11; Leiden: E.J. Brill, 1997], pp. 81-95), though this is the exception rather than the rule, as I believe Knauf himself would argue.

56. Relying on S.R. Bin-Nun, 'Formulas from the Royal Records of Israel and of Judah', *VT* 18 (1968), pp. 414-32.

57. Halpern, *The First Historians*, pp. 207-216. He states, 'Most scholars concede that H(Dtr) had a rich fund of materials...' But 'rich fund' is not the same as 'accurate' or 'reliable'; some of this rich fund was prophetic legends that scarcely count as dependable historical sources.

sources: legends, tales, hearsay, oral tradition, court stories. The real question is how he worked, what his aim was, and whether he exercised critical judgment. The question of his aims is an important one. Here Halpern is concerned to give him 'antiquarian interests'. This may be true, but what was his overall aim? Was it to write an accurate reconstruction of past history or was it to give a theological interpretation to which historical data and aims took a back seat? The answer seems to be obvious, as Halpern himself evidently accepts when he refers to 'DtrH: a cultic interpretation of history'.[58] The author has indeed exercised judgment, but it was theological judgment. Such judgments may have some characteristics in common with critical judgment, but they are not the same. I see no evidence that the Deuteronomistic History exercised critical historical judgment as we normally understand it.

Halpern accepts that the writer's idea of causation is theological, but he goes on to state, 'Israelite historiography differs from modern chiefly in its doctrines of causation, its sense of what the ultimate object of study should be'. I cannot accept that this is so. The question of causation is only one area in which modern historiography and the biblical writer's differ. The enquiry into all sources of information, the critical evaluation of sources, the testing for bias and ideological colouring, the scepticism towards explanations contrary to normal experience are all elements within modern historical study and reconstruction. It is much more than the question of causation.

The question is: is the biblical use of earlier legendary traditions any different from the Greek historians who made use of the early Greek mythical and legendary traditions traditions? Did the Greek historians believe in their own myths? Paul Veyne asked the question in the title of his book, *Did the Greeks Believe in their Myths?* As has already been indicated, the attitude of the Greek historical writers to their past seems to have been rather different from that of the biblical writers. The matter is complex and cannot be discussed at length here. However, their approach to their traditional myths was not the same as the Israelites' view of their past. The Greeks questioned their myths and traditions in a way for which we have no evidence among Jewish historians (with possibly one or two exceptions noted below).

58. Halpern, *The First Historians*, p. 220.

Critical Historical Thinking among the Jews

We know that critical history-writing developed among the Jews. The prime instance is Josephus, though someone such as Justus of Tiberias may also have been an example.[59] Unfortunately, Josephus is the only Jewish historian preserved more or less intact. Nevertheless, some other earlier Jewish writings give examples of explicit attempts to address perceived problems and contradictions in the sacred tradition.

The first writer to consider is Demetrius the Chronographer.[60] He is probably the earliest of the Fragmentary Historical Writers in Greek, with an indication that he wrote in the late third century BCE.[61] Of the fragments preserved, a number of them clearly have as at least one of their aims the reconciliation of apparently contradictory data in the biblical text. For example, he attempts to explain how it is that as newly released slaves, the Israelites had weapons when they went out of Egypt. He does this by the simple but ingenious argument that they picked up the weapons washed ashore from the Egyptian army that drowned in the Red Sea.[62]

Another question concerns the 'Ethiopian woman' who came to Moses and claimed to be his wife (Num. 12.1).[63] For Moses to have

---

59. We have Josephus; we do not have Justus. If we had the writings of both, we might well feel that Justus was the superior historian, but the vicissitudes of history have so far deprived us of the means of making such a judgment. I have often been critical of Josephus (*Judaism from Cyrus to Hadrian*, I-II, *passim*), and I do not regard him as particularly high on the list of ancient historians, but he seems to me to be a typical Hellenistic historian—worse than some but better than others.

60. Carl R. Holladay, *Fragments from Hellenistic Jewish Authors*. I. *Historians* (SBLTT, 20; Pseudepigrapha Series, 10; Atlanta: Scholars Press, 1983); Robert Doran, 'The Jewish Hellenistic Historians before Josephus', *ANRW II* (1987), XX.1, pp. 246-97.

61. This is calculated from his reference to the time of Ptolemy IV as a fixed point from which he calculates a number of biblical events. Some have attempted to emend this to Ptolemy III. However, such emendation is based on attempts to reconcile Demetrius's data, whereas this may simply be impossible. See the discussion in E.J. Bickerman, 'The Jewish Historian Demetrius', in Jacob Neusner (ed.), *Christianity, Judaism, and Other Greco-Roman Cults*, III (SJLA, 12; Leiden: E.J. Brill, 1975), pp. 72-84 (= *Studies in Jewish and Christian History*, II [AGJU, 9; Leiden: E.J. Brill, 1980], pp. 347-58).

62. Quoted in Eusebius, *Praep. ev.* 9.29.16.

63. Quoted in Eusebius, *Praep. ev.* 9.29.1-3.

married a foreigner was an embarrassment. Demetrius resolves the problem by claiming that this woman was none other than Zipporah, the wife taken by Moses when he fled Egypt. She was not an Israelite, of course, but Demetrius makes her a descendent of Abraham from Keturah. But if she was a descendent of Abraham, can she be shown to be Moses' contemporary by means of the genealogical record, since Zipporah is only six generations from Abraham and Moses is seven? Demetrius solves the problem by showing that Abraham was 140 years old when he took Keturah, whereas he had fathered Isaac at age 100. This is 40 years—a complete generation—earlier; hence, the difference in the number of generations from the same ancestor.[64]

Another writer who evidently produced a history of the Jews making use of the biblical narratives was Eupolemus. He is generally identified with the Eupolemus, son of John, mentioned in 1 Macc. 8.17 and 2 Macc. 4.11.[65] He was of the priestly family of Hakkoz (Haqqoṣ in Hebrew; Akkos in Greek: 1 Chron. 24.10; Ezra 2.61; Neh. 3.4, 21; 7.63) and evidently had a Greek education. He even seems to have made use of Herodotus and Ctesias in his book,[66] yet it is difficult to find anything suggesting a critical spirit in the preserved fragments. We find the exaggerated apologetic well known from other Jewish sources, such as the view that Moses gave the alphabet to the Jews, and everyone got it from them, or the magnificence of Solomon's temple. His embellishment of the biblical account may in some cases come from the exercise of rationalization or the use of other sources of information, and he attempts to sort out some chronological problems. Overall, though, the spirit of critical examination seems to have by-passed him.

The books of Maccabees need to be considered. There is no question that these books contain valuable historical data; the question is whether they show critical judgment. No statements are made as to any historiographical principles, and we find none of the questioning or discrimination between reports that the better Greek historians show. If the author of either of these works gathered diverse sources of information, judged them critically, and then reported only that which seemed to

---

64. For a further discussion, see L.L. Grabbe, 'Chronography in Hellenistic Jewish Historiography', in P.J. Achtemeier (ed.), *Society of Biblical Literature 1979 Seminar Papers*, II (SBLSPS, 17; Missoula, MT: Scholars Press, 1979), pp. 43-68, especially pp. 45-48.

65. See the edition and discussion in Holladay, *Fragments*, I, pp. 93-156.

66. Holladay, *Fragments*, I, p. 95 (and 101 n. 16); Wacholder, *Eupolemus*, p. 13.

pass muster, he says nothing about it. It has been argued that some battle descriptions are by eye-witnesses, but this view has been challenged.[67] 2 Maccabees has made use of certain sources, in particular the letters in ch. 11.[68] Besides this must be set the presence of martyr legends in ch. 7, the bias towards Judas Maccabee, and the strong prejudice against Jason. If the writer has selected his material on the basis of historical judgment, we have little indication of this. Perhaps we know too little to be sure at this point, but it seems doubtful that true critical investigation is found in either 1 or 2 Maccabees.

Another of the Fragmentary Historians in Greek is Artapanus who wrote probably in the second century BCE.[69] He contains some of the Jewish apologetic known from other sources, such as that Abraham taught astrology to the Egyptians or that Joseph was the first to divide Egypt into allotments. Artapanus has clearly interpreted the biblical story in light of Graeco-Roman history and culture, as a number of other earlier Hellenistic commentators do. There is a certain rationalizing principle at work here and there; for example, the Nile is not turned to blood but simply overflows; it begins to stink when the water becomes stagnant.[70] This may be an embryonic example of some critical thinking, though it is rather muted.

Demetrius especially but perhaps also some of the other writers show the opening up of the critical spirit among the Jews. Yet even they are not full-fledged examples of critical historians. A writer such as Herodotus, however much he might use older traditions, is willing to say that some traditions are wrong; it is difficult to find quite that spirit in any of the Jewish writers when it comes to the biblical text. Even Josephus does not appear to query the biblical text as such, regardless of the vast amount of reworking, re-organizing, and rewriting he does with it. His critical acumen is exercised with other sources, but with the sacred tradition he seems to have been as uncritical as his predecessors among the Fragmentary Writers.

---

67. Bezalel Bar-Kochva, *Judas Maccabaeus: The Jewish Struggle against the Seleucids* (Cambridge: Cambridge University Press, 1989), pp. 158-62; opposed by Seth Schwartz, 'Israel and the Nations Roundabout: 1 Maccabees and the Hasmonean Expansion', *JJS* 42 (1991), pp. 16-38, especially p. 37 n. 64.

68. For a summary of scholarship on these, see Grabbe, *Judaism from Cyrus to Hadrian*, pp. 259-63.

69. See Holladay, *Fragments*, I, pp. 189-243.

70. Quoted in Eusebius, *Praep. ev.* 9.27.28.

Indeed, the true critical spirit seems to be attested in only one Jewish writer of antiquity: Qohelet. Some have accused Qohelet of atheism; although I do not interpret him in this way, I believe that he would be willing to question even the sacred tradition in a way not exhibited by any other Jewish writers known to me. A good case can be made that he is only displaying the spirit of the Hellenisitic age and thus gained his critical spirit from the Greeks.[71] On the other hand, a good case can also be made that he owes his roots to the ancient Near Eastern traditions and not to Greek influence.[72] In any event, his scepticism looks sufficient to have been willing to challenge the biblical tradition itself. No other Jewish writer questions the tradition as acutely as he does.

Conclusions

This has been of necessity a rapid survey of a complex subject. One could easily devote a book to the topic, as several scholars have done. Nevertheless, I think several points have been established even in this brief study:

1. One may legitimately use a variety of definitions for determining what is 'history' or 'history-writing' in antiquity. The definition chosen may go a long way towards determining one's conclusions; at least the particular definition used will limit the possible conclusions. However, any definition chosen must not exclude important works from antiquity that have long been considered examples of history-writing, and it certainly must not exclude the work of modern historians.

2. One might argue for a definition which makes portions of the biblical text examples of history-writing (e.g. the Deuteronomistic History or the Yahwist). But if such a definition is chosen, it must not

71. Many commentators have interpreted him in this way, but two of the most important are probably the following: E.J. Bickerman, 'Koheleth (Ecclesiastes) or The Philosophy of an Acquisitive Society', in *idem, Four Strange Books of the Bible: Jonah/Daniel/Koheleth/Esther* (New York: Schocken Books, 1967), pp. 139-67; R. Braun, *Koheleth und die frühhellenistische Popularphilosophie* (BZAW, 130; Berlin: W. de Gruyter, 1973).

72. See especially the recent argument of Choon-Leong Seow, *Ecclesiastes: A New Translation with Introduction and Commentary* (AB, 18C; New York: Doubleday, 1997); *idem,* 'Linguistic Evidence and the Dating of Qohelet', *JBL* 115 (1996), pp. 643-66. See also Otto Loretz, *Qohelet und der alte Orient* (Freiburg: Herder, 1964), though I understand he has more recently accepted the case for Greek influence.

artificially exclude other similar examples among the ancient Near Eastern literature, such as the Babylonian Chronicles. The admitted accuracy of the Babylonian Chronicles implies critical judgment; the fact that the Chronicles do not tell us how this was exercised is unfortunate, but it should not blind us to the obvious. However much one might admire the product of the Deuteronomistic Historian, he has not produced a work of the accuracy or completeness of the Babylonian Chronicles. To call the one 'history' and the other merely 'historiography' is either remarkably naive or strangely perverse. Therefore, the attempt to make the Israelites the 'first historians' is misplaced since no definition which makes the Deuteronomistic History an example of historical writing can exclude some earlier examples in the Mesopotamian or Anatolian literature. Here I find the discussion of Van Seters and Halpern, different as they are, both examples of special pleading.

3. My concern in this essay has been with the first to produce critical historical writing, a somewhat narrower preoccupation than some other writers on the subject. Although the work of modern historians shows certain differences in comparison with historians of antiquity, I do not agree that a sharp distinction can necessarily be made. Even though the run-of-the-mill Hellenistic historian falls below modern standards, there are many examples of critical historical writing in antiquity, with a few comparing quite favourably with the products of historians in the last couple of centuries.

4. In the light of all the information currently available to us, the first to engage in critical historical writing were the Greeks, beginning at least as early as Herodotus. Although most Greek and Roman historians dealt with contemporary history, we have examples of those who tried to write about ancient history (from their point of view) and who made a credible job of it. As so often, Momigliano has put his finger succinctly on the real issues:

> Each Greek historian is of course different from the others, but all Greek historians deal with a limited subject which they consider important, and all are concerned with the reliability of the evidence they are going to use. Greek historians never claim to tell all the facts of history from the origins of the world, and never believe that they can tell their tale without *historia*, without research... The point, however, is that he had to claim to be a trustworthy researcher in order to be respectable...
>
> Thus to the Hebrew historian historiography soon became a narration of events from the beginning of the world such as no Greek historian ever conceived. The criteria of reliability were also different. Jews have

always been supremely concerned with truth. The Hebrew God is the God of Truth... Consequently reliability in Jewish terms coincides with the truthfulness of the transmitters and with the ultimate truth of God in whom the transmitters believe... What Josephus seems to have missed is that the Greeks had criteria by which to judge the relative merits of various versions which the Jewish historians had not...In Hebrew historiography the collective memory about past events could never be verified according to objective criteria. If priests forged records...the Hebrew historian did not possess the critical instrument to discover the forgery. In so far as modern historiography is a critical one, it is a Greek, not a Jewish, product.[73]

Thus, if someone asks, 'Who were the first historians?' I would have to answer, 'It depends on your definition of "historian"'. But if you ask, 'Who were the first critical historians?' the answer is definitely the Greeks.

73. Arnaldo Momigliano, *The Classical Foundations of Modern Historiography* (Sather Classical Lectures, 54; Berkeley: University of California Press, 1990), pp. 18-20.

THE MYTH OF ISRAEL: BETWEEN PRESENT AND PAST

David M. Gunn

The renewal of interest in 'late' dates (Persian, Hellenistic periods) for the composition of major portions of the (Hebrew) Bible, including much of Genesis–Kings, is creating an intriguing new episode in the great modernist project of historical criticism. Write the history of the literature, and then the history of 'Israel' or 'ancient Israelite religion' or 'Old Testament theology' can be written. Today understandings of what is involved in the project's pursuit have changed considerably from what they were half a century, let alone a century or two, ago— they have become, for one thing, less confident of comprehensive 'solutions'. Whether we are seeing a radical change or merely the old project in new garb is another question, not one I intend to answer here, but one I ponder as I watch the present episode (or is it a new story?) unfold. Nor is it my intent to try to settle questions of provenance. As will become obvious as I proceed, I think many of these are probably un-answerable. But I do think that the recent burst of 'history-writing' has been immensely important in forcing biblical scholars to confront seri-ously a much wider range of possibilities regarding not only what used to be called the 'history of ancient Israel' but also the significance of the biblical literature that has allured historians of 'ancient Israel' and still allures.

I shape my thoughts around three interconnected topics. First I ask some questions about methods of determining the provenance (date and location of composition) of biblical texts. I then deal further with the nexus between biblical literature and history (or literary criticism and historical inquiry) as it appears in some recent history-writing, in particular, Thomas L. Thompson's most recent book, *The Mythic Past*.[1]

---

1. Thomas L. Thompson, *The Mythic Past: Biblical Archaeology and the Myth of Israel* (New York: Basic Books; London: Jonathan Cape, 1999). The UK edition bears the title, *The Bible in History: How Writers Create a Past*.

Finally I make a proposal for reading contemporary historical construction in terms of the 'politics of provenance': specifically, I suggest some ways in which to view the interrelationship between constructions of biblical literature and ancient history, on the one hand, and of the foundation myth and history of the modern State of Israel, on the other.

I

If texts cannot be dated their use as source material for historical reconstruction is seriously impaired. Unfortunately, it has long been known that dating (and locating) biblical texts does not come easily. One fairly common procedure is what Bob Becking (in his essay for this volume) calls the lock-and-key method, what I call sociopolitical allegory. One 'matches' a sociopolitical context or even a historical event or set of events (context A—target) to a biblical text which is ostensibly treating some quite other context or event(s) (context B—source). One then 'discovers' the true intent of the text, namely to disclose an understanding or rendering of context A. There is nothing improbable about such a function of literature. A famous example that springs to mind is Jean Anouilh's play, *Antigone*, written and performed in German-occupied Paris during the Second World War, ostensibly dealing with classical antiquity but open to be interpreted as an account of the occupation.

Thus Thompson in *The Mythic Past* describes the enemies in Judges and Samuel as Philistines, 'established in a Hellenistic grouping of five cities, a pentapolis on Palestine's southern coast'.[2] Or, in 2 Kings, the biblical dichotomy between old Israel and its enemies is recast with new players: 'Judah and [Samaria?] take over the primary roles of nations opposed in conflict and hatred, as Jacob and Esau had been in Genesis'. This literary motif, he argues, 'mirrors' the breakup of Alexander's empire between a Seleucid north and a Ptolemaic south.[3] On Deut. 28.66, containing a reference to returning to Egypt, he comments: 'The text engages a subtext of political commentary involving the real world of the author... Do we here have a thinly veiled, Taliban-like polemic against the substantial number of diaspora Jews living in Egypt at the time that Deuteronomy was written?' And he goes on to nominate the time in question: 'Josephus refers to many Jews who moved "back" to Egypt, and especially Alexandria, during the course of the third

2. Thompson, *The Mythic Past*, pp. 40-41.
3. Thompson, *The Mythic Past*, p. 41.

century BCE. Does the story talk about a present, which is projected into the past it creates?'[4] On the story in Kings of the breakup of the united monarchy, we read:

> The pattern for this story is the break-up of the Hellenistic empire, which had separated into two integral parts: the southern Ptolemies of Egypt ruling from Alexandria, and the Seleucids of the north ruling from Antioch and Babylon. Seleucid Syria and the hated religious syncretism of Antiochus IV is reflected in II Kings' descriptions of Samaria, whose king goes to war with Solomon's successor.[5]

John Hyrcanus is a focal point of the allegory: 'Many have found both David and Josiah reflected in the image of John Hyrcanus, one of the Hasmonean kings of this period. Surely our philosopher king Solomon is a Hebrew-speaking Alexander. The stories of the golden age of the United Monarchy reflect the fantasy and ambitions of Jerusalem of the Maccabees.'[6] Parallels are to be observed between the stories in Kings of Hezekiah's and especially Josiah's reforms and Josephus's account of John Hyrcanus.[7] The implication is that in this figure we have an anchor point, our target context A.

Let me be clear: I do not question that such a context may provide a plausible provenance for some biblical texts. The problem I see is that, given the large number of 'events' recounted in Kings (let alone Genesis–Kings) from which to choose as the matching points of the allegory, Thompson's chosen context has to be but one of many that a competent scholar could construct. Moreover, when it comes to John Hyrcanus the argument leaves us rather at the mercy of Josephus who may, of course, be read most plausibly as fashioning his hero as Josiah and not the other way round. (I am not sure Thompson would disagree.)

Dating by allegory is an effective rhetorical device, however, especially where the parallels are 'events' such as the breakup of a kingdom, or an institutional reform, because the 'evidence' seems so precise, so concrete. The more so, when equally concrete alternatives are not laid alongside one another. But also effective are more abstract allegories that relate parallel ideas, ideologies, thought-forms, political agendas, and emotions. (I think Lemche's concept of a mental matrix arguably belongs here, at least in part.) Indeed, Thompson is careful to

---

4. Thompson, *The Mythic Past*, p. 66.
5. Thompson, *The Mythic Past*, p. 97.
6. Thompson, *The Mythic Past*, p. 207.
7. Thompson, *The Mythic Past*, p. 273; cf. pp. 265, 296.

buttress his key 'events' with key 'ideas'. Accordingly, in talking of the biblical schism paralleling the Seleucid-Ptolemaic split, he goes on to invest the events with ideology:

> The biblical polarity of north and south does not have its roots in politics and wars of Palestine's past. It is, rather, a sectarian way of thinking that reflects an understanding of the world as it appears to the writers of our texts… It is a moral world of black and white, of good and evil locked in eternal conflict. The reader is offered a radical choice. One walks either in the 'path of righteousness', in the 'way of the torah', in 'God's way', or one 'walks in the way of sinners' and 'seeks the counsel of the godless'. There is no middle way and no alternative to this choice. This sectarian mode of seeing reality is behind the varying contrasts so constantly reiterated in the biblical narrative of old Israel as rejected, standing against a new Israel of promise.[8]

Thus when we read that 'Seleucid Syria and the hated religious syncretism of Antiochus IV is reflected in II Kings' descriptions of Samaria', we already have at hand the parallel ideas which enliven the parallel events. All that is needed is another move to the concrete, by invoking the Taliban as a model of sectarianism in the context of Maccabees and John Hyrcanus, in order to reify the allegory.[9]

Of course, few scholars let their dating arguments rest on these kinds of grounds alone. Thompson appeals, in addition, to evidence regarding a social context in which the conditions of the production of the literature might plausibly be sought. This is a method Philip Davies deploys with characteristic skill in his recent *Scribes and Schools*, as also Niels Peter Lemche in *The Israelites in History and Tradition* and in his essay in the present volume (pp. 200-24).[10] In Thompson's case, he moves from the account of the texts saved by Judas Maccabee according to 2 Maccabees 4 to the sociopolitical situation in Palestine (Jerusalem?) following the rededication of the temple in 164 BCE. It is 'first in the historical context of the Hasmonean state, created by the Maccabees, that Palestine possesses the national coherence implied by the development of a library… Unlike many earlier periods in Palestine, we

---

8. Thompson, *The Mythic Past*, p. 41.
9. Thompson, *The Mythic Past*, p. 97; pp. 198-99, 296.
10. Philip R. Davies, *Scribes and Schools: The Canonization of the Hebrew Scriptures* (Library of Ancient Israel; Louisville, KY: Westminster John Knox Press, 1998); Niels Peter Lemche, *The Israelites in History and Tradition* (Library of Ancient Israel; Louisville, KY: Westminster John Knox Press, 1998).

know that the Hellenistic period was both creative and literate.'[11]

National coherence, creativity and literacy. These are relative vague categories under which to accumulate evidence. It does not take widespread literacy to produce the conditions for literary creativity;[12] and other scholars reasonably see other possible social locations for Hebrew textual creation (see, e.g., Albertz on the Persian period).[13] Nor do I see the issue of location factored in: given the extent of the 'Jewish' diaspora from at least the sixth century, there are strong candidates other than 'Palestine' for locating substantial composition (as Thompson readily acknowledges elsewhere). Moreover, the argument depends on privileging what we happen to know in the context of a large degree of ignorance. Lemche makes a similar case in his present paper when he characterizes Persian period datings for biblical compositions as a kind of 'black box' model within which 'everything is possible' because we know so very little about the period—'The "black box" concept makes everything possible and allows the scholar to propose all kinds of theories that cannot be controlled' (p. 216 below). But while it is true that Persian period hypotheses must remain largely speculative, it is not clear that hypotheses built around our better knowledge of the Hellenistic period should alone be accorded legitimacy. In principle, other evidence being equal, they may stand as much chance of being true or false as Persian—or for that matter Babylonian—period hypotheses. If speculation connecting texts to the Hellenistic period looks plausible, such hypotheses still stand under the shadow of our paucity of knowledge of the earlier period. They will always stand subject to the unknown, since while that unknown remains so we have no comparative measure of their strengths or weaknesses.

Defining the starting-point of the dating process is clearly an important procedural move in determining the outcome. Lemche has argued as follows:

> The starting point for the [dating] analysis must be the time where there can be no doubt that this biblical literature existed. When an agreement is reached on this point, we may begin the next step and see whether some part of the tradition has a prehistory. This can sometimes be done

11. Thompson, *The Mythic Past*, p. 294.

12. On this topic see now especially Davies, *Scribes and Schools*.

13. Rainer Albertz, *A History of Israelite Religion in the Old Testament Period.* II. *From the Exile to the Maccabees* (OTL; Louisville, KY: Westminster/John Knox Press, 1994 [original German edn, 1992]).

on the basis of information given by the literature itself. Regardless, whenever it comes to the fixation of a date, the latest possible one will always be preferable.[14]

He cites the example of Numbers 22–24, dating the text finally to the late fourth or the third century because of the reference at the end of Balaam's poem to the Kittim taken as a reference to the Macedonians. This is a reasonable argument to make about method in principle. In practice, there are some problems.

First, as Lemche himself notes in his present paper, some datable elements may well be the work of a glossator tinkering with the text long after it took substantially its extant form. Years ago, looking for evidence to date the so-called 'Court History' or 'Succession Narrative' in 2 Samuel, I noticed that the widely accepted reading of 2 Sam. 13.18 made a date close to the time of the events depicted (as was commonly accepted) improbable: 'Now [Tamar] was wearing a long robe with sleeves [*k^etonet passim*]; for thus were the virgin daughters of the king clad of old [reading *me 'olam*]'. Yet the narratorial comment is too easily characterized as a gloss for it to carry much weight in the dating game (though I myself believe it is integral to the narration). Lemche's example of Abraham being described as coming from 'Ur in Chaldaea' is a nice case in point: while the information probably can come from no earlier than 800 BCE it could easily have been added by a 'secondary hand'. On the other hand, his contrasting example of the camel as integral to the structure of the Abraham story because part of the technology, so to speak, of long distance travel, illustrates the fine lines that must be drawn in this kind of assessment. Long distance travel in ancient south-west Asia was not invented with the domesticated camel, rather certain kinds or conditions of travel so transpired. Could the stories of Abraham's journeying have been told otherwise than in the company of camels? I suspect so. The point at issue is what counts as the 'structure' of a story. This leads me to my next observation.

A second problem with Lemche's rule concerns the identification of the text under consideration. What text are we dating?[15] We can pose the question as Lemche does: what is 'structurally' integral to the text?

14. Lemche, *The Israelites in History and Tradition*, p. 159; cf. Thompson, *The Mythic Past*, p. 293.

15. For an excellent illustration of this question as a literary problem, see David Jobling, *1 Samuel* (Berit Olam: Studies in Hebrew Narrative and Poetry; Collegeville, MN: The Liturgical Press, 1998), ch. 2.

And then we get into all the problems associated with attempting to define literary 'structures'. Or we could pose the question in terms of boundaries: where does this text begin and where does it end? Either way we are faced with some radical choices that are almost entirely dependent upon 'literary' considerations. But now we are back to the dilemma of historical-criticism. How to date the text without reference to some 'external' history? But how to construct the history without knowing the date of the texts?

Lemche himself is justifiably circumspect about the classic procedures of literary criticism in its historical-critical mode, especially in its attention to 'parts' rather than the 'whole'.[16] But what is the whole? Is the story of Jephthah and his daughter in Judges 11–12 (a nice parallel to the Antigone story) a whole? What about Judges? Do we include 18–21? Are the books of Kings a whole? Is the 'Succession Narrative' a whole (as Auld and Van Seters believe) and does it include 2 Samuel 2–4 (as Davies believes)?[17] Is there such a thing as a Deuteronomistic History, and, if so, what exactly is its extent? Clearly to attempt to date each of the 'texts' mentioned is to engage in a discrete operation, each an operation upon a hypothetical subject defined by literary/source/ redaction criticism. And we have only mentioned the easy 'wholes'. Things go downhill from here. Let's not even mention 'J'.

Lemche rightly points out (in his present paper) that 'A piece of literature may reflect ideas and concepts that trace their origins way back in the history of humanity. If, however, such a piece also includes elements that are young and belong to another age, the textual context that includes old as well as new elements will always be the context of the youngest item.' I agree, but do not see that this dictum settles the problem of dating biblical narratives like those of Genesis–Kings. While I think 'tradition history' as practiced this century in biblical studies has been largely the pursuit of the impossible, I do not think that the historian as literary critic can simply dismiss the 'old' by subsuming it under the 'new'. That is to say, finding the 'new' among the 'old' does not make the 'old' any less 'old'. But of course the issue is determining what is old in the first place! So let me put it another way round.

16. Lemche, *The Israelites in History and Tradition*, p. 160.
17. A. Graeme Auld, *Kings without Privilege: David and Moses in the Story of the Bible's Kings* (Edinburgh: T. & T. Clark, 1994); John Van Seters, *In Search of History: Historiography in the Ancient World and the Origins of Biblical History* (New Haven: Yale University Press, 1983); Davies, *Scribes and Schools*, p. 142.

If some parts of Kings resemble royal annals and find some measure of external corroboration for their details, I see no good reason initially (though I am happy to be shown one) why dating some other parts of the Primary Story, say Numbers 22–24, to the third century should have some decisive impact on my assessment of the likelihood of the Kings material being 'old' and potentially useful as a historical source.

In a nutshell, the problem for dating here is that historical criticism, while largely failing at the level of details and dating to write a history of biblical literature, has largely succeeded in showing the 'whole' of Genesis–Kings to be a composite with a complex compositional history. We know its composition is complex because after 200 years of detective work no one has been able to work it out! Every attempt to date the text, therefore, comes up against the same problem, namely the speculative nature of 'the text' itself. What, in any given instance, is its essential structure? What are its boundaries? What, in short, are we choosing to date? Historians are held hostage to the vagaries of literary criticism. It is not clear to me how new initiatives are going to break free of the problem.

Lemche's insistence, therefore, that we date according to the 'latest' feature of the text, does not solve the problem of the composite text. At best such a date is likely to tell us something about the provenance of that particular feature of the text (whatever we designate that to be). Without a compelling general theory of the composition of the larger text of which this particular text is a component it will tell us nothing about the provenance of that larger text. And however much we tighten or broaden the boundaries of either the 'component' or the 'whole' we will always be engaged in a literary speculation, *our* construction of the text. (And are we really dating a text's composition, or offering a plausible account of how a text might have been read at a certain time and in a certain location?) It is not hard to see that questions of date and boundaries/structure/meaning become interlocked, facilitating the production of whatever result is desired. If we want a late date for the widest extent of text, then we can readily make appropriate literary choices, that is to say, construct a text, a 'whole', that includes within it 'late' features. For years scholars have been doing the same thing but with an opposite goal, namely constructing texts that *exclude* 'late' features.

II

It is an important feature of Thompson's new book that it recognizes the force of this connection between literary construction and dating. Much of the book is a literary construction (or reduction) of 'the text' in mythic or theological terms that lend themselves to being dated by, and mapped on to, Hellenistic and Roman socio-historical situations. (In some respects, Lemche's present paper adopts a similar strategy in seeking to produce textual 'elements' belonging to a datable socio-historical 'mental matrix'.)

Thompson needs to reduce complex literature to manageable dimensions by isolating characteristic themes and ideology. Thus he can take the broadest possible definitions of what counts as the text and yet have a very specific template with which to match his desired target context. His expositions of the literature cover a wide range of texts, including constructs such as the Primary and Deuteronomistic Histories, and some favourites such as the story of Saul, David at the Mount of Olives, Jonah, and the Psalter. He often speaks of 'the tradition' in an encompassing way (to the point where I am unsure sometimes what specific tradition or textual body is being referred to). His reader is moved towards a holistic conception of the Bible, a conception that Thompson articulates. He characterizes it frequently (as in the quotation above) as sectarian and uncompromising in its understanding of 'the way of Yahweh'. The bearers and collectors of the tradition understood themselves as belonging to a 'new Israel' as opposed to a failed 'old Israel'. The story is drawn in black and white and pits evil against good. The recounted conflicts 'are merely illustrations of what is for the tradition a transcendent conflict between good and evil' in the search for a new people who will commit themselves as a new Israel to torah.[18] Clearly, from here we do not have to travel far to find a match with Hasmonean sectarianism.

Now it is not that I do not recognize this obnoxious sectarian voice in biblical literature. Of course, I do. It is ubiquitous and continues to feed bigotry and intolerance in the present day as it has over many centuries in both Christianity and Judaism. (I live in the 'Bible belt' of the USA— I hear the voice *ad nauseum*.) Yet to characterize, say, Genesis–Kings as epitomized by this voice, dominated by it, is to do less than credit to the richness and elusiveness of this body of writing. Black and white,

18. E.g. Thompson, *The Mythic Past*, pp. 28-30.

good and evil? I do not think so. Where is the dialectic between the voices of 'authoritarian dogmatism' and 'critical traditionalism' that Robert Polzin so persuasively reads in the 'deuteronomistic' corpus? Where is the 'triumph of irony' that critics have traced through the 'Primary Story'? Peter Miscall's explorations in the indeterminacies of Samuel, Lyle Eslinger's sardonic readings in Samuel and Kings, or Mieke Bal's analyses of countercoherence in Judges? Of course I am only scratching the surface of the literary-critical enterprise of the past quarter-century and the variety of readings it has produced, many wholly at variance with the construction Thompson privileges.[19]

But then Thompson himself is as adept at reading for variance and complexity—and perhaps even paradox—as he is at delineating the monotoned sectarian voice that fits his target compositional context. He distinguishes, for example, between exclusive and inclusive monotheism,[20] with the 'exclusive' variety sounding like the Hasmonean sectarian voice (and Polzin's 'authoritarian dogmatism'). In the David story or in the Exodus tradition, he sees 'good' defined not as a moral category but as what God determines it to be in any given instance: 'one does not find a contest between a good Moses and an evil pharaoh, nor between an innocent Israel and demonized Egyptians'; rather Moses is feckless, the Egyptians poor 'faceless recipients of destruction', and pharaoh 'hardly worse that a fool'. Yahweh frees the oppressed and enslaved, yet he has created them for the sake of his contest with pharaoh, for the story is not about independence and freedom but

19. Robert Polzin, *Moses and the Deuteronomist: A Literary Study of the Deuteronomic History. Part One: Deuteronomy, Joshua, Judges* (New York: Seabury Press, 1980); *idem, Samuel and the Deuteronomist: A Literary Study of the Deuteronomic History. Part Two: 1 Samuel* (San Francisco: Harper & Row, 1989); *idem, David and the Deuteronomist: A Literary Study of the Deuteronomic History. Part Three: 2 Samuel* (Indiana Studies in Biblical Literature; Bloomington & Indianapolis: Indiana University Press, 1993); Lillian R. Klein, *The Triumph of Irony in the Book of Judges* (Bible and Literature 14; Sheffield: Almond Press, 1988); Peter Miscall, *The Workings of Old Testament Narrative* (SBLSS; Chico, CA: Scholars Press); *idem, 1 Samuel: A Literary Reading* (Indiana Studies in Biblical Literature; Bloomington: Indiana University Press, 1986); Lyle M. Eslinger, *Into the Hands of the Living God* (Bible and Literature, 24; Sheffield: Almond Press, 1989); Mieke Bal, *Death and Dissymmetry: The Politics of Coherence in the Book of Judges* (Chicago: University of Chicago Press, 1988). A fine entry point into issues of ideology and textual complexity is David Jobling's recent *1 Samuel*.

20. Thompson, *The Mythic Past*, pp. 295-301.

loyalty and submission.[21] Or on Saul:

> Unquestionably, Saul is rejected not because of any wrong that he has
> done, nor even because of any personal failure. He is rejected because he
> has done what he understood to be right. Such understanding is evil in
> Yahweh's eyes! It is the very theme of these stories that what is good
> and what is evil stands apart from human perceptions of justice and the
> right. Loyalty and allegiance are fundamental to this concept of a
> personal God. Sin is epitomized by apostasy and betrayal. True belief is
> submission and unquestioning obedience to the divine will.[22]

Or on the end of Kings: 'The closure of Kings, with its reassertion of
the divinely arbitrary, disrupts any sense of the morally ordered world
of justice of the sort that we find in Jeremiah and Chronicles. Yahweh's
moral disorder receives faint mockery in the narrative's comparison
with the human Evil-merodach's contrasting mercy to the captive Jehoiachin'.[23]

Nicely read, I would say, but I wish he would dwell further on how
the theme of good as submission to an ostensibly (i.e. from human perspectives) amoral or immoral God relates to the sectarian 'moral world
of black and white, of good and evil locked in eternal conflict' where
good is 'the way of righteousness'. It is not that I cannot see how the
one could be understood in terms of the other (which I assume is how
Thompson sees it). Rather my point is that the very expression of such
an understanding of 'good' and 'evil' immediately raises into view
what is deeply problematic about it. This is particularly so in the
accounts of David, Saul and the Exodus, where the narrative plays out
tangibly the ruination of lives, the human detritus, created by God's
need to be 'in charge', to be recognized, glorified. It takes but a small
shift in perspective (back to the human) for a reader—ancient or modern—to read such stories as validation of human morality and precisely
the reason why sectarian claims to power through the authority of an
incomprehensible god (whom, however, the sectarian always compre-
hends) should be viewed with deep suspicion. The tension in the writing is set up precisely because justice/morality is the context in which
divine and human perspectives operate. This is especially so when the
narratives are put into the context of the 'law', especially the 'deuteronomic' law. Theodicy really *is* the issue—for monotheism. Thompson

21. Thompson, *The Mythic Past*, pp. 58-59, 310.
22. Thompson, *The Mythic Past*, p. 315.
23. Thompson, *The Mythic Past*, p. 307.

asks of Job: 'What, then, is the whirlwind demon's message about the divine? Is it truth? Or caricature?' The question is exactly to the point: is 'submission' really a perversion of 'justice' and 'righteousness'? But then if Thompson can ask this of Job, why not an ancient reader of Exodus, Saul and David—as well as of Job?

Reception history makes my point: scholars have worked overtime for centuries to resolve the problem that Thompson's analysis exposes—resolving it by making submission the dominant 'message' but God's actions (by human standards) moral.

None of this means that this material could not have taken substantial shape in the context of Hasmonean sectarianism. That's not a conclusion I wish to draw. My argument is that these texts (and especially when read in the context of a larger Primary Story including much 'law' and significant appeal to categories of justice and morality widely known in the ancient world) should not be characterized as obviously sectarian. They should be recognized as radically multivalent. There is no figure or institution depicted from Genesis to Kings which cannot be read, reasonably, as ambiguously evaluated. If the Primary Story is to be read in the context of the Hellenistic period then it is not at all clear to me who all the parties are who might be the subject of its socio-political allegories. Perhaps there is something here for everyone? In this regard, Davies's insight regarding the power of the scribe to subvert the ideology of the commissioning patron at the same time as ostensibly serving that person or group is very helpful in understanding a work so ideologically slippery as Genesis–Kings.[24]

III

An important ingredient of the revision of ancient history pursued by members of this group and by others during the past decades have been questions of ideology, ethnicity and group identity (mostly in respect to ancient texts, but also on modern history-writing, notably in the work of Keith Whitelam).[25] These are important points of departure for literary critics of biblical texts also. What is clear to me as I have tried to follow

24. Davies, *Scribes and Schools*, p. 19.
25. Keith W. Whitelam, *The Invention of Ancient Israel: The Silencing of Palestinian History* (London: Routledge, 1996); and cf. Burke Long's work on the Albright school, *Planting and Reaping Albright: Politics, Ideology, and Interpreting the Bible* (University Park: Pennsylvania State University Press).

the course of the debate about history, from its beginnings in the work of George Mendenhall, Norman Gottwald and the 'Social World of Ancient Israel' group in the Society of Biblical Literature is that the ramifications of this research have reached well beyond the immediate context of academic interest, which is always in the first instance 'turf' protection or the making, taking, developing and trading of intellectual property. The 'history of Israel' has its own peculiar tie-ins to religious and political institutions, whose structures and power centers, while not those of academia, often afford reciprocal lines of access (churches, synagogues, religious-affiliated universities and colleges, museums, archaeological sites, etc.). One may conceivably talk about the ramifications of revisioned history as if it were a matter of reception, or about the ideological program or political intent of its proponents, as if it were a matter of agency. Let me talk of it here in the former mode, since it is always easier to suggest a reading than it is to construct an author's 'purpose', at whatever level of consciousness, if it is possible at all. (Curiously, historians' readings of biblical texts seem still largely dedicated to an understanding of literature in terms of 'intent'.)

Thompson writes: 'Texts do not give direct evidence for the construction of a history of any world of the past asserted by their authors, but rather for the history and perspective of the authors' own world as implied in the texts' projections'.[26] How then might I read Thompson's own text in terms of its projections regarding its author's own 'world'?

I see two obvious implications. The first concerns religion, and more particularly Christian theology and use of the Bible. The categories of myth and history have a long and contentious history in Christian theology and biblical criticism, and certainly where I live the term 'myth' used of the Bible is likely to provoke strong contention from certain quarters. There are other issues, however, including the function of these categories in contemporary Catholicism, as well as in liberal Protestantism where Thompson's rhetoric of myth ruptures an uneasy status quo reached between the demands of humanism and those of revelatory fundamentalism, a status quo marked out by an agreement that there are some texts that can be called myth and others history— and we know which are which. But this is not what I wish to speak about here.

I dwell rather on the second 'implication' of his text. Let me read his

---

26. Thompson, *The Mythic Past*, p. 254.

book in such a way that it becomes implicated in a dialectic set of relationships between biblical literature and the foundation myth of the modern State of Israel, between ancient and modern history, between past and present.

The foundation myth is a story of sovereign glory, displacement (exile) and restoration (redemption). In one form or another the narrative runs as follows. The Jewish people/nation along with their religion and culture are born in the Land (Eretz-Israel). However, they are forcibly removed, exiled from the Land. They endure vicissitudes in far lands (oppression), looking always with yearning to their lost Land. Then, after long centuries, the Zionist movement begins to forge for them a return, an 'ingathering of exiles', to their ancestral homeland. On return they (are to) redeem Israel/the Land, establish law, and exercise justice and equity.

It is readily apparent how thoroughly 'biblical' is this narrative. As the biblical story of return from Egypt (and possession of the land) is recapitulated in the return from Babylon (and possession of the land), so now a new post-biblical story of exile and return (and possession of the land) recapitulates both biblical stories.

In epitomizing this story, I have used here the term 'foundation myth'; or we might call it a 'legitimation story' or even 'master commemorative narrative'.[27] It is ubiquitous in modern Jewish/Israeli literature, may be found in sundry pages on the website of the Israeli Ministry of Foreign Affairs (www.Israel.org), or in its official print publications.[28] One notable rendition of the narrative (to which others on the website make rhetorical allusion constantly) is the 'Declaration of the Establishment of the State of Israel' (14 May 1948).[29] As the Declaration makes very clear, the myth is not understood in the rhetoric of this modern state formation as 'myth' but as 'history', where the former

27. On 'foundation myth', see Lemche, *The Israelites in History and Tradition*, pp. 86-97; on 'master commemorative narrative', see Yael Zerubavel, *Recovered Roots: Collective Memory and the Making of Israeli National Tradition* (Chicago: University of Chicago Press, 1995), pp. 3-12; cf. David M. Gunn, 'Yearning for Jerusalem: Reading Myth on the Web', in Fiona C. Black, Roland Boer and Erin Runions (eds.), *The Labour of Reading: Desire, Alienation, and Biblical Interpretation* (Semeia Studies; Atlanta: Scholars Press, 1999), pp. 123-40.

28. See, e.g., *Facts about Israel* (Jerusalem: Israel Information Center, 1996).

29. See www.Israel.org/peace/independ.html or www.Israel.org/mfa/go.asp? MFAH00hb0.

term takes on the popular connotation of 'fiction' and the latter term, 'fact'. The distinction is very important for the state's protagonists because the myth has been invoked in a quasi-legal fashion to legitimate an actual claim to the land—Jews, it is argued, are the rightful 'owners' by virtue of a 'historic' connection to the land.[30] We see this understanding of the myth as history in a Ministry website account of Jerusalem (which, of course, is the epitome of 'Israel'):

> Throughout the millennia of its existence, Jerusalem has never been the capital of any other sovereign nation. Jerusalem has stood at the center of the Jewish people's national and spiritual life since King David made it the capital of his kingdom in 1003 BCE. The city remained the capital of the Davidic dynasty for 400 years, until the kingdom was conquered by the Babylonians. Following the return from the Babylonian exile in 538 BCE, Jerusalem again served as the capital of the Jewish people in its land for the next five and a half centuries.[31]

The Christian link with Jerusalem is essentially a religious one, the text goes on to assure us, with no political or secular 'connotations' (apart from the 'short-lived' Crusader kingdom). As for Muslim rule, whether Arab or otherwise, Jerusalem was never the capital of any political entity 'or even a province'. Though British administration made Jerusalem its seat during the Mandate, it was not until 1948 that the city was restored once more to its place as a capital, 'the capital of a sovereign Jewish state'. So while Christians and Muslims may have religious investments in Jerusalem it is 'the Jewish people' who alone have a millennia-old stake in the city as the capital of a sovereign state.

This recitation, then, is framed as a narrative of the 'facts'—'what actually happened', so to speak. It is composed this way, including the biblically derived episodes, because for centuries these biblical narratives have been read by Jews and Christians, and not least by biblical scholars, as a more or less literal account of what happened.

Revisionist (biblical) history undermines this ideological prop for the modern state, just as revisionist Israeli history has been undermining some of the established verities concerning the establishment of the state in 1948 and its early years.[32] The very invocation of the term

---

30. The argument appears, e.g., in influential evidence to, and the findings of, the Peel Commission in 1937.

31. See www.Israel.org/mfa/go.asp?MFAH00j30.

32. See, e.g., Laurence J. Silberstein (ed.), *New Perspectives on Israeli History: The Early Years of the State* (New York: New York University Press, 1991).

'myth' to describe the biblical story of exile and return is potentially unsettling. The attack on the historicity of the united monarchy under David, the effective starting-point of the master narrative, threatens to shift the primary basis of claims to ancient 'sovereignty' from history to fiction. But these are only the more obvious aspects of the undermining. There is more to the relationship between modern Israeli foundation narratives and the revisionist histories than the broad categorizing of the stories of David and the Exile as myths. Let us consider just a few other implications.

Thompson's account of the Maccabees as Taliban[33] is unlikely to sound flattering to many Western readers, including Jewish Americans, nor to many Jewish Israelis for whom the Maccabees are a significant part of the national master narrative—an episode of heroic struggle against foreign oppression/occupation and sovereignty regained, a model for the 1948 war of 'liberation'.[34] Moreover, his depiction of them as clients of foreign powers, Egypt and especially Rome, tarnishes their image as emblems of independence. It does not help, either, that patron Rome is the arch-enemy in the master narrative's next episode, the revolts of 70 CE and Bar Kokhba which mark the beginning of the great exile that will end in the Zionist return and the establishment of the modern state. Viewed another way, the politics of 'independence' as a client state raises, of course, the question of the extent to which the establishment and sustaining of modern Israel can be understood in terms of colonialism.

One of the striking things about the biblical story of Babylonian exile is that there is virtually no narrative of the exile itself.[35] Likewise, the modern Zionist foundation narrative steps rapidly from Bar Kokhba to the First Aliyah, pausing only to characterize the intervening period as one of suffering and yearning for the land (cf. Lamentations; Ps. 137). This reduction of the exilic episode itself (including the Holocaust) has been not simply a matter of texts but of cultural practice in Israel; only in recent years has the pressure of alternative memories of flourishing communities, distinctive ethnic customs and rich cultural contributions begun to make inroads into the myth, straining the Zionist character-ization (caricature?) of Exile as only disaster, an episode best skipped, an event whose meaning lies wholly in the episode to which it gives

33. Thompson, *The Mythic Past*, pp. 196-99.
34. Zerubavel, *Recovered Roots*, pp. 19-20.
35. Cf. Thompson, *The Mythic Past*, p. 218.

place, namely return and the (re-)constitution of the people as State. Under the strain of such pressures, however, the singularity of the subject, the Jewish people who suffer in exile, begins to break down. The reality of an extremely diverse citizenship (as measured by almost any social or cultural category, including religion and ethnicity) is therefore slowly fracturing the foundation myth's tight plot. The exile is to be celebrated as well as mourned over, its people were many and not simply one; and they did, after all, have homes in far countries which they cherished. All of which begins to suggest that Exile was not actually exile.

Yael Zerubavel describes the period of Exile in the Zionist narrative as representing a 'hole' between the two national periods, an acute lack of positive characteristics attributed to it. 'As a Zionist Revisionist youth articulated this idea: "I stand stirred by the heroism and greatness of the Maccabees, Bar Kokhba, and Elazar ben Yair, but all that happened thousands of years ago. We lack someone in the middle".'[36] She goes on:

> The Zionist suppression of positive aspects of exilic life to promote the centrality of the people-land bond was reinforced by its denial of centuries of Palestinian life in that land. This double denial made it easier to reshape the period of Exile as a temporary regression between the two national periods, metaphorically suspending time and space in order to appropriate both into the Zionist commemorative narrative. Ironically, the recovery of the nation's roots in the ancient past implied playing down its roots in Exile as well as the renunciation of the Palestinian's roots in the same land.[37]

It is interesting to bring this analysis into relation with the similar 'hole' in the biblical story (if we construe Genesis–Kings and Chronicles, Ezra and Nehemiah as the story). The comparison suggests for one thing the ideological importance of establishing a 'continuous' national history for a settler community: the 'new' nation directly continues the 'old' nation, as the story moves (more or less) directly from deportation to settlement. (At the same time, the silent break has the advantage of rhetorically 'emptying' the land in preparation for its [re-]settlement.)[38] The comparison also indicates how the reduction of the hiatus (exile) to little more than a blank allows the settlers to claim that they are the

---

36. Zerubavel, *Recovered Roots*, p. 19.
37. Zerubavel, *Recovered Roots*, p. 22.
38. Cf. Lemche, *The Israelites in History and Tradition*, pp. 121-22.

subject of the whole story (they are true 'Israelites') without exposing their claim of exclusive identity to too much scrutiny. 'What did *you* do in the Exile, Dad?' That is not a proper topic for conversation.

Perhaps, then, Thompson and Lemche may be overstressing the ideological significance of the Exile as signifying the decisive break between a rejected 'old' Israel and the looked-for or reconstituted 'new' Israel. That reading, with its strong Lutheran, law-gospel connotations is not the only way to understand the relation between the 'subjects' (Israel, all Israel, Judah, etc.) of the various component narratives. Throughout the Hebrew Bible, the term 'Israel' is used of the pious and the rebellious, notes James Linville: 'Even in the expression, "God of Israel", Yahweh is posited as the deity for a nation, not a pure community'.[39] Likewise,

> the 'north' in Kings does not simply represent that which has corrupted itself and can no longer be called 'Israel'. Rather, it remains 'Israel', as its retention of the very name indicates. The 'north' and Judah are each other's alter ego, and their independent existences, so strongly affirmed in many places in the book, are blurred in many others.[40]

As Nehemiah tears people's hair out at the end of that book, the 'old' Israel is palpably still present and the 'new' one is looking pretty silly!

Of course, Thompson himself is well aware of the political importance of continuities. Elsewhere in his book he writes:

> Even the great displacements of the twentieth century, leading to the establishment of the state of Israel, have been understood in terms of return. They are spoken of in the language of continuity. From such a perspective, one must say that Palestine's population has ever set a high price on its continuity. Even the disruptions of imperial population policies had been reinterpreted in favour of continuities. Indigency was given the immigrants as their birthright.[41]

And as he writes the present into the past and the past into the present, I have to wonder for just a moment: and which immigrants is he talking about?

---

39. James Richard Linville, *Israel in the Book of Kings: The Past as a Project of Social Identity* (JSOTSup, 272; Sheffield: Sheffield Academic Press, 1998), p. 29; he cites Graham Harvey, *The True Israel: Uses of the Names Jew, Hebrew and Israel in Ancient Jewish and Early Christian Literature* (Leiden: E.J. Brill, 1996), pp. 148-88.

40. Linville, *Israel in the Book of Kings*, pp. 99-100.

41. Thompson, *The Mythic Past*, p. 255.

HOW DOES ONE DATE AN EXPRESSION OF MENTAL HISTORY? THE OLD TESTAMENT AND HELLENISM

Niels Peter Lemche

In the good days of old—not so far removed from us in time—a biblical text was usually dated according to its historical referent. A text that seemed to include historical information might well belong to the age when this historical referent seemed likely to have existed. At least this was the general attitude. The historical referent was the decisive factor. If the information included in the historical referent was considered likely or even precise, the text that provided this information was considered more or less contemporary with the event—that is, the historical referent—although the only source of this event was often the text in question that referred to it.

In those days, everybody knew and talked about the 'hermeneutic circle'. It was generally accepted that the study of ancient Israel was from a logical point of view based on a *circellus logicus vitiosum*, a false logical circle, but nobody within biblical studies believed that it was possible to avoid this logical trap.

A classical example of this 'methodology'—or lack of methodology—is the way biblical studies have dealt with the last years of Judah's history. Today it is becoming almost mainstream scholarship to argue that the united monarchy of David and Solomon never existed. It is also accepted that, as far as the early days of the independent kingdoms of Israel and Judah are concerned, most of the information in the books of Kings is legendary. In spite of this, when it comes to the final part of the history of the kingdom of Judah, scholars still consider large sections of the Deuteronomistic History to include vital historical information about Judah in the seventh and early sixth centuries BCE. Thus the reformation of King Josiah in Jerusalem is still generally assumed to have taken place in 623/622 BCE, more or less as described by the authors of 2 Kings. That Chronicles have a different story to tell about the reformation does not worry scholars who all too readily accept the version presented by 2 Kings. Chronicles believe King Hezekiah and not Josiah to have been the great reformer (2 Chron. 29–31). Although Chronicles know the story about Josiah's reform (2 Chron. 34–35), it is Hezekiah and not Josiah who reinstalls the celebration of the Passover as it used to be in the days of old. Evidently, even if the author of Chronicles borrowed from the Deuteronomistic History, he did not accept the image of the past created by the author of 2 Kings. Here he demonstrates that he is a more independent mind than many scholars of the present century who have in great numbers simply paraphrased 2 Kings, thereby disregarding the warning provided by Chronicles.

It is obvious that ancient historiographers could handle so-called historical narrative in many different ways. Sometimes they elaborated on a text describing a well-known historical event, such as Sennacherib's attack on Hezekiah in 701. Here the biblical historiographers include a short note simply stating a series of 'facts' relating to Sennacherib's campaign (2 Kgs 18.13-16). This short note that might well have been found in some kind of an archive.[1] It is, however, more than likely that the biblical historiographers cited it in order to present it as a jumping-off point for an elaborate, however invented story about the liberation of Jerusalem from the mighty army of the Assyrians (2 Kgs 18.17-19.37).[2] At other times the historiographers found historical information about the past within their tradition but were not able (from a historian's vantage point) to localize it properly.[3] But they were also able to create 'history' almost from scratch.[4] All in all it is clear that biblical

---

1. Compare this note in 2 Kings with the version presented by Sennacherib (*ANET*, pp. 287-88). Although the two versions are not identical or in total agreement about the course of events, they more or less include the same information.

2. Cf. further on this my 'Om historisk erindring i Det Gamle Testamentes historiefortællinger' ['On Historical Remains in the Historical Narratives of the Old Testament'], in Geert Hallbäck and John Strange (eds.), *Bibel og Historieskrivning* (Forum for Bibelsk Eksegese, 10; Copenhagen: Museum Tusculanum, 1999), pp. 11-28 (20-24) (ET in preparation).

3. Examples of this are the anachronistic note about Pithom and Ramses in Exod. 1.11, the settlement of the Benjaminites, and the kingdom of David; cf. my 'Is It Still Possible to Write a History of Ancient Israel?', *SJOT* 8 (1994), pp. 163-88.

4. In Lemche, 'Om historisk erindring', pp. 24-26, the example that illustrates this is 2 Kgs 3, the legendary story about the Israelite and Judaean campaign against Moab. Here the only historical element could well be Mesha, the name of the king of Moab.

historiographers did not share any modern idea of history as a scholarly discipline.[5] They simply made the tradition about the past fit the version of the history of Israel which they presented to their audience. The biblical historiographers shared this sentiment of tradition with their colleagues in the ancient world.[6] The past was not something that just happened once upon a time and was thereafter forgotten. It was part of a living tradition—or was simply the tradition—and was brought to life again and again whenever an ancient author decided to call upon the past to illustrate the present but always in a form that suited the actual situation.

Because of such standards of dealing with the past, it is unlikely that we can date a biblical historical narrative on the background of its historical referent. It is obvious that the historical truth and nothing but the truth was not a criterion employed by historiographers of the ancient world who reconstructed or simply constructed the past in this way.[7]

5.   It is a revealing fact that Greek ἱστορία (from the verb ἱστορέω, 'to enquire') primarily means 'inquiry', and comes closest to 'history' in our sense when it is used about the report of the enquiries (cf. LSJ, p. 842). Herodotus opens his report in this way: Ἡροδότου Ἁλιχαρνησσέος ἱστιρίης ἀπόδεξις ἥδε, ὡς μήτε τὰ γενόμενα ἐξ ἀνθρώπων τῷ χρόνῳ ἐξίτηλα γένηται, μήτε ἔργα μεγάλα τε καὶ θωμαστά, τὰ μὲν Ἕλλησι, τὰ δὲ βαρβάροισι ἀποδεχθέντα, ἀκλεᾶ γένηται, τά τε ἄλλα καὶ δι᾽ ἥν αἰτίην ἐπολέμησαν ἀλλήλοισι ('The enquiries of Herodotus from Halicarnasus presented here, in order that what people have done should not vanish with time, or that the great and wonderful deeds of the Greeks and the Barbarians should not fall into oblivion, but also why they engaged in a war among them' [Herodotus, *Historiae* 1.1]). He does not present himself so much a scholar as a journalist.

6.   Cf. further on this with reference to the similarity to Greek and Roman historiography, my 'Good and Bad in History: The Greek Connection', in Steve McKenzie and Thomas Römer (eds.), *Rethinking the Foundations: Historiography in the Ancient World and in the Bible. Essays in Honour of John Van Seters* (BZAW, 294; Berlin: W. de Gruyter, 2000), pp. 127-40. On the whole process of creating the past, cf. Thomas L. Thompson, *The Bible in History: How Writers Create a Past* (London: Jonathan Cape, 1999).

7.   Whereas the Greek and Roman authors have been well served by modern students of ancient literature, the historiography of the ancient Near East has not evoked the same kind of interest. For a recent overview cf. John Van Seters, 'The Historiography of the Ancient Near East', in *CANE*, IV, pp. 2433-444, but also John Van Seters, *In Search of History: Historiography in the Ancient World and the Origins of Biblical History* (New Haven: Yale University Press, 1983), and finally

The historiographers evidently had a programme and historical narrative was the medium selected by them to present their case. Specific ideas and sentiments, religious convictions as well as ideas about the nation and people of Israel, directed their thinking.[8] We may call it propaganda or educational literature as we wish. The aim of this kind of literature was not only to entertain people of the present but also, and much more importantly, to make an impression on the next generation.[9]

Political ideas and religious sentiments all come together to form the 'mental matrix' of a person. Such a 'mental matrix' governs the expressions of all writers—ancient as well as modern. Moreover, biblical historiographers carried within themselves mental matrices that were decisive when they were about to choose what to include and what to leave out in their retelling of the past. The student of this literature should investigate whether or not it is possible to reconstruct their mental matrix(matrices). Were they governed by ideas that originated in ancient Palestine, or in Mesopotamia or Egypt, or had Greek philosophy already influenced them to such a degree that knowledge of Greek (Hellenistic) civilization seems evident? What did the biblical historiographers know?

They were of course governed by an antiquarian interest. They were simply interested in the past. Ancient historiographers shared such an interest with their modern colleagues, the historians of the present. However, this is a superficial similarity that only says that ancient historiographers wanted to tell people of their own time the meaning of the past.

In order to understand this interest in the past it has to be stressed that ancient societies were by all accounts very conservative—not to say reactionary—societies. This is nowhere better reflected than in the

the discussion in John Van Seters, *Prologue to History: The Yahwist as Historian in Genesis* (Louisville, KY: Westminster/John Knox Press, 1992), Chapter 2, 'Myth and Tradition in Ancient Historiography', pp. 24-44.

8.   Cf. also on this my *The Israelites in History and Tradition* (Library of Ancient Israel; Louisville, KY: Westminster/John Knox Press, 1998), esp. Chapter 4, 'The People of God: The Two Israels in the Old Testament', pp. 86-132.

9.   Cicero's characterization of history, in his *De or.* 2.9.36, *Historia vero testis temporum, lux veritatis, vita memoriae, magistra vitae, nuntia vetustatis…* ('history [is] truly the witness about the ages, the light of truth, the life of memories, the teacher of life, and the messenger of ancient times…'), should never be left out of consideration when we evaluate ancient historiography. Cf. further on this my 'Good and Bad in History', BZAW, 294, pp. 127-40.

antique tale of the ages of the world, the original 'golden age' that was supplanted by the less prosperous 'silver age' that was for its part supplanted by the ferocious 'brazen age'.[10] Everything was from the beginning perfect: 'And God saw every thing that he had made, and, behold, it was very good' (Gen. 1.31). Any innovation was carried out to reestablish the original world order. This was the ideology behind, for example, the *mîšarum* acts of the old Babylonian world when debts were abolished and property handed back to its original owner.[11] Ancient societies were not 'primitive' societies but 'traditional' societies, a term adopted by anthropologists of the present day as a general term for so-called 'primitive cultures'. The past had to be preserved to provide guidelines for the present and future generations. The past carried a meaning that should not be lost, and it was the duty of the historiographer to retell the past in such a way that the meaning was not lost.[12] The meaning was more important than what really happened: 'Is this true or something that just happened?'[13]

The past as a concept and a reality also created a chronological distance to the present, and thus made unlikely things possible, that is, things that are unlikely in the present 'brazen age'. The past—the 'golden age'—was a kind of never-never world. Anything that happened in this never-never world, once upon a time, has a meaning for the present. Because ancient writers had no definite ideas about history in the modern sense of the word, they did not distinguish between the many kinds of information about the past but mixed all genres together. In this way it is understandable that literary genres such as fairy-tales, legends, myths, and so on, are joined by biblical authors in a—to our

---

10. Cf. Hesiod, *Op.*, pp. 110-55, and Ovid, *Metamorphoses*, I.90-162.

11. The classical studies on these decrees are F.R. Kraus, *Ein Edikt des Königs Ammi-Ṣaduqa von Babylon* (SDOAP, 5; Leiden: E.J. Brill, 1958) and *idem, Königliche Verfügungen in altbabylonischen Zeit* (SDOAP, 11; Leiden: E.J. Brill, 1984).

12. Which has little to do with modern ideas of history as the reconstruction of the past for its own sake—*wie es eigentlich gewesen*, as expressed by Leopold von Ranke. Cf. also the 'Prolegomena' to my *The Israelites in History and Tradition*, pp. 1-8.

13. I found this wonderful line some years ago in a Danish newspaper in a review of a book about the Islandic sagas. I have forgotten both the author of this line, and the exact place where it was originally printed. It does, however, express in a most precise way the difference between pre-modern and modern ideas of history.

eyes—most uncritical way. According to ancient historiographers, there were no qualitative differences between a fairy-tale and a proper historical report. The past was the subject of both the fairy-tale and the report. Therefore both fairy-tale and report contained evidence about the meaning of history.[14]

Describing and dating the mental matrix of an ancient writer is difficult. It is especially difficult when the author in question is anonymous and not dated by external evidence. We only have one way to go, and that is to concentrate on the written piece of evidence produced by the writer in question, in this case the biblical texts, in order to see whether it is possible to establish an intellectual 'profile' of this author. If this is possible, we may continue our quest and even propose—but no more than that—the situational background of the author, which also nails this person to a certain stage in the development of human thinking.

The authors of biblical literature are always anonymous. The text is the only evidence we possess. It is important evidence. After all, all texts come into being within a certain intellectual environment and are to be considered expressions of their environment.

Allow me to illustrate my point. In a discussion about the similarities and dissimilarities between the Dead Sea Scrolls and the New Testament, my Copenhagen colleague in New Testament studies, Niels Hyldahl, talks about 'structural similarities'.[15] Scholars have pointed out the many parallels as evidence of a physical relationship between the Essenes (supposed to be the authors of the Dead Sea Scrolls) and the early Christians.[16] In the same way other scholars have stressed the

14. This is definitely a subject that could be expanded upon. The 'meaning of history' has nothing to do with modern concepts like 'la longue durée' of Les annales school which says that certain conditions are likely to produce certain developments over time, i.e. that in a certain geographical area the natural geography is likely to promote specific historical processes. 'La longue durée' promotes a kind of historical determinism that could at best be termed 'quantitative'. The meaning of the 'great deeds of the past' was, in antiquity, rather qualitative.

15. Cf. Niels Hyldahl, 'Qumran og den ældste kristendom: En kort introduktion og problemorientering', in Niels Hyldahl and Thomas L. Thompson (eds.), *Dødehavsteksterne og Bibelen* (Forum for Bibelsk Eksegese, 8; Copenhagen: Museum Tusculanum, 1996), pp. 9-16.

16. This is certainly not the place to get involved in the present discussion about the origin of the library found at Qumran. I have a certain preference for the theory of a library with a mixed content probably from Jerusalem and stored away in the Judaean Desert perhaps by 63 BCE. This theory requires a new dating of the scrolls

many divergences between the New Testament and the scrolls from
Qumran. Although it is a fact that the New Testament and the Dead Sea
Scrolls are related in one way or the other—both group of texts belong
to more or less the same age—it would be wrong to maintain that the
authors of the Dead Sea Scrolls were Christians. However, the similarity between the two bodies of literature still remains. This similarity
should not be misunderstood to establish any kind of identity. It does
not allow us to identify early Christians with the Essenes. It is a similarity that has to do with the type of issues raised by the Dead Sea
Scrolls as well as by the New Testament.

Every period will include specific questions and subjects of discussion. An overview of scholarship within Old Testament studies in the
twentieth century will tell us that this is not only obvious, it is a truism.
Thus around the turn of the nineteenth century, the Babel-Bibel controversy was at the centre of scholarly (and public) interest following
the discovery of the ancient civilizations of Mesopotamia.[17] This controversy died out before the outbreak of the First World War. All
studies that centre on this discussion can accordingly be dated safely to
the period between the decipherment of Akkadian cuneiform in the
nineteenth century and 1914. After that date it became mainly irrelevant. It was never the case that all scholars of the period agreed on a
certain position in relationship to this controversy; it was rather that
they all had to address it in some way or another.

In historical studies, the amphictyony became a major subject after
the publication in 1930 of Martin Noth's famous study of Israelite society in the period of the Judges.[18] For the next 40 years this hypothesis
dominated every single study about pre-monarchical Israel. Although
most scholars adopted the hypothesis as their own, a few important
divergent voices were heard, but even scholars who rejected the amphictyony had to address the question of such a tribal organization. If
not, nobody would have paid any attention to what they wrote.[19] For the

to show that they belong to the first century BCE rather than the first century CE.

17. A recent overview of this discussion can be found in Mogens Trolle Larsen,
'The Babel/Bible Controversy and its Aftermath', in *CANE*, I, pp. 95-106.

18. Martin Noth, *Das System der zwölf Stämme Israels* (BWANT, 4.1; Stuttgart:
W. Kohlhammer, 1930).

19. Among the scholars who never accepted the hypothesis about the amphictyony, we may mention two important names: Otto Eissfeldt and Georg Fohrer.
Cf. on the criticism of the amphictyony my *Israel i Dommertiden: En oversigt over*

last two decades there has been an almost total silence about the amphictyony, after a series of studies that appeared in the early 1970s removed any historical foundation for its existence. In 1984 I was able to conclude the discussion in this way: 'The hypothesis of the amphictyony by now is irrelevant to the investigations into Israel's past history'.[20]

Between 1954 and 1970 as a consequence of the publication of George Mendenhall's articles about the relationship between the Sinai covenant and Hittite vassal treaties from the Late Bronze Age, Old Testament scholars invested a great deal of interest in covenant theology.[21] For the next decade and a half everything centred on the covenant that was supposed to appear here, there and everywhere in the Old Testament. After 1969, when Lothar Perlitt simply announced that covenant theology was invented by the circle of Deuteronomist theologians towards the end of independent Israelite and Judaean history, nobody continued to discuss the subject, which went into oblivion as if the discussion had never happened.[22]

These are of course only rather insignificant examples from a minor field within the academic world. However, they show how every period in the history of humankind will give birth to a number of questions— within philosophy, religion or simple politics—that are specifically related to this period, hot subjects for a while and then forgotten.

The same was the case in ancient times, although because of limited resources of communication, the stream of ever-changing ideas did not flow as fast as in modern times. Every era included a number of issues that specifically related to this period, and subjects of a lively discussion among the intellectuals of the time. We should not be surprised when two corpora of texts squarely belonging to the same period can display so many similarities and yet be so different as the texts of the

diskussionen om Martin Noths 'Das System der zwölf Stämme Israels' (Tekst og Tolkning, 4; Copenhagen: G.E.C. Gad, 1972), pp. 31-38.

20. Cf. my 'Israel in the Period of the Judges: The Tribal League in Recent Discussion', *ST* 38 (1984), pp. 1-28 (28); cf. also Georg Fohrer, 'Methoden und Moden in der alttestamentlichen Wissenschaft', *ZAW* 100 Supplement (1988), pp. 243-54 (244-48).

21. Cf. George E. Mendenhall, 'Covenant Forms in Israelite Tradition', *BA* 17 (1954), pp. 50-76.

22. Lothar Perlitt, *Bundestheologie im Alten Testament* (WMANT, 36; Neukirchen–Vluyn: Neukirchener Verlag, 1969).

New Testament and the Dead Sea Scrolls. The New Testament and the Dead Sea Scrolls need not agree on every single point because they might be more or less from the same time. It is simply an old scholarly hoax that people belonging to one and the same period should agree on anything and everything; on the contrary, in a society of the real world outside the academia, there are almost as many opinions around as people to discuss them. It is not the variety of opinions but the number of issues that is limited. Niels Hyldahl accordingly does not speak about individual points of contact but about a systemic kind of relationship: the same questions but different answers.

Since the beginning of academic discussion it has been a favoured pastime to indulge oneself in comparative studies. I do not intend to elaborate on this theme here. I only have to refer the reader to James G. Frazer's *The Golden Bough* as a famous but also contested specimen.[23] It is much too easy to find similarities between the literary expressions of different cultures when they basically belong to the same stage of development, especially when we talk about relatively simple societies with a more or less uniform socio-economic system such as basic agriculture. In basic agrarian cultures, peasants all over the world share many ideas without ever having been in mutual contact. This is in itself an interesting scholarly occupation and can—when put together—result in something like Stith Thompson's index of folk-motifs in fairy-tales and legendary stories originating in a mostly oral environment, later elaborated upon in writing.[24]

When, however, cultures get more complicated and the diversification of occupation in the old Durkheimian[25] fashion begins to create separation within one and the same society, cultural expressions also become more elaborate and sophisticated. In this case a systemic similarity such as the one discussed above is more likely to reflect not only political but also and especially cultural interchange between two interrelated cultural zones, such as, for example, Mesopotamia and Western

23. James G. Frazer, *The Golden Bough: A Study in Magic and Religion* (New York: St Martin's Press, 1990 [1890]).

24. Cf. Stith Thompson, *Motif-Index of Folk Literature: A Classification of Narrative Elements in Folktales, Ballads, Myths, Fables, Mediaeval Romances, Exempla, Jest-Books and Local Legends* (Bloomington: Indiana University Press, 1966 [1955–58]).

25. Cf. Emile Durkheim, *De la division du travail social* (Paris: Presses universitaires de France, 1996 [1893]).

Syria and the Levant in the Bronze Age, or Mesopotamia and Egypt already before the dawn of history. The famous saying that 'Graecia capta ferum victorem cepit', 'conquered Greece conquered its barbaric conqueror',[26] says precisely that the Romans became Hellenized when they entered into contact with Greece and were overwhelmed by its superior civilization and cultural tradition.

The moment we approach the problem of dating an Old Testament text—not to say the Old Testament itself—we are confronted with the literary remains of a culturally very rich civilization. No primitive literature is found in the Old Testament. Every part of the collection of Scripture included in the Old Testament displays a sophistication that brings us far beyond the cultural borders of an undeveloped basic agrarian society. The Primary History (Genesis to 2 Kings) is a fine example of this and need not be discussed in this context.[27] Of more interest in this connection are the patriarchal narratives. Although these stories include many motifs from folk-literature or simply reflect popular stories, they are much too complicated to have originated within a milieu that was almost exclusively oral—Gunkel's notorious campfire society—or which had just changed from oral to a written stage of literary transmission. I do not intend to reiterate the ideas of André Jolles that oral literature is perforce simple and devoid of literary elaboration[28]—there are plenty of examples of the complexity of orally transmitted literature. I do, however, say that the complexity is different from the one found in, say, the Ugaritic epics, or from another age, the Serbo-Croatian heroic epics collected by Parry and Lord.[29] The complexity of a literary corpus such as the patriarchal narratives depends on the number of themes that are combined by the authors of these narratives and are difficult to separate. It also has to do with themes such

26. *...et artis intulit agresti Latio.* Horace, *Ep.* 2.1.156-57.

27. Of interest in this connection is John Van Seters's comparison between Greek and biblical primaeval histories in his 'The Primeval Histories of Greece and Israel Compared', *ZAW* 100 (1988), pp. 1-22; cf. also his *Prologue to History*, pp. 78-103. Van Seters definitely sees a clear relationship between the two traditions about the origins of humankind and the world, but does not accept that this connection excludes other traditions like the Mesopotamian primaeval traditions.

28. Cf. André Jolles, *Einfache Formen, Legende, Sage, Mythe, Rätsel, Spruch, Kasus, Memorabile, Märchen, Witz* (Tübingen: Max Niemeyer, 1974 [1930]).

29. Milman Parry and Albert B. Lord, *Serbo-Croatian Heroic Songs Collected by Milman Parry* (Publications of the Milman Parry Collection; Text and Translation Series, 1-2, 4, 12; Cambridge, MA: Harvard University Press, 1953–86).

as 'how God educates human beings', illustrated by the unique humoresque that constitutes the Abraham-complex[30] or 'the struggle between creator and creation' that governs the traditions united in the Primary History.

It goes without saying that the form of these very narratives, almost exclusively prose narrative, is also an indication of a milieu of written literature that is almost unique in the ancient Near East. Literary fiction in the form of prose narrative was not widely distributed among the cultures of the ancient Near East. Mesopotamian literary creations were—like the literature from, say, Ugarit—mostly preserved in the forms of written poems or epics. The literary elite of the Middle Kingdom made an extended use of prose stories. From a literary point of view this is probably the best comparison with the milieu that created literature such as the patriarchal narratives, but it is removed from this by at least 1000 years—perhaps more.[31] Prose was of course known and dominates royal annals, Hittite as well as Babylonian and Mesopotamian, but although the forms of, for example, Assyrian royal annals may show up within biblical literature, the Old Testament does not include royal annals but, at most, literature that borrows its form from such reports.[32] The patriarchal narratives have of course nothing to do with royal official literature. The author(s) who wrote these stories were evidently well-educated people who could both write and read. They did not write with gods in mind.[33] They wrote literature to be read by other people. Their literature was composed with other educated people in mind, people who were able to understand and appreciate it.

30. This says that Abraham was old before he became wise, and probably never got it right—until the very moment when he was about to sacrifice his son, his hope for the future and the essence of Yahweh's promise to him.

31. Although it cannot be ignored that part of this literature, such as the story of 'Sinuhe' or the 'tale of the two brothers' that was preserved also at a much later date, may have influenced biblical authors.

32. Cf. K. Lawson Younger, Jr, *Ancient Conquest Accounts: A Study in Ancient Near Eastern and Biblical History Writing* (JSOTSup, 98; Sheffield: JSOT Press, 1990), who mixes an acceptable form-critical analysis with impossible historical conclusions.

33. Cf. the examples of Assyrian annals written on both sides of stone slabs, also on the side of the stone that turned inside and could not be read by anyone except the gods. Other examples are the many Assyrian foundation stones buried in the fundament of temples which commemorated the mighty deeds of the king who built this temple.

When we change to the subject of 'how to create profiles of the authors of Old Testament texts', we have to keep these remarks in mind when we want to describe the mental matrices of these authors.

In his *In Search of 'Ancient Israel'*, Philip R. Davies distinguishes between three different kinds of 'Israel'. One is 'historical Israel', that is, the state otherwise known from Assyrian sources as *Bît Ḥumriya* or *Samarina*. This Palestinian state came into being some time in the ninth century BCE and was destroyed by the Assyrians 722 BCE. Historical Israel did not include the Palestinian petty state called Judah that only appeared on the historical scene as a state, say, after 800 BCE and was in existence as a semi-autonomous political entity until 597 or 587 BCE.[34] The second Israel is 'biblical Israel', the Israel of the Old Testament. This Israel is the creation of the authors of the Old Testament and can only partly be related to historical Israel. Thirdly, modern scholars created still another Israel, the so-called 'ancient Israel'. This ancient Israel represents a curious mixture of biblical Israel and historical Israel.[35] Although I have always respected the Dumézilian theory about the importance of the number three in the Indo-European tradition, Davies's theory about the three different 'Israels' is one short of being correct. There are not one, but two biblical 'Israels'. In my recent study *The Israelites in History and Tradition*, a comprehensive section has as its subject 'the People of God'.[36] The term 'the People of God' includes the concept of the Israelite nation as the creation of the authors of the Old Testament prose narratives from Genesis to 2 Kings. It is my argument that in the Old Testament there is more than one biblical Israel; there are, as a matter of fact, two 'Israels' here. One of them is the 'old Israel', understood to be the people of the covenant written in stone (cf. the Sinai-complex but also Josh. 24); the second is the 'new Israel', the people of the covenant written in the heart (Jer. 31.31-4).

---

34. I do not wish to re-open the discussion about the origins of these states in this essay. The important study by David W. Jamieson-Drake, *Scribes and Schools in Monarchic Judah: A Socio-Archaeological Approach* (JSOTSup, 109; The Social World of Biblical Antiquity, 9; Sheffield: Almond Press, 1991) that argues in favour of these dates has been the subject of much criticism. It should, however, be noticed that Israel Finkelstein supports such dates, cf. his 'The Beginning of the State in Israel and Judah', *EI* 26 (1999), pp. 132-41 [Hebrew session, p. 134; English resumé, p. 233*].

35. Cf. Philip R. Davies, *In Search of 'Ancient Israel'* (JSOTSup, 148; Sheffield: JSOT Press, 1992).

36. Lemche, *The Israelites in History and Tradition*, pp. 86-132.

According to the Old Testament, the Babylonian exile constitutes the line of division between the old and the new Israel. Old Israel is destroyed and its people banished from their country because they rejected their God and broke the covenant. The new Israel is the Israel supposed to arise in the future as the true people of God. It has at various times been identified with the Jewish nation, or with the Christian Church (cf. Rom. 9–11). Any sectarian group within Judaism or Christianity is expected to refer to itself as the true 'new Israel'.

Most often it is argued that the same nation that the Babylonians forced into exile returned to Palestine in the Persian period. Now it is to this day an unsolved question whether there ever was a return of the dimensions envisaged by the Old Testament, namely, a movement of a people from one part of the Middle East to another.[37] I will maintain that the 'exile' in Babylonia never ended, and that the presence of exilic people from Palestine lasted at least until 1951 CE.[38] We probably have no other sources than the texts of the Old Testament that say that a major migration actually took place. Most of the constructions of Jewish history in the Persian period depend on the same type of hermeneutic circular exegesis as already described here. It is, however, an extraordinary fact that scholars have paid so little attention to the meaning of the different images of Jerusalem and Judah found in Chronicles, the book of Ezra and the book of Nehemiah. When we read Nehemiah, it is as if the author of Nehemiah 1–4—the so-called 'autobiography of Nehemiah'—has never read Ezra. We cannot say with absolute certainty that 'Nehemiah's autobiography' is a historical document that reflects conditions in Jerusalem in the fourth century BCE. It could be a kind of novel from a much later period, that is, the Hellenistic period. However, whether or not it is a piece of literature going back to a historical person of the name of Nehemiah, Nehemiah 1–4 describes conditions in Jerusalem and its environment that are almost totally different

---

37. On the historical value of the biblical idea of Palestine as 'the empty land' in the exilic period, cf. Hans M. Barstad, *The Myth of the Empty Land: A Study in the History and Archaeology of Judah during the 'Exilic' Period* (Symbolae Osloenses, 28; Oslo: Scandinavian University Press, 1996). Jamieson-Drake is not of the same conviction. According to his analysis of the evidence, a total breakdown of Judaean society took place in the sixth century BCE. Cf. his *Scribes and Schools in Monarchic Israel*, pp. 145-47.

38. That is, until the seventh 'Alia' that transferred most of the Iraqi Jewish community to Israel.

from the impression of Jerusalem in the Persian period found in other biblical books. Has a Jewish community already appeared in this place in the fourth century BCE? This is an open question. And from an archaeological perspective: do we possess evidence that a major migration took place at the end of the sixth century BCE from Mesopotamia to Palestine? If this was the case, if Jews from Babylonia really returned to Jerusalem and Judah in numbers between, say 538 and 516 BCE, where are their Babylonian cooking-pots? Would women leave their homes without bringing their utensils with them?[39]

The point is that the 'old Israel' is a construction of biblical authors, whereas the 'new Israel' is a utopia created by the same authors as an expression of their religious and national programme for the future. There never was an 'old Israel' in the biblical sense but the 'new Israel' is also an invention. It includes a project for the future: God-loving persons will found the 'new Israel'. Only the righteous are going to survive and to assemble at Zion protected by the Lord himself (cf. Isa. 4).

Two ideas are central to the concept of the 'new Israel'. On one hand the covenant between God and Israel and on the second God's *torah*. The covenant of Sinai failed miserably to unite the people of Israel with its God. The new covenant of Jeremiah 31 will substitute the old one and cannot be broken because it is not something from the outside but a part of the person who has entered the covenant. Together with the covenant goes God's *torah* or *instruction*. This *instruction* will guide the new Israel that it shall one day enter Zion. Without the *torah* there is no way to God. Most people will perish before they ever reach this place of blessing, 'because they have cast away the law of the Lord of Hosts, and despised the word of the Holy One of Israel' (Isa. 5.24).[40]

39. I made this point in my 'Jordan in the Biblical Tradition: An Overview of the Tradition with Special Reference to the Importance of the Biblical Literature for the Reconstruction of the History of the Ancient Territories of the State of Jordan', to be published in the proceedings of the Congress of the Archaeology of Jordan in Copenhagen, June 1998.

40. Cf. further on this my ' "For de har forkastet Hærskarers Herres lov"—eller "vi og de andre!"—Om forfatterne, der skrev Det Gamle Testamente', in E.K. Holt (ed.), *'Alle der ånder skal lovprise Herren': Det Gamle Testamente i tempel, synagoge og kirke* (Frederiksberg: Anis, 1998), pp. 63-90 (ET ' "Because They Have Cast away the Law of the Lord of Hosts"—Or "We and the Rest of the World!": The Authors Who Wrote the Old Testament', to be published in Thomas L. Thompson (ed.), *Changing Perspectives in Biblical Interpretation* [Sheffield: Sheffield Academic Press, forthcoming]).

The new Israel *is* the people of God. It is a people of 12 tribes assembled around a holy centre, the shrine of Yahweh at Zion. It is believed to include people with a common blood and a common religion—to a lesser degree with a common language, but with a land of its own.[41]

The mental matrix of biblical authors centres around the establishment of the new Israel. This matrix can be nothing less than the expression of a sectarian view of society. It creates a division between two kinds of people: the righteous that belong to this society and the unjust who will be condemned and thrown out. The criterion for deciding who is righteous and who is not is exclusively a religious one: do people keep the covenant and follow the instructions? The image of the new Israel is one of a sectarian community that—as other similar organizations in the Hellenistic world—excludes itself from the greater society that surrounds it.[42]

Without the *torah* there will never be a new Israel. What does this tell us about the authors who introduced the concept of the *torah*? The Decalogue opens the *torah* (Exod. 20.1-21; in Deuteronomy it serves the same purpose: 5.6-21). Irrespective of its origin and tradition-history, it probably serves as an index for the following sections of the legislation of Moses. This legislation opens with the 'Book of Covenant', Exodus 21–23. The Assyriologist Raymond Westbrook has argued that the first, so-called 'secular' part of this collection represents Mesopotamian law tradition.[43] He is certainly right—we only have to refer to the extensive degree of similarity analysed by, among others, Shalom Paul and Eckhart Otto.[44] Westbrook believes that this proves the Book of Covenant to be old. However, in Mesopotamia the tradition

41. Cf. the virtual 're-establishment' of the amphictyony in my *The Israelites in History and Tradition*, pp. 97-107. This amphictyony is not the old one invented by Noth. It has no part in the history of ancient Israel; it is a kind of mental structure put in writing.

42. Cf. the conclusion to Isa. 6. Only the elect among the elect will survive the ordeal (vv. 11-13). It is safe to assume that the author who wrote these verses will not reckon himself to be among the condemned ones.

43. Cf. Raymond Westbrook, *Studies in Biblical and Cuneiform Law* (Cahiers de la Revue Biblique, 26; Paris: J. Gabalda, 1988).

44. Cf. Shalom Paul, *Studies in the Book of the Covenant in the Light of Cuneiform and Biblical Law* (VTSup, 18; Leiden: E.J. Brill, 1970), and Eckhart Otto, *Wandel der Rechtsbegründigungen in der Gesellschaftsgeschichte des antiken Israel: Eine Rechtgeschichte des 'Bundesbuches' Exod. XX 22-XXIII 13* (Studia Biblica, 3; Leiden: E.J. Brill, 1988).

of the law codes lasted for millennia, from Sumerian times until at least the coming of the Greeks and probably even longer (the cuneiform literary tradition did not die totally out before the first or second centuries CE). This law tradition was rather stable and not easily exported. More importantly, it was not a law tradition in the usual sense of the word, but rather an academic tradition only remotely related to the life in court. It was nourished in the universities of the time (the misnamed 'scribal schools') and belonged exclusively to this milieu. In short: the Mesopotamian law codices are not primarily expressions of forensic experience but belong among wisdom literature and represent an academic pastime.[45]

The biblical collectors or authors of the law traditions that were included among the instructions of Moses evidently chose one of the Mesopotamian law codes (or created their own within the Babylonian law tradition) as the first part of the divine legislation. These collectors hereby reveal where they got their education. They must have studied in university institutions of their own time, most likely in Mesopotamia (this is a safe assumption as long as we have no evidence of comparable institutions outside of Mesopotamia—at least in the Iron Age [first millennium BCE]). It is clear that our collectors and/or authors had an *academic* background. They evidently belonged to academic circles and were brought up within a system of education that in their time had lasted for more than 2000 years.[46]

We now know two things about our authors. First, from a religious standpoint they were sectarians, people who believed themselves to belong among the chosen few who are destined to escape from extermination when God returns his people to Zion. Second, they were also academics and part of an age-old educational system.

45. In my 'Justice in Western Asia in Antiquity, Or: Why No Laws Were Needed!', *The Kent Law Review* 70 (1995), pp. 1695-1716, I try to explain why no written law was really necessary in Western Asia in antiquity. On the Babylonian 'law codes', cf. the literature quoted in 'Justice in Western Asia in Antiquity', p. 1698 n. 5, to which we have to add the introduction to Martha T. Roth, *Law Collections from Mesopotamia and Asia Minor* (SBLWAWS, 6; Atlanta: Scholars Press, 2nd edn, 1997), pp. 4-7.

46. This assumption is valid irrespective of whether we choose an Iron Age date of these authors or think that they belonged to the Persian or Hellenistic-Roman periods.

None of this proves our authors to be late, not to say from the Hellenistic-Roman period. They must obviously postdate the events of 587 BCE (if this is a historical date—the Old Testament is the only testimony to the second destruction of Jerusalem) or at least 597 BCE (the date of the conquest of Jerusalem confirmed by the Babylonian Chronicle).[47] The destruction of Jerusalem is a necessary part of the construction. It is of fundamental importance for the future return of the 'new Israel' to Zion. The question is only whether the authors belonged to the Persian or the Hellenistic period.

It is probably not a fair argument to say that the Persian period has been popular among scholars because we know so little about this period—as far as Palestine is concerned. However, the esteem for the Persian period among modern scholars compares well with the estimation of 'early Israel' as the cradle of Israelite civilization a generation ago. Like 'early Israel', the Persian period constitutes a kind of 'black box'. We know so very little about early Israel and only slightly more about the Persian period.

Many scholars think that in the Persian period the biblical tradition either originated or developed into the literature known from the Old Testament. The capacity of being a 'black box' makes the Persian period a likely candidate for such an assumption as it cannot be refuted by extant evidence that says the opposite. The 'black box' concept makes everything possible and allows the scholar to propose all kinds of theories that cannot be controlled. The procedure is illegitimate as it provides us with a hypothesis that cannot be falsified.[48]

It is of course possible that a religious idea such as the dualism between good and evil that is found in Old Testament texts, but much more expressly in para-biblical literature such as the War Scroll from

---

47. Cf. D.J. Wiseman, *Chronicles of Chaldaean Kings (626-556 B.C.) in the British Museum* (London: The Trustees of the British Museum, 1956), BM 21946, rv. 11-13. It is so easy to forget that 587 BCE is exclusively a biblical date. That the one of 597 BCE is confirmed by external sources does not prove that 597 BCE really took place. It is probably likely that something like 587 BCE happened, but it cannot be proven. The presence of members of the Judaean royal family at the Babylonian court in Neo-Babylonian times does not presuppose the destruction of 587 BCE— not even according to the Old Testament—it only presupposes the abduction of Jehoiachin in 597 BCE (cf. *ANET*, p. 308).

48. Adopted from the falsification claim of Karl Popper, which says that a hypothesis must be the subject of a falsification process, and if this is not possible, the hypothesis is redundant.

Qumran (clearly Hellenistic-Roman in date). is the result of influences from Persian religion.[49] It may also be the case that the idea of a theocratic government in Yehud has been moulded on the basis of the citizen-temple-society system that developed elsewhere in the Persian Empire.[50] The evidence of such a theocratic system from Judah, however, hardly predates the second century BCE.[51]

At the end of the day we simply have to admit that we know too little about the Persian period to make it a viable option and thus not only wishful thinking that the Old Testament was largely written during the centuries of Persian occupation of Palestine. If there are reflections in Old Testament literature of ideas current within the Persian Empire in, say the fifth or early fourth centuries BCE we cannot identify such ideas with any certainty. We cannot place biblical texts within an intellectual development that is otherwise unknown to us.

Matters gradually improve as we turn to the Hellenistic and Roman periods, as we are well informed about the general development in the intellectual history of humankind in this era. We are acquainted with the history of philosophy in the Hellenistic world, and we possess a fair share of Hellenistic literature, mostly but not exclusively of Greek origin. We also have an impression of the impact of Greek civilization in the Near East. At the moment we know too little about the precise history of this development, especially in remote areas such as the nooks and crannies of Palestine. We must hope that in the future it will be possible to describe how Greek civilization during the third and second centuries gradually extended its influence from region to region. The initial centres of Greek-Hellenistic influence were located in Egypt and Mesopotamia but subsequently Hellenistic civilization spread to other areas including also Palestine and Jordan in the second century BCE.[52]

---

49. The origin of the idea of dualism (i.e. the war between good and evil) that became popular within Judaism towards the end of the first millennium BCE has traditionally been reckoned to be Persian. Cf., e.g., Helmer Ringgren, *Israelite Religion* (Philadelphia: Fortress Press, 1966), pp. 314-15.

50. Cf. esp. Joel Weinberg, *The Citizen-Temple Community* (JSOTSup, 151; Sheffield: Sheffield Academic Press, 1992).

51. Well, this statement is probably gratuitous as we would know next to nothing about the second century BCE if not for the information provided by Josephus of the late first century CE.

52. But not before the second and first centuries BCE. The Hellenization of the Southern Levant has hardly been a major area of interest to students of Hellenistic

Now the question is: is it possible to find traces of the general intellectual climate of Hellenism within biblical literature?

The traditions of the ancient Near East are very much in evidence in biblical literature. It would be foolish to say anything else. From the very beginning of the collection of writings in the Old Testament, Near Eastern tradition manifests itself both in single stories and in more complex narratives. If we are to present an image of the authors and collectors of biblical literature we must keep this evidence of ancient Near Eastern culture in mind.

The procedure of analysis can alternatively be compared to an archaeological excavation. In the text of the Old Testament a variety of items dating from different places and times are available. Mesopotamian material is quite evident. Thus the story of the creation in Genesis 2 is definitely embedded within Mesopotamian tradition and the story of the flood in Genesis 6–8 is closely related to the Neo-Babylonian version in the Gilgamesh Epic. Some textual material comes from Egypt, for example, the chapters of Proverbs that are shared by the Egyptian wisdom book of Amenemopet (Prov. 22.17–24.22).[53] More Egyptian or 'Egyptianized' material can be found in stories about Israel in Egypt.[54] Ideas and notions from Syrian and the Levant abound, for example, in the allusions to the battle between God and the sea included in many Old Testament psalms. Biblical authors share many genres of literature with their Near Eastern colleagues, such as the already mentioned law-tradition but also wisdom literature in its many forms.

Although this Near Eastern influence is evident, it is not enough to date its literary context exactly. Just as in archaeology, a literary stratum must be dated according to the youngest item found within and not according to the oldest evidence. Any piece of literature may reflect ideas and concepts that trace their origins way back in the history of

---

culture, and probably with some justification as—apart for some major cities— Hellenization only slowly became a major cultural factor in the remote nooks and crannies of Palestine and Jordan. 'The Early Hellenistic archaeological lacuna and the late Hellenistic expansion and prosperity in the southern Levant can be understood within the context of the attitudes, policies and practices of the Ptolemaic and Seleucid governments': conclusion to Robert H. Smith, 'The Southern Levant in the Hellenistic Period', *Levant* 22 (1990), pp. 123-30 (130).

53. Amenemopet, cf. *ANET*, pp. 421-25.

54. Especially in the Joseph story, cf. Donald B. Redford, *A Study of the Biblical Story of Joseph (Genesis 37-50)* (VTSup, 20; Leiden: E.J. Brill, 1970).

humankind. If the text also includes elements that belong to a more recent period, the context that includes old as well as new material will always be the context of the youngest item *at the earliest.*

This hardly comes as a surprise to students of the Old Testament who have for centuries looked for solutions to the problem, not least by splitting biblical literature into several literary strata—sources or documents. In a recent contribution I argued that it is important whether information is part of the structure of the text or simply added to the text during its transmission.[55] Thus the idea that the content of the patriarchal narratives somehow goes back to an alleged 'patriarchal age' or belongs to an age not too far removed from the patriarchs makes it necessary to consider the information that Abraham came from 'Ur in Chaldaea' anachronistic (Gen. 11.31). Ur could only be considered a 'Chaldaean' city from, say, 800 BCE.[56] This piece of information could have been added to the story about Abraham's migration by a secondary hand. The information that the patriarchs used camels (cf., e.g., Gen. 24) is different although equally anachronistic as the camels had not been domesticated when the patriarchs are supposed to have lived. If the information about the camels in, say, Genesis 24 is secondary, this chapter has been the subject of a far more elaborate rewriting to make it fit the conditions of the first millennium BCE. The camel was domesticated shortly before 1000 BCE.[57] As it now appears in Genesis 24 the camel may not be absolutely essential to the plot (the bringing of Rebecca to Isaac), but it would demand a number of changes to the narrative to substitute with, for example, a donkey.

Such examples say that a single piece of information might not be sufficient evidence to date a text. Even if undisputed 'Hellenistic' material was present in the Bible it will not automatically make the Old Testament a Hellenistic book. We need more than isolated examples,

---

55. Cf. my *Prelude to Israel's Past: Background and Beginnings of Israelite History and Identity* (Peabody, MA: Hendrickson, 1998), pp. 62-63.

56. The Chaldeans do not appear in Mesopotamian sources before the ninth century BCE. The earliest mentioning is by Assurnirari II in 878: ^{KUR}Kaldu. Cf. on this Dietz Otto Edzard, 'Kaldu (Chaldäa)', *RLA*, 5 (Berlin: W. de Gruyter, 1976–80), pp. 291-97.

57. The date was established by R. Walz in his 'Zum Problem des Zeitpunktes der Domestikation der altweltlichen Cameliden', *ZDMG* 101 (1951), pp. 29-51, and *idem*, 'Neue Untersuchungen zum Damestikationsprobblem der altweltlichen Cameliden', *ZDMG* 104 (1954), pp. 45-87. To the best of my knowledge, Walz's date still stands.

items found 'out of context'. We need to find parts of what might belong to the 'mainstream intellectual tradition' of the period in question, not primarily single texts but larger pieces of literature, even genres.

A few isolated points of contact between Old Testament literature and the Hellenistic world will not satisfy us. We might decide to make a systemic comparison and see whether or not an analysis of the literature of the Old Testament will open it up for extended comparison so as to indicate that these texts could be related to an intellectual development that presupposes the blending together of Near Eastern and Greek traditions.

This comparative procedure may lead us in many directions. I do not intend to present an exhaustive catalogue of possibilities. Recently scholars and laypeople alike have been active, not least on the Internet, showing the Old Testament to belong to the Hellenistic Age. I will, however, concentrate on one genre only: the presence of history-writing in the Old Testament and in the Hellenistic world.

This subject has been of interest not least since John Van Seters more than 15 years ago made classical history-writing relevant to biblical studies.[58] His point of contact were the early 'logographers' of the Greek world, writers who in the sixth century BCE began to collect memories and traditions from 'ancient times'. The comparison, however, does not end here. We may question how Near Eastern intellectuals got to know the tradition of the logographers already in the Iron Age. Although contacts between the Aegean Archipelagos and the Levant existed, there are no traces of any influence of the logographers in any Iron Age source known from Syria or Palestine, not to mention Mesopotamia. Van Seters's idea of an early transmission of Greek culture to the Levant is obviously a part of his general appraisal of the exilic period and his dating of the Yahwist source to the sixth century. It is the weak link in his argumentation.

Other scholars have gone further. Recently a series of studies has appeared or are going to be published shortly that argues a dependence between biblical history writing and Herodotus's *Histories* of the middle fifth century BCE. Thus Jan-Wim Wesselius has published a series of articles—partly in Dutch—about Herodotus and the Old Testament,

---

58. John Van Seters, *In Search of History* (New Haven: Yale University Press, 1983).

among them a recent contribution to the *Scandinavian Journal of the Old Testament* where he argues a dependency between the primaeval history in Genesis and Herodotus' work.[59] This comparison is to be expanded in a forthcoming monograph by Wesselius.[60]

Obviously Wesselius like Flemming A. Nielsen in his recent work on Greek history writing and the Deuteronomistic History,[61] concentrates on the striking similarity between Herodotus and Old Testament historical prose narrative. Evidently the focus of attention has moved from the sixth to the fifth century BCE!

Still, the comparison between the Bible and Herodotus's *Histories* seems directed by the same tendency as is evident in Van Seters's already mentioned link to the logographers. Herodotus stands at the beginning of the Greek historiographical tradition and although he borrows from the logographers, the later Greek and Roman traditions probably correctly considered him 'the father of history'. There is no reason why we should limit our investigations only to the relationship between Herodotus and the Bible.

In a forthcoming publication I present a different approach to the study of biblical and Hellenistic history writing.[62] In this study it will be argued that the *History of Rome* by Livy is actually closer to the biblical history than Herodotus's 'investigations'. It is not because biblical literature presupposes the existence of Livy's extensive work dating from the end of the first century BCE but because it presupposes the historiographic tradition within which Livy's history should be situated. Livy's work is part of the Hellenistic tradition of writing history as it developed within the Greek system of education in the third and second centuries BCE.

Flemming A. Nielsen's study on Herodotus and the Deuteronomistic History demonstrates an extensive similarity as far as it involves the general arrangement of the two works. He accordingly makes use of the

59. Jan-Wim Wesselius, 'Discontinuity, Congruence and the Making of the Hebrew Bible', *SJOT* 13 (1999), pp. 24-77, see esp. pp. 38-48.

60. Jan-Wim Wesselius, *The Origin of the History of Israel: Herodotus' Histories as Blueprint for the First Books of the Bible* (Sheffield: Sheffield Academic Press, forthcoming).

61. Flemming A. Nielsen, *The Tragedy in History: Herodotus and the Deuteronomistic History* (JSOTSup, 251; Copenhagen International Seminar, 4; Sheffield: Sheffield Academic Press, 1997).

62. 'Good and Bad in History'.

systemic approach advocated above. It is possible to apply this approach to a wider field that also includes other aspects of biblical narrative, not least philosophy (theology and anthropology). In such a study the Hellenistic quest for the 'good person' might be of interest as the goal of education.

History is therefore a main point of contact between biblical and Hellenistic literature. Although the authors of the history of the Old Testament sometimes employ old literary forms or borrow from, for example, the annalistic tradition of Mesopotamia,[63] the concept of history as a process with a purpose unites Greek and Old Testament historical narrative.

The 'historical' mode of interpreting the fate of humankind, which biblical as well as Greek historiographers employ, is an important part of the mental matrix. Now we can see at least a shadow of our writers. They are sectarians with a definite sectarian view of humankind: few are elected, most will vanish because they have forsaken God's *torah*. How it happened belongs to history and it is the historiographers' duty to explain how and why it happened so that it never happens again. Our sectarians are clearly academically educated persons. They are well acquainted with oriental mythology and traditions as well as the Greek tradition of history-writing. Furthermore, they combine both the Greek and oriental traditions in an organic fashion that shows that they are brought up within an intellectual milieu that is at the same time both Greek and oriental. Such a milieu is hardly likely to have existed before the Hellenistic period and even then probably only in a few major urban centres, especially in Mesopotamia or Egypt.[64]

We therefore assume that the historical literature of the Old Testament belongs to the Hellenistic period. It is not unique. At the same time as the biblical historical literature came into being other similar constructions of the past were published, such as Manetho's history of

63. As is probably the case in 2 Kgs 18.13-16.
64. Syria and Phoenicia are other options but the extent of Hellenization of these parts of the Near East in the third century BCE may not have reached a level that could support such an intellectual climate that is presupposed to have formed the background of biblical history writing as early as the third century BCE. Because Philo of Byblos (see below) belongs to the first or second centuries CE, we can hardly conclude with Van Seters that Philo indicates that the pre-Roman Phoenician society was highly literate (cf. *In Search of History*, p. 208).

Egypt, or Berossus's history of Mesopotamia.[65] Philo of Byblos's *Phoenician History* is much later.[66] Little has been preserved of the works of Manetho and Berossus, but the fact that they appeared more or less at the same time (early second century BCE) in different places illustrates the early impact of Greek literary tradition on the major centres of the Near East.

When we put the evidence together and ask for a place where the amalgamation between oriental and Greek traditions might have taken place, the fact that the historical literature of the Old Testament pre-supposes an amalgamation between Greek and Oriental academic tradi-tions is important. Within the Hellenistic-Roman educational system, history was an integral part of the academic curriculum identified with the dominating discipline of rhetoric. We therefore have to look for a place where oriental and Greek traditions came together in an educa-tional system or academic environment that included both traditions.[67]

Many years ago I joyfully proposed a new theory about the origin of the Pentateuch that should never be published. It has later publicly been referred to as 'Lemche's famous "three pub hypothesis"'. The 'hypoth-esis' claims that the Pentateuch came into being over a very short time in the third century BCE in three different pubs in a Jewish suburb in

65. None of these authors has survived intact. Most of the remains of their work have been found in much later Christian sources. The remains of Manethos's his-tory has been published by W.G. Waddell, *Manetho* (LCL, 350; Cambridge, MA: Harvard University Press, 1940). Berossus's Βαβυλωνιακά was dedicated to Anti-ochus I. For a recent discussion cf. Stanley Mayor Burstein, *The Babyloniaca of Berossus* (Sources for the Ancient Near East, 1.5; Malibu: Undena, 1978).

66. The fragments of Philo's history of Phoenicia have been published by Harold W. Attridge and Robert A. Oden, Jr, *Philo of Byblos: The Phoenician History. Introduction, Critical Text, Translation, Notes* (CBQMS, 9; Washington: Catholic Biblical Association, 1981). This edition has now been supplemented by J. Cors i Meya, *A Concordance of the Phoenician History of Philo of Byblos* (Aula Orientalis Supplementa, 10; Barcelona: Editorial AUSA, 1995). One of Philo's sources may have been Menander from Ephesus whose 'excerpts' from the history of Phoenicia were used by Josephus.

67. All this does not detract from the fact that our authors were also acquainted with Western, i.e. Palestinian, traditions. They certainly were, and this may betray the origin of this group of authors (and theologians). They—or most of them—belonged among the immigrants or (more likely) the descendants of immigrants from Palestine to Babylonia. Whether or not such immigrants were part of a planned deportation as argued by the Old Testament or turned up in this place at a later date—or both—is a moot question.

Babylon. One of these was called 'Y', another 'E' and the third 'P'. It took little more than three months of lively interchange between the three pubs to finish the first four books of Moses. Although no more than a joke, it may nonetheless be closer to reality than we perhaps realize. We should probably not look for the intellectual milieu of our authors in Babylon. In the third century BCE people gradually deserted Babylon and resettled in newly founded Seleuceia, the present Baghdad. The Seleucid Empire was, however, excellently set up to provide the intellectual conditions for an amalgamation between Mesopotamian and Greek traditions that could also have provoked the appearance of Old Testament historical prose literature.

It is probably more than likely that the centre of this intellectual development was Mesopotamia itself. Syria might be considered an alternative (Damascus?). The utopian character of the concept of the 'people of God' and its likewise utopian concept of the land of Israel in the Old Testament speak in favour of an origin of the historical literature in the Old Testament outside of Palestine. If Hellenism came late to Palestine we may have still another argument in favour of a non-Palestinian origin of this literature.

A JIGSAW WITHOUT A MODEL?
THE DATE OF CHRONICLES

Kai Peltonen

Introduction

In modern biblical research, the date accorded to Chronicles is a particularly controversial topic.[1] The *terminus post quem* can naturally be set easily on the basis of the books' content. Since the presentation of Israel's history ends with the rise of the Persian Empire, it is obvious that the books have been composed after 539/538 BCE. References to the existing books of Chronicles have usually been found in Ben Sira, whose 'Praise to the Fathers' probably presupposes the chronistic description of David (cf. 47.8-10), and in the preserved excerpts of the work of the Jewish historian Eupolemus, who appears to have made use of Chronicles in a Greek translation. Since both works date from the first half of the second century BCE (Ben Sira 190–175; Eupolemus approximately 150), one may conclude that the original Hebrew Chronicles had to be ready by the beginning of the second century BCE at the latest.[2] What one can say with any certainty, then, is that Chronicles were written some time after the exile but before the first century BCE.

---

1. For recent summaries of the discussion, see R.W. Klein, 'Chronicles, Book of 1–2', *ABD* 1 (1992) pp. 992-1002 (994-95); P.B. Dirksen, 'Kronieken in de recente literatuur: Een overzicht van recente publikaties betreffende Kronieken', *NedTTs* 47 (1993), pp. 6-20 (13-14); G.H. Jones, *1 and 2 Chronicles* (OTG; Sheffield: JSOT Press, 1993), pp. 92-94; I. Kalimi, 'Die Abfassungszeit der Chronik: Forschungsstand und Perspektiven', *ZAW* 105 (1993), pp. 223-33; J.W. Kleinig, 'Recent Research in Chronicles', *CRBS* 2 (1994), pp. 43-76 (46-47).

2. The possibility of using Ben Sira and Eupolemus as a means of setting a *terminus ante quem* for Chronicles has been recently contested, however; see G. Steins, 'Die Bücher der Chronik', in E. Zenger *et al.*, *Einleitung in das Alte Testament* (Kohlhammer-Studienbücher Theologie, 1.1; Stuttgart: W. Kohlhammer, 3rd edn, 1998), pp. 223-34 (231). According to him, the composition of Chronicles should be set in the early Maccabaean period.

The timespan between the earliest possible and the latest possible date is thus over 300 years. What makes the issue really problematic is that unambiguous evidence for saying something more precise does not exist. The word unambiguous must be underlined here. Scholars have naturally found hints—or what they interpret as hints—in Chronicles of a more precise date, but there is no agreement as to how trustworthy the alleged hints are and how they should be understood. As a result, virtually every imaginable point of time throughout the 300 years has been put forth in recent decades as a possible date of Chronicles. At the one extreme, there are scholars who believe that the message of Chronicles can be properly understood only against the background of the restoration of a Jewish community in Jerusalem immediately after the edict of Cyrus and the return of the first exiles. Chronicles should thus be dated to the closing years of the sixth century BCE. This view, complemented with numerous modifications in detail and redactional hypotheses it necessarily entails about the original shape of Chronicles, has been advanced in recent years by F.M. Cross, J.D. Newsome, D.L. Petersen, S.L. McKenzie, R.L. Braun, R.B. Dillard, M.A. Throntveit, and D.N. Freedman and B.E. Willoughby, for example.[3] The other extreme position is represented by scholars who argue that Chronicles derive from the Hellenistic era, either from the third[4] or even from the second[5] cen-

3. F.M. Cross, 'A Reconstruction of the Judean Restoration', *JBL* 94 (1975), pp. 4-18; J.D. Newsome, 'Toward a New Understanding of the Chronicler and his Purposes', *JBL* 94 (1975), pp. 201-217; D.L. Petersen, *Late Israelite Prophecy: Studies in Deutero-Prophetic Literature and in Chronicles* (SBLMS, 23; Missoula, MT: Scholars Press, 1977), pp. 57-60; S.L. McKenzie, *The Chronicler's Use of the Deuteronomistic History* (HSM, 33; Atlanta: Scholars Press, 1985), pp. 25-26; R.L. Braun, *1 Chronicles* (WBC, 14; Waco, TX: Word Books, 1986), pp. xxviii-xxix; R.B. Dillard, *2 Chronicles* (WBC, 15; Waco, TX: Word Books, 1987), p. xix; M.A. Throntveit, *When Kings Speak: Royal Speech and Royal Prayer in Chronicles* (SBLDS, 93; Atlanta: Scholars Press, 1987), pp. 97-107; D.N. Freedman and B.E. Willoughby, 'I and II Chronicles, Ezra, Nehemiah', in B.W. Anderson (ed.), *The Books of the Bible*, I (New York: Charles Scribner's Sons, 1989), pp. 155-71 (155-59). The 'early Persian period' as the best setting for the Chronicler's emphasis on the temple has recently been suggested by W.M. Schniedewind; see *The Word of God in Transition: From Prophet to Exegete in the Second Temple Period* (JSOTSup, 197; Sheffield: Sheffield Academic Press, 1995), pp. 249-52. For a more comprehensive listing of scholars who have advocated a sixth-century date, see Kalimi, 'Abfassungszeit', p. 227.

4. So most recently M. Noth, *Überlieferungsgeschichtliche Studien: Die sammelnden und bearbeitenden Geschichtswerke im Alten Testament* (Tübingen:

tury BCE.[6] Between the extremes, there are a great number of scholars who have rejected attempts to date Chronicles either to the early Persian era or deep into the Hellenistic period and sought a middle course instead. The view supported by the majority of them is that Chronicles had been composed some time in the fourth century BCE, be it before or shortly after the fall of the Persian Empire to Alexander the Great in 333 BCE.[7] One may recognize behind this mediating position, first, a

Max Niemeyer, 3rd edn, 1967), pp. 150-55; P. Welten, *Geschichte und Geschichtsdarstellung in den Chronikbüchern* (WMANT, 42; Neukirchen-Vluyn: Neukirchener Verlag, 1973), pp. 199-200; *idem*, 'Chronikbücher/Chronist', *NBL* 1 (1991), pp. 369-72 (370); R. Smend, *Die Entstehung des Alten Testaments* (ThW, 1; Stuttgart: W. Kohlhammer, 3rd edn, 1984), p. 228. Kaiser says more vaguely that Chronicles derive with great probability from the Hellenistic era; see O. Kaiser, *Einleitung in das Alte Testament: Eine Einführung in ihre Ergebnisse und Probleme* (Gütersloh: Gütersloher Verlagshaus, 5th edn, 1984), p. 189. The Hellenistic period is also favoured by K. Strübind, *Tradition als Interpretation in der Chronik: König Josaphat als Paradigma chronistischer Hermeneutik und Theologie* (BZAW, 201; Berlin: W. de Gruyter, 1991), pp. 23-25, 200; and A. Ruffing, *Jahwekrieg als Weltmetapher: Studien zu Jahwekriegstexten des chronistischen Sondergutes* (SBB, 24; Stuttgart: Katholisches Bibelwerk, 1992), pp. 301-302.

5.   See, e.g., Steins, 'Bücher', p. 231; *idem, Die Chronik als kanonisches Abschlussphänomen: Studien zur Entstehung und Theologie von 1/2 Chronik* (BBB, 93; Weinheim: Beltz Athenäum, 1995); *idem*, 'Zur Datierung der Chronik: Ein neuer methodischer Ansatz', *ZAW* 109 (1997), pp. 84-92. It is well known that the pioneer of the late dating of Chronicles was the Jewish philosopher B. Spinoza who as early as 1670 suggested that Chronicles may come from the time after the restoration of the Jerusalem temple during the Maccabaean era; see G. Gawlick and F. Niewöhner (eds.), *Benedictus de Spinoza, Opera: lateinisch und deutsch.* I. *Tractatus theologico-politicus* (Darmstadt: Wissenschaftliche Buchgesellschaft, 2nd edn, 1989), p. 345.

6.   For a summary of different views, see Kalimi, 'Abfassungszeit', pp. 227-28.

7.   To mention but a few modern scholars who have advanced a fourth-century date for Chronicles, see H.G.M. Williamson, *1 and 2 Chronicles* (NCB; Grand Rapids: Eerdmans, 1982), pp. 15-17; S.J. De Vries, *1 and 2 Chronicles* (FOTL, 11; Grand Rapids: Eerdmans, 1989), pp. 16-17; I. Gabriel, *Friede über Israel: Eine Untersuchung zur Friedenstheologie in Chronik I 10—II 36* (ÖBS, 10; Klosterneuburg: Österreichisches Katholisches Bibelwerk, 1990), p. 2 n. 3; M. Oeming, *Das wahre Israel: Die 'genealogische Vorhalle' 1 Chronik 1-9* (BWANT, 128; Stuttgart: W. Kohlhammer, 1990), pp. 44-47; Klein, 'Chronicles', p. 995; S. Japhet, *I and II Chronicles: A Commentary* (OTL; London: SCM Press, 1993), pp. 23-28; Jones, *Chronicles*, p. 94; Kalimi, 'Abfassungszeit', pp. 228-33; I. Kalimi, 'Könnte die aramäische Grabinschrift aus Ägypten als Indikation für die Datierung der Chronikbücher fungieren?', *ZAW* 110 (1998), pp. 79-81; J.W. Kleinig, *The Lord's*

willingness to avoid certain methodological, especially literary-critical, procedures necessitated by the early Persian date of Chronicles and, secondly, a serious appraisal of the observation that there are no obvious signs of Hellenistic influence in Chronicles (cf. below).

The spectrum of radically differing opinions about the date of Chronicles is not the only remarkable element of the scholarly discussion. Even more remarkable is the fact that there is so much disagreement among scholars about the historical context into which Chronicles best fit. It is not just a matter of academic curiosity to ask whether a date in the fifth, fourth, third or even second centuries BCE should be assigned to Chronicles. During those centuries, the Jewish community in Palestine witnessed and experienced significant political, economic, religious and cultural upheavals, and one would naturally expect to find at least occasional traces of them in a work that allegedly comes down to us from that era. It is still an open question, however, which of the tumults of the second half of the first millennium BCE are reflected in the theological/ideological disposition of the author(s) of Chronicles—or, conversely, whether any of them is present there.

Issues Affecting the Dating of Chronicles

Every attempt to date Chronicles more precisely in the general framework sketched above is dependent on several factors and their interplay. The issues affecting the dating of Chronicles can be roughly divided into two groups: internal and external evidence.

Internal Evidence
Internal evidence refers here first of all to occasional pieces of information in Chronicles that allegedly have a bearing on the books' date. Additionally, the questions concerning the literary composition and redaction of Chronicles, the historical development of Israelite cult as

Song: The Basis, Function and Significance of Choral Music in Chronicles (JSOTSup, 156; Sheffield: JSOT Press, 1993), p. 22; W. Riley, *King and Cultus in Chronicles: Worship and the Reinterpretation of History* (JSOTSup, 160; Sheffield: JSOT Press, 1993), pp. 24-26; M.J. Selman, *1 Chronicles: An Introduction and Commentary* (TOTC; Leicester: Inter-Varsity Press, 1994), pp. 69-71; B.E. Kelly, *Retribution and Eschatology in Chronicles* (JSOTSup, 211; Sheffield: Sheffield Academic Press, 1996), pp. 26-28; J.E. Dyck, *The Theocratic Ideology of the Chronicler* (Biblical Interpretation Series, 33; Leiden: E.J. Brill, 1998), p. 33.

described in the books, and the language of Chronicles must be briefly mentioned here. In what follows, the relevant issues will be more or less just listed, since one can find a more thorough discussion of them in every standard commentary on Chronicles.

The passages usually regarded as having some relevance to the dating of Chronicles are 1 Chron. 3.17-24; 29.7; 2 Chron. 8.3-4; 16.9; 26.15.[8] The first one contains perhaps the most important single indication of a possible *terminus a quo* for the composition of Chronicles. It lists the genealogy of the sons of King Jehoiachin, who was exiled in 597 BCE. The text is unclear at a number of points, and as yet there is no consensus over its proper reading. The Massoretic Text (MT) appears to extend for six generations after Zerubbabel, while LXX counts still five generations more. There has been a lot of debate as to whether and to what extent the MT should be regarded as corrupt or whether and to what extent LXX represents a secondary clarification of the difficult MT. To find a system of counting the generations is not the only problem that encounters the scholar here, however. The scholar must also decide the point of time from which to start counting the generations after Zerubbabel and how many years one should assume per generation. Depending on how these questions are answered, one reaches either the latter part of the fifth or the first third of the fourth century BCE for a *terminus a quo* if the MT is preferred. If the LXX text is followed, the *terminus a quo* must be moved at least 100 years later.[9]

1 Chronicles 29.7 is generally understood to refer to darics, a Persian coin that was first minted during the reign of Darius I (522–486 BCE). Since a certain lapse of time would be necessary for the Chronicler and his audience to tolerate the anachronism of the use of darics during David's regime, his work cannot have been written as early as the sixth or early fifth century BCE. A similar sort of anachronism is possibly contained in 2 Chron. 8.3-4. The association of Tadmor and Hamath-

---

8.   The materials of the books of Ezra and Nehemiah are not discussed here, since it is a commonly held scholarly opinion nowadays—and a correct one, in my view—that Chronicles and Ezra–Nehemiah are independent works by different authors.

9.   It has been suggested that Anani, who is mentioned in an Elephantine text from the fourteenth year of Darius II Ochus (424–404 BCE), should be identified with the person of the same name in 1 Chron. 3.24. If correct, such an identification would support the view that Chronicles should be dated to c. 400 BCE; see Kalimi, 'Abfassungszeit', p. 231.

zobah has been regarded as reflecting the Persian system of provincial administration. If the association goes back to the Chronicler himself, it provides an indication of the Persian period as the time when the Chronicler was composing his work. 2 Chronicles 16.9 appears to contain a citation of Zech. 4.10. Since Zechariah was active during the last quarter of the sixth century, Chronicles must have been composed late enough for his prophecy to have acquired an authoritative status comparable to that of the pre-exilic prophets which the citation in Chronicles indicates.

These passages provide clues for setting the earliest possible date for Chronicles. To make more precise conclusions from them is problematic, however, since they allow no concrete possibilities for a scholar to say, for example, how long darics must have been in use or the text of Zechariah ready before they could be used in the way they now are in Chronicles. The most common conclusion from the evidence of the passages just mentioned is that a date in the late fifth or early fourth century for Chronicles would appear as the most probable one. To these considerations must be added the fact that there are two passages in Chronicles which are apparently borrowed from Ezra–Nehemiah, namely the list of the inhabitants of Jerusalem in 1 Chron. 9.2-17 (cf. Neh. 11.3-19) and the edict of Cyrus in 2 Chron. 36.22-23 (cf. Ezra 1.1-3a). It is a matter of controversy whether these passages belong to the original Chronicles (see below), but if they do, it would set the composition of Chronicles later than that of Ezra–Nehemiah.

The war machines mentioned in 2 Chron. 26.15 have been suggested by P. Welten to refer to catapults, the use of which as defensive weapons would probably not have been known in Judah until the third century BCE. Welten is also of the opinion that the chronistic information concerning building projects, military arrangements and wars of the Judaean kings is in harmony with what the author saw in his own day. Basically, the late Persian period could be regarded as providing a satisfactory background for such data, but the reference to catapults, together with the Chronicler's representation of the structure of the Judaean army—which in Welten's view follows the Greek model— necessitate a Hellenistic date.[10] Welten's views have not received

10. See Welten, *Geschichte*, especially pp. 98-114. Welten's view has recently found support in an article by Bianchi and Rossoni that deals with the description of the army of Uzziah in 2 Chron. 26.11-15. According to them, philological and archaeological examinations of this passage indicate that it is the Chronicler's own

unanimous approval, however, and the Hellenistic date of Chronicles on the basis of such uncertain and ambiguous evidence has been regarded as highly problematic.[11]

The matter is further complicated by the fact that there is no agreement among scholars as to whether or not the above-mentioned passages of 1 Chronicles, in particular, have been part of the Chronicler's original composition. The literary-critical aspect naturally exerts a significant influence on how their relevance to the issue of Chronicles' date can be assessed. In the course of the history of research, large-scale redactional hypotheses about the literary composition of Chronicles,[12] as well as suppositions that a number of secondary additions and adaptations has been introduced to the original text of the Chronicler without their constituting coherent layers,[13] have been brought forward as explanations of the various literary phenomena in Chronicles. The secondary material is found mainly in the lists of 1 Chronicles (all or portions of chs. 1–9; 12; 15–16; 23–27); the closing verses of 2 Chronicles (36.22-23) have occasionally been regarded as secondary additions

composition and not based on an eighth-century source. The structure of the army, its weapons and the Hebrew word referring to catapults suggest that the passage should be dated between the end of the fourth and the beginning of the third century BCE; see F. Bianchi and G. Rossoni, 'L'armée d'Ozias (2 *Ch* 26, 11-15) entre fiction et réalité: Une esquisse philologique et historique', *Transeuphratène* 13 (1997), pp. 21-37.

11. See, e.g., Klein, 'Chronicles', p. 995; Jones, *Chronicles*, pp. 92-93; H.G.M. Williamson, *Israel in the Books of Chronicles* (Cambridge: Cambridge University Press, 1977), pp. 85-86; *idem, Chronicles*, pp. 337-38.

12. Of the older theories, the best known are probably those presented by J.W. Rothstein and J. Hänel, A.C. Welch, and K. Galling; see J.W. Rothstein and J. Hänel, *Kommentar zum ersten Buch der Chronik* (KAT, 18.2; Leipzig: D. Werner Scholl, 1927); A.C. Welch, *The Work of the Chronicler: Its Purpose and its Date* (The Schweich Lectures of the British Academy 1938; London: Oxford University Press, 1939); K. Galling, *Die Bücher der Chronik, Esra, Nehemia* (ATD, 12; Göttingen: Vandenhoeck & Ruprecht, 1954). More recently, F.M. Cross's theory of the composition of the Chronicler's history in Chronicles, Ezra and Nehemiah in three stages has found considerable support; see Cross, 'Reconstruction', pp. 11-14. Cf. also the recent theory of the composition of Chronicles by G. Steins. According to him, the formation of Chronicles took place in a relatively short literary-scribal process in which the basic text was augmented and supplemented with materials of varying thematical orientations; see Steins, *Chronik, passim*.

13. See, in particular, Noth, *Studien*, pp. 110-55; W. Rudolph, *Chronikbücher* (HAT, 21; Tübingen: J.C.B. Mohr [Paul Siebeck], 1955).

by a later hand, too. Modern scholarship tends to be quite critical towards different redactional hypotheses, however. It emphasizes the literary unity and integrity of Chronicles, and, concerning the sections mentioned above, regards them as part of the Chronicler's original composition either in their entirety or at least for the most part,[14] though it must be stressed that there is no such thing as scholarly consensus about these matters.[15] Regarding the date of Chronicles, a lot depends on what kind of attitude an individual scholar adopts towards the literary-critical issues. If the list materials are regarded as secondary additions, then nothing stops the scholar from supporting a considerably earlier dating (e.g. the late sixth century) than would be appropriate on the basis of a contrary view. The possible existence of later additions precisely where the most important single indications of the date of Chronicles are to be found makes sweeping claims from the internal evidence shaky and inconclusive.

Thus, there are some hints in Chronicles as to when the books were composed, but they are vague and allow different interpretations. Unfortunately, that is all the scholars have got by way of internal evidence. As S. Japhet has recently put it, the 'date and provenance of Chronicles must...be determined mostly on the basis of general considerations, with no support from reference to precise historical events'.[16] As general considerations of internal nature, one may refer to the content and language of Chronicles.

It is pertinent to say that linguistic observations support a postexilic date for Chronicles.[17] The language of Chronicles clearly represents late biblical Hebrew,[18] with features common to the late corpus of biblical (Ezra–Nehemiah, Daniel, Esther) and extra-biblical (Dead Sea Scrolls, Samaritan Pentateuch) works. Within this general phase of the development of Hebrew language, Chronicles displays a number of unique linguistic and stylistic features. On the basis of present knowledge, however, it is not possible to make clear distinctions between the general linguistic usage of late biblical Hebrew, on the one hand, and the characteristics of the Chronicler, on the other, for the purpose of setting a

14. See, in particular, Japhet, *Chronicles, passim.*

15. See Jones, *Chronicles,* pp. 82-84.

16. Japhet, *Chronicles,* p. 25.

17. Kalimi, 'Abfassungszeit', p. 223.

18. Cf. R. Polzin, *Late Biblical Hebrew: Toward an Historical Typology of Biblical Hebrew Prose* (HSM, 12; Missoula, MT: Scholars Press, 1976).

precise chronological framework for the composition of Chronicles.[19]

An undeniable fact is that the portrayal given in Chronicles of the development of the pre-exilic cultic institutions and the organization of the temple personnel is anachronistic and reflects either the circumstances or the dreams of the postexilic Jewish community. Such a conclusion is justified by the observation that the chronistic picture of the cultic administration with its meticulous system of 24 divisions of all clerical classes clearly represents a more advanced stage than the one found in Ezra–Nehemiah. To quote Japhet again, in 'the absence of comparative material it is difficult to draw precise chronological conclusions from this general portrayal of the cult organization, but since a prolonged and complex process is involved, a late provenance, certainly later than the one assumed by Ezra–Nehemiah, must be presupposed' for Chronicles.[20] Even though Japhet's view is undoubtedly correct, the utilization of this factor for setting a date for Chronicles is complicated by the fact that the late development of cultic organization is to be found in 1 Chron. 23-26, that is, precisely in the chapters that several scholars have regarded as later additions to the Chronicler's work. If we follow Japhet and accept these chapters as an authentic part of the Chronicler's view of the temple service, we get an important clue about the *terminus a quo* for the composition of Chronicles. If we disagree with Japhet and accept the literary-critical excision of these materials, as a number of scholars have done, an analysis of the development of cultic organization in postexilic Israel only yields a *terminus a quo* for the additions made to Chronicles, not for Chronicles themselves.

The net result gained from an assessment of the internal evidence in Chronicles of the books' date is meagre indeed: the work undoubtedly derives from the postexilic era, but this triviality is the end of unambiguous evidence. Several indicators appear to point towards the late Persian period as the most probable chronological setting of Chronicles, but every suggestion in this direction can be quite easily shot down with a literary-critical theory—or with a catapult.

External Evidence
There are several issues that can be dealt with under the rubric *external evidence*. They are naturally more or less closely intertwined with each other.

19. See Japhet, *Chronicles*, pp. 25, 41-43.
20. Japhet, *Chronicles*, p. 27.

The first aspect of external evidence concerns the question of who wrote Chronicles. There is no clear hint of the author's person in the books themselves, and contemporary biblical and extrabiblical sources throw no further light on this issue. The rabbinical tradition, which tried to get rid of the anonymity typical of biblical writings by ascribing them to well-known biblical figures, knows more about the author of Chronicles, however. According to *b. B. Bat.* 15a, Ezra wrote his book and the genealogies of Chronicles up to his own time. Regardless of the uncritical nature of rabbinical traditions, the view that the author of Chronicles had been Ezra the Scribe has received some support in the history of Chronicles research.[21] It has found especial favour among scholars who have wanted to regard Chronicles as highly as possible as a source for historical reconstruction. By far the best known among the twentieth-century scholars who have advanced the view of Ezra as the author of Chronicles is the American exegete, historian and archaeologist W.F. Albright.[22] If Ezra or some other person whose activity can be dated at least with reasonable certainty[23] is identified with the author of Chronicles, the problem of the date is of course settled automatically. It must be emphasized, however, that the idea of Ezra being the Chronicler is a minority view with no noteworthy support in modern scholarship. Characteristic of the mainline research today is to admit that the author of Chronicles remains unknown and, consequently, one must not draw exact conclusions about the date of Chronicles from a speculation of the author's personality.

An issue that is closely connected with the previous one concerns the existence or non-existence of the Chronistic History Work (henceforth CHW). Since the theory of Chronicles and the book(s) of Ezra (–Nehemiah) constituting a literary entity composed by one and the same author was put forth almost simultaneously by L. Zunz and F.C. Movers

21. Kalimi, 'Abfassungszeit', p. 224.

22. See W.F. Albright, 'The Date and Personality of the Chronicler', *JBL* 40 (1921), pp. 104-24 (119-21); *idem*, 'The Judicial Reform of Jehoshaphat', in S. Lieberman (ed.), *Alexander Marx Jubilee Volume on the Occasion of his Seventieth Birthday: English Section* (New York: Jewish Theological Seminary of America, 1950), pp. 61-82 (69-74).

23. The nature, aims and precise date of Ezra's mission as well as its relation to that of Nehemiah is at least as controversial an issue in biblical research as that concerning the date of Chronicles, however. Depending on whether the seventh year of Artaxerxes (Ezra 7.7-9) is seen to refer to Artaxerxes I or Artaxerxes II, the year of Ezra's arrival to Jerusalem should be set either in 458 or in 398 BCE.

in the 1830s,[24] it became widely accepted, even to such an extent that, as late as the middle of the twentieth century, it was regarded as a truism, a fact that needed no further substantiation. The supporting pillars of the hypothesis were the alleged similarities of style, language, interests and historiographical approach between Chronicles and Ezra–Nehemiah. The common author was either Ezra or an anonymous Chronicler—the latter view became generally accepted when the critical research progressed—who wrote the history of his people up to the great figures and events of either his own day or the immediate past.

In the last few decades, however, the CHW hypothesis has come under increasing criticism. Although it still receives some support, the burden of proof has shifted from the opponents of the hypothesis to its supporters. Most scholars nowadays accept as their starting-point the conviction that to make historical, theological and other conclusions about Chronicles on the basis of materials in Ezra–Nehemiah is methodologically unsound. The comparison of linguistic, historical, historiographical and theological factors (e.g. concept of retribution, attitude towards the North, roles assigned to the Davidic monarchy and Exodus traditions, prophetic influence) between Chronicles and Ezra–Nehemiah is today seen to lend considerably more support to the diversity of authorship rather than to the traditional CHW hypothesis.[25]

The CHW hypothesis is closely connected with the question of the date of Chronicles in that if it is accepted, straightforward conclusions concerning the date of Chronicles can be made on the basis of the entire Chronicles–Ezra–Nehemiah corpus. If the hypothesis is rejected, such conclusions are naturally out of order. A stand in favour of or against the CHW hypothesis exerts thus a decisive influence on how much material one has at his or her disposal for the analysis of Chronicles' date. A supporter of the hypothesis can argue that Chronicles cannot

---

24. L. Zunz, *Die gottesdienstlichen Vorträge der Juden, historisch entwickelt: Ein Beitrag zur Alterthumskunde und biblischen Kritik, zur Literatur- und Religionsgeschichte* (Berlin: A. Asher, 1832), p. 21; F.C. Movers, *Kritische Untersuchungen über die biblische Chronik: Ein Beitrag zur Einleitung in das alte Testament* (Bonn: T. Habicht, 1834), p. 14.

25. See, in particular, Williamson, *Israel*, pp. 5-70; *idem*, *Chronicles*, pp. 5-11; S. Japhet, 'The Supposed Common Authorship of Chronicles and Ezra-Nehemia Investigated Anew', *VT* 18 (1968), pp. 330-71; *idem*, 'The Relationship between Chronicles and Ezra-Nehemiah', in J.A. Emerton (ed.), *Congress Volume: Leuven 1989* (VTSup, 43; Leiden: E.J. Brill, 1991), pp. 298-313; *idem*, *Chronicles*, pp. 3-5.

have been written before the missions of Ezra (arriving in Jerusalem 398 BCE at the latest) and Nehemiah (445–433 BCE), in which case the early Persian dating advocated by some scholars drops out at once. An opponent of the hypothesis is in a much worse position in that a different attitude towards the hypothesis necessarily leads to a substantial loss of the kind of source material that would give the much sought-after exact data for setting a date to Chronicles.

The third aspect of the external evidence for dating Chronicles has to do with the books' relationship to the biblical source material used in their composition. The influence on Chronicles of Ezra–Nehemiah (in the case that the relevant passages in Chronicles are considered genuine) and Zechariah has already been mentioned. It is generally accepted that the chronistic theology presupposes the Pentateuch as a whole, which means that the completion of the Pentateuch also signifies the *terminus a quo* for Chronicles. These observations indicate that the fourth century BCE would be the most probable time for the composition of Chronicles, but they do not enable us to say whether the books belong to the Persian or to the Hellenistic era. It is obvious, further, that the Chronicler had utilized the Deuteronomistic History as his source basically in the form we now know it. It is conspicuous, however, how freely and without restraint the Chronicler deviates from this source even on several important points. This gives us reason to suppose that even though the Deuteronomistic History had already attained an established form, it nevertheless did not enjoy such canonical status and respect that its content and information could no longer be touched upon. The composition of Chronicles should thus be set between the completion of the Deuteronomistic History and its final canonization, whatever this could mean in terms of a definite date. It is of especial importance here to try to clarify why and in what situation the content and message of the Deuteronomistic History had lost its relevance to the extent that a 'revised edition' like the chronistic one was needed. The relationship of Chronicles to their biblical sources thus brings forward more pointedly than the previous aspects of external evidence the problem that concerns the matrix and circles in which the chronistic theology and message were considered indispensable.

Another aspect that influences the dating of Chronicles is the historical value accorded to the books. The manner with which the historical reliability of Chronicles has been assessed by scholars has for a couple of hundred years divided them into different sorts of conservatives and radicals, although today historicity is no longer the number one issue in scholarly discussion.[26] The connection between the dating and reliability of Chronicles is obvious: the closer Chronicles are set to the events described in them, the more trustworthy they are as a presentation of history—and vice versa, of course. What we have here is an indirect—and also perilously close to circular—argumentation that is clearly more theologically/ideologically than historically motivated; for example, it is obvious that a work composed soon after the events it purports to describe can be as tendentious as a substantially later work dealing with the same events, since it is the author's purpose that determines the treatment of source materials. The methodological hazards of an argumentation that directly connects Chronicles' date and historical value are nowadays truly recognized, and it is therefore only rarely that one comes across such interpretations in serious discussion about the age of Chronicles.[27]

As out of date as the question of Chronicles' historical value may seem to be from the standpoint of modern scholarship, it nevertheless raises a question that is important to the dating of Chronicles. If the books of Chronicles are thought to describe the pre-exilic history in a reliable way, one has to surmise that the Deuteronomistic historiography is historically less reliable when it is at variance with the chronistic version. It follows from this that one has to ask, first, for what purpose the Deuteronomistic History, revealed as unreliable already in the biblical period, was composed, and, secondly, in what phase of Israel's postexilic history a need arose to replace it with an entirely new

26. The history of research on Chronicles from the standpoint of the books' historical reliability has been surveyed by me in a work entitled *History Debated: The Historical Reliability of Chronicles in Pre-Critical and Critical Research* (Publications of the Finnish Exegetical Society, 64; Helsinki: The Finnish Exegetical Society; Göttingen: Vandenhoeck & Ruprecht, 1996).

27. In a way, however, such an approach still lives on in Chronicles research. A position that holds to the historical trustworthiness of Chronicles can abandon defending their early date and still maintain the books' historical value by holding to their early dating in an indirect, speculative way. This can be done by supposing that the compiler of Chronicles had had old and trustworthy non-biblical sources at his disposal. See K. Peltonen, 'Function, Explanation and Literary Phenomena: Aspects of Source Criticism as Theory and Method in the History of Chronicles Research', in M.P. Graham and S.L. McKenzie (eds.), *The Chronicler as Author: Studies in Text and Texture* (JSOTSup, 263; Sheffield: Sheffield Academic Press, 1999), pp. 18-69.

historical work. In other words, the latter inference leads one to search for a historical context in which, to use modern terminology, a historical interest striving for objectivity had become acute enough to produce a corrective such as Chronicles to earlier historiography. To ascribe such a modern Western historical interest to the author of Chronicles creates a very anachronistic impression. Furthermore, an interest like that is quite obviously destitute of a real historical setting during the biblical era. If it is argued that Chronicles picture the pre-exilic history from an ideological-theological point of view of the postexilic Jewish community or of a section of it, scholars do not have to speculate about the historicity of the Deuteronomistic historiography. Then they are faced precisely by the above-mentioned fundamental questions about the message of Chronicles and the matrix in which it would have had a socio-ideological order. Seen in this light, the question of Chronicles' reliability opens up the need for reconstructing the historical milieu in which a work like Chronicles would have had a meaningful *Sitz im Leben* and served a tangible purpose.

One more aspect exerting an influence on the dating of Chronicles is the existence/non-existence in the books of traces of the cultures that dominated the Near Eastern region in the second half of the first millennium BCE. The absence of Greek words in Chronicles and the lack of Hellenistic influence on its ideology is commonly recognized among scholars. This phenomenon, as all the previous ones, is open to different interpretations. It may be an indicator of the fact that the Chronicler knew nothing about Hellenism, for which reason his work must be set into the Persian era or to the beginning of the Hellenistic one, at the latest, when the Hellenistic cultural imperialism with its considerable impact on Jewish religion and literature from the third century BCE onwards had not had time to start exerting its influence. An alternative interpretation that is as possible as this is that precisely because of the pressures of the Hellenistic culture the Chronicler consciously avoided all Hellenistic expressions and views.[28] One has to admit in the same breath, however, that if Chronicles are dated to the Persian era due to the lack of visible Hellenistic influence on them, there arises the problem that the degree of Persian impact on Chronicles is very meagre, too. The Persian administrative system is not reflected in Chronicles

---

28. A reference to a catapult in 2 Chron. 26.15, if that is really what the Chronicler had in mind, could then be regarded as an unintentional slip—or, alternatively, it is not a Greek war machine that is meant here.

(2 Chron. 8.3-4 is a possible exception; see above), and there are very few clearly Persian words in the entire work. The absence of Persian influence can be interpreted in the same way as in the case of Hellenism. Either we have to do here with a deliberate phenomenon, an implicit polemic against the Persian power in a work composed under its dominion, or simply with the fact that for the Chronicler the Persian era was dead and gone. In the latter case, there was no need for him to reflect upon the events of that period, and, as to vocabulary, he was almost a complete success in avoiding Persian anachronisms.[29] Again, a different interpretation of evidence, here that of a cultural influence of some kind on Chronicles and the reasons behind it, enables scholars to suggest quite different dates for the Chronicler's work.

The net result from the external evidence concerning the date of Chronicles is basically as meagre as it was in the case of internal evidence. The relationship of Chronicles to their biblical sources appears to suggest a late date in the postexilic era rather than an early one, but definite conclusions about either a Greek or a Persian setting for Chronicles are not possible. The entire issue of the date of Chronicles allows so many different interpretations of their basic elements that tenable arguments can be made for widely diverging views.

Socio-Ideological Context and the Dating of Chronicles: Two Recent Approaches

Every bit of internal and external evidence of the date of Chronicles is like a piece in a big and complex jigsaw. Someone trying to make sense out of it has to fit the pieces together without having a model, a picture of what the result should look like. A number of finished jigsaws have been presented in the course of research, some of them looking quite alike while in some cases one wonders whether the same pieces have really been used. It is not my aim here to bring forward yet another combination of the pieces—a task that would really stretch one's imagination—for the purpose of defending a date in the Persian or Greek or Maccabaean or whatever period. I am of the opinion that an attempt to find out why and for whom a work like Chronicles would have been written and in what social and ideological context it would have got a favourable reception and have had a positive—from the author's view-

---

29. See Japhet, *Chronicles*, pp. 25-26.

point, of course—influence on the existing conditions (for that is surely
what the author had in mind) is much more important to the understanding of Chronicles than to propose another more or less possible or
probable date for the work.

The quest for the social and ideological relevance of Chronicles has
by no means been a self-evident enterprise in Chronicles research.
Scholarly work was long dominated by strictly historical presuppositions. Furthermore, the great number of variables included in every
attempt to date Chronicles have made scholars cautious and even sceptical of all undertakings to explain the books' content and purpose
on the basis of some supposed historical setting. Recent years have
witnessed a certain change in this respect, however, with scholars
beginning to pay more attention to the theology of Chronicles and its
presuppositions. Consequently, various proposals have been made concerning the religious and social milieu out of which the peculiar chronistic world of thought grew. Well known is M. Noth's view of Chronicles as a polemic against the schismatic Samaritan cult that was set up
around the end of the Persian empire. F.M. Cross, as well as a number
of other advocates of the early date of the original version of Chronicles, regarded the first edition of the Chronicler's work as structured
around the figure of David and his dynasty. According to Cross, the
original Chronicler's work, written between the founding of the temple and its completion (520–515 BCE) and breathing monarchist fire,
reviewed and reshaped Israel's historical traditions to support the programme for the building of the temple and the restoration of the kingdom under the Davidide Zerubbabel. The second edition (about 450)
combined the Ezra-narrative with the older work. It contained a strong
hierocratic disposition, whereas the messianic themes of the earlier
edition had vanished. Towards 400 BCE, a final editor combined the
Nehemiah Memoir with the Chronicler's work, prefixed it with genealogies (1 Chron. 1–9), and edited the whole.[30] P. Welten saw in Chronicles a work of considerable actuality for the situation of the cult community of Jerusalem in the political and military conflicts of the third
century BCE Palestine. Surrounded by overpowering opponents, the
community felt itself permanently threatened from all over. In such a
trying situation, Chronicles wanted to teach that hope and salvation
were to be found in obedience to Yahweh and his will alone.[31] In a

30. Cross, 'Reconstruction', pp. 4-18.
31. Welten, *Geschichte*, pp. 195-206. Cf. also Ruffing, *Jahwekrieg*, pp. 361-62.

somewhat similar vein, J. Kegler has argued recently that the theology of Chronicles represents an attempt to define and defend the proper Jewish identity during a period of intensive pressure on the part of foreign cults. Such a religious crisis had been occasioned by the developing Hellenism.[32] According to the recent suggestion of G. Steins, the restorative efforts of the early Maccabaean period provide a plausible ideological setting for both Chronicles and the closing of the third part of the Hebrew canon. The purpose of Chronicles was to close the canon of the Hebrew Bible and thus create a strong basis for a reform of Jewish faith after the profound religious and cultural crisis occasioned by the pressure of Hellenism.[33] It can be said, therefore, that the Chronicler had been 'the first theologian of the canon'.[34] The Chronicler has often been seen as coming from the (possibly Levitical) circles of the temple of Jerusalem. It has been claimed that he was a narrow-minded, law-crazed propagator of the interests of his own party. He wrote history not as it really was but as as it should have been in order to support the attempts to improve the status of his own circles in the postexilic Jewish community.[35] It has been suggested, further, that the Chronicler was a learned scribe who composed his work for other scribes. His history is a learned exposition of Jewish faith for those who were familiar with these issues and who could comprehend his intentions.[36]

The list of examples could naturally be lengthened, but even this sample of scholarly opinions is enough to demonstrate how differently the historical background and social milieu of Chronicles have been outlined. The reason for such a variety of opinions is the amount of the jigsaw pieces and their openness to different interpretations. In what follows, it is my intention to draw closer attention to two recent attempts at sketching the historical and ideological context in which the chronistic enterprise on the history of Israel allegedly becomes under-

32. J. Kegler, 'Prophetengestalten im Deuteronomistischen Geschichtswerk und in den Chronikbüchern: Ein Beitrag zur Kompositions- und Redaktionsgeschichte der Chronikbücher', *ZAW* 105 (1993), pp. 481-97.

33. Steins, 'Bücher', p. 172.

34. Steins, 'Datierung', pp. 90-92. He follows here the earlier remark of P.R. Ackroyd, *The Chronicler in his Age* (JSOTSup, 101; Sheffield: JSOT Press, 1991), p. 284.

35. The classic formulation of this view was presented by J. Wellhausen in his *Prolegomena zur Geschichte Israels* (Berlin: W. de Gruyter, 6th edn, 1927), pp. 165-223.

36. See, in particular, Oeming, *Israel*, p. 206.

standable. A comparison of them is helpful in several respects. First, it brings to light the eclectic nature of the chronistic theology: it can be accommodated quite smoothly to diverse historical and ideological contexts. Secondly, it illustrates the importance of seriously asking about the social matrix of Chronicles and their basic function therein. Thirdly, and as a consequence of the foregoing points, the comparison illuminates—if it still needs it—the methodological problems involved in utilizing Chronicles for a historical reconstruction of a certain era. Finally, the comparison calls forth some guidelines along which, in my opinion, the question of Chronicles' date should be assessed in the future.

Joel P. Weinberg

In the last few decades, the Latvian scholar J.P. Weinberg has actively propagated a theory of the existence of what he calls a 'citizen-temple community' as the sociopolitical structure that provided the matrix for the composition of Chronicles. His point of departure is the conviction that the spread and establishment of Hellenism in the Near East required certain preconditions. The set of political, social and economic factors paving the way for Hellenism proper is called by Weinberg 'pre-Hellenism'. According to him, pre-Hellenism in the Near East is a period of two centuries of historical development when a number of crucial social and ideological preconditions for Hellenism proper took shape. These are: a remarkable increase of production and a relative individualization and democratization of the links of socio-economic development; an expansion of the commodity-money economy; an intensive process of urbanization; a political unification in the realms of centralizing empires; emergence and expansion of self-governing local powers (one of which was the citizen-temple community in places such as Mesopotamia, Syria, Asia Minor and Armenia); intensive and wide-ranging inner Near Eastern migration embracing large masses of people and stimulating an interaction and rapprochement of different cultures; interaction of and opposition to universalistic openness and particularistic closedness; a sceptical attitude towards tradition and predisposition to innovations; and a cultivation and autonomization of human individuality together with a dissemination of agnatic and/or territorial units. Under these circumstances from the sixth to the fourth centuries BCE, an active economic development and administrative expansion of local communities took place in the areas conquered by the Achaemenids. This process was accompanied by the local communities' separation from the mechanisms with which the central royal administration exercised its domination. Weinberg argues that the separation from the royal sector was carried out by a unification of the local communities with the temple. The merger of temple personnel, who had formerly constituted the exclusive intelligentsia of a certain settlement, with free, property-owning and economically productive citizens of a local city community produced an essentially new type of sociopolitical structure: the citizen-temple community, which came into its own during the centuries of Achaemenid rule in the Near East and persisted even beyond the Seleucid period. An autonomous and privileged social entity, the citizen-temple community afforded its members the means for organizational unity and collective self-management, and provided for internal political, social and economic welfare.[37]

As an important example of the citizen-temple community of the *Achsenzeit*, though one with its own peculiar features, Weinberg refers to the postexilic community in Jerusalem. Its origin and special nature were determined by the national catastrophe of 587/586 BCE, the exile, and the events that followed. They resulted in fundamental changes in the structure of Jewish society. In Judaea, a simplification and unification of the social structure of the Jewish population took place under the influence of the agrarian-social arrangements implemented by the conquerors. At the same time, local territorial communities were reinforced as substitutes for the destroyed agnatic institutions. Among the exiles, new agnatic communities emerged as the means to preserve the Jewish national identity. The postexilic citizen-temple community in Jerusalem emerged as a social organization based on these preconditions. During its formative period between 539 and 458/457 BCE,[38] the community had a bipartite structure. On the one hand, there were the returnees from Mesopotamia, who had voluntarily accepted the opportunity granted by

---

37. Weinberg has presented his concept of the citizen-temple community mainly in a series of articles. Several of them are presently available in English in a volume entitled *The Citizen-Temple Community* (trans. D.L. Smith-Christopher; JSOTSup, 151; Sheffield: JSOT Press, 1992). For Weinberg's discussion of pre-Hellenism in the Near East, see, in particular, *Community*, pp. 17-33.

38. The latter year introduced some important changes in the sociopolitical status of the postexilic community, according to Weinberg. The edict of Artaxerxes I (Ezra 7.11-26) granted the community members tax exemption, their own jurisdiction and other privileges. All this signified a step towards an official establishment of the postexilic community as a recognized sociopolitical unit with its own self-administration. See Weinberg, *Community*, p. 136.

the edict of Cyrus to go back to the land of their fathers. On the other hand, there were the 'collectives named by toponyms' that consisted of the inhabitants, laypeople as well as priests, of northern Judaea organized in local territorial units. These people, who had never been in the exile, entered the emerging community and were enlisted in the catalogue of its members.[39] These basic groups had different attitudes and apprehensions about many vital aspects of the community (in particular, different plans about the basic elements of its restoration, reflecting either an orientation of continuity or discontinuity with the past), the contradiction and coexistence of which was a characterizing factor of the community's mentality.[40] The postexilic community was essentially a consciously and voluntarily formed association of free and fully enfranchised people. As such, it represented a uniform and homogeneous social formation. The primary form of social organization in the citizen-temple community was constituted by a *bet 'abot*, an agnatic association. It included not only laypeople but priests and Levites as well. The postexilic *bet 'abot* was a result of a conscious convergence of the earlier agnatic units that had been dissolved during the exile and in early postexilic times.[41] The centre of economic activity for the postexilic citizen-temple community was the city of Jerusalem, which in normal circumstances was self-administered by elders and judges. In the situation of a gradual and protracted voluntary consolidation of the postexilic community's social structure and the groups of which it consisted, the temple provided the primary unifying centre. The *bet 'abot*, the city and the temple were, according to Weinberg, 'three typologically and functionally different institutions, but they did not form a vertical hierarchic structure with strict order of supremacy and subordi-

---

39. The list has been preserved in Neh. 7/Ezra 2. In it, the Jewish inhabitants of the former Babylonian Judaea formed a separate group, according to Weinberg, since they differed from other community members by the way they were identified. The returnees were identified with the formula 'the sons of X' (X designating an agnatic formation, a *bet 'abot*), while the other group was mainly identified with the formula 'the men of Y' (Y designating a toponym). Weinberg argues that such a difference of designation justifies the idea that the collectives named by toponyms consisted chiefly of the local territorial units that represented the Jewish population of northern Judaea (Weinberg, *Community*, p. 132).

40. See J.P. Weinberg, 'Die Mentalität der jerusalemischen Bürger-Tempel-Gemeinde des 6.-4. Jh. v.u.Z.', *Transeuphratène* 5 (1992), pp. 133-41.

41. See Weinberg, *Community*, pp. 49-61.

nation, but were rather a loose horizontal combination of interacting and counterbalancing institutions'.[42]

Weinberg admits that the designation of the social structure of the Jewish community in Jerusalem after the exile as a citizen-temple community is not the only possible one. However, as he argues, such a designation allows one to see the postexilic Jerusalem community in a typological connection with other contemporary analogous organizations and to study them synchronically. In Weinberg's opinion, one obvious advantage of the hypothesis of the citizen-temple community is that such an 'appellation accentuates the dichotomy "continuity-discontinuity" on the diachronic vertical axis of Jewish history and fixes the essential differences as well as the common features between this organization and those preceding and following it'.[43]

According to Weinberg, Chronicles[44] are an exponent of the views of one specific group within the postexilic citizen-temple community in Jerusalem.[45] This group consisted of the collectives named by toponyms, that is, of units from northern Judaea whose members had not been exiled. Weinberg points out that, in modern scholarship, Chronicles have repeatedly been regarded as a creation of a priestly, especially Levitical, milieu because of the author's obvious interest in the temple and temple service and in the clergy, particularly the Levites. It should not be neglected, however, that the alleged *Sitz im Leben* of Chronicles in priestly and/or Levitical circles does not conform to such fundamental features of the author's worldview as his consistent demythologizing and desacralizing *Tendenz*, his emphasis on the central role of the autonomous person in history, and his virtually non-existent interest in events of history which self-evidently were of prime importance to priestly circles (e.g. creation of the world and man, Exodus). On the

42. Weinberg, *Community*, p. 135.

43. Weinberg, *Community*, p. 137.

44. Weinberg has dealt with numerous aspects of Chronicles in a series of essays. Most of them are listed in I. Kalimi, *The Books of Chronicles: A Classified Bibliography* (Simor Bible Bibliographies; Jerusalem: Simor, 1990). The main results of Weinberg's work on Chronicles are now to be found in a convenient form in his monograph *Der Chronist in seiner Mitwelt* (BZAW, 239; Berlin: W. de Gruyter, 1996), and it is to this work that reference will be made below. The questions concerning the author, date, *Gattung* and audience of Chronicles are discussed on pp. 277-90 of this work.

45. On the citizen-temple community of Jerusalem as the Chronicler's immediate *Mitwelt*, see Weinberg, *Chronist*, pp. 34-118.

basis of these observations, Weinberg argues that the *Sitz im Leben* of Chronicles must be sought in the scribal circles of the postexilic citizen-temple community, among the 'families of the scribes that dwelt at Jabez', to be more precise.[46] The writer of Chronicles was an individual author of considerable skill and artistry. Such an assumption was justi-fied by the basic features of his work, such as the fundamental integrity and coherence of his worldview, the uniformity and consistency of his selective-critical attitude towards the historical tradition at his disposal (as shown by the numerous essential modifications introduced by the Chronicler into his important source, the Deuteronomistic History), his consistent stress on individual responsibility, and the personal bias which his work repeatedly manifests.[47] As to its *Gattungsbestimmung*, Chronicles were of course basically historiography, but whereas the Deuteronomistic historiography resembled the epic history-writing of the classical antiquity, Chronicles were closer to the biographies of the same period. This observation enables one to present a definition of Chronicles' *Untergattung*: it was a cycle of royal biographies prefaced with a genealogical introduction. This generic affiliation provided an explanation of the differences in nature and manner of presentation bet-ween Chronicles and the Deuteronomistic History.[48]

These considerations already give a rough idea of how Chronicles should be dated, but an even more precise date within the framework of the postexilic citizen-temple community can be set. Weinberg main-tains that Chronicles had been composed during the latter half of the fifth century BCE, about the time of Nehemiah's mission in Jerusalem. This claim can be substantiated by the inference that since the Chron-icler's worldview reflects the specific views of the collectives named by toponyms, this group either had to be in existence as a socio-ideological quantity in the Chronicler's era or it had ceased to exist only a little

46. Weinberg, *Chronist*, pp. 278-81. According to him, the complicated text in 1 Chron. 2.54-55 lists really existing pre-exilic scribal clans that belonged to the tribe of Judah, resided in the northern parts of Judah before the exile, and probably had close connections with the Davidides. Like several other inhabitants of northern Judah, these clans were not deported by the Babylonians. After the exile, they joined the emerging citizen-temple community together with other collectives named by toponyms. Weinberg is convinced that it is precisely this milieu of agnatic clans of scribes that produced a work such as Chronicles.

47. Weinberg, *Chronist*, p. 281.

48. Weinberg, *Chronist*, pp. 284-87.

earlier. Since the collectives had merged into the larger social structure of the citizen-temple community after 458/457 BCE and thus lost their independent significance, Chronicles could not have been written long after 458/457. A period after 458/457 was suggested by the considerable attention directed to priests and especially Levites in Chronicles. Weinberg links this fact with his observation that the citizen-temple community evidenced a significant increase in the number, authority and prestige of the priests and Levites after the above-mentioned year. The connection between Chronicles and the era of Nehemiah is established by the fact that the list of the inhabitants of Jerusalem in 1 Chronicles 9 is largely parallel with the list in Neh. 11.1-19. The latter list, regarded by Weinberg as historically authentic, catalogues the inhabitants of Jerusalem after the synoecism executed by Nehemiah. The changes which the Chronicler introduced into the list show that while the books of Ezra and Nehemiah portray the tribes of Judah and Benjamin, that is the repatriated exiles, as constituting the Jewish community in Jerusalem, the Chronicler insisted that the postexilic community in its entirety, not just the former exiles and their offspring, was the legitimate heir and representative of the whole Jewish 'we'. The Chronicler had taken the core of his list from Nehemiah and modified it in accordance with his purposes. Put together, these observations justified the conclusion that Chronicles had to be dated to the period soon after the synoecism and the book of Nehemiah.[49]

The proposed date and *Sitz im Leben* of Chronicles can be further supported, in Weinberg's opinion, by a comparison of some important theological accentuations in Chronicles and Ezra–Nehemiah. The former was the exponent of the views of the collectives named by toponyms, while the *Sitz im Leben* of the latter was to be sought in all probability within the other important section of the postexilic community, the returnees from Mesopotamia and their descendants. Ezra–Nehemiah gave expression to the attitudes and apprehensions, hopes and ideas of this group in the citizen-temple community. First, for the returnees who had experienced their own exodus from Mesopotamia, the ancient Exodus from Egypt was not just an event of the remote past. On the contrary, it was a model for their own liberation, a manifestation of divine charity not only on their ancestors but also on themselves. Therefore, Neh. 9.9-21 contains a detailed description of the Exodus.

49. Weinberg, *Chronist*, pp. 281-84.

The fact that the Chronicler pays only limited attention to this decisive event of Israel's past is due to the fact that for the group he represented, the inhabitants of northern Judaea who had never been deported, Exodus really was a thing of the past with no theological significance to their thinking and ideals in the social context of the postexilic era. Secondly, another important biblical tradition, the Conquest, receives analogous treatment in Chronicles and Ezra–Nehemiah. For the returnees, whose forefathers had lost their land and property during the 587/586 catastophe, the restoration of their rights and claims on the land of their ancestors was one of their prime problems. It is thus quite in accordance with what one would expect that the book of Nehemiah (9.23-25) gives an enthusiastic description of the Conquest. For those who had never been in exile, the Conquest was more a problem than a tradition to be warmly remembered, since it appeared as a threat to their position and welfare. So it is only natural that the Chronicler did not record it. Thirdly, among the collectives names by toponyms, the hope of continuity between the past and the present dominated. One expression of it was a hope for a renewal of the former glory days under the Davidic kingship. Consequently, David and Davidides occupy a central place in the Chronicler's history. The dominant interpretation of the history under the Davidic kingship among the repatriated was one of discontinuity, however. A critical attitude towards the Davidides was much more common than a hope for the restoration of David's dynasty. This view is given a clear expression in Ezra–Nehemiah, the exponent of the deported and returned people.[50]

On the basis of the date, *Sitz im Leben* and *Gattung* of the Chronicler's work, it is obvious that the audience that the author had in mind was the contemporary postexilic citizen-temple community in Jerusalem. It is to this community that the Chronicler attempted to convey the ideas and hopes of his own background. Weinberg argues, with a very good reason, that what one must expect from the audience is that it is able to understand and appreciate the author's goals. If the contradiction between the notions and intentions expressed by the author in his text and what the audience reads and hears from it and interprets in accordance with its own views and intentions is too big, there is always the danger that the text is not understood and taken seriously and, as a result, that it is rejected and forgotten. That is why the audience had to

---

50. Weinberg, *Chronist*, pp. 280-81.

be 'included' in the system and structure of the work if the author wanted a positive reception for it. Conclusions concerning the author of Chronicles could also be drawn along these guidelines. According to Weinberg, a significant feature of the Chronicler as a writer of history is his constant striving to remove all superfluous linguistic means of expression and to substitute a 'contracted' polysemy, sometimes even a monosemy, for a 'dispersive' one, a feature which was characteristic of the mentality of the intellectual elite of the *Achsenzeit*. The Chronicler possessed a consistent selective-critical attitude towards the historical tradition at his disposal, and another fundamental feature of his working method was his habit to use source citations to direct his readers' attention to important texts supplementing his own narrative. Such features could be appreciated only by an audience that understood and accepted the Chronicler's basic approach, knew the canonical historical tradition as well as the other texts used by the Chronicler, and was therefore able to evaluate his innovations.[51]

These observations substantiate the claim, in Weinberg's opinion, that the Chronicler's primary audience consisted of the social and intellectual elite of the contemporary citizen-temple community. His readers belonged mainly to the same milieu as he did, to the well-to-do, literate and intellectual circles. His audience was limited—even though the admittance of Chronicles into the canon is an indication of the books' popularity—and it stayed that way in later Judaism as well.[52]

Based on the conviction that the postexilic citizen-temple community in Jerusalem must be located not only on the diachronic axis of Jewish history but also in the synchronic context of its Near Eastern environment, Weinberg's conception provides insights into the basic questions concerning the dating of Chronicles: why, for whom and in what social milieu was this work composed? The socio-ideological macrocontext was the Persian dominance during the fifth century BCE. Within it, the citizen-temple community in Jerusalem constituted the immediate context for the Chronicler's work. The author wrote his work for the influential and intellectual people of the community, probably for the purpose of demonstrating to them the expectations and aims of his ideological framework in a situation where the citizen-temple community had already passed its formative stage (539–458/457 BCE). Within the compass of this reconstruction, Weinberg makes a number of apt

51. Weinberg, *Chronist*, pp. 289-90.
52. Weinberg, *Chronist*, pp. 287-90.

observations about many characteristic features of the Chronicler's theology as relevant elements of the patterns of thought of his socio-religious framework.

A fundamental question raised by Weinberg's conception is of course whether such a sociopolitical phenomenon as the citizen-temple community, which could produce the kind of worldview the Chronicler advocates, ever really existed. If the answer to this question is negative, that is the end also for Weinberg's interpretation of Chronicles' date. If the answer is affirmative, several questions still remain open. Why was it only the local intelligentsia that the Chronicler had in mind as his audience? Should one see his programme as religio-political propaganda, aimed at changing something in the circumstances in which he and his group lived? If this is the case, why did he direct it to the circles close to his own and not to the potential revolutionaries in the society who had reasons to be dissatisfied with the prevailing conditions? One must surely suppose that the well-to-do, literate, intellectual audience of the Chronicler hardly had such a predisposition towards the citizen-temple community that promoted social peace and stabilized the relations between different social groups and subgroups. If the Chronicler did not want to change anything around him, why did he compose his work in the first place, bearing in mind Weinberg's assertion that it was not merely a scribal exercise for other scribes? It is precisely the question of the function of Chronicles within the social context of the citizen-temple community that is clearly left unanswered by Weinberg. If, as it seems, Chronicles was a sort of party propaganda for the views of the non-exiled people of northern Judaea who had not been left out of the citizen-temple community but already belonged to it, what was it needed for during the second half of the fifth century when the citizen-temple community had already been consolidated, the economy was rapidly growing, and the early post-exilic agnatic groups had lost much of their relevance? It must be noted that what Weinberg does not say is that Chronicles would have been needed for solving some acute inner-Judaean social problem in the citizen-temple community—or for blocking the socially and religiously exclusive attitude towards 'outsiders' advanced in the books of Ezra and Nehemiah, for example. It very much seems that the social context sketched by Weinberg makes Chronicles look quite anachronistic: the books advocate views which had already been accepted at least for the most part or which had no possibility of being accepted, or which generally seem to be rather 'academic' issues against the backdrop of contemporary social reality. The social context outlined by Weinberg, if it ever existed, was perhaps able to produce a work such as Chronicles, but it remains unclear for what purpose it really needed it.

As far as the date of Chronicles is concerned, Weinberg is able to do with very few such assumptions that would put the pieces of the jigsaw in a conspicuously unnatural order. In fact, in most cases he can restrain from hypotheses that would essentially deviate from the general lines of modern scholarship (1 Chron. 3.17-24 is perhaps his biggest problem in this respect). With quite impressive style, Chronicles are set into the context of the historical and theological traditions of the Jews of the Persian era. There are no contacts whatsoever with Hellenism proper, only with its Near Eastern social and ideological preconditions. If, then, Weinberg's theory of the social milieu of Chronicles is accepted, it is methodologically perfectly sound to claim that these books are nothing to do with the Hellenistic period in Palestine.

Rainer Albertz

In his account of the history of Israel's religion in the biblical period,[53] R. Albertz argues that the CHW hypothesis is improbable. Chronicles and Ezra–Nehemiah apparently derive from the same milieu, but the books of Chronicles are later than the other two books. Since the description in Ezra–Nehemiah of the events of the fifth century BCE is inaccurate and reveals the author's poor acquaintance with historical facts, there is every reason to believe that these books had been composed considerably after the events themselves, that is, no earlier than about 350 BCE. Bearing this in mind and the fact that one can recognize in Chronicles a process of inner literary growth of quite a long duration, it is obvious that the latter work could not have been written after Ezra–Nehemiah but before the end of the Persian era. It seems, therefore, that Chronicles had been composed in the early Hellenistic era, probably some time between 330 and 250 BCE.[54]

---

53. R. Albertz, *Religionsgeschichte Israels in alttestamentlicher Zeit*. I. *Von den Anfängen bis zum Ende der Königszeit*. II. *Vom Exil bis zu den Makkabäern* (GAT, 8.1, 2; Göttingen: Vandenhoeck & Ruprecht, 2nd edn, 1996–97). Chronicles are discussed in II, pp. 605-623.

54. Albertz, *Religionsgeschichte*, II, pp. 606-607. According to him, the literary growth of Chronicles had taken at least a few decades, a fact that can be seen from the development and adjustments in the organization of the temple personnel, for

What Albertz has primarily done to explain the intentions of Chronicles is that he revives the old idea of the Samaritan schism as the work's ideological matrix. Earlier, the theory of the anti-Samaritan polemic as the driving force of the chronistic theology was enhanced by M. Noth, in particular. He argued that the Chronicler's work was a third-century polemical response to the rival cult in Samaria that had broken away from Jerusalem about the time of the conquest of Syria and Palestine by Alexander the Great. The Chronicler's purpose was to demonstrate that the legitimate Israel centred around Jerusalem and was ruled by the house of David. In the schismatic situation, the Chronicler argued that it was the Jerusalem cultic community and not the Samaritan one that must be regarded as the genuine successor of the legitimate Israel.[55] Already before Noth, C.C. Torrey had put forth a similar view,[56] and Noth's suggestions were followed by a number of scholars.[57] In recent decades, the understanding of Chronicles as an anti-Samaritan polemic has been out of fashion in Chronicles scholarship, however. It has been argued by numerous scholars that the decisive break between Jerusalem and the inhabitants of Samaria did not take place until considerably after the composition of Chronicles, either at the time of the alleged destruction of the sanctuary on Mount Gerizim by John Hyrcanus in 128 BCE, or even in a still later period. Furthermore, the abandonment of the CHW hypothesis has led to a reassess-

example. 1 Chron. 23-27 show clear marks of literary growth but the section as a whole can hardly be regarded as a massive insertion into Chronicles (*Religionsgeschichte*, II, p. 609 n. 20). The present form of Chronicles is best explained 'durch die Annahme mehrerer Verfasser einer geschlossenen Trägergruppe, die über eine längere Zeit tätig waren' (p. 607 n. 9).

55. Noth, *Studien*, pp. 161-66, 171-80. On Noth's contribution to the study of Chronicles, see H.G.M. Williamson, 'Introduction', in M. Noth, *The Chronicler's History* (trans. H.G.M. Williamson; JSOTSup, 50; Sheffield: JSOT Press, 1987), pp. 11-26; R.L. Braun, 'Martin Noth and the Chronicler's History', in S.L. McKenzie and M.P. Graham (eds.), *The History of Israel's Traditions: The Heritage of Martin Noth* (JSOTSup, 182; Sheffield: Sheffield Academic Press, 1994), pp. 63-80; Peltonen, *History Debated*, pp. 639-53.

56. C.C. Torrey, *Ezra Studies* (Chicago: University of Chicago Press, 1910).

57. For example, Galling, *Chronik*, pp. 14-15; Rudolph, *Chronikbücher*, pp. viii-ix. Recently, this view has been followed in a somewhat more cautious manner by Oeming, *Israel*, who states: '*Ein* wichtiger Skopus der Darstellung [of the Chronicler] ist die Polemik gegen die "Separatisten" im Nordreich' (p. 47; Oeming's italics). See also J. Becker, *1 Chronik* (NEB, 18; Würzburg: Echter Verlag, 1986), pp. 9-10.

ment of Chronicles' attitude towards the northern Israel. It has been recognized that it is actually far from being as negative as Noth and his early followers used to suppose, mainly on the basis of evidence from Ezra–Nehemiah. Thus, a majority of modern scholars have argued for the view that to regard the Chronicler as engaging in anti-Samaritan polemic in his work is a misunderstanding.[58]

In opposition to the anti-anti-Samaritan trend of modern Chronicles scholarship, Albertz argues that during the late Persian and early Hellenistic periods the Judaean community was far more interested in its internal matters than in world politics. An internal issue of burning actuality that engaged the Judaean community in these years was the challenge to its authority and theological substance presented by the Samarians. According to Albertz, the eventual separation between the Judaean and Samarian cultic communities was a lengthy process that was originated not primarily by the emergence of the postexilic community in Jerusalem as such but by the conflict with which the Samarians attempted to impede the establishment of the political structures of the southern community. The political issue was soon associated with another one that concerned the definition of Israelite identity in an ethnically mixed environment. The organization of the postexilic community

58. See, e.g., T. Willi, *Die Chronik als Auslegung: Untersuchungen zur literarischen Gestaltung der historischen Überlieferung Israels* (FRLANT, 106; Göttingen: Vandenhoeck & Ruprecht, 1972), pp. 190-93; R. Mosis, *Untersuchungen zur Theologie des chronistischen Geschichtswerkes* (FTS, 92; Freiburg: Herder, 1973); Welten, *Geschichte*, pp. 172-73; *idem*, 'Chronikbücher/Chronist', p. 370; R.L. Braun, 'A Reconsideration of the Chronicler's Attitude toward the North', *JBL* 96 (1977), pp. 59-62; *idem*, 'Chronicles, Ezra, and Nehemiah: Theology and Literary History', in J.A. Emerton (ed.), *Studies in the Historical Books of the Old Testament* (VTSup, 30; Leiden: E.J. Brill, 1979), pp. 52-64 (56-59); Williamson, *Israel*; S. Japhet, *The Ideology of the Book of Chronicles and its Place in Biblical Thought* (BEATAJ, 9; New York: Peter Lang, 1989), pp. 325-34; Klein, 'Chronicles', p. 994; Jones, *Chronicles*, pp. 102-103; Dyck, *Ideology*, pp. 33-37. According to Williamson (*Chronicles*, p. 24), 'all the scholarly monographs published on Chronicles in recent years', together with some works dealing primarily with the history of Samaritans themselves, inveigh against the interpretation of Chronicles as anti-Samaritan polemic. S. Japhet has recently remarked (*Chronicles*, pp. 43-44): 'It is doubtful…whether one single and unilateral purpose would account for such an enormous enterprise [i.e. as Chronicles], with all its complexities of content and form. Chronicles is not a manifesto devoted to a specific political movement but a more general and comprehensive theological stock-taking, striving to achieve a new religious balance in the face of a changing world.'

in Jerusalem was strongly dependent on the maintenance of tribal-ethnic structures, with which it wanted to protect its social and religious integrity. A natural result of this was that the northern followers of Yahweh were left out of the community proper: they were allowed to take part in the Jerusalem cult and they were bound by the religious obligations of the Yahweh faith, but they nonetheless did not have the same rights as the 'proper' Jews within the community. A way to circumvent such a discrimination and enter the tribally organized community structure was to join a 'proper' Jewish family through marriage. Eventually, the issue of mixed marriages became an acute theological problem, because the question had to be settled whether the true Israel included all who believed in Yahweh, including the Samarians, or whether it should be understood as a religiously and politically exclusive entity that had to protect itself from all outsiders. As the books of Ezra and Nehemiah show, the latter option won the day. Simultaneously, the political status of the Judaean community grew stronger and stronger until it finally became an independent province in Nehemiah's time, which from the Samarian viewpoint meant that the temple of Yahweh was now situated in a politically foreign territory. The judicial and theological discrimination as well as the new political circumstances left only one alternative open to the Yahweh-believing Samarians: a new cult centre had to be established in their own territory. The geographical aspect naturally explains why the Samarians accepted only Pentateuch as their sacred book but left the Deuteronomistic complex of traditions out of it. Since the latter emphasized the status of Jerusalem, the Judaean cult centre, it simply had to be abandoned. The actual cultic separation took place during the time of Sanballat III. According to Josephus, Sanballat took advantage of the fall of the Persian rule to obtain from Alexander his support to the building of the Samarian temple. The rising Macedonian empire was naturally willing to promote loyalty towards the new Greek rule in Palestine, and that is why the temple project of the Samarians got off to a rapid start.[59]

The emergence of the Samarian cult community seriously questioned the formerly self-evident legitimacy and authoritative position of Jerusalem. The latter took up the challenge and responded to it in two different ways. The Samarian claims for equal rights in the Judaean community during the late Persian period were given an inimical res-

---

59. Albertz, *Religionsgeschichte*, II, pp. 576-89.

ponse in Ezra–Nehemiah: no way! The Samarians could not be part of the true Israel, since it consisted only of the legitimate heirs of ancient Israel. The result of such a disobliging attitude on the part of the Jerusalem community was the erection of the Gerizim temple in the beginning of the Hellenistic era. What was particularly problematic for the Judaean community was that the Samarians legitimized their own cause by an appeal to precisely the same sacred writings as were in use in Jerusalem, too. According to Albertz, the Judaean community was compelled to believe that the attitude towards the north advanced in Ezra–Nehemiah was of no avail in the new situation. In order to save its authority, the Judaean community had to reassess the course and the fundamental elements of the pre-exilic history. Its main problem was that the Jerusalem temple and the dynasty of David, the basic elements on which the Jews theologically based their claims, were not explicitly mentioned in the already canonized writings. Because they could no longer be corrected, the Judaean community had to find some other means of promoting these elements to inseparable parts of the history that defined the self-understanding of true Israel. This means was found, and here we see the second answer to the Samarian challenge, in Chronicles in the early years of the third century BCE. This work exhibited strict continuity between the canonized early history of Israel and the monarchic period: both the ark of the covenant and the tent of meeting were brought into the temple of Jerusalem according to Chronicles; David was in several respects like a new Moses; precisely as Yahweh had chosen his people and its leaders in the early days of Israel's history, he had now chosen David as the founder of the cult and royal dynasty, Solomon as the builder of the temple, Jerusalem as the holy city, and even proper servants for his sanctuary. The promotion of the David-Solomon era to the climax of Israel's sacred traditions in Chronicles was nothing less than a canon revision, an operation in which the entire pre-exilic history received a new interpretation on the basis of contemporary issues.[60] According to Albertz, the authors of Chronicles were convinced that the decision taken in the Persian period, in the interest of opposition to domination and enthusiasm and with a view to the emancipation of the priesthood, to close the foundation history of Israel with Moses' death and thus largely exclude the ancient theology of kingship and state cult from the official religion of Yahweh

---

60. Albertz, *Religionsgeschichte*, II, pp. 607-609.

was in urgent need of revision. The canon should be enlarged in order to accommodate to the official theology the historical tradition of DtrG which had been omitted as well as the prophetic writings which brought out the special Jerusalem traditions of salvation. With their work the Chroniclers wanted to show the right direction for such a revision. So the Samarian split provoked an effort at integration within the community of Judah, an effort that aimed at extending the consensus concerning the foundations of the official religion of Israel beyond the framework set by the Torah.[61]

In a specific religious and sociopolitical conflict, the purpose of Chronicles was thus to articulate a synthesis of the differing religious traditions of Israel, a synthesis that would be as comprehensive as possible. Albertz argues that this purpose expresses itself in four synthetic aspects with which Chronicles paved the way for the canonization of the Deuteronomistic History and the prophetic traditions that had been pushed aside when the Torah had attained an authoritative status. The first of these was a synthesis between the Torah and Deuteronomistic History.[62] It was achieved by demonstrating that, properly understood, the Deuteronomistic presentation of Israel's history indeed was in harmony with the normative legal tradition of Israel.[63] What this meant in practice was that, in various connections of the monarchic history, the Chroniclers point out that everything happened in accordance with what was written, that is, with the regulations of the law. In a similar manner, their work informs the reader that priestly ordinances concerning cult personnel, sacrifices and religious feasts, for example, were observed during the pre-exilic history even though one may get a different notion from the Deuteronomistic account. In creating the synthesis between these two blocks of traditions, the Chroniclers did not merely quote passages from the Torah in a mechanical way. They also interpreted it, paid attention to the factual cultic circumstances of the postexilic era, and even introduced some ideas of their own about necessary cultic reforms, concerning, in particular, the extension of the cultic functions of Levites. The biggest problems in this respect were posed by kingship and state cult, that is, precisely the themes that were of the utmost importance to the post-exilic Judaean community. It was because of

61. Albertz, *Religionsgeschichte*, II, pp. 609-610.
62. See Albertz, *Religionsgeschichte*, II, pp. 610-15.
63. In other words, the aim of the Chroniclers was to depict Israel's history 'nach den Regeln der kanonischen Tora'; Albertz, *Religionsgeschichte*, II, p. 612.

them that the Deuteronomistic synthesis of the history of the pre-monarchic and monarchic periods had been discredited by those responsible for the Torah's canonization. To attain their basic aim, that of proving the legitimacy and authority of the Judaean community against the claims of the Samarians, the Chroniclers were compelled to direct their main attention to these issues and construct skilful theological compromises. As Albertz puts it, the Chroniclers were adamant that the Jerusalem cult was to be associated with the royal house of David in order to give it theological legitimation, but at the same time it must be carefully seen that the old mistake of the royal state cult with its fusion of altar and throne and its alienation from the people would be avoided.[64] The compromise concerning the other problematic and simultaneously highly important issue was quite similar. According to Albertz, the Chroniclers attempted to achieve a theological consensus over the Davidic kingship by resorting to the old ideal of the constitutional monarchy, an ideal which had never been realized but which left room for Israel's drive towards freedom and its claim to self-determination. This they tried to do without lapsing into the error of the old theology of the kingship, namely, that of ideologically exalting state power by fusing it with divine might.[65]

The second synthesis dealt with the position of prophecy in Israel's history. The Chroniclers wanted to say that prophecy should be accorded a bigger role in the true Yahweh religion than the fathers of the Torah had wanted to do because of their fear of enthusiasm, since, correctly understood, prophecy had much to teach about life in accordance with Yahweh's will in different historical situations. According to Chronicles, prophecy guaranteed that Yahweh remained faithful to the promises he had given to his people if they remained loyal to him.[66] The third synthesis concerned the reception of the Jerusalem psalm tradition. Albertz observes that the Chroniclers wanted to demonstrate that, correctly interpreted, cultic reality was ultimately identical with

---

64. Albertz, *Religionsgeschichte*, II, p. 613.

65. Albertz, *Religionsgeschichte*, II, pp. 614-15.

66. Albertz, *Religionsgeschichte*, II, pp. 615-16. Not every sort of prophecy was suitable for the Chroniclers' purposes, however. They gave priority to conditional prophecy of judgment and salvation, while radical prophecy of doom as well as the kind of unqualified prophecy of salvation that was advocated by Second Isaiah, e.g., were ignored by them.

the historical one.[67] Finally, the fourth synthesis emphasized the role of personal piety in the offical worship of Yahweh. In the cult political rivalry between Jerusalem and the Samarians, it was ultimately the individual believer who decided which of the two existing sactuaries, Jerusalem or Gerizim, he regarded as his religious home. What the Chroniclers tried to do in this situation was to make the Yahweh worship in Jerusalem appear as attractive as possible for personal devotion. It was therefore in their interests to affirm that the Judaean version of Yahweh worship was not burdened by nomistic and ritualistic ballast but anchored deeply in personal religious experience and commitment. So the Chroniclers underlined the close connection between Israel and its king, on the one hand, and Yahweh, their God, on the other. According to Albertz, such an intimacy is closely linked with idea of retribution so prominent in Chronicles. What is essential for the Chroniclers is not the idea per se but its individual and personal application. Every king, every generation and every individual could affect his vicissitudes positively or negatively through his relationship to Yahweh. As a consequence, it was never too late for Israel to turn back to Yahweh and seek shelter in his mercy. Although the history of the northern Israel had gone completely wrong in the monarchic era, and the situation in Samaria was now everything but desirable, the former Israelite tribes and their descendants were nevertheless not forbidden to return to Yahweh and true faith within the context of the cult that was in operation in Jerusalem.[68]

According to Albertz, the orientation of Chronicles is clearly anti-Samarian. Though modern scholarship has regarded such a view as a misunderstanding and emphasized Chronicles' pan-Israelite concept and positive attitude towards the inhabitants of the former northern kingdom, it should be noted, as Albertz argues, that such elements could be part of the Chroniclers' anti-Samarian programme as well. Even if the cultic separation was reality from the second half of the fourth century BCE onwards, the final and irreconcilable schism did not take place in the time of the Chroniclers—its turn did not come until the Hasmonaean

67. 'Die Geschichte Israels wurde im Jerusalemer Kult aufgehoben, ihre zentrale Heilsperiode in ihm gottesdienstliche Gegenwart; und die im Jerusalemer Kult zelebrierte und besungene Realität heilvoller Gottesnähe liess sich bis ins einzelne am Verlauf der Geschichte Israel bewahrheiten, wenn man nur akzeptierte, dass ihr Zentrum im Süden lag' (Albertz, *Religionsgeschichte*, II, p. 616).

68. Albertz, *Religionsgeschichte*, II, pp. 615-18.

era. Strict exclusivism as that proffered in Ezra–Nehemiah was no longer able to do any good to the Judaean claims for cultic and religious authority in the rivalry between the two communities, and that is why the Judaean side abandoned such a policy and adopted a new one. It set out to win back to the Jerusalem cult as many as possible of those who had begun to follow the Samarian form of worship, not primarily by 'anti-Samaritan polemic' but by convincing them of the theological superiority of the Judaean standpoint and the good will of the Judaeans.[69]

The social and political milieu of Chronicles explains also the books' non-eschatological orientation. Since it aimed at articulating an inner-Jewish consensus about the true nature of Israel's faith, eschatological hopes and expectations of coming social and political upheavals, which undoubtedly gained considerable support within the 'lower classes' of the Jewish society, did not further the Chroniclers' cause. On the contrary, they would have had an injurious effect on the assertion that Yahweh's gifts were already present in devout faith and in the celebration of the true cult of Yahweh in Jerusalem. The same applied to different sorts of messianic expectations. The Chroniclers consciously avoided promoting them and concentrated on the realization of the theocratic ideal within the Jerusalem cult and cultic community.[70] Furthermore, the social milieu and theological orientation of Chronicles explained why there was no Hellenistic colouring in it even though it was a product of the Hellenistic era.[71] It was undoubtedly a premeditated measure on the part of the authors. As Albertz puts it, their lasting appeals to seek the God of the fathers with all one's heart and to refrain from all pagan influences can be understood as an admonition to preserve the Jewish identity in the face of modern Hellenistic seductions. Nonetheless, the Chroniclers had no interest whatsoever in presenting an antithesis to the new cultural environment, since their education and

69. Albertz, *Religionsgeschichte*, II, pp. 584, 620-21.

70. Albertz, *Religionsgeschichte*, II, pp. 621-22.

71. Albertz (*Religionsgeschichte*, II, p. 622) regards the details of the allegedly Hellenistic military technics in Chronicles, discussed by P. Welten, as an exception to this general rule. Such a concession to inconsistency on the part of the Chroniclers is unnecessary, however, since Welten's interpretations are by no means beyond controversy among scholars. Albertz's argumentation would be still more convincing if they were simply rejected.

training, focused entirely on their own Israelite tradition, probably did not allow any alternative to sealing themselves off.[72]

From the socio-historical point of view, the theological synthesis constructed by the Chroniclers had most probably originated in the scribal circles of the late Persian and early Hellenistic times. One can deduce this from the authors' profound familiarity with the wide spectrum of Israel's religious traditions.[73] The picture given by them of the theological and, more generally, socio-religious harmony between king and people leads one to assume that, sociologically, the learned scribes who wrote Chronicles had belonged to the 'middle class' people. They adopted a mediating and harmonizing policy, a kind of good public-relations attitude, towards the different social and religious groups among contemporary Jews and the controversies that existed between them, and consciously pushed acute inner problems within their social context out of sight. As Albertz puts it, they offered all leading forces of Judah a new religious consensus with a specifically Judaean stamp which was to unite them in a defensive war against the Samarian rivals, and therefore they deliberately put all internal divisions in the background.[74] The Chroniclers had considerable sympathy towards the religious and political aspirations of the 'upper class' circles of their society, not towards the hopes cherished by the 'lower classes' for radical changes in their social structures. What the chronistic enterprise ultimately achieved in this particular respect was not much. The bourgeois middle-class propaganda was not enough to repair the break between Judaeans and Samarians, and the zeal of the Chroniclers for a cult covering all notorious social problems of the day under the veil of pious solidarity, the zeal with no place for the social criticism of the prophets or the social legislation of the Torah, was unable to deal with the social conflicts the elements of which were already in existence in the Chroniclers' era—only to explode violently in the Maccabaean revolt. In the end, the chronistic theology succeeded in

72. Albertz, *Religionsgeschichte*, II, p. 622.

73. 'Die Verfasser waren nach Ausweis ihres Werkes nicht nur intensiv mit der gesamten religiösen Literatur Israels vertraut, sondern verstanden sich auch auf das Geschäft der Auslegung und Angleichung unterschiedlicher Positionen und hatten sich bei ihren Studien einen Sprachstil angeeignet, der von Anspielungen, Zitaten und Versatzstücken aus anderen Schriften strotzte' (Albertz, *Religionsgeschichte*, II, p. 619).

74. Albertz, *Religionsgeschichte*, II, pp. 619-20.

alarming the 'upper classes' of the Judaean society no more than it was able to satisfy the the social and religious needs of the 'lower classes'. On the contrary, the lack of courage in the face of the upper class and lack of sensitivity to the suffering of the lower class in this last great synthesis of Israelite of Israelite religion in the Hebrew Bible was to have devastating consequences for subsequent history.[75] The most important effects of Chronicles must be sought in another direction, namely, in the important position achieved by the interpretative and integrative type of literature in later Jewish tradition.[76]

Albertz's concept of Chronicles as a product of Judaean scribal activity in a specific social and religious conflict of deep and far-reaching significance manages to give quite clear-cut answers to the questions of who wrote Chronicles, for whom the books were written, and what was their function in their social context. The scribes of the early Hellenistic period composed the chronistic history in order to offer the contemporary leading circles of Judaea the theological instruments for solving the Samarian problem that threatened the political status and religious identity of the Jerusalem community. The authors of Chronicles were thus Jews of the Hellenistic era, but they did not try to deal with problems primarily generated by the Hellenistic era with Hellenistic tools. The political and religious issues of the Chroniclers' era as well as the social structure and atmosphere in which they took shape and grew worse were inherited from the Persian period.

A Jigsaw without a Model? Concluding Remarks

Weinberg and Albertz have attempted to understand Chronicles as part of a larger social, ideological and religious context in which the books had a relevant message and function. According to the former, the best candidate for such a context is to be found from around the middle of the Persian period, while the latter argues for the early Greek period. Temporally, these suggestions are around 150 years apart, which, considering the general differences of opinion about the date of Chronicles, is actually not all that long a period. Despite the basic disagreement between Weinberg and Albertz here, they have quite a lot in common in their respective positions, too. Both maintain that the Chronicler(s)— according to Weinberg, the Chronicler was an individual author, while

75. Albertz, *Religionsgeschichte*, II, p. 623.
76. Albertz, *Religionsgeschichte*, II, pp. 622-23.

Albertz reckons that there were more than one Chronicler—had belonged to the learned circles of his time, the scribes. Further, both of them contend that the Chronicler(s)'s work, excluding Ezra–Nehemiah, was directed to the learned and prestigious people in the Jewish community who were able to understand the author(s)'s profound theology and appreciate his (their) intentions. Weinberg and Albertz also agree on the fact that the peculiar theological interpretation of history in Chronicles needed a specific socio-religious situation for such an undertaking to make sense. Chronicles was not primarily a polemic or a piece of theological controversy directed against someone with the aim of strongly disproving something. On the contrary, it represents a synthesis, merging as much as possible different theological opinions into a model of faith and action on which not only a theologically but also socially workable Jewish community could be based at a time when the Jews were forced to live under foreign rule. Weinberg believes that such a synthesis was relevant within the Jewish community during the Persian era, whereas Albertz sees in Chronicles a response to the problem actualized by the entrance of the Samarians onto the stage of Israel's history. One could perhaps say that, in Albertz's opinion, the Chroniclers tried to turn the clock back in order to restore the tolerable conditions of the Jewish community in the Persian Empire before the Samarians seriously started rocking the boat, while Weinberg appears to think that the purpose of the Chronicler was to create a new theological and social status quo in which the citizen-temple community would be capable of both preserving its distinctive religious identity and integrating itself into developments that took place in the contemporary political macrocontext. Chronicles was thus a learned theological programme for learned people, composed for the purpose of ending, preventing or smoothing out social and religious conflicts among the people of Israel. It was a legitimization of 'we', not primarily as opposed to 'them' but as a means to develop the understanding of Jewish identity so as to rectify and heal the traumas of the not-so-distant past.

It seems to me that when the dating of Chronicles is considered from the standpoint of the questions of why, for whom, and in what context, Albertz's position has obvious advantages over that of Weinberg. The latter's theory of the citizen-temple community is after all a hypothesis, a general appellation for a number of more or less obvious social and economic trends in the Near East during the second half of the first millennium BCE.[77] In this hypothesis, the postexilic Palestinian version of the citizen-temple community has served as a model for the reconstruction of this particular sociopolitical organization, since it is, as Weinberg himself admits, the best documented case of a citizen-temple community in the sources of the Achaemenid period.[78] The Palestinian form of citizen-temple community, in its turn, has been reconstructed by Weinberg mainly on the basis of information derived from Chronicles, Ezra and Nehemiah. The danger of circular argumentation looms large when the interpretation of Chronicles' historical and theological nature is deduced from the general theory created to a not inconsiderable extent with the help of it. The advantage of Albertz's position is that the Samarian schism, the early developments of which are reflected in Chronicles in his opinion, has obviously existed as a political and theological issue of some acuteness and intensity about the time of the composition of Chronicles, Ezra and Nehemiah. The stronger position is always the one that has to assume less.

The same is true also with regard to the particular situation on which the author(s) of Chronicles has attempted to influence with his work. At least the present writer was left in the dark by Weinberg about the actual problematic situation which could have been solved with the help of the Chronicler's work. By all accounts, Chronicles was not meant to draw a line between the Jews and outsiders (Samarians, for example) but to promote the inner balance and congruity of the Jewish community in circumstances where, as it seems on the basis of Weinberg's own discussion, the Jewish citizen-temple community had already passed the initial and most complicated stages of its existence in the early postexilic years, and the role of the temple and cult, so vehemently underlined by the Chronicler, was not disputed. If the books of Chronicles were composed by scribes to other scribes in such a context, what were they really needed for? It appears, further, that of the characteristic features of the Chronicler's theology discussed by Weinberg,

---

77. See H. Kreissig, 'Eine beachtenswerte Theorie zur Organisation altvorderorientalischer Tempelgemeinden im Achämenidenreich: Zu J.P. Weinberg's "Bürger-Tempel-Gemeinde" in Juda', *Klio* 66 (1984), pp. 35-39. For scholarly assessments of Weinberg's theory or parts of it, see, e.g., the essays of J. Blenkinsopp, P.R. Bedford and R.A. Horsley in P.R. Davies (ed.), *Second Temple Studies 1: Persian Period* (JSOTSup, 117; Sheffield: JSOT Press, 1991). See also the references in Weinberg, *Community*, p. 127.

78. Weinberg, *Community*, p. 26.

the conspicuous neglect of the Exodus and Conquest traditions would have been most appropriate in the years immediately after the end of the exile and not about 100 years later. It may be supposed, moreover, that after the disappearance of Zerubbabel from the scene, the enthusiasm of the repatriates about the Davidic kingship had calmed down by the time of Nehemiah, but about the time of the return from the exile they would hardly have had anything against the restoration of the dynasty of David. It seems, therefore, that the emphases recognized by Weinberg in Chronicles vis-à-vis those of Ezra–Nehemiah do not fit in as coherent parts of the religious context into which he wants to set Chronicles. This is not a problem for Albertz, because he regards Chronicles as a repository of theological ideas against something that does not belong to 'us', against those who are presently adversaries and will remain so if they do not do the right thing and change their disposition towards Jerusalem. When Chronicles are not described as a polemic intended to make a final separation between Judaeans and Samarians but as an endeavour to return those who have erred back to the bosom of the Jerusalem cult,[79] the theological characteristics of Chronicles discussed by Weinberg fall into place quite smoothly in Albertz's model.

A big question mark that hangs over Albertz's reconstruction of Chronicles' historical matrix naturally concerns the dating of the Samaritan schism. He argues quite convincingly that an interaction of political, social, ideological and religious factors brought about and upheld the controversy between the two communities, and in the early Hellenistic era the authors of Chronicles produced an ambitious theological synthesis of older traditions for the purpose of removing the acute and ever-worsening conflict from the agenda with 'peaceful' means. Samaritans are not explicitly mentioned in Chronicles, however, and such an important Deuteronomistic passage as 2 Kings 17 receives no attention from the Chroniclers. In fact, they make no mention of the presence of foreign peoples in the land of Israel in the entire historical narrative, and the regions that according to other evidence were populated by foreigners at that time are portrayed by them as being inhabited

---

79. A typical feature of Chronicles is that before Yahweh's judgment falls on his people, prophets come forward with a warning and a charge to repent and reform. If Chronicles are set within the context of the emerging Samarian conflict, the books themselves may be regarded as representing the same kind of obligatory prophetic warning and call to repentance before anything worse might happen.

by members of the northern tribes alone. Does this not seem quite odd in view of the Chroniclers' alleged theological orientation? Did they not know anything of the schism they were supposed to solve—or were there any schism at all in their day? But considering the peace-making aim of the work, one is entitled to ask why the old and new sins of the adversaries should be catalogued in detail. What could the authors possibly have gained from a presentation of the probably well-known origins of the Samarians? Undoubtedly, they regarded the history of the northern kingdom as illegitimate, but their message is that it was nevertheless not unforgivable. If the grand-scale explication of conciliatory attitude on the part of the Chroniclers towards the inhabitants of the area of the former northern kingdom is taken at face value, not just as a statement of sublime principle, one cannot escape the conclusion that there really were tensions of considerable nature within the postexilic community. It is natural to suppose, then, after the fashion of Albertz, that the tension was generated by some serious issue or group—or community. The natural candidate for the trouble-maker's role is without doubt the Samarians. These considerations contribute to the dating of the Samaritan schism only indirectly at the most, but what they do mean is that it is possible to set, as Albertz does, the chronistic theology within the sociopolitical context of the dawning schism— basically independently of the dating of the schism itself. Consequently, the problem of the dating of Chronicles in Albertz's position is in fact a problem of dating the separation of the Samarian/Samaritan community from Jerusalem. Since it is easy to be caught in a circular argumentation between these two problems, the latter must be solved on the basis of other evidence, not with the help of Chronicles. This is because of the simple reason that there are very few unambiguous pieces of evidence in Chronicles of the books' date and provenance.

The utilization of Samaritan schism in the reconstruction of the historical context of Chronicles has its problems, too, which even Albertz's approach is unable to solve fully. First, modern Chronicles scholarship has naturally recognized a certain ideological/theological tension as a factor that has shaped the Chronicler's thinking. He has been regarded as trying to steer a middle path between strict theological and national extremists in the fashion of Ezra–Nehemiah and more loosely orientated assimilationists. H.G.M. Williamson, for example, has argued that the Chronicler promoted a programme of political and theological reconciliation, the purpose of which was to demonstrate that the division of the Israelite monarchy after Solomon did not put either of the groups hopelessly beyond the boundary of true Israel if they repented and focused again on the true worship of Yahweh in Jerusalem. This programme, which echoed the spirit of the early restoration period, failed, however, and the stricter party of Ezra's and Nehemiah's successors gained the upper hand over the postexilic community. Tangible expressions of the different attitudes drifting to a breaking-point were the construction of a sanctuary on Mount Gerizim and the establishment of a rival religious community at Shechem, later to be known as the Samaritans, in the second half of the fourth century, even if the irreversible break did not follow for another century or so.[80] Although there are clear similarities between the views of Albertz and Williamson, the essential difference is that, contrary to the former's view, Williamson sees in Chronicles a kind of precautionary measure in a tense situation, an attempt to prevent the break in the Jewish society before it actually happened. S. Japhet admits that the position of the Chronicler regarding the Samaritans is understandable only at a time when there were tension between them and the Judaeans. The tension had not yet resulted in a full-blown separation, however. Instead, there was still hope of unification, and that is why the Chronicler composed his work. He called for an end to opposition and rivalry among the people of Israel and summoned all Israel to come together to worship Yahweh in Jerusalem. Japhet emphasizes that the Chronicler's definition of Israel is far too broad and comprehensive for one to assume that he considered the Samaritans a separate community. The Chronicler was convinced that everyone living in the land of Israel constituted an organic part of the people of Israel irrespective of their status—and this at a time when there certainly were large groups of foreigners in Israel.[81] Thus, while Albertz argues not only for the very existence of the community of Samaria but also for the break between it and Jerusalem already before the Chroniclers, Williamson and Japhet maintain that the Samaritan community came into being and eventually broke away from Judaea despite the Chronicler's attempts to speak for reconciliation and unity.

Now, which one of these propositions concerning the Chronicler's

80. See H.G.M. Williamson, 'The Concept of Israel in Transition', in R.E. Clements (ed.), *The World of Ancient Israel: Sociological, Anthropological and Political Perspectives* (Cambridge: Cambridge University Press, 1989), pp. 141-61 (156-57).

81. See Japhet, *Ideology*, pp. 333-34.

failed theological undertaking and its context does better justice to the chronistic view of the people of Israel? Before anything can be said about this, another problem should be mentioned. Both Weinberg and Albertz suppose that Chronicles require a certain type of scribal authorship and a privileged audience that could comprehend the author's intentions. Both conclude that the Chronicler(s) wrote primarily for their own circles, for other scribes and/or authorities of the Judaean community. These suppositions make Chronicles very much look like 'insiders's literature'. Weinberg's position is able to accommodate such an inference without further ado, since he has maintained all the way that Chronicles were written for insiders only, that is, by a person for other persons like him. Albertz's concept runs into some difficulties here, since, according to it, Chronicles were clearly inside stuff by the work's basic nature and intention but the group of people on which it ultimately tried to influence (those following the Samarian cult) was anything but a part of the inside circles of the Judaean society that actually read it. One is entitled to ask here whether a piece of insiders's literature like Chronicles could ever achieve such far-reaching goals as envisaged for it by Albertz—and allegedly by the chronistic circles themselves. To use Weinberg's terminology, was not the contradiction between the work's intent and the 'final' audience's interpretative horizon far too big for the work's message to become accepted? And a negative reaction was precisely what it met: the alleged programme of Chronicles failed to attain its goal. Should one think, therefore, that the Chroniclers got their operative strategy wrong for such an undertaking—and, consequently, the canon revision discussed by Albertz appears mainly as a kind of a happy by-product of an otherwise unsuccessful project? Or were they plain utopists who knew right from the start that this was not going to work? When due attention is paid to the observation that Chronicles was read by 'insiders', it would seem rather natural to suppose, unlike Albertz, that the author(s)'s vision of his audience was 'all Israel' with its inner tensions but without inner separation. This would mean that his/their concept of the people of Israel was based on an attempt to rectify some of the grave mistakes of the Ezra–Nehemiah period by constructing a theological concept which would keep Israel together as a unity despite its inner political, social and religious problems. Albertz, for his part, has to regard Chronicles as 'insiders's literature' aimed at changing the attitudes and behaviour of 'outsiders', or to put it another way, as an attempt to drive home a certain concept of Israel in circles where it probably appeared as nothing more than party propaganda.

There is no doubt that Albertz is aware of these issues. At least that is what one gathers from his emphasizing the non-finality of the separation between the Samarians and Jerusalem to such an extent that his reader cannot help wondering how the Chroniclers really perceived the actual dimensions of the separation and its consequences. It seems, then, that a reflection of the concept of Israel in the light of the literary-sociological nature of Chronicles has not yet resulted in conclusive results in Albertz's position. Despite its problems, Albertz's interpretation has much to commend itself, however, especially as regards Chronicles' social context and function. This is simply because it contains a tangible idea of them, a property that is usually missing from scholarly discussions of Chronicles. Lest the Chronicler's programme of reconciliation—or however one defines the theological synthesis of different traditions it contains—should get too speculative and theoretical, scholars such as Japhet and Williamson have to assume that he saw clear signs of a breaking-down of Israel's integrity in the air and set out to compose his work in order to prevent the worst from happening. One can see that such a view is actually not very far away from Albertz's somewhat unclear idea of the Samarian problem as perceived by the Chroniclers. In my opinion, the failure of the chronistic programme is better explained by assuming that the Chronicler(s) tried to deal with a problem that was already bad than by supposing that he/they took steps to prevent something that was perhaps not even regarded as a problem by all. From the socio-functional point of view, the Chronicler's contribution is more believable as a reaction to existing circumstances (so Albertz) than as a speculative action—but it is sure that in some other's eyes the degree of probability would favour precisely the opposite alternative. The question of whether the Chronicler acted before the Samaritan schism or reacted to it brings a new component to the jigsaw imagery used above and shows how complex and many-sided the issue of the date of Chronicles really is and how much it is affected by external considerations.

One more aspect of Albertz's work deserves a brief mention here. His view of Chronicles as theology of the canon that builds bridges and establishes links rather than breaks them accords well with the general trend of modern Chronicles research. Albertz places a lot of emphasis on the role of Chronicles as a pioneer and forerunner in a process that he calls canon revision, however. Attention is due here to the question made recently by G. Steins. He asks whether Albertz is correct in considering the process of canonization as a consequence of the Chroniclers' work and not as its prerequisite.[82] In other words, can Chronicles, with its failed programme of theological reconciliation and other peculiar features, really provide a sufficient basis and guidelines for the formation of the second and third sections of the Hebrew canon? This question is particularly acute with regard to Chronicles' relation to the Deuteronomistic History. When one takes into account the considerable number of changes, additions, corrections, omissions and outright contradictions that the Chronicler introduced to the work obviously used by him as an important source, it is somewhat difficult to escape the conclusion that the older historical tradition was such a millstone around the Chronicler's neck that he would have got rid of it very willingly if that would have been possible. Since he did not—could not—do that, it is more natural to assume that the books of Samuel and Kings possessed a canonical status of some sort even before the Chronicler than to suppose in the fashion of Albertz that one purpose of his work was to promote their canonization. Precisely the same is true in the case of the books of Ezra and Nehemiah with their theological exclusivism. The way the Chronicler used older traditions in his theological syntheses indicates that they had such an authoritative status that he could neither ignore nor completely rewrite them. Basically, a need for a synthetization of existing traditions reveals that the seemingly problematic elements, such as the Deuteronomistic History for the Chronicler, were firmly established and could not be removed or rejected, whether one wanted it or not. Steins's criticism of Albertz's idea of canon revision thus seems justified, but it does not automatically follow from this that the dating of Chronicles proposed by the latter should be abandoned. Even if the books of Chronicles are not regarded primarily as a canon revision but a *relecture* or reinterpretation of canonical traditions, they can still derive from the Hellenistic era and/or from the context of the Samaritan conflict.[83]

82. Steins, 'Datierung', pp. 89-90.

83. In fact, Steins himself dates Chronicles considerably later than Albertz. He is of the opinion that Chronicles were probably composed for the purpose of marking the closing point and final summary of the third section of the canon and joining the whole together with Torah and the Prophets. He concludes from this that Chronicles must be dated as late as the early Maccabaean period. Steins's view of

When the contributions of Weinberg and Albertz to the discussion of Chronicles' date are compared to the variety of pictures created by a constant juggling with the above-mentioned jigsaw pieces, one can well say that the socio-historical and socio-ideological approach has significantly narrowed the spectrum of different pictures of the date of Chronicles without having to resort to some novel hypotheses of the proper order of the individual pieces. Albertz's pursuit of a clear and methodologically consistent intepretation of Chronicles from this standpoint, in particular, represents a step forward in Chronicles research,

the social and ideological context of Chronicles is, *mutatis mutandis*, in many respects analogous with that of Albertz. Albertz's reconstruction is better substantiated, however, in my opinion, since it provides not only the ideological framework but also an actual social function for Chronicles within the conspectus of the Samarian conflict, while Steins has to be content with a somewhat more speculative situation (restorative efforts of the early Maccabaean period under the pressure of Hellenization) here. See Steins, 'Datierung', p. 91. The view that Chronicles was written with the intention of closing the biblical canon has also been advanced recently by H.J. Koorevaar. According to him, Chronicles' basic function as a closure of the canon can be seen from the author's careful overall planning of his work as well as from his emphasis precisely on the theological themes (David and his dynasty, the special role of the Jerusalem temple) that are central to all other books of the Hebrew Bible, too. But while Steins dates Chronicles very late, Koorevaar goes in the opposite direction. He is convinced that Chronicles bear a Persian stamp all over, not a Greek or Maccabaean one. By assuming that Shallum/Meshullam mentioned in 1 Chron. 9.17-18 and Neh. 12.25-26 was a contemporary of both the Chronicler and Ezra and Nehemiah, Koorevaar reaches the conclusion that Chronicles were written during the last quarter of the fifth century BCE, probably around 425–420. It appears from Koorevaar's discussion that he would even be ready to accept the idea that the author of Chronicles was in fact no lesser a person than Nehemiah himself. Koorevaar argues that the period of the restoration and reorganization of the social order and religious life of the Jewish people under Ezra and Nehemiah constituted an ideal background for establishing the canon of the entire Bible, since this particular measure, in which Chronicles played an important role, had the function of providing the Persian judicial authorities with a kind of constitutional document for the Jewish people. See H.J. Koorevaar, 'Die Chronik als intendierter Abschluss des alttestamentlichen Kanons', *Jahrbuch für evangelikale Theologie* 11 (1997), pp. 42-76. It is obvious that Koorevaar's theory is based on a number of precarious suppositions concerning the date and provenance of the books of the Hebrew Bible. As far as Chronicles and their date are concerned, his answers to the basic questions of why, for whom and in what context these books were written are in need of much more concrete substantiation before they can displace the views of Albertz and Steins.

since it offers a persuasive—even though not unproblematic—combination of insights into the basic issues of why and for whom the enormous theological synthesis of Chronicles was created and in what historical context it answered an acute need.

The final point must be reserved for the question that concerns Chronicles and Hellenistic historiography in general. If an early Hellenistic date of Chronicles is accepted, as Albertz does, for example, it should be noted that the problems of a contemporary situation that the author(s) implicitly dealt with were not evoked by Hellenism as such. They were inherited from the Persian period. Methodologically, now, such an observation allows only very trivial conclusions from chronistic materials: first, the dawn of the Hellenistic period did not signify the end of the ideological and social problems of the Persian era but, at least in the case of Chronicles, their intensification and actualization in a new political and social context. However, to try to shed substantial new light on this context on the basis of chronistic materials alone is a precarious undertaking, due to the paucity of tangible and unambiguous historical data in Chronicles. Secondly, Hellenism possibly presented such a threat to Jewish identity that a Jewish writer like the Chronicler saw it wise to remain tight-lipped about the entire phenomenon. If argumentation from silence is allowed as a methodological procedure, then Chronicles can contribute something to the knowledge of Hellenism and its impact on Jewish history and thought. This state of affairs does not change even if Chronicles are dated later into the Hellenistic period than Albertz does—or significantly earlier in the wake of Weinberg, for that matter, only that the word 'Hellenistic' must then be substituted by the word 'Persian'. The voice of Chronicles would also then be the voice of silence. The course of research should therefore run only from the study of Hellenism to conclusions about Chronicles but not in the opposite direction.

Part III

OTHER CONTRIBUTIONS

THE BIBLE AND HELLENISM: A RESPONSE

Thomas L. Thompson

Robert Carroll

Robert Carroll's contribution to the discussion should form our point of departure. I think we can all agree with this. He begins by distinguishing what we know from what we do not know; namely, we do not know when the Hebrew Bible originated: neither when the earliest scrolls were first committed to writing nor when a collection that approximated one of our canons was first assembled. Our first reliable knowledge derives from the Dead Sea Scrolls, and this presents us with a strong case for origins in the late Persian or early Hellenistic period. Carroll's outline of the potentially historically significant processes of writing, editing, collating and canon building (which would carry us well into the Roman period) and his argument against equivocation on these principles is important. We might well consider the 'biblical' texts among the Dead Sea Scrolls—or shortly before—as our *terminus a quo* and the completed canon as our *terminus ad quem* for dating the Bible. There is a sense of clarity in the argument which will be difficult to gainsay. However simplistic these principles may seem, they have the advantage of dealing directly with the fatal anachronism that lies implicit in the question of the Bible's origin, which this seminar set out to address. If one were to try to date texts which have been included in the Bible to a time before a given section of the collective and collating process had acquired a definable mass—such as we find with the Isaiah Scroll—we would be forced also to include in our discussion those literary productions that are no longer part of the Bible: for example, the implied versions of David stories that are clearly referenced by the dramatizing headings in such canonical psalms as 34, 52 and 56.[1] Once

---

1. T.L. Thompson, 'Historie og Teologi i overskrifterne til Davids salmer', *Collegium Biblicum Årsskrift* (1997), pp. 88-102.

that step is taken, one can hardly stop: should not *Jubilees* be considered at least as proto-biblical? What about the Bileam inscription or Idrimi? It is in fact an aspect of the literary process lying somewhere between Gilgamesh and Genesis 6–9, between Ugarit and the Psalter and between Amenemope and Proverbs, that we are trying to define when we discuss any biblical reality before the canon closes. As a common point of departure for our discussion, we need to define a given literary development that has created a text we can all call biblical. This, Carroll suggests, we can do with a few of the Dead Sea Scrolls. Comparative literature long ago gave up efforts to follow the chains of borrowing that were inevitably and endlessly drawn out of questions of origins.[2] Biblical studies might learn from this.

Niels Peter Lemche

The contribution of Niels Peter Lemche to the meeting in Cracow expands on and qualifies his question about whether the Bible may after all be best studied as a Hellenistic work.[3] He makes his first point with delightful perversity. Having started his career with a prize essay in 1968 that helped undermine Martin Noth's illustrative theological expansion of Albrecht Alt's amphictyony hypothesis,[4] Lemche now strives to reinstate it. While his argument is more fully developed in his recent book *The Israelites in History and Tradition*,[5] it functions in his essay to the European Seminar (pp. 200-224 above) as a supportive argument for his understanding of the Hellenistic context of biblical tradition: here, the so-called Deuteronomistic History. In his second

---

2. One might think here either of James Frazer's chain of tradition linked to a single motif which expanded over a study of seven expansive volumes (*The Golden Bough* [London: Macmillan, 1913–22]) or of such reductionist works as P. Jensen, *Das Gilgamesh Epos in der Weltliteratur* (2 vols.; Marburg, 1906, 1928).

3. N.P. Lemche, 'The Old Testament—A Hellenistic Book?', *SJOT* 7 (1993), pp. 163-93.

4. N.P. Lemche, *Israel i dommertiden: En oversigt over diskussionen om Martin Noths 'Das System der zwölf Stämme Israels'* (Copenhagen: G.E.C. Gad, 1972); M. Noth, *Das System der zwölf Stämme Israels* (BWANT, 10; Neukirchen–Vluyn: Neukirchener Verlag, 1930); A. Alt, 'Ein Reich von Lydda', *ZDPV* 47 (1924), pp. 169-85; also A. Alt, *Die Landnahme der Israeliten in Palästina* (Leipzig: A. Deichertsche Verlag, 1925).

5. *The Israelites in History and Tradition* (Library of Ancient Israel; Louisville, KY: Westminster/John Knox Press, 1998).

argument, which illustrates the 'Taleban' mentality of biblical sectarian discourse, Lemche suggests a social and political perspective of our texts that is theologically orientated towards the establishment of a theocracy. Together with his discussion of amphictyony, this argument has expanded his understanding of the Hellenistic quality of biblical origins to embrace both the history of ideas and the social-historical context of the Bible. Lemche's discussion seems implicitly to argue against Van Seters's earlier chronologies for the Pentateuch by offering the Hellenistic period as a favorable alternative for Van Seters's Greek tradition. Lemche's illustrative arguments are likely to make it quite difficult to argue for any intellectual context that is much earlier than a dating of texts as suggested in Carroll's article. Yet, we need to press Lemche to define what he means by a Hellenistic intellectual context apart from the merely chronological debate with Van Seters, and particularly how his Hellenistic world differs and distinguishes itself from worldviews within earlier forms of the empire.

Lester L. Grabbe[6]

Lester begins his Cracow article with a list of 'assumptions'. These he defends as principles of historical reconstruction, which are in turn based on some fundamental assumptions. First, that 'historical knowledge is possible'. One must object to Grabbe's assertion that this principle is shared by his colleagues, particularly in so far as he tames the statement unacceptably by denying a distinction between what we might know of our own past and the 'more difficult' knowledge of antiquity. I must object to both. The possibility of historical knowledge about antiquity is lacking in both the elusive and deceptive categories of personal memory and in a stabilizing structure of continuity of sources. Moreover, one hardly needs to 'reject one's own past' to be aware that one has precious little of that past as knowledge.

---

6.   Lester Grabbe presented papers at both Cracow and Helsinki. My response here concentrates on his paper from Cracow. At the Helsinki congress, Lester Grabbe gave an extensive review (L.L. Grabbe, 'Hat die Bibel doch Recht? A Review of T.L. Thompson's *The Bible in History*', *SJOT* 14 [2000], pp. 117-39) of my book, *The Bible in History*, together with a response (T.L. Thompson, 'Lester Grabbe and Historiography: An Apologia', *SJOT* 14 [2000], p. 140-61) that focuses on the differences of our perspectives and approaches to historical reconstruction. Because of this, I refer here briefly only to two small issues which are not discussed there: that of the principles of historiography and the use of Ben Sira to date texts.

Secondly, that 'all sources of information are legitimate'. One might see this assumption as an implicit denial of Robert Carroll's earlier discussion of 'bogus sources'.[7] Here again, Lester implicitly ignores important distinctions in his argument that all sources are interpreted. That has never been the issue in distinctions made between archaeologically *derived* information and literarily *asserted* information. Furthermore, Grabbe also ignores a fundamental distinction between primary and secondary sources.

Thirdly, that 'writing history is an exercise in weighing probabilities'. I argued long ago that the probabilities of ancient history, in fact, are not and cannot be weighed.[8] It is rather a hypothesis that can be confirmed which is significant for history-writing. This has nothing to do with probability. An unconfirmed possibility is simply a statement awaiting refutation: only a guess in an nearly infinite sea of possibilities. Consider for a moment a historical argument constructed of a chain of argument associating five distinct elements of evidence, each of which is judged to have a probability of being 50 per cent accurate (e.g. an event datable in either 597 or 586). Such arguments are commonplace among the details of historical arguments in antiquity. An accumulation of so many different elements interpretable as evidence would encourage most of us quite favorably towards the reconstruction's probable. In fact, however, its probability can be calculated ($0.5 \times 0.5 \times 0.5 \times 0.5 \times 0.5$) as hardly more than 3 per cent probable! And before we begin to assume that even such probability is meaningful historically, we should ask whether our judgment of 50 per cent probability of our first element of evidence is trustworthy in any way. How would anyone know what might probably have been? The language of Grabbe's principles is not so much tendentious as anachronistic, belonging to an older, uncritical stage of history-writing. In the ancient history of Palestine or Syria, multiple and independent sources hardly exist. We have data (textual and artifactual) which we interrelate and define as specific results or effects in an effort to reconstruct what is implicit in them. This fragile, reconstructive process provides us with sources for history.

7.   R.P. Carroll, 'Madonna of Silences: Clio and the Bible', in Lester L. Grabbe (ed.), *Can a 'History of Israel' Be Written?* (JSOTSup, 245; ESHM, 1; Sheffield: Sheffield Academic Press, 1997), pp. 84-103.

8.   T.L. Thompson, *The Historicity of the Patriarchal Narratives* (Berlin: W. de Gruyter, 1974), pp. 51-54.

Practice, however, is always different from theory, and Lester Grabbe is a very good reader of texts. In reading, for example, Hecataeus on Jews, Grabbe finds that Hecataeus is discussing Jews of his own time—regardless of the text's claim. In honouring this fundamental principle of texts as historical sources—that texts are sources of implied not asserted information—his analysis supports understanding.

There are of course a few caveats. He assumes that names of West Semitic or Hebrew derivation are Jewish, a common fallacy in our field.[9] The Tobias variations might reflect literary variations on a stock character: much in the spirit of Philip Davies's Moses.[10] Similarly, Grabbe's confidence in the historicity of the Ben Sira collophon does not consider the stock literary overtones since Amenemope that hardly allow us to date this text to the time of an authorial grandfather. Similarly, when Ben Sira refers to a pentateuchal tradition, we must remember that the text remains variable for some centuries yet. Finally, Grabbe's discussion of the traumatic events of deportation not only assumes that biblical traditions in some form already existed at the time, but also that these traditions were national and ethnic in their orientation. These implicit assumptions are far from anything we know! Grabbe, moreover, ignores multiple known deportations over centuries in order to favour one of the much later biblical stories that places Jerusalem's deportation in 587.[11]

While Lester Grabbe's third principle echoes John Bright's well-known 'history of the possible' which Bright had proposed in opposition to the more aetiologically sensitive historiography of his German contemporaries Martin Noth and Gerhard von Rad,[12] and his second principle is a tautology flirting with the banal, his starting principle is an act of faith. Given the title of the first session which brought this

9.   Especially tendentious in this regard is J. Tigay's statistically based study *You Shall Have No Other Gods: Israelite Religion in the Light of Hebrew Inscriptions* (HSM, 31; Atlanta: Scholars Press, 1986).

10.   See further below, pp. 279-82.

11.   See, however, Lester L. Grabbe (ed.), *Leading Captivity Captive: 'The Exile' as History and Ideology* (JSOTSup, 278; ESHM, 2; Sheffield: Sheffield Academic Press, 1998), *passim.*

12.   J. Bright, *Early History in Recent History Writing* (SBT, 19; London: SCM Press, 1956); cf. esp. the responses: M. Noth, 'Der Beitrag der Archäologie zur Geschichte Israels', *VT* 7 (1960), pp. 262-82, and G. von Rad, 'History and the Patriarchs', *ExpTim* 72 (1960–61), pp. 213-16.

seminar together ('Can a "History of Israel" Be Written?'), one must also say that he begs the very question he should be addressing.

Philip Davies

While Grabbe's historiographical reading of texts is far more *au courant* than his principles, as well as far more convincing, Philip Davies's article goes directly to the heart of the problem of written 'sources' for our historiography. One might be well served by reading Robert Carroll's question about 'bogus sources' between the lines of Davies's essay. I suspect that after reading Davies' essay, Grabbe needs to modify his second assumption. While he is so engaged, we need to ask ourselves whether—in considering the question of Israel's origins— Davies's 'bogus sources' aren't at least as legitimate as the only possibly earlier, yet canonized, 'sources' that we all have accepted as legitimate. The association with events—whether of a biblical national history or biography, or of one or other of Davies's bogus sources—is an association which we scholars have created within our imaginations, and it is that imaginative perspective which allows us to identify the one as a source 'worth considering' and another as bogus. Behind this debate is an *assumption of events*, what Burke Long identified more than a decade ago as a 'fundamentalist's assumption' in scholarly historiography of ancient Israel, namely, that sacred texts render history.[13]

While Davies might appear somewhat equivocal in his gentle rebuttal of some of the historicist arguments which have allowed historians to maintain the assumption of event behind the canonical variants of our Moses tradition,[14] and while I have some rather emphatic doubts that

---

13. B.O. Long, 'On Finding the Hidden Premises', *JSOT* 39 (1987), pp. 10-14. See also his 'Historical Narrative and the Fictionalizing Imagination', *VT* 35 (1985), pp. 405-416.

14. For example, the assertion that slavery in Egypt is a motif which is unlikely to be invented in a national history of origins, first of all assumes that we are dealing with perceived events of national origins: an implicit assumption of events of origin (however known) in the classification of the tale's genre. However, the motif of the oppression in Egypt itself is a wonderful example of the singularly most frequently used plot-motif in the Bible, namely 'the success of the unpromising'—a motif which is fundamental to the text's theological argument of Israel as the people of God, rather than a people like others. The problem of such a historicist reading is that it ignores what is fundamental to the text. Similarly, the creatively contradictory fragmentation and parade of variants which make up the

Davies's 'history of a story' is in fact possible, the methodology implicit throughout the essay is fundamentally at odds with Lester Grabbe. This opposition is apparent from the very beginning when Davies introduces non-canonical tale variants of the Exodus/Moses story. Grabbe handles historiographical variants with distinction, with the definition of event as his arbiter. Here, however, grounds for arbitration are absent, and the variants must fight on the very unsystematic grounds of rhetoric and reception.

For purposes of debate, Davies proposes a history of a story as an alternative to historicist questions relating to a history of events. While I can only applaud the heuristic function of this search, one must doubt the legitimacy of the quest itself. One does not have a story with a history, but rather a wide range of narrative variants with an interlocking narrative discourse at play. For example, already at the close of the paradise story and again in the Tower of Babel tale, the protagonists are driven out; the Joseph stories share the motifs of exodus and return, just as the 18th Dynasty's Hyksos tale has motifs of entrance and expulsion. So, too, the biblical Moses story has a leper motif that remains unresolved within the biblical tradition itself. Davies's argument loses some of its edge as he centres the coherence of his story's history in the language of event; as if the story were, in fact, one of the many stories about a specific past. He asserts an accumulation of a genre of fictive historiography, much as the very best of our historic critics have done.[15] The assumption of such a genre, however, forces him unnecessarily to separate his story collections on grounds of diverging ideologies, even though the received tradition betrays little distress with variable themes, scenes or episodes. So, the presentation of Saul's death displays several variations on the theme of fear in the transition from 1–2 Samuel; variable creation aetiologies are offered in Genesis's prologue, just as the nations are spread in both Genesis 10 and 11, each its own reiteration of the expulsion of Gen. 3.23-24.

---

bulk of the wilderness tradition are fundamental aspects of our texts, even as they form an emphatic—though implicit—rebuttal of arguments that we are dealing with either biography or historiography.

15. So, most recently, J. Van Seters, *The Life of Moses* (Louisville: Westminster, 1992). Cf. T.L. Thompson, 'Tradition and History: The Scholarship of John Van Seters' in S.L. Mckenzie and T. Römer, *Rethinking the Foundations: Historiography in the Ancient World and in the Bible* (BZAW, 294; Berlin: W. de Gruyter, 2000), pp. 9-21.

While Davies is undoubtedly correct in seeing Manetho's account as a close cousin of Hecataeus's—given only the dozen or so variants that have survived—it also shares fundamental motifs with both the Hyksos tradition and the Exodus–Numbers accounts, and, as one begins to assemble pertinent variants, one can hardly leave out the exile stories of 2 Kings or the tales of return in Ezra and Nehemiah. It is not so much a story as such that has travelled and developed and had a history; rather it is motifs that travel, each with its own passport to other lands of story. Scribes have given these motifs to cluster around reiterated themes, rendering implicit critical commentaries, that give reference to and echo their colleagues working within a wide variety of a society's literary functions. The streams of tradition in which the themes of 'being driven out' and of 'escaping', of exodus and exile fluctuate with variable protagonists, goals and contexts, hardly allows a hunt for historical matrices for the development of such specific literary motifs. Davies' two-tradition hypothesis—particularly viewed in opposition to Van Seters's fictional biography of Moses—while offering a very strong step in the right direction, can nevertheless blind us to the no less than six variations of the 'Moses story' within the book of Exodus alone and to the well more than a dozen implicit tales of this type within the canon. It may also blind us to the many other tales—biblical and non-biblical—that serve the same function, but lack the particular name of Moses as hero. Davies is emphatically right that, if we are to do a literary history, we must break the canon and look at the Bible's greater context in the world of such story. At the same time, one must not arbitrarily limit oneself to a single hypothetical tale-type as Davies has done. For example, the development of the biblical theme of the process of the soul's movement from slavery to son-ship, which informs so much of the exodus narrative, is not so much an intellectual movement reflecting on Israel's historical origins in the past, as it is a theological discourse which heuristically casts old Israel in the 'way of all flesh'.

It has to be repeated: theories of borrowing and the historiography of tales was given up in comparative literature more than half a century ago. When one has but two or three variants of a story episode, one might well be found discussing which had led to which.[16] However, our literary worlds are larger than the historical, and we should not forget

16. T.L. Thompson, 'A New Attempt to Date the Patriarchs', *JAOS* 98 (1978), pp. 76-84.

what we learned from Frazer's collection of flood stories.[17] Similarly, biblical stories of salvation, testing and backsliding, motifs of the desert and the new creation, which arise from it like the phoenix from the ashes, display a compositional interrelationship that ever escapes the narrowness of a historicist perspective. This, I think, is made emphatically clear in Davies's discussion of the Egyptian king Amenophis leading an expedition to Ethiopia during a revolt of lepers and their allies from Jerusalem. Such revolt motifs are correctly marked as stock motifs in Egyptian narrative. They belong to a very specific cluster that we find reiterated in a broad stream of creation motifs.[18] Following folklore's common dichotomous view of the world, one finds two patterns developing: uniting the two lands of upper and lower Egypt or destroying the enemies of the North and the South. For example, the Memphite theology's divine pharaoh's struggle against Seth and the powers of death is found reiterated in the Narmer Palette, whose proto-hieroglyphs present King Narmer smiting the *ȝmw* in the Delta.[19] The Narmer Palette offers us a creation story, not historiography. Meri-Ka-Re offers us a lamentation from the First Intermediate period of the Delta dwelling *ȝmw* 'becoming people everywhere'.[20] The *ȝmw* of both these texts play a cosmic role similar to 'the nations', the enemies of Yahweh and his Messiah, who play out their mythic roles in Psalms 2, 8, 89 and 110. This same motif is implicit in the *Execration Texts,* in the 18 Dynasty's creation story centring on the expulsion of the Hyksos, and throughout the many stories referenced in Davies's essay. By carrying us outside the canon, Davies has freed these narratives from some of the historical anchors created by our assumptions and expectations. He also carries us out of the field of history and into that of comparative literature. If we followed him there, it would bring about an important shift in our discussions.

17. James Frazer, *Folklore in the Old Testament* (3 vols.; London: Macmillan, 1919).

18. To see some of the broad range of motifs that are involved in the Moses exodus tale, see T.L. Thompson and D. Irvin, 'The Joseph and Moses Narratives', in J.H. Hayes and J.M. Miller (eds.), *Israelite and Judean History* (Philadelphia: Westminster Press, 1977), pp. 149-212; esp. pp. 181-209.

19. *ANET*, pp. 4-5; *ANEP*, frontispiece.

20. *ANET*, pp. 414-18.

David Gunn

David Gunn's open puzzlement about the histories of Israel, of its religion and the many Old Testament theologies that have been created on the basis of a history of a literature is well expressed. I doubt that any such histories can be written any longer—even as I still believe that we can continue to talk meaningfully about the social, literary and theological worlds implied by our texts. This, however, would have little to do with a 'history' of the literature, however much we might think of such contexts as historical. 'Late dating' is a term that Gunn uses, or—given the quotation marks—perhaps one he has borrowed. Although I don't find chronology particularly informative, the issue is hardly indifferent. Apart from the issues of Robert Carroll's discussion, we should be cautious in moving away from a chronology that is conservatively close to the Dead Sea Scrolls. Much earlier dates push us into a discussion based on texts we don't have. They also push us into an understanding of a society (namely, of 'ancient Israel') which is more or less identical with what one normally calls a story world. This problem is not done away with merely by adding a sum of 500 years to all of our known dates. Chronology is meaningless without some quite detailed societal content to link it with. At the moment, we have precious little more than a biblical past to work with.

I believe that there are two issues on which Gunn and I miss each other. I believe the responsibility is mine. In using a concept of 'tradition', I have chosen to be both coy and intentionally vague. My purpose is to buy time to develop a hypothesis in process. The book which he reviews[21] intends to be comprehensive, but the discourse is only begun. What Gunn refers to as 'the complexity of the tradition's composition'—a complexity that he judges I have not sufficiently acknowledged—is, of course, a well-established dogma of historical critical scholarship. I had hoped to raise doubt about that dogma, without challenging it too directly. My effort was limited to an attempt to illustrate what I saw as the tradition's surprising coherence and relative simplicity. That this simpler explanation might function as Ockham's razor to a prior generation's puzzled complexity was not my explicit intention. Having chosen to cast the historical context of biblical composition in

---

21. T.L. Thompson, *The Mythic Past: Biblical Archaeology and the Myth of Israel* (New York: Basic Books, 1999) (= *The Bible in History: How Writers Create a Past* [London: Jonathan Cape, 1999]).

terms of literary, intellectual and social worlds, I felt the more generic term 'tradition' helped me to avoid the anachronism of limiting myself to those specific texts that later took on their reception's character as biblical—defined by convention's canon. At least theoretically, I needed to open my discussion to the larger world of early Jewish composition. Even this broad perspective needed to be expanded in order to include both all the many 'Judaisms' or 'New Israels' known among social groups of the Hellenistic and Graeco-Roman periods, as well as to include other non-biblical texts which shared some of the central ideological pivots within a literary world whose 'biblical' core provided but an arbitrary centre, among so many possible perspectives that one might choose to take. In this respect, I see Davies's essay supporting my maximalist terminology. Of course, such expansiveness needed restraints to prevent my 'tradition' from encompassing most anything ever written or thought in antiquity! Yet, any such restraints create barriers to be overcome. For example, my understanding of the development of inclusive monotheism required that the intellectual context of my texts be open to an inclusion of universalist thought from at least the Assyrian period and later.

It was through the analysis of Genesis's and *Jubilees*'s discussion of the Cain Story that I first became aware that both of these texts reflected secondary refractions of the tradition. They also presented a discussion—implicitly and explicitly—commenting and interpreting the story they held in common. The emerging theory implied in this perception is buttressed by my discussions of *Testimonia*'s (4QTestim) 'lego-blocks' as illustrative of composition techniques which built on literary variants and the ubiquitous Semitic rhetoric of parallelism. The relationship of one of the redactional aspects in the book of Psalms, implying a distinctive version of the David narratives, convinced me that my 'secondary discourse' had taken over the authorial voice of the text in transmission. In this discussion, 'tradition' came to refer to the intellectual and literary world which was engaged in an implicit discourse that repeatedly marked the process of collecting, revising and interpreting our texts.

Although 'sources'—whether historical or literary—might be theoretically excavated with various synoptic exercises, comparative folklore studies amply warn us away from trying to establish chains of borrowing even in regard to well-known and nearly contemporary traditions. I find it difficult to privilege any of our extant texts as 'primary'. Not only are both *Jubilees* and Genesis quite distinctive works, each holding its own right to existence, but both show a level of discourse that marks them as secondary stages within an ongoing, much larger discourse—had it not been that the movement towards canon has tried to close and define them. Having said so much, I can hardly reasonably avoid the issue Gunn raises about historical criticism's confidence in a sufficient complexity of composition to justify its two centuries of scholarly analysis—or what he more appropriately calls 'failed detective work'. That this encourages Gunn to avoid a discussion of dating is unfortunate, since the liberal protestant theology, which historical criticism expresses, has much at stake in separating the Bible's theological centre from early Judaism. I also find myself disagreeing with him as he identifies the problem as one of dating; rather than, for example, as one of failed reading. In positing such hopeless complexity at the centre of his composition theory, Gunn makes biblical literature special even before it becomes biblical: again a protestant perspective.

That historical criticism's project has ended in failure should hardly discourage us from choosing other avenues. I am convinced our texts were written—at least those among the Dead Sea Scrolls—one word after another, like most texts before the invention of movable type. I don't find these texts so terribly complicated; I find their antiquity and their lack of context much more difficult to deal with. I can find only relatively few big themes in the Bible, and hardly more than a few hundred significant motifs and motif clusters. The implied processes of composition seem easily transparent, so far as human language goes. Certainly Egyptian and cuneiform literature is more daunting. For the sake of procedure, I have suggested that we begin to read across our texts that we might better recognize the many common dimensions throughout this literature. We need to begin collecting and classifying the component units of the tradition that are fixed in our texts and establish some comparative taxonomies as aids in working out the specific techniques and literary functions of this material. This will help us speak quite concretely about composition in antiquity. Neither chronology nor historical development seem very promising in such a discussion. In 200 years, such efforts have not rendered history. I think that chimeric goal—whatever its theological value for our origin story of Christianity—has to be given up.

I would like to close my response with a discussion of the one issue on which I believe Gunn and I emphatically disagree: the function of my 'theology of the way' as a hallmark of the tradition. The ideology expressed in the 'theology of the way' as an intellectual worldview seems to be a perception that is pervasive in biblical literature. It implicates the bulk of the narrative, poetic and wisdom literature of the Bible. It offers an ideological basis that is fundamental to sectarianism: from the sectarian strains of Ezra and the Damascus covenant to modern fundamentalist movements within Islam, Christianity and Judaism (here listed in the reverse order of their supersessionism). The world is divided into two opposing mythical forces and ways of life; it is dualistic. It is also an intellectual and learned tradition which involves a habit of philosophical critique and alienation from both the ordinary political world and established religion. This theology seems to colour the primary voices implied in the texts which motivate tradition collection. It is idealistic and socially utopian. As such, it is potentially violent towards any society that supports or tolerates it. The search for righteousness and divine understanding alienates the practitioner from any who are perceived as living outside such fellowship. While the story problems of the past can be cast into future hopes, they can also be used to demand changes of the present—hence my use of Lemche's Talebans as illustration, and hence my suggestion that some elements among the Jews of the Maccabbaean period had attempted to create just such a society. Just as easily, one could point to Calvin's Geneva. The Maccabbees offered me an illustration of some of the more virulent strains of hatred connected with this ideology that surfaces in so many of our texts from Ezra to Matthew. Apart from such sectarian perversions of this 'philosophy of the path', Gunn's efforts to suggest alternative ideologies seems more to reflect aspects of this intellectual discourse than real departures from such a worldview. Think of the Cain story with pietism's epitomizing instruction: 'One need only do the good; then one might hold one's head high'. This does not force the discourse towards a proverbial matching of slogans; one can just as well force an opposition: 'What if one does what is evil?' is a question implicit to such thinking. A god of promise also repents of his promise; creation already implies it is opposite the cosmic desert of destruction's *tohu wa-bohu* (Jer. 4.23, etc.).[22]

---

22. For the reiterative significance of *tohu wa-bohu* in biblical narrative, see T.L. Thompson, 'Historiography in the Pentateuch, Twenty-Five Years after Historicity', *SJOT* 13 (1999), pp. 258-83.

THE OLD TESTAMENT—A HELLENISTIC BOOK?[*]

Niels Peter Lemche

1. *The Septuagint and the Hebrew Bible—Some Basic Issues*

It may be rather imprecise to call the Old Testament a Hellenistic book —as not all Old Testaments can be Hellenistic.

It is obvious that the Septuagint must be considered Hellenistic, since it was not translated before the Hellenistic period. The Hebrew Bible is, on the other hand, not a Hellenistic book, for the simple reason that it— in its present shape—is a Jewish rabbinic collection of writings no earlier than the second century CE (although the beginning of this process of canonization can be traced further back).

Thus it is reasonable to connect the appearance of the Hebrew Bible with the historical catastrophes that drastically influenced the life of the Jewish communities, especially in Palestine, at the end of the first century CE, and in the first half of the 2nd century CE, and which threatened to remove the Jews from history. Also a new threat to the Jewish faith may have been important, that is the Christian religion, which— although originally part of the Jewish world—developed into a major opponent to Jewish religious society. Moreover, Christianity argued that it had simply replaced the Jewish religion as the only legitimate faith.

According to James Barr, R.H. Lightfoot once claimed that the origin of the New Testament should be sought in the moment the early Christians, under the impression of the first Roman persecutions, lost faith in the survival of their religion. As a result of their fear, they decided to write down their traditions and recollections, in order that

*   This article represents a rewritten and greatly expanded version of my article in Danish, 'Det gamle Testamente som en hellenistisk bog', *DTT* 55 (1992), pp. 81-101. The Danish original goes back to a public lecture held in Copenhagen, 31 March 1992. It was first published in English in *SJOT* 7 (1993), pp. 163-93, of which this is a slightly revised version (published with permission of *SJOT*).

these might not be lost or deliberately perverted.[1] The canonization of the Hebrew Bible may also have been caused by motives like these, not to be separated from the fact that the Jews had seen their religious centre, the temple, defiled and destroyed, and—probably already before the canonization process had reached its goal—had had to evacuate their traditional religious home, Jerusalem, to become foreigners in their own country.[2]

A number of differences exist between the Hellenistic Septuagint and the later Hebrew Bible. One of them consists in the fact that a number of books in the Septuagint are not included in the Hebrew Bible, although they are certainly to be considered holy writ in the Septuagint. We also find other differences in the organization of the individual books; these are more or less extensive differences of wording or different arrangements of chapters and paragraphs. The major differences are: (1) the arrangement of the books in the Hebrew Bible in comparison to the Septuagint; and (2) the absence in the Hebrew Bible of several books already included in the Septuagint.

The first part, the different arrangements of canonical books in the Septuagint and the Hebrew Bible, is well known to most people, as it is perpetuated in the difference of arrangement of books in the Hebrew Bible and in most modern bibles of the present age. The issue of interest here is that the modern versions generally follow the arrangement present in the Septuagint, and disregard the organization of the Hebrew Bible. It is a matter of discussion how, in the first place, such a difference emerged. From a chronological point of view, it is likely that the Septuagintal order of books should be considered older than the one found in the Hebrew Bible, which was hardly in existence in pre-Christian times, and it may be assumed that the different arrangement of the Hebrew Bible had polemical reasons. The original order in both Greek and Hebrew traditions was the Law followed by the Prophets, while they differed when it came to the incorporation of other writings. We may suppose (but it is only a supposition) that the decisions made by the Greek-speaking Jews of Alexandria to place the writings between the Law and the Prophets, in a Palestinian Jewish environment of a later

---

1.   Cf. James Barr, *The Bible in the Modern World* (London: SCM Press, 1973), p. 43.

2.   In 135 CE, after the insurrection against the Romans under Hadrian.

date, may have looked too obviously like a Christian choice (Law and Prophecy followed by the fulfillment of Prophecy).[3]

As far as the selection of writings is concerned, it is well known that all books in the Hebrew Bible are to be found in the Septuagint, while several books of the Septuagint have no place in the Hebrew canon. One principle seems to have governed the selection of writings in the Hebrew Bible: no book can officially belong to a period later than the days of Ezra the scribe, in the biblical historiography. Of course, this is an ideological reason for accepting or rejecting books, as quite a few among the Old Testament writings must be considered considerably younger than Ezra, including, among others, the Song of Songs, Daniel, Ecclesiastes and Job. However, so far as these books had obtained canonical status, they have all been provided with an 'author' considerably older than Ezra, such as Solomon, or they have been placed in a historical situation that clearly antedates Ezra, as happened to Daniel which was placed back in Neo-Babylonian and Achaemenid times. This principle may, however, be owing to a rather late development and may not have been in force when the Septuagintal selection of writings was determined. Ezra's position as the one who finally installed the Law seems to be a creation of fairly late Jewish thinking. In favor of this, the fact that Jesus Sirach does not know Ezra but—in his historical overview (Sir. 42–50)—skips over the period from Nehemiah to the high priest Simon, the son of Onias (Sir. 49.13; 50).[4] The persons responsible for the selection of books to be included in the Septuagint[5] were thus not constrained to acknowledge only books that could be attributed to figures of ancient Israelite history; they were free to include whatever kind of writing—maybe even contemporary writings—they pleased.

---

3.   Thus the references to the Tana(kh) in other writings, e.g. in the Prologue to Jesus Sirach, and in the New Testament, can hardly be considered conclusive evidence of the originality of the order in the Hebrew Bible. This information is more likely an indication of a hierarchical kind of order: (1) the Law; (2) the Prophets; and (3) whatever else; without reference to the actual place of the ketubim inside the Tanakh. For recent overviews of this problematic, cf. J.A. Sandars, 'Canon', *ABD*, I, pp. 837-58, and also M.K.H. Peters, 'Septuagint', *ABD*, V, pp. 1093-1104.

4.   The point is well made by G. Garbini, *History and Ideology in Ancient Israel* (London: SCM Press, 1988), p. 152.

5.   In order not to be misunderstood this should be stressed: it is most likely that more than one selection of books was made, and that the standardization into only one canon may have been a phenomenon of a fairly late period.

However, when we compare the books of the Septuagint to the ones of the Hebrew Bible, the importance of the author—that he must per-force be pre-Ezraen—seems not always to have been decisive, as some books in the Septuagint, such as the Psalms of Solomon, the Wisdom of Solomon and the first book of Esdras, were not found worthy to be incorporated into the Hebrew Bible. In this case, some other principles may have governed the decisions, perhaps only the mechanical one that no Hebrew manuscript of these books was extant.[6] It should be rela-tively easy to isolate two such major principles: (1) the requirement that the content of a certain book not be in conflict with dominating Jewish-theological doctrines of the day; and (2) the requirement that books of special interest to religious groups such as the early Church—especially apocalyptic literature—be discarded, or be represented as little as pos-sible.[7]

Although these issues are interesting—and at the same time provoca-tive—this is not the place to go further. Very little has been done here from an Old Testament point of view, because of a lack of interest on the part of Old Testament scholars, since the Hebrew Bible in the Chris-tian scholarly tradition has obtained a position as the only relevant subject of study.[8] To the extent that the already mentioned particular-ities of the Septuagint and the Hebrew Bible may be considered facts (so far as we are entitled to speak about 'facts' in Old Testament stud-ies), the argument here cannot be considered controversial. It is there-fore time to return to the theme of this article: whether or not the Old Testament was a Hellenistic book.

2. *Tanakh and Hellenism*

a. *The Samaritan Schism*
When New Testament authors refer to writings in the Old Testament, however, according to the order of the Hebrew Bible, it is arguable that the first two parts of the Tanakh are attributed a special importance in

---

6.   Whether or not such a Hebrew 'Vorlage' for these books has ever existed is irrelevant to the present argument.

7.   The exception to this rule is, of course, the book of Daniel. This is not to deny that some earlier witnesses of the embryonic apocalyptic tradition were also accepted, say, Ezekiel and Zechariah.

8.   *Pace* the hard-working and learned minority of Septuagint specialists, form-ing the body of the IOSCS.

their Jewish context. The Law must be considered all-important, closely followed by the Prophets. The Writings, on the other hand, are certainly less important, if they are included at all in the Tanakh.[9] This hierarchical subordination of the different groups of books is normally attributed to their redaction history, the Pentateuch being the oldest collection, followed by the Prophets, whereas the Writings are understood to be no more than a late amalgamation of different types of literature. The translation of the first two groups, however, took place already before the appearance of the third group.

Scholars often refer to the existence of the Samaritan Pentateuch as an additional proof of this redactional history of the books of the Hebrew Bible. Because the Samaritan congregation only accepted the Law as holy writ, and not the Prophets and the Writings, it may be assumed that the Pentateuch was the only part of the Hebrew Bible in existence when the Samaritan schism occurred. This schism is usually dated to circa 300 BCE, which suggests that at least the Law should not be considered a work of the Hellenistic age.[10] When it comes to the Prophets, the date of composition may be the subject of discussion. Parts of the collection of prophetic books may certainly be very late, such as Trito-Isaiah and Malachi. Of course, most of the Writings can be considered literature of the Hellenistic period. This argument, which is based on the traditional dating of a Samaritan schism, is not a very strong one.

First of all, it may be assumed that ideological as well as political reasons were of decisive importance when the Samaritans had to choose what was to become their 'Bible'. In those days there may have been plenty of reasons for the Samaritans to accept only the five books of Moses and to exclude all other parts of the present Old Testament (whether Greek or Hebrew). The religious center of Judaism as expressed by the greater part of the Old Testament is certainly Jerusalem,

---

9. Cf. Mt. 5.17; 7.12; 22.30; Lk. 16.16; Acts 13.15; 24.14: exclusively ὁ νόμος καὶ οἱ προφῆται; cf., however, the enigmatic Lk. 24.44: πάντα τὰ γεγραμμένα ἐν τῷ νομῷ Μωϋσέως καὶ τοῖς προφήταις καὶ ψαλμοῖς. Sirach, Prologue διὰ τοῦ νόμου καὶ τῶν προφητῶν (cf., however, also Sir. 39.1: again only the Law and the Prophets).

10. On this recently, B. Otzen, *Judaism in Antiquity: Political Developments and Religious Currents from Alexander to Hadrian* (The Biblical Seminar, 7; Sheffield: JSOT Press, 1990), p. 29. It is the opinion of Otzen that the Samaritans deliberately broke the relationships to mainstream Jewry, rather than being ostracized by the community of Jews in Jerusalem.

and not Shechem or Mount Gerizim. Contrasting this, Jerusalem plays a very reduced role in the books of the Pentateuch, where much more interest is invested in the homeland of the Samaritans. We should therefore simply ask the question: why should any Samaritan, who found himself in outspoken opposition to Jerusalem, want to include writings in his Bible that accepted Jerusalem as the one and only center of the worship of God? This may be the reason why the historical books were not to be part of the Samaritan Bible, but it also explains the absence of prophets from the Samaritan canonical literature, because the prophets —including Amos and Hosea—were certainly considered proponents of the worship of Yahweh in Jerusalem. And it goes without saying that a collection like the book of Psalms could never become a Samaritan favorite—provided, of course, that the psalms were in fact mostly connected with the temple of Jerusalem!

Secondly, the date of the Samaritan schism is not an established fact. It may have happened before 300 BCE, but it could just as well be considerably younger—or to put it bluntly: we do not know when or how such a separation occurred.[11]

b. *Literary Matters*

The objections that can be directed against the Samaritan schism as the main witness to the existence of the Pentateuch before, say, 300 BCE, will of course not make the Old Testament a Hellenistic book. It will therefore be necessary to broaden the perspective of the discussion by including other aspects, literary as well as historical

It seems obvious to most scholars that our estimate of the age of a certain book of the Old Testament must be founded on information contained in the book itself and not on other information, and the estimate should certainly not be based on the existence of a historical background that may never have existed. Although seemingly self-evident, this method is not without fault, and it may easily become an invitation to 'tail-chasing', to quote Philip R. Davies.[12] By this we intend to say

11. Cf. the excellent although rather compressed discussion in J.A. Soggin, *Einführung in die Geschichte Israels und Judas* (Darmstadt: Wissenschaftliche Buchgesellschaft, 1991), pp. 219-22. According to Soggin the schism was in the later Jewish tradition referred back to the time of Ezra and Nehemiah, although Soggin also acknowledges that the schism was not an indisputable fact before the Hellenistic period.

12. Cf. Philip R. Davies, *In Search of 'Ancient Israel': A Study in Biblical*

that the scholar may soon become entangled in a web of logically circular argumentation which is conveniently called the 'hermeneutical circle' (in order to make it more acceptable among exegetes because of its supposed inevitability). Another point is that it is also supposed that the reading of a certain piece of literature will automatically persuade it to disclose its secrets—as if no other qualifications are needed.

The first point to discuss will be the circular argumentation that is based on a too close 'reading' of the biblical text. Here the first example will be the books of Samuel. Some assume that these books must be old simply because they say that they are old.[13] The exegete who claims that the books of Samuel must perforce be old will, as his point of departure, have to accept the claim of the books themselves by either rather naively assuming that Samuel could be the author (as the later Jewish tradition did claim) or by more sophisticated argumentation, for example, of the kind formerly often used to prove narratives like the 'Succession Story' to be old because only an eye-witness would have been acquainted with the particulars of the family of David.[14] In order to escape from the trap created by this circular method of argumentation and the rather naive understanding of the biblical text that lies at the bottom of such claims, it will be necessary to go further and find arguments not necessarily part of the biblical text itself but coming

Origins (JSOTSup, 148; Sheffield: JSOT Press, 1992), p. 36, here used in connection with the reconstruction of the so-called 'ancient Israel' based on information contained in much later (Old Testament) literature.

13. The example is only one among plenty of other possibilities. The example might just as easily have been the Pentateuch or any part of the Deuteronomistic History. We could easily include also the prophetic books in the argument. Cf. N.P. Lemche, 'The God of Hosea', in E. Ulrich, J.W. Wright, Philip R. Davies and Robert P. Carroll (eds.), *Priests, Prophets and Scribes: Essays on the Formation and Heritage of Second Temple Judaism in Honour of Joseph Blenkinsopp* (JSOTSup, 149; Sheffield: JSOT Press, 1992), pp. 241-55.

14. Cf A. Weiser, *Einleitung in das Alte Testament* (Göttingen: Vandenhoeck & Ruprecht, 6th edn, 1966), p. 151; cf. the somewhat more interesting argumentation in L. Rost, *Die Überlieferung von der Thronnachfolge Davids* (1926), reprinted in his *Das kleine Credo und andere Studien zum Alten Testament* (Heidelberg: Quelle & Meyer, 1965), pp. 119-253, see p. 234. If so, scandals in royal families may not be the subject of only modern boulevard journalists! However, it should never be forgotten who will be best acquainted with inner thoughts of the participants in a narrative or play: of course, the author himself who invented his figures.

from other sources. Such information alone will be able to disclose to the reader that the books of Samuel were composed, not at the moment when Israel's got its first king, but at a much later date.

The case of the books of Samuel is hardly unproblematic. Samuel cannot, of course, be the author, since he passes away already in 1 Samuel 25, yet like a ghost reappears three chapters later. However, after this point anybody could be the author and the only thing that can be said for sure is that the *terminus a quo* for the composition of the books must be at a date following the death of Samuel, which might be dated, according to both biblical and modern scholarly tradition, in the late eleventh century BCE. The logical *terminus ad quem* for the composition must, however, be the moment when we possess the first complete scroll or book containing the text of the two books of Samuel as a whole. This is not the case before, at the earliest, the first half of the fourth century CE, the date of the presumably oldest Greek manuscript (the Vaticanus) of the Septuagint. As a consequence, we involve a span of time of no less than 1300 to 1400 years and, in principle, need to maintain that the books of Samuel could have been written at any time between 1000 BCE and 350 CE. Here it will certainly be very important to choose the right kind of procedure to follow! Should we start at the earliest possible date, the eleventh century BCE, or at the latest possible, that is the fourth century CE? Or, to rephrase the sentence: should we begin at the point where we are left with postulates and hypotheses, that is 1000 BCE, or is it preferable to start the procedure of finding a date for the composition of the books of Samuel at the point where we can be certain that these books existed, that is 350 CE? *The brutal fact is simply that we do not know that the books of Samuel existed around 1000 BCE, but we are certain that they did in 350 CE!*

Although it has become a standing procedure in the study of the Old Testament to begin where we know the least and to end at the point where we have safe information in order to explain what is certain by reasons uncertain and from an unknown past, it is obvious to almost everybody else that this procedure has no claim to be called scientific. We should rather and as a matter of course start where we are best informed. Only from this vantage point should we try to penetrate into the unknown past. *The point of departure for a discussion of the date of the books of Samuel can only be 350 CE and not 1000 CE.* This does not, however, mean that the books of Samuel were written down—not even in their present form—between 340 and 350 CE, but it does mean that we have to provide reasons for an earlier date, as no evidence exists that these books must be older.

Now it is quite easy to provide a reasonable argument in favor of an earlier date. Such an argument might, for example, be based on the fact that fragments (but so far only fragments!) of the books of Samuel have turned up among the Dead Sea Scrolls. It will presumably also be possible to argue in favor of an even earlier date than these Dead Sea Scroll fragments, and to base our argument on the fact that these books were incorporated into the form of the Septuagint that has been transmitted by the Codex Vaticanus. Nor can it be ruled out that they are much older, but in this case it is difficult to find hard evidence for such an early date.

It is an established fact that a literary product must be considered a reflection of its age of origin, as nobody can escape being a child of his or her own time. This is absolutely commonplace but, on the other hand not to be forgotten by, say, narrative analysts who may claim that it is possible to understand an argument by a person in the past without knowing in advance the specific values attached in his age to certain beliefs and concepts. The same applies to the study of biblical literature, although written by anonymous authors. It is surely extremely naive to believe that the meaning of biblical books can be properly exposed without knowledge of their date of composition, about the ideas current in that age or the beliefs common to their audience; and it is of no consequence whether the subject is a narrative as a whole or parts of it or just single concepts and phrases.[15]

To cite another, less controversial, example: Genesis 1. In the account of the origin of the world, God first creates the light and the darkness, followed by the water and the earth, although it is better to say that God does not exactly create these elements, but makes a kind of division between them.[16] Now, this description of the creation in Genesis 1 may

---

15. Cf. also the proposal by Diana Vikander Edelman, *King Saul in the Historiography of Judah* (JSOTSup, 121; Sheffield: JSOT Press, 1991), pp. 11-26, to read the story of Saul and David as an ancient reader would have done it (although this is certainly a vain hope, as Diana Edelman herself readily admits).

16. The creative activity of God in Gen. 1 is usually described by the verbs ברא and עשה. However, the light (v. 3) and the darkness (v. 9) appear, not because they are his creation, but on his direct order, (neither ברא nor עשה is used in this connection). After the appearance of the light, God makes a division (Hebrew בדל, in the hiphil) between the light and the darkness (v. 4). After this God personally

seemingly be read without further knowledge of the background of its author; although a number of misinterpretations have occurred, for example, that we here have a *creatio ex nihilo*. But if, on the other hand, we should have a look at the story of the creation of the four elements, light and darkness, water and earth, from an ancient point of view, then it is obvious that God 'creates' these elements in a manner that accords with some ideas current among Greek natural philosophers from the sixth century onwards. The creation of the light and the darkness says that God creates the hot element and the cold element. Water and earth can also be compared to two elements, respectively the dry element and the wet element. Taken together, the four basic elements of creation are simply the four elements of antique philosophy: the hot and the cold and the dry and the wet. Certainly old Thales from Miletus would not have been disappointed by these acts of God!

As already indicated, this is hardly to be considered controversial, as most scholars would be prepared to accept that the author of Genesis 1 cannot predate the Babylonian Exile. Rather, he belongs to the sixth or fifth centuries, if not later. If the author of Genesis 1 knew the ideas of Thales and his colleagues or his information came from some other source (perhaps the supposed oriental background of Thales's theory), then this would not be in conflict with the generally accepted date of Genesis 1.

In this case, Thales and the Greeks could only be considered as the *terminus a quo* for dating Genesis 1; they are certainly not to be identified with the *terminus ad quem*. If the dating of Genesis should follow the same procedure as the one relevant to the dating of the books of Samuel, the result will be that this text must have been written down between the sixth century BCE and the fourth century CE. However, the presence of some Dead Sea fragments of the book of Genesis makes it highly likely that this book of Genesis was already in existence in the first century BCE. The span of years from the earliest and latest possible dates for Genesis 1 is much shorter than the one relevant to the dating of the books of Samuel, although from a methodological point of view

---

makes the firmament (v. 7: עָשָׂה), but this firmament is to be considered another division, only now between different kinds of water. The waters below the firmament are collected in one place, on God's order and the dry land appears as a consequence of this. Again it should be realized that the dry land is not a creation of God; it just appears as a consequence of division between the water and the land.

the problem of dating Genesis 1 and the books of Samuel is very much of the same kind.

c. *Historical Matters*

At this point, a shift of emphasis from literature to history would be most appropriate to continue our discussion of the Old Testament as a Hellenistic book. By way of introduction we may ask the question: how important is the historical information provided by a biblical book for dating the book itself? We should also here proceed in very much the same way as already indicated above, although literary issues have now been replaced by historical ones. Instead of looking for the place of origin of some ideological elements that may be discerned in a certain biblical text, we are now trying to establish the time and place for whatever historical information the text in question provides. In this section, I shall use two examples: first, the book of Joshua; and second, the books of Samuel.

The first example is easy to handle today, since it has been evident for a long time that the historical 'reality' referred to in the book of Joshua has disappeared. The book of Joshua has simply nothing to tell us about the historical origins of the Israelite nation. No prolonged discussion of the *Forschungsgeschichte* is necessary here, although I may refer to the discussion in my *Early Israel*.[17] However, in order to introduce my subject here, it should be stressed that the often fervent discussion between the two great schools of historical studies in the past, on one hand the German school of Albrecht Alt and Martin Noth, and on the other the American one of William F. Albright, resulted in the victory of the American school, although it may at the same time be argued that it 'died' in the process.

To put it briefly, the German school was principally interested in analyzing Old Testament texts to dig out historical facts from the biblical narratives, while the Americans were mostly interested in creating harmony between archaeological artifacts and historical information that derived from the biblical text. The American school triumphed because archaeology was destined to deal a death blow to the German approach

17. Cf. N.P. Lemche, *Early Israel: Anthropological and Historical Studies on the Israelite Society Before the Monarchy* (VTSup, 37; Leiden: E.J. Brill, 1985), pp. 1-79. A much shorter resumé can be found in my *Ancient Israel: A New History of Israelite Society* (The Biblical Seminar, 5; Sheffield: JSOT Press, 1988), pp. 104-116.

and its results; archaeology simply showed these German ideas about Israel's origin and oldest history to be wrong. The German procedure mainly consisted in creating a rationalistic paraphrase of the stories of the Old Testament and it was its intended goal to present a picture of the historical development that would not disturb our sense of what may possibly have happened (no miracles, please!). At the same time the German scholars almost slavishly followed the historical layout of the Old Testament itself, and they had no intention of departing from the general succession of periods and events that had been presented by the biblical writers. We may say, to quote the German scholar Bernd Jørg Diebner of Heidelberg, that the German method should be likened to a text-archaeological procedure.[18] The most important German results were (1) that the early Israelites did not conquer Palestine but moved into the country as mostly peaceful semi-nomads; the actual Israelite subjugation of the indigenous population only followed at a later date; and (2) that following their settlement in Palestine, the Israelite tribes proceeded to create an amphictyony or sacred tribal league, that became the home of most of Israel's traditions about its past.[19]

As already mentioned, so-called 'dirt' archaeology, that is field archaeology proper, finally led to the downfall of the German position, but the idea of an Israelite conquest nourished by Albright and his students had be to discarded. Archaeology did not prove the Bible to be true; to the contrary, it has shown that the Israelites (whoever they were) never conquered Palestine but should be considered part of the ancient population of Palestine going back to the Bronze Age. Only at a much later date did the 'Israelite' society develop the characteristics of the 'Israel' to be found in the Old Testament.[20]

18. Cf. B.J. Diebner, 'Wider die "Offenbarungs-Archäologie" in der Wissenschaft vom Alten Testament. Grundsätzlicher zum Sinn alttestamentlicher Forschung im Rahmen der Theologie', *DBAT* 18 (1984), pp. 30-53.

19. The classical German description of this period is certainly Martin Noth, *Geschichte Israels* (Göttingen: Vandenhoeck & Ruprecht, 1950). In more recent German histories of Israel, such as (the probably best informed) Herbert Donner, *Geschichte des Volkes Israel und seiner Nachbarn in Grundzügen* (ATD, 4.1; Göttingen: Vandenhoeck & Ruprecht, 1984) the construct has begin to crumble, and the amphictyony is no longer part of it anymore.

20. A kind of *status quaestionis* can be found in Diana Edelman (ed.), 'Toward a Consensus on the Emergence of Israel in Canaan', *SJOT* 5.2 (1991), pp. 1-116 (including contributions by N.P. Lemche, G.W. Ahlström, I. Finkelstein and others), and in two comprehensive volumes that have just appeared, in T.L. Thompson, *The*

One historical fact cannot, of course, be denied, namely the very existence of the narratives about Israel's conquest of its land in the book of Joshua. However, these tales have nothing to do with historical circumstances at the end of the Late Bronze Age and the beginning of the Iron Age. This is not a postulate, but a fact, and we are therefore in the position to ask: what do the narratives in Joshua really tell us about if they do not inform us about a conquest of Palestine in ancient times? The answer is clear and obvious: the book of Joshua informs its readers about a conquest that never happened. The next question is then: why does this book of Joshua present information about a conquest that never happened? The answer to this last question may not be as clear as the former one, because we cannot say that it is based on hard evidence; it rather depends on scholarly theories and hypotheses. One possible answer could be that the tradition of Israel's foreign origin was invented at a later date in order to create a racially pure Israelite nation. An extensive number of passages in Joshua and other places in the Old Testament may be called upon in support of this answer, starting with the book of Genesis and continuing right through to the book of Ezra the Scribe. In case we prefer to continue along this line of thought, the next question will probably be: when did the impetus arise that created the milieu of such an idea of racial purity of the Israelite people in contrast to other nations living in its land, as this claim cannot be supported by historical evidence? The correct answer to that question will be that such an idea arose the moment certain individuals who considered themselves to be Israelites saw other individuals who they did not consider to be Israelites to be occupying 'their' land. Evidently—in light of what we know about Israel's origins—this claim to be pure Israelites destined to inherit the land must be a late development, and it most probably turns the book of Joshua into a post-exilic book written by an author—or a number of authors—who can scarcely have lived in the

Early History of the Israelite People (SHANE; Leiden: E.J. Brill, 1992), and G.W. Ahlström, *The History of Ancient Palestine from the Palaeolithic Period to Alexander's Conquest* (JSOTSup, 146; Sheffield: JSOT Press, 1992). So far no serious reaction has come from German scholars; a book such as R. Neu, *Von der Anarchie zum Staat: Entwicklungsgeschichte Israels vom Nomadentum zur Monarchie im Spiegel der Ethnosoziologie* (Neukirchen–Vluyn: Neukirchener Verlag, 1992), should rather, because of its total neglect of archaeology and because of its extensive rationalistic paraphrase of the biblical text, be understood as a clear step backwards.

land to be conquered. This says that the book of Joshua is (1) postexilic and (2) literature from the Jewish diaspora, or to use a Hebrew term, it originated among the Jewish *gola.*

When introducing my second example, I should like to return to the books of Samuel. Here the central figure is David, not Samuel nor Saul, and the narratives about Samuel and Saul should be considered a prolegomenon to the narratives about David. It is only right to say that David is truly the great hero of Israel's past (Joshua may be the only one to dispute that claim), and he was reckoned the creator of a great Israelite empire preceding the independent histories of the kingdoms of Israel and Judah.

Laypeople as well as scholars (including the present writer[21]) have always thought highly of the historicity of David and considered it an established fact. They also believe the main part of the traditions about David and his son and successor, Solomon, to be trustworthy information, although none of it, whether person or event, is confirmed or supported by external evidence, especially by written sources from other parts of the ancient Near East. The only written evidence about David and Solomon are—apart from the Old Testament—sources whose information about these two kings comes from the Old Testament itself. Only a few voices of protest have arisen that may cast doubt on the historicity of the early Israelite empire, including the historicality of its two kings[22] and the conclusions reached by David Jamieson-Drake can only be considered a temporary culmination of this.[23] It is the opinion of Jamieson-Drake that we find no evidence of a united Israelite kingdom in pre-exilic times. To the contrary, it is highly unlikely that a state called Judah came into existence before the middle of the eighth century. The Jerusalem of 'David's' time was hardly anything but a small

21. Cf. my article, 'David's Rise', *JSOT* 10 (1978), pp. 2-25. Although the historical part of the argument in that article as well as that of several other contributions by other scholars either following in its footsteps or progressing along comparable lines may now have to be discarded, the literary argument may still be of some importance, as maintained by G.G. Nicol, in his 'The Death of Joab and Accession of Solomon', *SJOT* 7 (1993), pp. 134-51.

22. Cf. the outspoken mistrust of the biblical tradition in Garbini, *History and Ideology*, pp. 21-32. Recently also D.B. Redford has presented a negative view of the historicity of David and Solomon, in his *Egypt, Canaan, and Israel in Ancient Times* (Princeton, NJ: Princeton University Press, 1992), pp. 297-311.

23. Cf. D.W. Jamieson-Drake, *Scribes and Schools in Monarchic Judah: A Socio-Archaeological Approach* (JSOTSup, 109; Sheffield: JSOT Press, 1991).

fortified village, occupying a territory of less than four hectares. and inhabited by a population of hardly more than 2000 persons, including women and children.[24] Although Jamieson-Drake's argument will certainly provoke other scholars to object, his case is so far a very strong one in favor of abandoning the time of the united kingdom as a historic age.

These two dubious cases, the historicity of the Israelite conquest and of the united kingdom of Israel, certainly point in the same direction. When we deal with the tradition of the empire of David, we obviously have to ask why this idea of a Davidic empire arose, if it had been totally without historical support. The exchange of answers and questions that may follow will be of the same kind as the one described in more detail above concerning Joshua's conquest. The result of such a discussion would probably be that a number of possible dates for the origin of this idea of David and his empire could be proposed, either a late pre-exilic, an exilic or even a postexilic one. The answer to the question why this story was invented at all will presumably be of this kind: in order to create an 'Israelite' great king comparable to the great kings said to have ruled other nations. The biblical historians consequently turned the mythical ancestor of the Judean royal family into such an ideal king to be compared to the empire-builders of the ancient world. It could also be argued that since this great ancestor-king never lived, it is impossible to consider the stories about the kingdom of David historical reports concerning the past. Rather, they present a program for the future, that will appear as soon as the contemporaries of the historians themselves have (re-)conquered their land. It could very well be the case that the stories about David as well as the conquest narratives in Joshua aimed at creating a program for the glorious future of Israel, rather than a report of past glory that never existed. Thus these narratives could very well derive from the Persian period, and the model for the great king may have been none other than the great founder of the Persian empire, Cyrus. In this connection it should not be forgotten that the careers of Cyrus and David reveal a number of comparable traits. It

24. The calculations of the population size is, however, not presented by Jamieson-Drake but is my own estimate, based on a calculation of population size like the one proposed in J.M. Sasson, *Jonah* (AB, 24B; New York: Doubleday, 1990), p. 312. It should, however, be clear that this is a very generous calculation. It would also be possible to say that the area covered only one or two hectares, and included a population of 1000 persons or fewer.

is, however, also possible that the idea of the great king David only arose in the Hellenistic period and for comparable reasons.

More than a few scholars will be prepared to think of the books of Joshua and Samuel as having propagandistic motives. Thus a number of studies have lately connected the composition of these books with the reign of King Josiah. One such example is provided by Magnus Ottosson who regards the book of Josiah to be a product of the Josianic age and a program for the Josianic restoration of the Davidic kingdom.[25] It should, however, be noted that while Ottosson thinks that the conquest stories in Joshua are fictional war reports and have little if anything to do with historical facts, he still considers the Davidic kingdom to be a historically established fact. Contrary to Ottosson's opinion, his analysis (probably correct) of the relationship between P-elements and the main D-narrative in Joshua actually proves Joshua to be not Josianic but postexilic, and later than P—provided, of course, that P should be dated in the postexilic era.[26]

Another scholar who thinks highly of the Josianic age as the time of history writing is Diana Vikander Edelman who considers the Saul-David narrative to belong to the time of Josiah, although the purpose of writing this story at exactly this moment in Judah's history seems more ambiguous.[27] It is a problem for her dating of these narratives that the Israelite people in 1 Samuel 8 demand to have a king like all the other nations. Why should anybody in the age of Josiah wish to have a king, as they already had one? As a matter of fact, this demand can hardly be pre-exilic.[28] It is therefore more likely that the author of 1 Samuel 8

---

25. Cf. M. Ottosson, *Josuaboken: En programskrift för davidisk restauration* (Acta Universitatis Upsaliensis, Studia Biblica Upsaliensia, 1; Uppsala: Textgruppen i Uppsala, 1991).

26. Ottosson generally considers the P-elements original parts of the Deuteronomistic narratives in Joshua. For that reason, they cannot, of course, be late additions to the narratives. It should at the same moment also be said that Ottosson, like so many other Scandinavian scholars of the past, reckons the P-elements to be leftovers from various sanctuaries like Shilo or Gilgal. The problem of such a theory is certainly that it is entirely based on guesswork, as no proof except the circular variety can be adduced in its favor.

27. Cf. Edelman, *King Saul in the Historiography of Judah.*

28. Unless we should choose to express a view on these narratives like the one in F. Crüsemann, *Der Widerstand gegen das Königtum* (WMANT, 49; Neukirchen–Vluyn: Neukirchener Verlag, 1978), who maintains that they are to be considered

wrote in a period and for a society without a king. Here too it is better to look to the exilic or postexilic periods.[29]

This predilection for the time of Josiah as the creative period in the history of Hebrew literature is, moreover, problematical. It must be realized that it is the Deuteronomistic historians who say that the period of Josiah was a splendid era, a restoration period and therefore the right time and place for writing great literature like Joshua and Samuel. If scholars should accept the picture presented by the Deuteronomistic circle without scrutinizing the reasons for turning Josiah's period into such an age of 'enlightenment', they would be falling into the same hermeneutical trap as did, formerly, scholars such as Gerhard von Rad, who thought highly of the Solomonic period as the background of Israelite history-writing.[30] Although this background for Hebrew history-writing seems now to be evaporating with the demise of the Hebrew empire of the tenth century BCE, scholars are indefatigably repeating the arguments in connection with an era of Josiah, which they consider to have been almost in the same class as, formerly, had been the time of Solomon. It should never be forgotten, however, that all we know about Josiah is told by Old Testament writers, as no external source ever mentions Josiah, except such as are clearly dependent on the Old Testament narrative. Mostly because the Old Testament itself says that Josiah tried at the end of the seventh century BCE to unify all of Israel into one

reflections of party politics in pre-monarchical times—not a bad idea at all if it was possible to claim that the Deuteronomistic traditions are as old as that.

29. It may be an alternative to the idea that David became the model of the later Judean kings, especially Josiah, to transfer this honor from the presumably non-existent David to a person whose historicity cannot be doubted, and here the obvious candidate would probably be Omri (followed by his son Ahab). The importance of the state that was governed by these kings is certain and is also reflected by Assyrian and Moabite inscriptions. It is also generally assumed that they reigned over a territory that included Jerusalem, if not all of Judah. It is a least a working hypothesis that in the period following the fall of Samaria the idea of the united kingdom, which was founded on the existence in the ninth century of the kingdom of Omri, was transferred to Judah, and that the greatness belonging to the old Israelite kings was at the same time bestowed on David, the mythical ancestor of the Judean kings.

30. Programmatically expressed in G. von Rad, 'Der Anfang der Geschichtsschreibung im alten Israel' (1944), now in his *Gesammelte Studien zum Alten Testament* (TBü, 8; Munich: Chr. Kaiser Verlag, 1958), pp. 148-88.

major state, biblical scholars believe this to be true.[31] However, the Josiah of 2 Kings need not be a historical figure at all (although it seems likely that shortly before the disappearance of the shortlived state of Judah there lived a king called Josiah in Jerusalem); he may be nothing more than the invention of the Deuteronomistic author(s) who wrote the books of Kings. The comparison between David and Josiah is of course also a product of Deuteronomistic thinking and it shows how the Deuteronomists worked a rather miserable king with an inglorious end into a major historical figure of Israel's history. It can also be argued that the Deuteronomists very much needed a Josiah to make their own religious program legitimate, and here it is of no consequence whether the Deuteronomistic History was a work of the exilic or of the postexilic periods.[32]

The discussion may stop at this point, and it may be argued that the time of Josiah, the so-called restoration period in the history of Judah,

---

31. This reminds me of the the the verdict of Mario Liverani, in his 'Storiografia politica hittita II: Telipini, ovvero: Della Solidarieta', *OA* 16 (1977), pp. 105-31, see p. 105: 'The indolence of the historians is of great extent, and when they deal with a certain period and they are confronting a continuous account of the course of events, which has already been included in some sort of "ancient" documentary source (which is perforce not contemporary with the events themselves), then they all too happily apply this account, and they limit their efforts to paraphrasing it or even rationalizing it' (trans. my own). Liverani is dealing with the scholarly reconstructions of the history of the ancient Hittite empire, normally based almost exclusively on the decree of Telipinus and generally accepting its views, and it is fairly easy for Liverani to deconstruct the content of the edict and to show that it is a totally propagandistic and partisan view of the history of the Hittites that is presented by the king who issued the decree.

32. It is, on the other hand, interesting to compare the description of Josiah in 2 Kings with the one in 2 Chron. 34–35. The Chronicler seems much less enthusiastic about this king than his Deuteronomistic source, although he duly quotes the Deuteronomistic narrative almost from one end to the other. However, when he comes to the death of Josiah, the Chronicler clearly expresses his contempt of this king who died an ignominious death because he disobeyed a direct order from Yahweh. The Chronicler also diminishes (or even ridicules: cf. the wording of 2 Chron. 35.18, 'No Passover like it had been kept in Israel since the days of the prophet Samuel', with the slightly different version in 2 Kgs 23.22!) the importance of Josiah's reform as described in 2 Kings by referring to Hezekiah as the real reformer who reinstated the Passover in its former glory (cf. 2 Chron. 30). According to the Chronicler, the reform of Josiah was no more than a copy of the one initiated by Hezekiah (cf. 2 Chron. 31.1).

which is only known from the Old Testament, is nothing except another product of the Deuteronomistic imagination, and it is not necessarily more historical than the age of David and Solomon.[33] Instead of transferring the period of Josiah into a great time for history-writing in Israel (or: Judah), only to repeat former mistakes, it will be safer to apply the same procedure as advocated above in connection with the dating of biblical literature; that is, to begin where we can be certain that the literature in question really existed, and after having established that fact to proceed with our quest for a possible earlier date. It should, however, be understood that there may be little reason to go back to the time of Josiah, which may itself be no more than a postulate made by Old Testament writers.

3. *Other Themes*

I believe that I have presented enough practical examples here to illustrate my point. It would have been possible to discuss also other important issues and themes that may be in the focus of the scholarly debate. I have to abstain from doing this here. Instead I will only mention a couple of very important themes for discussion here.

First, the religion of Israel. In this connection I shall only mention one recent contribution that may help us to clarify the history of the religion which, according to the Old Testament, should be considered old Israelite religion. In his highly interesting study *Der höchste Gott*,[34] Herbert Niehr proposes not to separate the emergence of monotheism in 'Israel' (we should rather think of postexilic Jews) from a contemporary trend towards a practical monotheism in other places. It is only true to say that Niehr's investigation can be understood as a confirmation of my own view: that the so-called pre-exilic Israelite religion was some sort of Western Asiatic religion, hardly distinguishable from religious

---

33. It should not be overlooked that some indications offered by Jamieson-Drake point at the possibility that the decline of Judah started well before the Babylonian destruction of Jerusalem, notably in the sector termed 'Public Works'. Cf. Jamieson-Drake, *Scribes and Schools*, p. 104, and charts 7 and 9, although a more comprehensive study of the period of Josiah is badly needed, especially from an archaeological point of view.

34. BZAW, 190; Berlin: W. de Gruyter, 1990.

belief in places such as Moab, Ammon, Phoenicia, etc.[35] As a result of Niehr's (and others) work we are entitled to ask whether it is not totally misleading to talk about an Israelite religion in pre-exilic times. Genuine Israelite religion as presented by the biblical tradition is no way Israelite, it is reflective of the religion of the postexilic Jewish society, and it is more than likely that the religious conflicts between the so-called Israelite religion and the so-called Canaanite religion that emerge from the Old Testament books have little to do with conditions in Palestine between, say, 1000 and 500 BCE. Rather this information refers to the situation between, say, 500 and 200 BCE.

Secondly, the national identity of the Israelite people. Just as the Israelite religion in the Old Testament turns out to represent Jewish religious thought, the Israelites of the Old Testament are Jews (it is ironical that this was anticipated by, e.g., the German sociologist Max Weber, when he published his study of Israel as ancient Judaism).[36] If this is compared to the modern view on the origin of the 'Israelites' (and we now have to put this concept of 'Israel' into quotation marks!), there is no longer any reason to talk about the Israelites as forming an ethnic unity in pre-exilic times. If anything, the so-called Israelites were Canaanites, or maybe it is better—to make this conform with the result of my study on the Canaanites—to say that the 'Israelites' are left without any specific ethnic affiliation at all. They simply reflect a regional selection of the inhabitants of Palestine, where they formed a late branch of the population that had been present in Western Asia since the beginning of history. The idea of 'Israel' in the Old Testament may

---

35. Cf. my *Ancient Israel*, pp. 197-257; as well as 'The Development of the Israelite Religion in Light of Recent Studies on the Early History of Israel', in J.A. Emerton (ed.), *Congress Volume: Leuven 1989* (VTSup, 43; Leiden: E.J. Brill), pp. 97-115. I have little to say against a verdict like this: '...there was very little distinction between Canaanite and Israelite religion, at least in practice. The rituals were virtually the same, even if one assumes that Israel's Yahwistic theology was an innovation and that is not always evident' (W.G. Dever, *Recent Archaeological Discoveries and Biblical Research* [Seattle: University of Washington Press, 1990], p. 166).

36. *Das antike Judentum: Gesammelte Aufsätze zur Religionsgeschichte*, III (repr., Tübingen: Mohr, 1988 [1921]). It should on the other hand be noted that the distinctiveness of what is 'Israelite' and what is 'Jewish' may not always have been as obvious to Max Weber's contemporaries as it was to become afterwards.

be nothing except a very late ideological concept, as maintained by Philip R. Davies.[37]

Thirdly, the Babylonian exile. This is certainly an issue that is growing in importance as the greater part of the Old Testament is now being considered fairly late. The whole issue of the exile could be summarized in this fashion: we have excellent information about the beginning of the Babylonian exile, at the early half of the sixth century BCE; it is, however, far more uncertain when it stopped. The 'official' date of return is, of course, 538 BCE, when the exiled were allowed to return as a consequence of Cyrus's decree, or this is what is normally assumed. However, if such a decree was ever issued, with the particular intention to send the Jewish people home again, it could be maintained that this time the Jews of Babylonia were offered something which they could easily refuse. Most of them preferred to stay in Babylonia and to die there as did also their descendants for many generations. They found little reason to leave the center of the Persian Empire in order to move to its fringe to one of its poorest and most desolate provinces. It is quite ironical that the end of the Jewish communities of Mesopotamia only came in 1948 CE, when the majority of the Jews of Mesopotamia were forced to leave and to return to Palestine as a consequence of the establishment of the modern Jewish state.

I wish to stress this point, as most scholars who are prone to date the major part of the Old Testament to the Babylonian exile may after all be right: this literature is really exilic. It should at the same time also be stressed that few of the said scholars have realized that the exile continued—almost forever—although it was from now on a self-inflicted one. The sons and daughters of the deportees happily continued to live in Mesopotamia as long as the Persian Empire existed, but also under the following empires of the Seleucids, the Sassanides and the Parthians. It may even by maintained that the idea of an exile became a kind of obsession to the Jews of the Diaspora because it provided them with a legitimate excuse for keeping away from that barren place called Palestine.

---

37. On the Canaanites, cf. N.P. Lemche, *The Canaanites and their Land: The Tradition of the Canaanites* (JSOTSup, 110; Sheffield: JSOT Press, 1991). The consequences of this are more sharply drawn up by Davies, *In Search of 'Ancient Israel'*. Most of this development was, however, foreseen by the late Gösta W. Ahlström, in his *Who Were the Israelites?* (Winona Lake, IN: Eisenbrauns, 1986).

4. *The Old Testament—A Hellenistic Book?*

The following points may speak in favor of a Hellenistic date of the Old Testament:

1. It is a fact that the history of Israel as told by the Old Testament has little if anything to do with the real historical developments in Palestine until at least the later part of the Hebrew monarchy. It cannot be excluded (and there is, as a matter of fact, no reason to exclude) that we here and there may possess genuine historical recollections, but it should at the same time be argued that from a historian's point of view we have to consider the historical literature in the Old Testament a poor source of historical information.

2. An extensive part of this literature should be considered the creation of the Jewish Diaspora, first and foremost the patriarchal narratives, the story in Exodus about the Israelites in Egypt and their escape from Egypt, but also the conquest narratives in Joshua. All of these aim at one and the same issue, at the more or less utopian idea that a major Jewish kingdom—even empire—should be (re-)established in Palestine, an idea that emerged in spite of the fact that it had no background in an ancient Israelite empire.

3. The writers who invented the 'history of Israel' seem to have modeled their history on a Greek pattern. The first in modern times to stress this point is presumably John Van Seters,[38] although his reference to

---

38. Cf. J. Van Seters, *In Search of History* (New Haven: Yale University Press, 1983), and now his *Prologue to History: The Yahwist as Historian in Genesis* (Louisville, KY: Westminster/John Knox Press, 1992). In his new book, Van Seters argues that two currents are presented in the Yahwistic parts of Genesis, one of them displaying an interest in history proper, while the other is more of an 'antiquarian kind'. The first current can be traced back to the Greek historical tradition while the second is genuinely oriental, and has its roots in Mesopotamia, in the Babylonian tradition. According to Van Seters, the meeting-place of both currents cannot be pre-exilic, but must be dated to the Babylonian exile in the strict sense of the word. In favor of this, Van Seters discusses the possibility that the Phoenicians were the carriers of the Greek tradition to the Orient. This sounds like an unnecessary complication and is totally unattested. In spite of Van Seters's splendid defense of his exilic date, a more relevant moment can and should be proposed for the confluence of Greek and Oriental tradition, that is the time of the Seleucid and Ptolemaic empires when the Greeks ruled the East. In this age, the Jews of Mesopotamia would have had easy access to the Greek as well as the Babylonian traditions.

Hecataeus of Miletus may seem gratuitous, as we no longer possess Hecataeus's history, except in the form of rather diminutive fragments. It would be preferable to propose the history of Herodotus as the earliest point of comparison and to indicate that there are a number of similarities between the histories of Herodotus and the Old Testament. Both histories have as their beginning a perspective that encompasses the world as such, and this perspective narrows down to single nations only at a later point, respectively the Greek and the Hebrew. I should like to stress this point without ignoring the many significant differences between Herodotus's history and the Old Testament historical literature.[39] It is only my intention to indicate that the biblical historians display a knowledge of the Greek tradition, and that this could hardly have been the case before Greek historians were to become known and read in the Near East.

4. The Persian period does not seem to meet the requirements of being the time when the historical books of the Old Testament were written down. First of all it would have to be proved that Greek authors were known and extensively read in the Persian empire, and I very much doubt that this was the case. Furthermore, we have to look for a suitable place where the biblical historical narratives may have been written down.

One of the major problems in this connection is the fact that we have very little information about the Persian age, at least as far as the Jewish population is concerned. Thus we know practically nothing about the situation in Palestine except from the books of Ezra and Nehemiah, and although these books have generally been highly regarded as first-hand sources of information, some critical voices have arisen lately, arguing (1) that the mission of Ezra never took place and (2) that the authenticity of the so-called 'autobiography' of Nehemiah may also be doubted—with reference to the fact that autobiographies constituted an acknowledged and widespread literary genre in the Greek world.[40]

39. Other Greek historical works should of course be consulted as relevant to the discussion, in particular Hellenistic authors, but also Livy, although Livy, being a Roman author, can only be an elaborate example of history-writing in the Hellenistic world. The fact, however, remains that a number of parallels can be found between Livy and the Old Testament history, even structural ones. This may not be a coincidence but may be a testimony of a common 'spiritual' (i.e. Hellenistic) background.

40. A number of interesting viewpoints relevant to this discussion can be found

Palestine in the Persian period hardly seems to have embraced the kind of society in which to look for the authors of literature like that found in the historical parts of the Old Testament. From a material point of view the Persian conquest seems to have brought little positive to Palestinian society in general. The rebuilding of Jerusalem was evidently only on a minute scale, the Jerusalem of Nehemiah being even smaller than the one that existed before the extensions to the city area made by Hezekiah.[41] It is certainly true that much work has to be done in order to clarify archaeologically the conditions of the Persian period, if we wish to create the impression that great literature may possibly have been composed in this age.[42]

An utterance such as the following by Philip J. King, 'The Persian Period was a time of peace and prosperity, when Judah was allowed a

in P.R. Davies (ed.), *Second Temple Studies*. I. *Persian Period* (JSOTSup, 117; Sheffield: JSOT Press, 1991); notably Lester L. Grabbe, 'Reconstructing History from the Book of Ezra', pp. 98-107; and R.P. Carroll, 'Textual Strategies and Ideology in the Second Temple Period', pp. 108-124. On Nehemiah's biography, cf. now also D.J.A. Clines, 'The Nehemiah Memoirs: The Perils of Autography', in his *What Does Eve Do to Help? And Other Readerly Questions to the Old Testament* (JSOTSup, 94; Sheffield: JSOT Press, 1990), pp. 124-64. It is, as a matter of fact, an age-old position which hereby makes its re-entrance on the scene: cf. C.C. Torrey, 'The Exile and the Restoration', in *idem*, *Ezra Studies* (Chicago: University of Chicago Press, 1910), pp. 285-340, and especially C.C. Torrey, *The Composition and Historical Value of Ezra–Nehemiah* (BZAW, 2; Giessen: Alfred Töpelmann, 1896). See also the discussion in Davies, *In Search of 'Ancient Israel'*, pp. 78-87, and, of course, in Garbini, *History and Ideology*, pp. 151-69.

41. It is strange to realize how uninformative even the most recent descriptions of Jerusalem in the Persian period are. Thus P.J. King, in *ABD*, III, p. 757, has nothing to add to such old books as K.M. Kenyon, *Digging up Jerusalem* (London: Ernest Benn, 1974), pp. 172-87. Both King and Kenyon merely paraphrase the books of Nehemiah and Ezra.

42. In spite of the existence of a work like E. Stern, *Material Culture of the Land of the Bible in the Persian Period* (Warminster: Aris & Phillips, 1982), a study like Jamieson-Drake, *Scribes and Schools*, is most needed for this period and the available material should be statistically analyzed. The deplorable lack of material is also reflected by the rather short description of the age from an archaeological point of view in Helga Weippert, *Palästina in Vorhellenistischer Zeit* (Handbuch der Archäologie, 2.1; Munich: C.H. Beck'sche Verlagsbuchhandlung, 1988), pp. 687-718. Her remarks on p. 697 ('Forschungsstand') are most revealing. It is also the case that most of the material from this period is found in sites north of present-day Haifa, an area that can hardly be considered part of the Persian province of Jehud!

great deal of administrative independence', should awaken suspicion. How do we know this, except that it is the convenient common opinion of many scholars? Modern examples of crumbling societies left on their own and with 'a great deal of administrative independence' provide a sad picture of local incompetence, and Jamieson-Drake's demonstration of the total collapse of Judean society around 600 BCE points to socio-economic conditions in Palestine in the following centuries that will have demanded more than the occasional visit of a Persian emissary to settle. As a matter of fact, the often praised leniency of the Persians towards their subject nations may have been nothing more than a display of an absolute lack of responsibility from the Persian part. Maybe they did not interfere in local affairs because they did not care! A re-evaluation of Persian rule and a realistic appraisal of the Achaemenid administrative system are also most needed. The possibility that the community in Jerusalem was organized as a 'Tempel-Bürger' society, as maintained by some scholars following a proposal made by Joel Weinberg (for example, Joseph Blenkinsopp and David Petersen), seems to me to be a moot question, as very little except hypotheses speaks in favor of such a theory.[43] I have little to offer here, except that I have severe doubts about the efficiency of Persian administration in those days, doubts caused by a report like Xenophon's *Anabasis*. Here, in the heyday of the Persian empire (at the end of the fifth century BCE), Xenophon together with a small army of Greek mercenaries (c. 5000 men) participated in an expedition that brought them to the very heart of the Persian Empire. The expedition was, however, not to end here when their Persian warlord was killed in a battle. Now the Greeks simply turned around and walked home. In spite of having lost their commanding officers, they were not only able to get rid of their Persian persecutors but to proceed on their journey right through—at the beginning—the richest provinces of the Persian Empire. They were only met by really serious opposition when they crossed the borders of Anatolia,

---

43. On this see J. Blenkinsopp, 'Temple and Society in Achaemenid Judah', in Davies (ed.), *Second Temple Studies 1*, pp. 22-53, and D. Petersen, 'Israelite Prophecy: Change Versus Continuity', in J.A. Emerton (ed.), *Congress Volume: Leuven 1989* (VTSup, 45; Leiden: E.J. Brill, 1991), pp. 190-203, see pp. 195-203. The original formulation of this hypothesis can be found in Joel Weinberg, 'Demographische Notizen zur Geschichte der nachexilischen Gemeinde in Juda', *Klio* 59 (1972), pp. 45-59, and *idem*, 'Das *bēit 'ābōt* 6.-4. Jh. v.u.Z.', *VT* 23 (1973), pp. 400-414.

although their opponents here were not the Persians proper but local mountain tribes, seemingly the subjects of the Persian king. The report by Xenophon thus hardly indicates that the adversaries of the Greeks were citizens in an efficiently governed state or empire! It would certainly also be ironical—in case a view on the appearance of the Old Testament like the one promoted by, for example, Philip Davies should be vindicated—if most of the archaeological material of the formative period of the Old Testament literature should belong to the much neglected Persian period, as this material has often been thrown away or placed in dumps—in order that the archaeologist may quickly get down to the truly 'Israelite' layers.[44]

It should never be forgotten that the revitalization of the ancient Near East only became a fact after the Greek takeover. It is an established fact that city life vastly expanded after the conquest of Alexander. Here we must realize what happened in Jerusalem and in Palestine, innovations that were comparable—although on a smaller scale—to the cultural developments in Syria, Mesopotamia and Egypt. I hardly have to develop this theme any further. It is my impression that we now, finally, get a glimpse of a society in which great literature may have been composed, kept and loved. Scholars may nurse very romantic ideas about what may have happened in the nooks and crannies of pre-Hellenistic Palestine, in a society considerably poorer than the one found there, for example, during the Late Bronze Age (a society that was not the home of any great literature, as becomes clear when we turn to the Amarna letters, which by no means can claim to be 'great literature'). A more worldly and realistic assessment of facts suggests that the Persian period was not the time when the Old Testament could have been written down. Hardly any parallel exists to such a development, but a lot of evidence that says that the Hellenistic Age was the formative period of early Jewish thought and literature as witnessed by the Old Testament itself.[45]

44. An outspoken example of the lack of interest (i.e. contempt for) especially among Israeli archaeologists, for the Persian period is the recent 'standard' archaeology by A. Mazar, *Archaeology of the Land of the Bible 586 B.C.E.* (New York: Doubleday, 1990). His case is certainly not exceptional!

45. So far, the theme of discussion has been the historical literature. That the writings are mostly Hellenistic literature seems self-evident in the light of the present discussion, and there is no need to elaborate further on this here. The prophetic literature, however, poses a special problem, because this collection is

There is no reason to gloss over the fact that the majority of Old Testament scholars of the present day will not readily accept new ideas like these concerning the date and ideological background of the Old Testament. A number of reasons may be found, not all of them based on the irrational, if understandable, disbelief and reluctance to accept what goes against the *opinio communis* of several generations of scholars. I hereby intend to say that exclamations like 'This is nonsense!', 'This cannot be true!' or 'This is impossible!' are often heard, although the argument in favor of such 'criticism' will usually be of the circular kind: that is, it cannot be true, because it goes against the once generally accepted view, which is, in turn, based on the assumption that such things cannot be correct.

However, some objections of a more serious kind will likely be launched against a position like the one held in this article:

1. How is it possible that a period, which must be considered the time of production of 'literature' such as Chronicles, could also produce a Yahwist or the book of Joshua, and not least the engaging stories of the books of Samuel?
2. We are acquainted with the linguistic evidence in certain parts of the Old Testament that are acknowledged as Hellenistic, such as Ecclesiastes or the Song of Songs. When this evidence is known and compared to, for example, the language of the Deuteronomistic literature, how could anybody be prepared to accept the Deuteronomistic literature as being about the same age as Ecclesiastes or the Song of Songs?
3. Where should we look for the home of the Old Testament in such a late period? Is the Old Testament in its Hebrew shape not so far removed from the Septuagint in spirit and language

normally understood to be younger than the Pentateuch and the Deuteronomistic History, which, according to the Jewish tradition, is also prophetic. There will be no time to go further here, except that Julius Wellhausen's verdict should be remembered, that the Prophets predate the Law. The possibility that the historical literature may be late does not preclude that the prophetic literature is even later (the collection may be, but that is another case). The analysis in my *Early Israel*, pp. 306-336, showed that the historical tradition was unknown to the pre-exilic prophets. My estimation of the time of composition of the so-called pre-exilic prophetic collections may be wrong after all, but the conclusion could still be valid that these prophetic collections predate the appearance of a larger historical narrative of the kind found in the Pentateuch and in the Deuteronomistic History.

that these Hebrew writings must be much older than their Greek translations?

It should be possible to answer all three questions at one and the same time, by introducing ethno-linguistic as well as socio-economic arguments, although these need not be very sophisticated, as the issues are, in fact, quite plain. The remarkable qualitative distance between Chronicles and the Deuteronomistic History is not only a distance in time (the Chronicler is generally citing the Deuteronomistic History, so this history must therefore predate Chronicles), which may be short or long; it may just as easily bear witness to the fact that the two histories were composed in very different environments, and it is quite safe to assume that the persons responsible for publishing the books of Chronicles were less able narrators than the Deuteronomistic Historians.

This discussion sounds like a new version of the debate concerning the respective date of J, E and P that has lasted for more than a century. It is well known that much of this discussion was based on arguments like differences of religious or political outlook, on linguistic matters, etc. It was also assumed that the Yahwist was a more simple-minded fellow (although by all means a great narrator) than his Elohist colleague, and that the persons behind P display a view of religion (if not theology) that is very different from the one found in J and E. Such differences were explained a long time ago by Johannes Pedersen as not necessarily the consequence of a difference in time; they could just as well be the outcome of different milieus and/or abilities and preferences of their authors.[46] To deny that Pedersen's argument is valid would be the same as maintaining that Plato could not be a contemporary of Xenophon!

When we turn to linguistic matters, it is true that the language of Ecclesiastes is much nearer to the Middle Hebrew of the Mishna, and it is far removed from the classical Hebrew which is the idiom of the Pentateuch and Deuteronomistic History. It should nevertheless be realized that it is impossible to say whether such differences should be explained as the result of differences of time or of milieu (or place). Where should we look for the author of Ecclesiastes, and who wrote the Deuteronomistic books? Although I will not deny that such differences may reflect different times of composition, I will at the same time stress

---

46. Cf. J. Pedersen, 'Die Auffassung vom Alten Testament', *ZAW* 49 (1931), pp. 161-81.

the fact that Hebrew was known (if not spoken) in postexilic times among Jews living in places as different as Mesopotamia, Egypt and Palestine. So far dialectal differences that must have existed between any of these places have been poorly studied. It may also be impossible to find evidence of these differences as linguistic differences have been harmonized although certainly not totally eradicated.

Finally, in order to counter the argumentation that refers to differences between the Septuagint and the Hebrew books of the Old Testament, it should be remembered that it is a safe assumption that the Septuagint came into being in Egypt. There is, on the other hand, no safe indication that the Hebrew writings also originated in this place. It is not unreasonable to think of a mixture in the Hebrew Bible of writings which came from Mesopotamia (especially the major part of the historical literature) and from Palestine (maybe Ecclesiastes, certainly Daniel, and others). Neither can we totally exclude the possibility that Hebrew—as represented by Hebrew Scripture—was no longer a living language. In this period, Hebrew may be what Ernst Axel Knauf has termed an artificial language, a kind of 'Latin' which was perhaps 'invented' as the idiom of sacred literature.[47] It is likely that the original Hebrew manuscripts which in their Greek disguise were incorporated into the Septuagint were simply translated after having been transferred to Egypt, because of the less than inadequate knowledge among ordinary Jews living in a city like Alexandria, and there is really no reason to believe that the Hebrew versions must perforce have been much older than their translations into Greek. To discuss an interval of, say, 100 years, or a decade, or just one year, is simply a hopeless affair, as no hard evidence of the correct interval between the appearance of the Hebrew original and the Greek translation can be found in favor of any of these positions.

5. *Theses*

It is my intention at the end of this article to present some 'theses' in order to show that the view of the Old Testament presented here may lead to a renewed appraisal of its status as sacred literature to both Jews and Christians in ancient times. These theses are all to be considered themes for future discussion. Here they will only be listed. First we will

47. E.A. Knauf, 'War Biblisch-Hebräisch eine Sprache?', *ZAH* 3 (1990), pp. 11-23.

have four theses concerning the relationship between the Septuagint and the Hebrew Bible.[48]

1. The position of the Septuagint in the Christian Church. It is often stressed, especially by specialists in Septuagint studies, that the Septuagint was the bible of the first non-Jewish Christians. However, insofar as it was still in use in the Jewish Diaspora, the Septuagint was also the bible of these communities. The Septuagint was thus clearly a Jewish bible. The reaction to the Christian use of the Septuagint, on the other hand, led to the appearance of Jewish revisions of the Septuagint as well as to the canonization of the Hebrew Bible.

2. The Hebrew Bible is a Jewish canon, selected by Jews for Jews, perhaps created in direct opposition to the Septuagint, now the Bible of the Christian Church, but certainly also under the influence of the catastrophes of the late first century and early second century CE.

3. The reason why the Hebrew Bible and not the Septuagint should be part of the Bible of the Church is to be found in a criterion of originality, which is certainly a mythical concept, in this case attached to the question of the original language of Old Testament books. Also ancient man was able to understand that there is a qualitative difference between an original text and its translations. Because of this, it is still reasonable to continue in the footsteps of European biblical humanism and the reformers, and read the Old Testament primarily in Hebrew.

4. On the other hand, from a specifically Christian point of view, it is questionable to continue in the footsteps of the protestant—in contrast to the Greek Orthodox and Roman Catholic churches—and disregard the books of the Septuagint which are not in the Hebrew Bible. Protestantism made a strange decision when it departed from the usage among fellow Christians and accepted a selection of writings originally made by Jewish scholars for their fellow Jews. From a theological perspective, the concept of 'apocryphal writings' should be suspect. There may be sound reason to re-introduce the parts of the Septuagint not included in the Hebrew Bible among the scriptures of the Western Church (although this will probably awaken little discussion today, as the importance of the Bible to modern Christians is, after all, diminishing).

---

48. Some preparatory work on this has already been published by my colleague Mogens Müller; see his 'Graeca sive Hebraica veritas? The Defense of the Septuagint in the Early Church', *SJOT* 3.1 (1989), pp. 103-124, and *idem*, 'Hebraica sive graeca veritas: The Jewish Bible at the Time of the New Testament and the Christian Bible', *SJOT* 3.2 (1989), pp. 55-71.

Finally, four theses concerning the relationship between the two Testaments.

1. The time lapse between the composition of the major part of the Old Testament and of the New Testament must, in light of the discussion above, be considered minimal. The Old Testament was no creation of a distant and foreign Israelite world, but it came into being in postexilic Jewish society, presumably during the Hellenistic Age. From a historical point of view the continuity between the Old Testament and the New Testament therefore consists in the continuity between the Jewish society that created and transmitted the writings of the Old Testament and the Jewish society that became the cradle of Christianity.

2. It is important that we realize that the Septuagint was originally a Jewish bible, and accepted as holy writ by early Christians only later. From a specifically Christian point of view, this means that the Old Testament cannot be considered an isolated entity, but theologically is an integral part of the Christian heritage.

3. A theology of the Old Testament is, accordingly, not an issue for Christian believers. The idea that Old Testament theologies should be founded on the Old Testament alone cannot be supported by the allegation that the early Christians inherited old writings from the ancient Israelites—not from the Jews—and turned these old Israelite books into their own sacred literature. The Christian acceptance of the Old Testament cannot therefore be likened to its acceptance by the ancient Jews (who wrote it). It should accordingly be a job for Jewish theologians to write Old Testament (or rather: Hebrew Bible) theologies in the strict sense of the word.[49]

4. A theology that also acknowledges the Old Testament as part of the Christian canon will, in a Christian environment, look to the New Testament for guidance, according to the scheme 'promise and fulfill-

---

49. This is not to deny that extraordinary intellectual achievements have been accomplished in this field, as, e.g., the probably most important Old Testament theology of this century, Gerhard von Rad's *Theologie des Alten Testaments* (2 vols.; Munich: Chr. Kaiser Verlag, 1957–60). It should, however, at the same time be realized that because of his definite historical and redaction-historical approach, von Rad wrote, not a proper theology of the Old Testament, but a mental history of the ancient Jews ('Israelites'), which in a Christian environment is an absolutely legitimate issue. A fine dissection of the problems involved in writing Old Testament theologies in the present century has been written by J. Høgenhaven, *Problems and Prospects of Old Testament Theology* (The Biblical Seminar, 6; Sheffield: JSOT Press, 1988).

ment'. As a result of this, a Christian theological discussion that also involves Old Testament matters will have to be an issue of interest for biblical theology; it is not a specifically Old Testament theme.[50]

These theses may eventually lead to a renewed interest in the Old Testament and save it from becoming theologically and intellectually a cul de sac among Christian believers. Traditional historical-critical research has, in spite of its many merits, made the Old Testament a book that 'only' provides information about the past, and which has little to say to modern (Christian) people. In connection with the New Testament, the Old Testament must be considered a main topic of interest for all Christians, laypersons and theologians alike. This approach should certainly not be considered an attack on the integrity of the Old Testament in a Christian environment, and does not prevent historical studies from continuing to be based on the Old Testament.[51] To the contrary, the Old Testament should be acknowledged as part of the Christian canon and as such important to Christian believers on a level with the New Testament. Nor should it be forgotten that the New Testament is such a small book with a comparable narrow theme only because of the presence of the Old Testament in the Christian Canon.

50. The opposite could be said of specialized theologies of the New Testament, as it was never intended to be an independent part of the Bible, but certainly presupposes the existence of the Old Testament.

51. It is not my case to judge whether a change of approach to Old Testament studies will bring any benefit to modern Jewry. I imagine that the majority of the modern Jews will consider these to be irrelevant, but it is my hope that they will at the same time appreciate their importance for the relationship between Christians and Jews, if the Christian communities will understand that the origin of the Old Testament as well as the cradle of Christianity should be sought, not among ancient Israelites, but in the Jewish society of the Hellenistic and Roman periods.

Part IV

CONCLUSIONS

REFLECTIONS ON THE DISCUSSION

Lester L. Grabbe

The summary that follows draws both on the essays and responses printed in this volume and on the discussion in the meetings of the Seminar. Participants are indicated by their initials; however, in order to differentiate between points made in the essays and points arising in the discussion, the full surname is given in parentheses when reference is to the individual essays and responses prepared for the Seminar. Comments in the discussion itself are indicated by the use of only the initials in parenthetical references.[1]

The topic for this volume was the Hellenistic period, without particular restrictions on what might be covered. As it turned out, however, most of the essays have focused in one way or another on the question of whether the Bible is primarily a Hellenistic production—with reference to the influential article by NPL, asking whether the Bible is a 'Hellenistic book'.[2] His article is in fact a quite wide-ranging study, but the thesis advanced responds to the question in the affirmative. TLT is, if anything, more outspoken in his recent book which seems to put the

---

1. The following initials are used:

RA	Rainer Albertz
BB	Bob Becking
HMB	Hans M. Barstad
RPC	Robert P. Carroll
PRD	Philip R. Davies
LLG	Lester L. Grabbe
DMG	David M. Gunn
NPL	Niels Peter Lemche
KP	Kai Peltonen
TLT	Thomas L. Thompson

2. 'The Old Testament—A Hellenistic Book?', *SJOT* 7 (1993), pp. 163-93, reprinted above (pp. 287-318), rewritten and expanded from the original Danish article, 'Det gamle Testamente som en hellenistisk bog', *DTT* 55 (1992), pp. 81-101.

emphasis on the Graeco-Roman period.[3] Together these represent a significant challenge to scholarship.

N.P. Lemche's Challenge

NPL's 1993 article is his most detailed development of his thesis. In it he made a number of points to answer the question of the title and to support the resulting thesis about the Bible, which may be summarized as follows.

The LXX is naturally a Hellenistic book; the Hebrew Bible is, on the other hand, a product of the second century CE, perhaps created by the two catastrophic wars with Rome in 66–70 and 132–135 CE. Also, the threat of Christianity by this time may have been influential. It has been suggested that the threefold division of the Hebrew canon is indicative of its historical development. However, the argument that the Pentateuch must have been canonized first, since the Samaritans use only those books, falls foul of two problems: we do not know when the Samaritan schism with Judaism took place, and there could be reasons why the Samaritans use only the Pentatech other than the development of the canon (e.g. the Former and Latter Prophets all emphasize Jerusalem, in contrast to the Samaritan holy site of Gerizim).

We cannot just use the writings themselves to determine their history because of the 'hermeneutical circle' (scholars have long recognized the problems with the 'hermeneutical circle' but still have not given due weight to them). The final date of a writing is when the complete text appears. For the Hebrew Bible, this is not until 350 CE. For example, we cannot say anything about the Samuel story with regard to 1000 BCE, but we certainly know it existed in 350 CE. This is where we must start, though it is easy to find some evidence that the text existed earlier. The question is how much earlier. A literary writing is the product of its age of origin and will show the marks of that age. For example, Genesis

---

3. *The Bible in History: How Writers Create a Past* (London: Jonathan Cape, 1999), or in America, *The Mythic Past: Biblical Archaeology and the Myth of Israel* (New York: Basic Books). The term 'Graeco-Roman' has several potential meanings, one being a generic term to mean the whole period encompassing the common history and culture of the Mediterranean beginning with the Greeks. Another is a way of referring to the period of Mediterranean culture after the Romans had conquered the Greek empires, which seems to be the way TLT uses it.

1 shows knowledge of the four elements which first appears in the Greek writer Thales; therefore, it is post-Thales.

Two more examples can be given. It is now recognized that Joshua describes an event that did not take place. The existence of the Joshua narrative is a fact, but it is also a fact that it describes a non-existent reality. Why was it written? One suggestion is that it wants to prove the racial purity of the Israelites, which would lead to the conclusion that it was written at a time when the land was possessed by foreigners. Therefore, the Joshua story originated after the exile and in the Diaspora. As for David, archaeology shows that Jerusalem was no more than about 2000 people until the mid-eighth century, and the story of the Davidic (Solomonic) empire is invention, but why? The story seems to have been created to give an Israelite hero to compare with the empire-builders of the other nations. It would provide a future programme for when the Jews themselves would conquer the land. Perhaps the story is Persian, with David modelled on Cyrus, but it could be even later.

It has been widely argued that Joshua and also Samuel originated in the Josianic period, but some aspects of both stories are postexilic. For example, there is no reason why the people of Josianic times would be demanding a king, since they already had one. Arguments once used to demonstrate a tenth-century origin for narratives are now being used for the time of Josiah. Yet just as with David and Solomon, there are no external accounts that mention Josiah. The work of Herbert Niehr shows that the pre-exilic religion is no different from that of the surrounding peoples (e.g. the Moabites). The alleged contest between Canaanite and Israelite religion fits 500–200 BCE better than 1000–500. The Israelites of the Old Testament are Jews. There is no reason to think that the pre-exilic Israelites were an ethnic unity.

The arguments for dating the Hebrew Bible to the Hellenistic period can be summarized as follows:

1. The Old Testament has little to do with real history until at least the later part of the monarchy. Although there may be genuine historical recollections, the Old Testament is a poor source of historical information.

2. A good portion of the Old Testament literature can be considered the creation of the Jewish Diaspora. The exodus and conquest narratives show the aspirations of the writers rather than historical memory.

3. The 'history of Israel' seems to be modelled on the Greek pattern, beginning especially with Herodotus, showing that the Old Testament writers had a knowledge of Greek literature.

4. The Persian period does not seem to meet the requirements of the context for when the Old Testament books were written down. A major problem is that we have so little information about the Persian period as far as the Jewish population is concerned. There is a problem with the archaeology because the Persian period has often been neglected by archaeologists;[4] however, the indication is that Jerusalem was very small and not likely to be conducive to authoring the historical literature of the Old Testament. The supposed benevolence of the Persian empire is not well documented; it may in fact have only been the Persian administration's neglect of the Palestinian area.

The revitalization of the ancient Near East only became a fact with the Greek takeover. Jerusalem expanded and there were parallels (on a smaller scale) to the cultural developments in Mesopotamia and Egypt. It seems self-evident that the Hellenistic age was the formative period of early Jewish thought and literature. NPL notes three 'serious objections' against his position:

1. How could a period which produced the Chronicler also produce such writings as the Yahwist, book of Joshua, or books of Samuel?

2. How can one explain the difference between classical biblical Hebrew and Late Biblical Hebrew?

3. Where would we find the home of the Old Testament in such a late period?

NPL responds that all three can be explained through an ethno-linguistic and socio-economic argument. The distance, real as it is, is not necessarily one of time. It could be a case of different environments and/or the abilities and preferences of their authors in each situation. Also, the Hebrew of the Bible was no longer a living language at this time. The Hebrew text was translated into Greek in Egypt, but there

---

4. See now for an analysis in detail of the available archaeological evidence: Charles E. Carter, *The Emergence of Yehud in the Persian Period: A Social and Demographic Study* (JSOTSup, 294; Sheffield: Sheffield Academic Press, 1999).

was no reason that it had to be much older than the translation.[5]

NPL's essay in the present volume (pp. 200-24) is a further development, though it also remains programmatic. It is already summarized above (p. 25), the main additional arguments seeming to be the following:

1. The Persian period is a 'black box', and to put the composition of the biblical writings there is to create an illegimate (in a Popperian sense) hypothesis because it is unfalsifiable.
2. Various Near Eastern elements can be found in the text, but many of these (e.g. the Mesopotamian law codes) continued to exist in the Hellenistic age.
3. The presence of elements which are unquestionably early in the text must be treated like old artifacts found alongside younger in an archaeological stratum: the text is dated by its youngest elements.
4. The amalgam of Greek and ancient Near Eastern traditions would argue for an origin in the Seleucid empire, perhaps in Mesopotamia, though a place like Damascus is also a possibility.

TLT seems to accept the main arguments of NPL about the Bible. His views can be summarized as follows.[6] The Hellenistic and Graeco-Roman periods (extending into the first century CE) are a necessary literary context for biblical texts. He thinks that NPL has made a strong case for looking to the Hellenistic period as the central period of collection and formation of the texts which later became the Hebrew Bible. Sound methodology requires that one look to the mid-second century BCE as the earliest possible date for the extant form of the Masoretic tradition of the Pentateuch. Not only is this argument based on the MT chronology's orientation to 164 BCE and supported by the variant

---

5. Based on his argument that the Hebrew Bible is basically a Hellenistic composition, NPL goes on to develop two sets of theses. The first set of four is about the relationship of the LXX and the Hebrew Bible, and the second set of four concerns the relationship of the two Testaments of the Christian Bible. These are not discussed here because they do not seem to be directly relevant to the discussion of this volume.

6. It would be impossible to deal adequately with his book in this section (cf. my review, 'Hat die Bibel doch recht? A Review of T. L. Thompson's *The Bible in History*', *SJOT* 14 [2000], pp. 114-38). TLT has kindly provided the summary given here.

chronological schemes in the near-contemporary versions of the LXX and the Samaritan Pentateuch, but it is also attested by the appearance in this period of texts (among the Dead Sea Scrolls) that can be recognized as those of the Bible. The Isaiah Scroll (in two versions, 1QIs[a] and 1QIs[b]) is a Hellenistic text. This is our *terminus ad quem*. Our *terminus a quo* for the process of tradition collection must be connected with the formation of the Jewish self-understanding as a 'people of God', with its implicit voice of the 'new Israel'. Since this ideologically created entity reflects on 'old Israel' as a thing of the past, some time after 597 BCE is indicated; however, an earlier period (though post-722) must be considered possible since the specifically Judaean traditions are secondarily attached to the Pentateuch.

TLT's views especially focus on the ideological nature of the text. Since the Judaean traditions centre on a Zion ideology, our *a quo* date for these Judaean traditions should post-date the literary construction of a temple ideology, that is, probably a date after temple reconstruction (because of the idealistic nature of the temple ideology). However, in disagreement with NPL, it is not necessary to understand the Hellenistic dating as implying specific Greek influence. The imperial ideologies of the Persian period are a direct ancestor of Hellenism, and the Mediterranean fringe of the Persian Empire came into contact with the Greek world very early. The *terminus a quo* chronology is therefore weak, in contrast to the relatively firm *terminus ad quem* dating given by Qumran. This means that the chronological parameters for the development of the text might be placed within early Jewish literature from the mid-fifth century BCE to the first century CE.

RPC's article has a number of points that seem to be sympathetic to aspect's of NPL's paper. He notes that the Hebrew Bible was not completed until the second century CE, and that to begin with the Hellenistic period is 'the beginning of wisdom'. However, he does seem to allow here and there that the Persian period may be equally viable for certain aspects of development that NPL wishes to push to after the coming of Alexander. PRD's paper also argues that the Hellenistic period is certainly a candidate for the exodus tradition as found in the present book of Exodus, though he is not at all dogmatic. What he is especially concerned to show is that a number of contexts (apart from the Late Bronze/Early Iron period) could have given rise to the exodus story. He also wants to emphasize the fact that there may be a non-Israelite/Jewish version of the story.

Responses and Objections to Lemche

Responses and Objections to Lemche

In one way or another quite a few of the contributions to the present volume address various aspects of NPL's paper. As the next section shows, there were a number of significant agreements, a fact which must not be forgotten. First, however, this section will look at some of the areas where the papers and discussion threw up specific disagreements with NPL at various points. Any attempt to summarize these critiques inevitably leads to some distortion in presenting the arguments of the different writers, but it is only fair to indicate not only that the majority disagreed with some aspects of NPL's position but also the main areas where this disagreement was expressed.

The question of the Greek background to the Old Testament books is very significant to NPL. It is the argument perhaps most directly pressed in both his original 1993 article and his more recent article (Lemche). Indeed, the earlier emphasis on Herodotus has given way to one on the work of Livy. Most scholars would say that the Dead Sea Scrolls decisively rule out a composition of any book in the Hebrew canon as late as the time of Livy (died early first century CE), which NPL readily admits. The argument of Greek influence is an important one, but there is a real problem: how do you demonstrate Greek influence? Unfortunately, NPL has not so far given detailed analyses to demonstrate his assertions. Indeed, TLT himself has noted in his one criticism of NPL that the latter has not defined what he means by 'Greek intellectual content'.[7]

Apart from the difficulty in pinning down 'Greek influence', there is a strong argument that the earliest influence was in the other directon— from the Orient to the West. There is still much to be done in this area, but there are some significant studies.[8] Thus, when NPL states that Genesis 1 could not be earlier than Thales because the Genesis writer uses the four elements of Thales, this is hardly a conclusive argument. A number of classical scholars have claimed that Thales was actually drawing on Near Eastern traditions, and that his cosmology is a Bab-

---

7.   TLT himself does not appear to have focused on the question of Greek influence to the extent of an explicit discussion in his book, though he refers to it in passing in a number of passages; see n. 13 below.

8.   Among general studies, one might note most recently W.L. West, *The East Face of Helicon: West Asiatic Elements in Greek Poetry and Myth* (Oxford: Clarendon Press, 1997). See also next note.

ylonian one.[9] If so, Thales is irrelevant to the dating/origin question of Genesis 1, and there is room for those who see a Babylonian background and its composition in the 'exilic' or Persian period. For this reason, it is hardly surprising that NPL's Greek thesis has been met by the counter-argument that the Old Testament shows greater influence from ancient Near Eastern models than Greek ones (Barstad). What HMB finds is the 'common theology' of the ancient Near East strongly reflected in the Old Testament. Indeed, one could turn the argument on its head and argue that Herodotus modelled himself on the Deuteronomistic History. It would be perfectly possible to develop such a thesis. Most would not, a priori, give this idea much credence, but it is also a fact that not many scholars currently give much credence to the thesis that the Deuteronomistic History is modelled on Herodotus (much less Livy).

The account of Hecataeus of Abdera (about 300 BCE) is considered significant by several writers, mainly with regard to his witness to the existence of the Pentateuch (Albertz, Becking, Davies, Grabbe ['Jewish Historiography and Scripture']). RA gives a lengthy discussion of Hecataeus, arguing that he must presuppose the existence of much of our present Pentateuch, primarily the books of Genesis to Numbers (Albertz). BB agrees (Becking); however, PRD is rather more circumspect. He sees Hecataeus's account as reflecting elements of both Jewish and Egyptian versions of an exodus story, suggesting that the story had already been traded between Egyptians and Judaeans by the time Hecataeus got hold of it (Davies). On the other hand, many of the details in Hecataeus's account would not have come from any such account but are likely to depend on contemporary information. The fact that so many of the Seminar mentioned Hecataeus shows a recognition of his importance for the state of Judah and Jewish religion about 300 BCE. BB and LLG noted some other early Hellenistic writers (Jewish in this case) who seem to show a knowledge of the LXX text (Becking, Grabbe ['Jewish Historiography and Scripture']).

RA and NPL differ sharply in their evaluation of the Greek period as

9. M.L. West, *Early Greek Philosophy and the Orient* (Oxford: Clarendon Press, 1971), pp. 208-213; G.S. Kirk, J.E. Raven and M. Schofield, *The Presocratic Philosophers: A Critical History with a Selection of Texts* (Cambridge: Cambridge University Press, 2nd edn, 1983), pp. 76-99. An early tradition even makes Thales of Phoenician origin, but on balance he was most likely Greek (Kirk, Raven Schofield, *The Presocratic Philosopher*, p. 77).

conducive to the development of Jewish literature and thought. I think I differ from both in my own evaluation. As I have argued at length elsewhere, Hellenization is a complex process often misunderstood by biblical scholars.[10] Something new was added to the melting pot of the ancient Near East, and eventually it had widespread effects, but these effects were more uneven, more gradual and more complicated than is sometimes appreciated. I would not agree that Greek rule was necessarily antithetical to the development of Jewish literature, partly because the Greeks were not primarily cultural imperialists. Greek culture spread mainly because the natives, especially those from the upperclasses, saw an advantage in gaining a Greek education and adopting certain aspects of the Greek way of life. We thus have the paradoxical example of Greek loanwords in Jewish Semitic writings. Some Greek words appear in an Aramaic inscription within decades of Alexander's conquest. Yet the number of Greek loanwords even down to rabbinic times in Jewish writings is remarkably few. I therefore agree with NPL that in the Hellenistic period many of the centuries-old ancient Near Eastern institutions continued to flourish (e.g. the legal traditions), making that period a good context for composing the Old Testament if it was created in Mesopotamia. But that is not the only appropriate context for such literary activity.

My view is that Jewish literary activity was neither encouraged nor discouraged by Hellenization; in fact, I doubt that things were much different from the situation under Persian rule. As time went on and many Jews took on Greek as their first language, a large Jewish literature in Greek eventually accumulated, but by this time I think there is no doubt that large sections of the Bible were already essentially in their present form. Contrary to NPL, the flourishing of the native cultures in the Seleucid period is a good indication that the coming of the Greeks did not bring a 'revitalization'; rather, it draws attention to the fact that a similar dynamic situation had also existed under Persian rule. NPL is quite correct that the Persians did not establish some sort of idealized rule in contrast to the Babylonians and Assyrians before them,

---

10. *Judaism from Cyrus to Hadrian* (Minneapolis: Fortress Press, 1992; London: SCM Press, 1994), especially ch. 3, 'The Jews and Hellenization' (pp. 147-70) and ch. 5, 'Seleucid Rule, the Maccabean Revolt, and the Hasmonean Priest-Kings' (pp. 221-311). To my bibliography needs to be added the excellent study by Susan Sherwin-White and Amélie Kuhrt, *From Samarkhand to Sardis: A New Approach to the Seleucid Empire* (London: Gerald Duckworth, 1993).

a fact already pointed out two decades ago by Amélie Kuhrt.[11] On the other hand, conditions for creating a Jewish sacred literature were as fully available in the Persian period as in the Greek.

The lack of Greek loanwords does not mean, however, that Jewish writings of the Greek period cannot usually be identified as such, and here the argument hinges on rather more definite indications than just a vague dependence on Greek models. First, for writings supposedly so influenced by Greek, there is surprisingly little reference to Greece in any of the Old Testament books before Daniel. Even in Qohelet, widely believed to be written in the Ptolemaic period, it is difficult to find clear Greek influence. So problematic is it that a recent scholar has been able to make a reasonable case for composition in the Persian period.[12] If KP's preferred dating of Chronicles in the early Greek period is correct, as many scholars would agree, it would not necessarily show any Greek influence, reflecting rather the situation in the Persian period. But those Jewish writings in the Greek period that refer to external events often have some obvious indication of the dating and of the reality to which they refer. For example, Daniel's symbolic visions and his 'king of the north and king of the south' cannot be mistaken as to what they refer. The Animal Apocalypse (*1 En.* 85–89), the references to Pompey in the *Psalms of Solomon*, the allusions to Rome in *4 Ezra* and the New Testament book of Revelaton, all use symbolism as a thin disguise for current events. Yet when NPL suggests that a biblical scenario is really a symbol for the Seleucids and Ptolemies,[13] there is no such obvious symbolism. There is in fact no reason why the story in question could not just as easily be taken as a straightforward reference to the actual entities in the story.

This does not mean that here and there an argument could not be made for such an interpretation, but NPL does not do so. He and TLT

---

11. 'The Cyrus Cylinder and Achaemenid Imperial Policy', *JSOT* 25 (1983), pp. 83-97.

12. See Choon-Leong Seow, *Ecclesiastes: A New Translation with Introduction and Commentary* (AB, 18C; New York: Doubleday, 1997); also his article, 'Linguistic Evidence and the Dating of Qohelet', *JBL* 115 (1996), pp. 643-66. He demonstrates the fragility of dating the book; however, despite some well-made points, in the end I think a Ptolemaic dating is on balance more probable.

13. TLT also indicates such an interpretation for certain passages, e.g. the pattern for the division of the Israelite kingdom is said to be the breakup of Alexander's empire (*The Bible in History*, p. 97).

seem to be content with merely stating that a particular biblical story could have in mind the Seleucids and the Ptolemies or whatever. One would expect detailed arguments for at least some examples. The same applies to developing a full-scale hypothesis of how the biblical text developed in the Greek period, with a discussion of the social and historical context. Considerable frustration has been expressed that this has not been done, even though there has been a willingness to rubbish the reconstructions of other scholars (e.g. by RA, both in his article [Albertz] and in the Seminar discussion). This is probably one of the reasons that a number of scholars, including some in the Seminar, have asked whether NPL and TLT are really interested in history as such. On the other hand, it should be noted that TLT has a section in his book giving a historical reconstruction of Palestine from the Stone Age to the Bronze Age, giving no hint that he has lost his interest in history.[14] Unfortunately, when the tenth century BCE is reached, he reverts to the familiar attacks on the use of the biblical text, and no historical reconstruction from archaeology is attempted.[15]

Another area is the question of whether history for the ancients was just another branch of rhetoric. Answering the question for Jewish writers is not easy because of no explicit statements, but we can at least discuss it in relation to Greek and Roman writers because we have statements to analyse. The implication of connecting history with rhetoric is, of course, to suggest that persuasiveness or beauty of language took precedence over accuracy or verisimilitude. Although this may well have been the case with some historians, it was not the way that history was normally viewed; on the contrary, the expectation was that historians were to make truth the first concern of their writings (Grabbe, 'Who Were the First Real Historians?'). This perspective is discussed at length in Thucydides and Polybius, as one might expect. However, even in a writer such as Cicero, known for his writings on oratory and

14. Pp. 103-199. See my comments in my review of his book ('Hat die Bibel doch recht?' pp. 134-35).

15. TLT points out that such a reconstruction is found in his book, *The Early History of the Israelite People* (Leiden: E.J. Brill, 1992); he also mentions that his *The Bible in History* has some discussion (pp. 210-17, 234-66). On the other hand, he accepts that RA's critique is correct in so far as he has turned increasingly to a reconstruction of social, literary and intellectual contexts rather than a history of Israel, whose possibilities he increasingly rejects (cf. *The Bible in History*, pp. 228-33, and his response to DMG's paper at p. 27 above).

his practice of the art of rhetoric, we find a distinction made between mere rhetoric and the truth of the statements being made. He criticizes those historians (such as the Roman annalists) who were practically unreadable because of their dry style, but he sees no incompatibility between writing well and telling the truth. Some who adopted the name 'historian' may well have subordinated proper historical enquiry to rhetoric, and we can list quite a few Hellenistic historians whose qualities as proper historians were poorly developed, if at all. But this is the difference between theory and practice. The common view was that historians should be factually accurate, and that history differed from poetry and rhetoric in making truth about the past its first concern.

The most clear indication to my mind, however, comes from Ben Sira's section in praise of the fathers (Sir. 44–49). This is not just vague praise of some of Israel's past heroes which could have come from general tradition. On the contrary, Ben Sira follows systematically through the biblical books from Genesis to Kings/Chronicles, then through the prophetic literature. He does not mention Ezra or Daniel. Some have tried to suggest that he knew Ezra but did not mention him; however, I argue that he either did not know Ezra or did not consider the book authoritative, showing that the book of Ezra–Nehemiah in our present canon was not before him.[16] But his failure to mention Ezra and Daniel highlights those figures from the Old Testament that he does mention. Thus, even though Ben Sira seldom quotes the biblical text, there seems clear evidence that he knew much of the Pentateuch, the Deuteronomistic History and the Latter Prophets in a form recognizably like those same books today. That the text continued to develop in some sections of these writings is a documented fact, but I would still conclude that these sections of the Bible had reached substantially their present form by Ben Sira's time. Allowing for a period of time for them to become authoritative and to form a conventional and widely accepted collection (note the term, 'the Twelve') suggests composition no later than the end of the Persian period.

TLT seems to recognize the significance of this with his critique of my dating of Ben Sira: 'Grabbe's confidence in the historicity of the Ben Sira colophon does not consider the stock literary overtones since Amenemope that hardly allow us to date this text to the time of an authorial grandfather' (Thompson). However, this is not in my opinion

---

16. *Ezra–Nehemiah* (London: Routledge, 1998), pp. 86-88.

a satisfactory response to my argument which does not simply depend on accepting the attribution of the colophon of the Greek version; indeed, a footnote gave several reasons for my dating.[17] But in any case the dating of Ben Sira is not exceptional among historians. It depends on the same sort of evidence as is used for Herodotus, Josephus or any other of writers from the Greek and Roman periods. The book of Ben Sira occurs in two forms. The Greek version has the statement allegedly by the grandson and the translator, and the Hebrew version does not. It also differs from the normal scribal colophons of copyists, though the latter are in fact generally accepted as authentic by scholars. The lack of a reference to the Maccabaean revolt or the 'abomination of desolation' in the Hebrew text is extremely important for making the original book pre-Maccabaean.

This brings us to an issue that has arisen before: is the Bible being treated as special? In the past, some scholars have privileged the biblical text rather than subjecting it to criticism and scrutiny by normal historical methods. But now the question has been raised as to whether the reverse is true—that the biblical text is being treated in a more critical and negative way than other potential historical sources.[18] In the discussion TLT did suggest that it was not history as such that was being got rid of but 'biblical history' (TLT), though NPL explicitly denied that there was an 'anti-biblical agenda' (NPL). Nevertheless, the feeling has still persisted that different criteria are being asked for con-

17. In my essay on Jewish historiography and scripture, I give three principles for doing history, one of which is that any proposition has to be argued for on the grounds of probability. Although I think most historians would take them as self-evident and normal working principles, TLT rubbishes them. I am puzzled by this since TLT is quite willing to quote history *based on the very methods he has criticized* when it suits his purpose, as I point out in my review ('Hat die Bibel doch recht?', pp. 123-26). In any case, I think that he has completely distorted what I said in this short section of my paper. I do not suggest, for example, that all sources are equal and can be used for historical reconstruction—on the contrary, I make it clear that some sources are of little or no value. All I ask the reader to do is compare what I said in my three principles with TLT's summary of them. No wonder he claims I am better at reading texts than formulating principles! The fact is that my reading and my principles *as stated* are in harmony.

18. See especially Hans M. Barstad, 'The Strange Fear of the Bible: Some Reflections on the "Bibliophobia" in Recent Ancient Israelite Historiography', in Lester L. Grabbe (ed.), *Leading Captivity Captive: 'The Exile' as History and Ideology* (JSOTSup, 278; ESHM, 2; Sheffield: Sheffield Academic Press, 1998), pp. 120-27.

firmation of biblical stories than for those found in other sources. An example of why this is so may be the dating of Ben Sira: it is only this dating that TLT questions, not that of Manetho or Hecataeus of Abdera or Herodotus, even though the dating methods all use the same general principles long accepted in scholarship. I come back to my plea in our first volume that we must apply the same historical principles to all our data, whether from the Bible or not.[19]

One argument that has been important in the debate has been that of the language of the biblical text. NPL argued that the differences in language between the various writings could be explained by ethno-linguistic and socio-economic criteria rather than diachronic develop-ment (Lemche 1993), though he did recognize that the data might be explained on diachronic grounds. BB pointed out that the Lachish and Arad ostraca contain a language that is likely to coincide to a high degree with contemporary spoken Hebrew, and its remarkable coincidence with the language of Kings and Jeremiah was a valid argument for dat-ing these books earlier than the Greek period (Becking). The fact that the Lachish letters can be dated archaeologically leaves no doubt that they present sixth-century Hebrew (BB). This got strong support from a number of those present in the audience. Timo Veijola pointed out that native speakers of modern Hebrew do not accept the argument that dif-ferences in the Hebrew of the Bible can be explained by non-diachronic factors. Saul Olyan noted that orthography is a good indication of de-velopment through time. Walter Dietrich mentioned that the Tel Dan inscription has correspondences with 'old' features of biblical Hebrew. Nadav Na'aman asked more generally whether a single anachronistic detail of the Deuteronomistic History from the Persian or Hellenistic period can be pointed out. TLT outlined several factors that affect the question.[20]

---

19. 'Are Historians of Ancient Palestine Fellow Creatures—Or Different Animals?', in L.L. Grabbe (ed.), *Can a 'History of Israel' Be Written?* (JSOTSup, 245; ESHM, 1; Sheffield: Sheffield Academic Press, 1997), pp. 19-36.

20. A brief summary of them is as follows: (1) the diachronic distinction be-tween Classical Hebrew (CH) and Late Biblical Hebrew (LBH) is a potentially important hypothesis which needs better formulation and chronological anchorage. (2) CH is obviously early in relation to the later development of LBH. However, it seems also to be contemporary, and whether LBH and CH are close or far from Qumran Hebrew has not been satisfactorily settled. (3) Are we looking at a chrono-logical shift or a distinction of specific groupings of texts, where authorial associa-tions such as sociolects play a role? (4) The stress on Aramaic influence as a crite-

The linguistic argument has been advanced before as one of the more objective means of determining dating. It is relative because the form of the language is difficult to pin down except in broad time periods, but it has long been concluded that it could be done. The argument that differences between sections of the Old Testament can rather be explained completely by sociological and ethno-linguistic considerations, without recourse to diachronic arguments, has not met with general favour among Hebraists and Semitists.[21] I think it would be fair to say that this is one area where NPL and others[22] are perhaps on their shakiest grounds in the eyes of contemporary scholarship.

Finally, there is NPL's 'black box' argument. He is of course quite right about our lack of knowledge for large sections of the Persian period. However, the argument that putting the writing of (large sections of) the Bible at that time is illegitimate misunderstands Popper's principle of falsification. It is like saying that if you lost your keys, you are only allowed to look where there is a street light—no matter where you lost them! To suggest the Persian period is not to present an *unfalsifiable* hypothesis, because the hypothesis can theoretically be falsified. The present stage of knowledge may mean that it cannot be tested now, but this is not the same as saying it is unfalsifiable. An unfalsifiable hypothesis is one framed in such a way that it *cannot* be falsified. The two concepts are quite different. Several aspects of Einstein's theories were incapable of being tested in his own time because the technology did not exist to do so.

Despite the problems with the biblical writings, we have more knowledge of the Persian period than NPL allows (Albertz).[23] Even where we

---

rion is exaggerated as, historico-linguisically, this is a relatively trivial issue. Noth, we must remember, used to date things early because of Aramaic flavours. (5) The chronology and the distinctions within complex texts are largely based on the documentary hypothesis which itself is based on a fictive history and chronology. (6) Iron Age inscriptions have distinctive dialectic characteristics—including closeness and distance from Aramaic. These all need to be considered.

21. Cf. Avi Hurwitz, 'The Historical Quest for "Ancient Israel" and the Linguistic Evidence of the Hebrew Bible: Some Methodological Observations', *VT* 47 (1997), pp. 301-315.

22. E.g. PRD read a paper, 'Dated Hebrew and Dated Scholarship', at the 1998 IOSOT conference in Oslo, though this has not yet been published. It was mainly an engagement with the arguments of Hurvitz.

23. Cf. also my attempts to bridge the Persian period without recourse to the biblical text, 'Israel's Historical Reality after the Exile', in Bob Becking and Marjo

do not have detailed information, we can infer certain developments because of information for an earlier or later period, the 'triangulation method'.[24] This is normal historical procedure and would not raise an eyebrow among classical historians. Far from being a violation of the Popperian principle, future discoveries might well provide sufficient data to falsify the Persian hypothesis. In the meantime, it is as legitimate to develop a Persian-period thesis for the essential origin of much of the biblical text as it is to propose a Hellenistic one. Each thesis must be evaluated on its merits.

Points of General Agreement

It is natural that the discussion has emphasized areas of disagreement. There are indeed significant disagreements which must not be minimized, and these have been aired as summarized above. Neverthless, there is substantial agreement on a number of important points by most members of the Seminar. This agreement is in many ways more significant than the disagreement, for it shows the extent to which scholars with quite different perspectives and backgrounds have come to similar conclusions. I hope that it is these agreements that will be the strongest impression taken away by readers.

1. It will first be recognized by everyone that the Hebrew Bible was completed no earlier than the Hellenistic period. Significant sections of the Old Testament are unquestionably Hellenistic in origin. For example, Daniel could not have been completed before the 'abomination of desolation' set up in the temple in 168 BCE,[25] and few if any critical scholars would query its Hellenistic date. Likewise, Qohelet is widely thought to be Ptolemaic in origin, though a case has recently been made for a Persian-period dating.[26] Most of us would also accept that various other writings, especially in the Prophets, would not have been com-

Korpel (eds.), *The Crisis of Israelite Religion: Transformation of Religious Tradition in Exilic and Post-Exilic Times* (OTS, 42; Leiden: E.J. Brill, 1999), pp. 9-32.

24. Discussed in ' "The Exile" under the Theodolite: Historiography as Triangulation', in Grabbe (ed.), *Leading Captivity Captive*, pp. 80-100; see also 'Israel's Historical Reality after the Exile'.

25. On this dating, see Lester L. Grabbe, 'Maccabean Chronology: 167-164 or 168-165 BCE?', *JBL* 110 (1991), pp. 59-74.

26. See n. 12 above.

pleted until the Hellenistic period (even if they already existed in some form earlier than this).

2. We should begin with the evidence of the Dead Sea Scrolls. Some epigraphers are rather more confident with paleographic dating than some of the rest of us, but the texts can be dated within broad limits. (Surprisingly, not a lot of this particular argument was made in the various papers in this volume, though it was mentioned in passing several times and clearly considered significant.) The Scrolls show the completion or substantial completion of a number of biblical books and thus give a *terminus ad quem* for their composition.

3. The Hebrew Bible in the form of the consonantal Masoretic Text and its present canon, at least for the bulk of Jews, is attested for the first century CE at the earliest and perhaps even the second century.[27] If that were the only point made by NPL, we could stop here because I think we would all agree that these are facts.

4. The literary and ideological nature of the text makes it problematic as historical writing; therefore, we cannot label any of the Bible as 'history' in any modern sense of the term (cf. Grabbe, 'Who Were the First Real Historians?'). Where the disagreement begins is whether, despite the ideology, sections of the narrative can be used as historiographic sources alongside other sources.

---

27. If by 'Hebrew Bible' we meant the Masoretic Text, then our present Hebrew Bible is no earlier than the Middle Ages. A proper discussion would take far too much space here, but some brief points can be made (for further information see ch. 8 of my study, *Judaic Religion in the Second Temple Period: Belief and Practice from the Exile to Yavneh* [London: Routledge, 2000]). The Masoretic Text is not only the consonants but also the vowel points, accents, versification, etc. Our earliest manuscript showing these is probably from the ninth century CE, the system of writing the vowels, etc., having apparently been developed from about the seventh century CE. This does not mean that the MT is a late artificial creation as was once argued; on the contrary, it is founded on a long solid tradition, on which see Lester L. Grabbe, *Comparative Philology and the Text of Job: A Study in Methodology* (SBLDS, 34; Missoula, MT: Scholars Press, 1977), pp. 179-97. Although the Masoretic text-type is attested early among the Qumran Scrolls, it was not the sole text-type in use among the Jews until after 70 CE. Similarly, the witnesses to the Hebrew canon do not attest the present collection until after 70. On the other hand, to ascribe the text and canon to the Yavnean period goes well beyond the evidence, and the designation of them as 'rabbinic' is unjustified. It may be that the present text and canon belonged to one segment of the Jews and became widely promulgated and exclusive only after 70. PRD has suggested that a proto-canon was created already by the Hasmoneans, though not everyone accepted it.

5. There are old elements and early traditions in the text, going back to well before the Hellenistic period, perhaps even as far as the Bronze Age in some few cases. Again, the issue is not whether these exist but the extent to which we have access to them through the present text.

6. The Pentateuch as a collection is not likely to be pre-exilic. The question turns on whether it is essentially a Persian-period composition or primarily the product of a later age (both views allow both Persian-period and Greek-period developments, with the real question centring on which period is the primary context for its composition).

Yes, the Bible is a Hellenistic (or Graeco-Roman) book, whether we are referring to the Hebrew Bible or the Septuagint. Exactly when the present collection of books in the LXX became more or less established is difficult to say since most of our evidence for the LXX is Christian. One could ask whether there ever was a 'LXX Jewish canon' apart from the Pentateuch. In any case, we know the LXX text continued to develop and change well into the early centuries of the Common Era, at least to the time of Origen. It is not clear that the Hebrew canon was established before 70, though it remains possible that for some circles (the Jerusalem priesthood?) it had been, but the first century CE seems the earliest date. The same applies to the consonantal form of the MT. The debate therefore does not centre on the issue of whether the Bible is a Hellenistic book—because in its completed form it is—but rather on the question of the state of the text before the Hellenistic period. To what extent were there already written versions of (some of) the books, and when and where did the concept of a collection of sacred writings make an impact on the Jewish community? It is over these issues that the debate runs, but it is easy to forget that these are to some extent subsidiary issues.

Final Thoughts on the Development of the Bible

At the end of the discussion, the question was asked as to how each person present saw the development of the Bible. The responses were as follows (including some submitted in writing by those who were not in the debate in Helsinki, which is why some entries are longer and more thoughtfully formulated than others):

RA: The Bible has a long history of about 1000 years. There are some compositions from the ninth and eighth centuries, such as the stories of Jehu and Jacob. The exile was decisive for

producing written texts. The Pentateuch is from the Persian
period and had become authoritative by the end of the third
century (as the Prologue to Ben Sira shows). Books from the
Hellenistic period such as Chronicles depend on sections of
the Old Testament, which is also the basis for Hellenistic commentaries (e.g. *Jubilees*). Works produced in the Hellenistic
period are Zechariah 9–14 (probably), Isaiah 24–27, and the
apocalyptic writings (Daniel, *1 Enoch*).

BB: The Bible is the intellectual form in which various groups of
Yahwists rendered account of their past. Some of it dates from
the Iron III period.

HMB: The canon is very late. It contains the final edition of ancient
Palestinian traditions and also the *Einheitskultur*. It is related
to ancient Near Eastern literature. As for the question of historicity, we must look at each tradition separately.

RPC: The production of the Bible is a fairly long-term *process*, starting perhaps in the Persian period, gathering momentum in the
Greek period and coming to full fruition in the Graeco-Roman
and Roman periods. This process relates to the production of
the substantive contents we now have as individual biblical
scrolls. The transformation of these scrolls into collations, collections and finally canons must be assigned to an even later
period, to the Roman and Late Antiquity periods. The question
I would like an answer to is this: which era or generation was
the first to clap eyes on what we would call 'a/the Bible', that
is, the full horror-show of 39/52+ books (taking into account
the various forms of the Bible in Hebrew, Greek, Latin, etc.)
or whatever would be recognized by ancient communities as a
'canon' (in whatever sense of the word *kanon*)? That is the
moment when the Bible *qua* Bible came into being as the
caterpillar of scrolls transformed into the butterfly of canon.
All our papers deal with caterpillars, but it is the butterfly we
should really be discussing.

PRD: The literature that came to comprise the canon was formed
very largely within the scribal communities of Jerusalem,
mostly connected to the temple which served political as well
as religious functions. At first the works written in the Persian
and Hellenistic periods made up an informal 'canon' such as
all literate societies generate, and reflected the classical scribal

genres of wisdom and liturgical poetry plus two other genes: historiography and collections of prophetic oracles. In the Hellenistic period, other works found their way into the repertoire, authored by independent intellectuals (like the author of Qohelet) or by laypersons (possibly female), as in the case of Song of Songs, Jonah, and Esther, though even here the scribal tradition can clearly be seen. The idea of a formal list of Judaean books in the native language(s) was almost certainly conceived and put into effect by the Hasmoneans as part of a programme of cultural definition, after which there was an official canon. The Qumran texts suggest this was not strictly recognized, though their less formal canon was comprised of much the same list (but probably also including *1 Enoch* and *Jubilees*). The rabbis did nothing to the canon except re-categorize the notion of holy books in terms of physical purity (whether they 'defiled the hands'). Functionally, the Jewish canon extends beyond the *Tanakh* to include the talmudic literature; in fact, it could be argued that Judaism has an open canon.

LLG: The Hebrew Bible as we know it is not earlier than the first century CE—or even mediaeval times if we accept the MT as the best version of the Hebrew Bible, as I would. Nevertheless, much of the text was written in a form substantially like our version (i.e. sufficiently close to be recognizable as a prototype of the Hebrew Bible) by the end of the Persian period, meaning the Pentatech, Deuteronomistic History and the Latter Prophets. The text continued to develop, and some books circulated in more than one version (e.g. Jeremiah) for centuries. Canonization was a process that probably began in the Persian period, but it was a long process (even the concept of canon as we know it may have taken a long time to develop), and the present Hebrew canon as a widely accepted collection among the Jewish people was probably not reached until at least the first century CE.

NPL: The first and second divisions of the Bible are theological discourse. The writings contain other sources. Continuous commentary was going on.[28]

---

28. These were the brief remarks made in the discussion in Helsinki, but NPL's views are summarized at length from his 1993 article on pp. 321-24 above.

KP: The Hebrew Bible is a collection of inventories of earlier tra-
       ditions made by various Yahwistic circles in various political,
       social, cultural and religious contexts. The inventories were
       created through a twofold process: (1) new ways of describing,
       presenting and understanding historical events and traditions
       were designed on the basis of conflicting experiences and
       learned study, not with the purpose of questioning or distorting
       the historical events and traditions as they were but of giving
       their positive relevance in a new situation. (2) Entirely new
       'historical events and traditions' had to be contrived on the
       basis of existing materials through the use of creative imagina-
       tion for parenetic, pedagogic and other relevant aims. Regard-
       ing the issue of historicity, the material in (2) is of no value for
       the time it purports to describe, but the results of the process in
       (1) must not be rejected out of hand without serious historical
       study of their origin and development. The most fertile period
       for the emergence of many of the written texts was presum-
       ably the Persian, while the generally accepted collection of
       sacred writings with an established text form (i.e. the present
       Hebrew canon) is certainly a late phenomenon.
TLT: The bulk of the tradition is a wisdom discourse on the past and
       is at least as late as the third or second centuries BCE. How-
       ever, within the collections are traditions going back as early
       as the Bronze Age.[29]

The Next Seminar Subject

The Seminar noted the fact that the topics chosen up to this point were
sufficiently broad that it was easy to talk past one another or to sidestep
what others perceived as difficulties with the position taken. Therefore,
for its next topic it was agreed to focus on a rather narrow, specific
topic: Sennacherib's invasion. Several Assyriologists and other specialists have been invited as guests to participate in the discussion.

---

29. This is what was stated in the discussion; for a more detailed summary see
pp. 324-25 above.

INDEXES

INDEX OF REFERENCES

OLD TESTAMENT

Genesis		11.2	108	23.9	45
1–11	67	12.36	108	23.23	45
1–2	102	12.38	108, 127	24.5-9	46
1	295, 296,	14	36	25–27	119
	327	19–24	43	25	41
1.3	295	20.1-21	214	25.1	45
1.4	295	20.3	68	25.23	41
1.7	296	20.4	69	26	60
1.9	295	21–23	214	27.1	45
1.31	204	25–31	43	27.34	44, 132
3.23-24	280	32–34	43		
4.25	144	35–40	43	*Numbers*	
4.26	144	39.1-31	144, 146	1	41
5.24	144, 147			7	41
6–9	275	*Leviticus*		11	120
6–8	218	1–16	43	11.4-34	45
6.9	144, 147	1–7	46	11.4	127
6.10	144	1.1	45	12.1-16	44
10	280	4.1	45	12.1	176
11	280	7.22	45	12.3	144
11.31	219	7.28	45	12.7	144
15.18	144, 147	8–9	43	14.6-38	144
17.5	144	10.1-10	45	16	144
22.18	144	10.11	45	18	46, 144
24	219	11.1	45	18.23-24	41, 45
37	144	12.1	45	18.24	132
39–50	144	15.1	45	18.25-32	40
50.25	144	16.1	45	22–24	187, 189
		17.1	45	25	144
Exodus		18.1-5	41	25.13	144
1.11	201	18.1	45	26	41
1.16	112	18.24-30	41	36.13	44, 132
5.1	126	19.1	45		
6.1	108	22.1	45	*Deuteronomy*	
11.2-3	108	23.1	45	1–2 Kgs 25	38

Deuteronomy (cont.)		17.49-50	145	3.17-20	61
4.15-19	69	18.7	145	6.15-18	61
5.6-21	214	23.4-5	61	7.5-7	61
5.8	69	25	294	13.20-21	145
7.3	40	28	145	17	26, 264
10.9	41, 45,			17.6-8	57
	132	*2 Samuel*		17.21-23	145
12–26	43	2–4	188	18–20	83
12.12	41, 45,	5.22-25	61	18–19	145
	132	7	145	18.13-16	222
18.1	41, 45	13.18	187	19.5-7	145
20	43			19.14-34	145
28–32	60	*1 Kings*		19.35-36	146
28.1	132	1–11	56	20.1-11	146
28.66	183	4.7-19	74	20.20	145
30	53	5–9	63, 64	21	56
34	53	5.9-14	145	22–23	146
34.10-11	44	5.14	145	23.22	304
		6	145	25	153
Joshua		8.22-53	64	25.26	123
8.1	61	8.25-26	64	25.27-30	39
10.11	61, 144	8.33-40	63		
10.12-14	144	9.1-9	64	*1 Chronicles*	
24	53, 211	9.4-7	64	1–9	231, 240
24.11-12	61	10.1	145	1–7	40
		10.21	145	2.54-55	246
Judges		10.23-24	145	3.17-24	229, 251
1.10-15	144	10.27	145	3.24	229
4.14-16	61	11	40	9	247
5.19	119	11.1-5	145	9.2-17	230
11–12	188	12.1-19	145	9.17-18	270
18–21	188	12.20	145	12	231
		12.25–13.5	145	15–16	231
1 Samuel		17–18	145	15.16	148
1.11	144	17.17-24	145	16	145
7.9-11	144	18.13-16	201	16.4-6	148
7.10	144, 147	18.17–19.37	201	23–27	231, 252
7.16-17	144	18.38	145	23–26	233
8–12	74	19.5-18	145	23.5	145, 148
8–10	144	19.19-21	145	23.31-32	148
8	302			24.10	177
8.6-7	74	*2 Kings*		29.7	229
9.9	144	1–2	151		
12.3-5	145, 147	1.10	145	*2 Chronicles*	
12.3-4	146	1.12	145	7.6	145
16	144	2.9	145	8.3-4	229, 239
17.34-37	145	2.11-12	145	16.9	229, 230
17.45-47	61	3	201	26.11-15	230

26.15	229, 230, 238	*Proverbs*		8.14	68	
29–31	201	1–9	47	10	146	
30	304	22.17–24.22	218	45.4-5	46	
31.1	304			48.10-14	46	
32.30	145	*Isaiah*				
34–35	201, 304	2.6	68	*Daniel*		
35.18	304	4	213	1–6	152	
36.22-23	230, 231	5.24	213	7–12	152	
		6	214			
Ezra		6.11-13	214	*Hosea*		
1.1-3	230	8.16	101	8.4-6	68	
2	244	19	124			
2.61	177	19.16-22	124	*Amos*		
3–6	146	19.18	124	8.14	68	
7	35, 40	22.9-11	145			
7.7-9	234	24–27	31, 47, 338	*Jonah*		
7.11-26	243			2.9	68	
7.26	35	27.9	68			
47.21–48.29	41	36–37	145	*Micah*		
		37.5-7	145	1.7	68	
		37.14-34	145			
Nehemiah		37.35-36	146	*Habakkuk*		
1–4	212	38.1-8	146	2.18-19	68	
2–4	119	40–55	119			
3–4	146	52.4	125	*Zephaniah*		
3.4	177	65–66	47	1.4-5	68	
3.21	177					
7	244	*Jeremiah*		*Haggai*		
7.63	177	1.5	146	1–2	146	
9.9-21	247	1.10	146	1.1	173	
9.23-25	248	4.23	286	1.15–2.1	173	
11.1-19	247	7.31	68	2.10	173	
11.3-19	230	11.13	68	2.20-23	39	
12.25-26	270	23.27-30	39	2.23	146, 147	
13.4-13	40	31	213			
13.25-27	40	31.31-34	211	*Zechariah*		
		32	119	1.1	173	
Psalms		36	101	1.7	173	
2	282	41.1-2	39	4.10	230	
8	282	43–44	123	7.1	173	
34	274	43.13	124	9–14	31, 47, 338	
52	274	44.1	123			
56	274	44.14	123	10.2	68	
89	282					
110	282	*Ezekiel*		*Malachi*		
137	197	1	146	2.7	44	
		6.6	68	3.23-24	145, 147	

APOCRYPHA

2 Esdras		45.25-26	144	49.9	146
14	102	45.25	146	49.10	146
		46.1-6	144, 146	49.11-13	147
Wisdom of Solomon		46.7-10	146	49.11	146
14.3	86	46.7-8	144	49.12	146
17.2	18.6	46.9-10	144	49.13	146, 289
		46.11-12	144, 146	49.14-16	147
Ecclesiasticus		46.13-20	144, 146	49.14	144
39.1	291	47.1	145, 147	49.15	144
42–50	289	47.2-11	145, 146	49.16	144
44–50	92, 143	47.8-10	225	50	138, 150,
44–49	331	47.9-10	148		289
44	143	47.12-22	145	50.1-29	147
44.1–50.24	90	47.23-25	145, 147		
44.16	144, 146	48.1-11	145, 147	*1 Maccabees*	
44.17-18	144, 146	48.12-14	145, 147	8.17	177
44.19-21	144, 146	48.15-16	147		
44.22	144, 146	48.17-25	145, 147	*2 Maccabees*	
44.23-24	144, 146	49.1-3	146, 147	3.11-12	138
45.1-5	144, 146	49.4-5	147	4	185
45.6-22	144, 146	49.6	146	4.11	141, 177
45.23-24	144, 146	49.8	146	7	178
				11	178

NEW TESTAMENT

Matthew		7.12	291	*Acts*	
5.17	291	22.30	291	13.15	291
5.32	99			24.14	291
7.1-5	100	*Luke*			
		16.16	291	*Romans*	
				9–11	212

POST-BIBLICAL JEWISH SOURCES

Pseudepigrapha		*4 Ezra*		*b. B. Bat.*	
1 Enoch		14.44-46	153	15a	234
85–89	329				
91.1-10	90	*Letter of Aristeas*		Josephus	
91.11-17	90	12–14	123	*Ant.*	
91.18-19	90	13	123	12.1.1.3-10	78, 131
92.1–93.10	90			12.3.3-4.	
		Rabbinica		138-46	140
3 Maccabees		*m. Ab.*		12.3.3-4.	
4.21	86	3.16	86	138-56	140
5.30	86				

12.4.1-11.
  154-236   136
12.4.1.
  157-59   150
13.5.9.
  171-72   86

19.5.2.
  280-85   344

Apion
1.8.37-43   153
1.136-37   123

1.183-204   42, 117
1.22.209-212   78, 131
1.228-52   114
1.73-105   114
1.93-105   116

OTHER ANCIENT SOURCES

Cicero
Inv.
1.21.29   169

De or.
1.5.17-18   169
1.14.60   169
2.9.36   203
2.15.62   169
2.82.337   169
120   169

Part. or.
9.32   169
25.90   169

Rhet. ad Her.
1.16   169

Diodorus Siculus
1-2   41
1.28.1-3   121
3   41, 42
4-5   41
4   41
5   41, 44

6   41, 42, 44
7   41, 42
8   41
40.3   117
40.3.1-8   132

Eusebius
Praep. ev.
9.27   127
9.29.1-3   176
9.29.16   176

Herodotus
1.1   202
2.118-20   163
3.61-87   164
4.42   164
7.54-56   37

Horace
Ep.
2.1.156-57   209

Plutarch
Art.
1.4   170

Polybius
1.14   167
2.56   169
2.56.10   167
3.7   167
3.20.3-45   169
3.47.6-48.9   169
3.57-59   167
4.28.4   167
12   168
12.25b.1   167
12.25g-25i   167
12.26d-28a   167
36.1.7   167

Strabo
16.2.35.760   116

Thucydides
Hist. Pel.
1.20-22   164
1.20.1   165
1.21.1   165
1.22.2-4   165
11.42-43   169

INDEX OF AUTHORS

Achtemeier, P.J. 177
Ackroyd, P.R. 241
Aharoni, Y. 87
Ahlström, G.W. 298, 299, 307
Albertz, R. 16, 20, 21, 26, 31, 32, 34, 35,
    38-40, 43, 45, 46, 69, 86, 88, 186,
    251-71, 320, 327, 330, 334, 337
Albrektson, B. 58, 76, 80, 156
Albright, W.F. 87, 193, 234, 297, 298
Alt, A. 275
Anderson, B.W. 226
Ankersmit, F.R. 79
Anouilh, J. 183
Appleby, J. 18
Arav, R. 80
Ash, P.S. 65, 74
Attridge, H.W. 78, 89, 223
Aufrecht, W.E. 72
Auld, A.G. 188
Avigad, N. 101

Bagnall, R.S. 135, 136, 155
Bal, M. 191
Balcer, J.M. 164
Balentine, S.E. 93
Bar-Kochva, B. 79, 88, 117, 130, 132,
    178
Barr, J. 156, 287, 288
Barr, M.L. 61
Barrick, W.B. 67
Barstad, H.M. 16, 17, 21, 50, 58, 68, 79,
    80, 82, 156, 212, 320, 327, 332, 338
Barton, J. 95
Beaulieu, P.-A. 66, 75, 77
Becker, J. 252
Beckett, S. 103
Becking, B. 16, 21, 57, 66, 69, 183, 320,

    327, 333, 334, 338
Bedford, P.R. 263
Beentjes, P.C. 143
Ben Zvi, E. 72
Benjamin, W. 107
Bergler, S. 47
Bertrand, J.M. 139
Bianchi, F. 230, 231
Bickerman, E.J. 140-42, 149, 176, 179
Bietenholz, P.G. 77
Bigwood, J.M. 170
Bin-Nun, S.R. 174
Biran, A. 80
Black, F.C. 195
Blenkinsopp, J. 109, 263, 311
Block, D.I. 67
Blum, E. 37, 44
Boer, R. 195
Bohlen, R. 32, 82
Bolin, T.M. 49
Braaten, C.E. 98
Braun, R.L. 179, 226, 252, 253
Brettler, M.Z. 66, 74, 160
Bright, J. 278
Brooke, G.J. 148
Broshi, M. 33
Brown, T.S. 162
Bruce, I.A.F. 166
Brunt, P.A. 169
Burstein, S.M. 223

Cagni, L. 67
Calvin, J. 286
Carroll, R.P. 18, 22, 26, 27, 92, 95, 96,
    98, 100, 119, 274-77, 283, 293, 310,
    320, 325, 338
Carter, C.E. 323

Childs, B.S. 109, 156
Clements, R.E. 266
Clines, D.J.A. 310
Cogan, M. 62
Collingwood, R.G. 19, 79
Collins, J.J. 32, 47, 152, 156
Conan Doyle, A. 105
Coppens, J. 67
Cors i Meya, J. 223
Cowley, A.E. 125, 150
Crenshaw, J.L. 48
Cross, F.M. 80, 87, 226, 231, 240
Crüsemann, F. 302

Damerow, P. 71, 75
Danot, A.C. 79
Davies, G.I. 72
Davies, P.R. 16, 22, 25-27, 74, 88, 92, 95,
    97, 119, 185, 186, 188, 193, 211,
    263, 278-82, 284, 292, 293, 307,
    310, 312, 320, 325, 327, 334, 338
Day, J. 62, 72
Deist, F.E. 49, 95, 96
Derow, P. 135, 163
Derrida, J. 18, 19
Descamps, A. 67
Dever, W.G. 72, 306
Dickens, C. 93
Diebner, B.J. 81, 298
Dietrich, M. 62, 68
Dietrich, W. 333
Dillard, R.B. 226
Dillery, J. 42
Dirksen, P.B. 225
Donner, H. 298
Doran, R. 176
Dorp, J. van 56
Drews, R. 162
Driver, S.R. 109
Due, B. 166
Durkheim, E. 208
Dyck, J.E. 228, 253

Edelman, D.V. 17, 79, 85, 86, 118, 159,
    160, 295, 298, 302
Edzard, D.O. 77, 219
Eilers, W. 170
Eissfeldt, O. 206

Elayi, J. 17
Emerton, J.A. 48, 72, 76, 235, 253, 306,
    311
Englund, R.K. 71
Eph'al, I. 62
Eskenazi, T.C. 92
Eslinger, L.M. 191
Evans, C.D. 65
Evans, R.J. 18
Eynikel, E. 56

Falkenstein, A. 66
Feldman, L.H. 115
Fensham, F.C. 60
Ferguson, E. 78
Finkelstein, I. 33, 72, 211, 298
Fischer, T. 139
Fishbane, M. 71
Fohrer, G. 47, 206, 207
Fokkelman, J.P. 51
Fornara, C.W. 162, 165, 168, 169
Foucault, M. 18, 19
Frazer, J.G. 208, 275, 282
Freedman, D.N. 52, 226
Freudenthal, J. 89
Friedman, R.E. 82
Frye, N. 51
Fuks, A. 133

Gabriel, I. 227
Gager, J.G. 115
Galling, K. 231, 252
Garbini, G. 289, 300
Gauger, J.-D. 140-42, 149
Gauley, S.W. 72
Gawlick, G. 227
Gera, D. 139
Gera, D.L. 166
Gerbrandt, G.E. 56
Glassner, J.-J. 77
Gnuse, R.K. 68
Gogel, S.L. 88
Golding, W. 93
Goldstein, J.A. 79, 137
Golka, F.W. 72
Goossens, G. 67
Gordon, D. 19
Gordon, R.L. 86

Gordon, R.P. 72
Gottwald, N. 194
Grabbe, L.L. 16, 17, 23, 24, 26, 27, 40,
    50, 74, 78-80, 82, 88, 89, 92, 102,
    117, 128-30, 137, 138, 141, 148,
    153-56, 177, 178, 276-80, 310, 320,
    327-more-
Grabbe, L.L. 330-33, 335, 336, 339
Graf, 109
Graham, M.P. 237, 252
Grayson, A.K. 171, 172
Greenfield, J. 60
Gruen, E.S. 128
Gunkel, H. 209
Gunn, D.M. 24, 27, 51, 195, 283, 285,
    286, 320, 330

Halbertal, M. 95
Hall, R.G. 90
Hallbäck, G. 201
Hallo, W.W. 58, 65
Halpern, B. 159, 160, 172-75
Handy, L.K. 174
Hänel, J. 231
Haran, M. 72
Hardmeier, C. 83, 84
Harvey, G. 199
Hayes, J.H. 282
Hengel, M. 117, 141
Hess, R.S. 66
Hill, A.E. 48
Hillers, D.R. 60
Hoffmeier, J.K. 109, 110
Hogenhaven, J. 317
Holladay, C.R. 89, 114, 154, 176-78
Holt, E.K. 213
Hornblower, S. 163, 164, 171
Horsley, R.A. 263
Horst, P.W. van der 66, 69, 89
House, P.R. 48
Hübner, U. 17
Huizinga, J. 157, 158
Hunt, L. 18
Hurovitz, V. 63
Hurvitz, A. 87
Hurwitz, A. 334
Hyatt, J.P. 109
Hyldahl, N. 205, 208

Irvin, D. 282

Jacob, M. 18
Jacoby, F. 170
Jaeger, W. 42
Jamieson-Drake, D.W. 72, 211, 212, 300,
    301, 305, 310, 311
Japhet, S. 48, 152, 232, 233, 235, 239,
    253, 266, 268
Jellicoe, S. 154
Jenkins, K. 18
Jensen, P. 275
Jenson, R.W. 98
Jeppesen, K. 17
Jobling, D. 187, 191
Johnstone, W. 111, 112
Jolles, A. 209
Jones, G.H. 225, 231, 232, 253
Joyce, J. 91, 100

Kaiser, O. 32, 48, 124, 227
Kalimi, I. 225-27, 229, 232, 234, 245
Kansteiner, W. 18
Kegler, J. 241
Kelly, B.E. 228
Kenik, H.A. 52
Kenyon, K.M. 310
Keulen, P.S.F. van 56
Kieweler, H.V. 32
King, P.J. 310
Kirk, G.S. 327
Kirkpatrick, P.G. 113
Klein, L.R. 191, 227, 231, 253
Klein, R.W. 225
Kleinig, J.W. 225, 227
Klibansky, R. 157
Klopfenstein, M.A. 68
Knauf, E.A. 17, 79, 174, 315
Knoppers, G.A. 52
Koch, H. 33
König, F.W. 170
Koorevaar, H.J. 270
Korpel, M. 335
Kraeling, E.G. 125
Kraus, F.R. 204
Kreissig, H. 263
Kuhnen, H.-P. 80
Kuhrt, A. 160, 161, 171, 328, 329

Landau, Y.H. 139
Lapp, N. 138
Lapp, P. 138
Larsen, M.T. 206
Lella, A.A. di 143
Lemaire, A. 39, 72, 85, 87, 159, 161
Lemche, N.P. 16, 17, 20, 21, 24-26, 30-
    38, 40, 46, 49, 81, 83, 86, 87, 104,
    129, 151, 153, 184-90, 195, 198,
    199, 201, 211, 223, 275, 276, 286,
    293, 297, 306, 307, 320, 321, 323-
    30, 332-34, 336, 339
Lenger, M.-T. 135
Leschhorn, W. 42
Lesky, A. 162
Lévêque, J. 48
Levine, B. 127
Levy, T.E. 72
Lewis, J. 153
Lieberman, S. 234
Liebesny, H. 135
Lightfoot, R.H. 287
Limburg, J. 47
Lind, M.C. 61
Linville, J.R. 199
Liverani, M. 17, 304
Livingstone, A. 66
Locke, J. 100
Lohfink, N. 32
Long, B.O. 54, 193, 279
Lord, A.B. 113, 209
Loretz, O. 62, 179

Macchi, J.-D. 52, 77
Magen, U. 58
Maier, J. 39
Malkin, I. 42
Malul, M. 60
Mandell, S. 52
Mannheim, K. 80
Mansfeld, J. 86
Marcus, R. 141
Marincola, J. 168
Martin, R. 18
Massaux, E. 67
Mauer, G. 58
Mayer, W. 69
Mayes, A. 17

Mazar, A. 72, 312
McCarthy, D.J. 60
McCullagh, C.B. 19
McGrath, A.E. 98-100
McKenzie, S.L. 202, 226, 237, 252, 280
Mendels, D. 42-44, 88, 118, 119, 122,
    132, 133
Mendenhall, G.E. 194, 207
Meshorer, Y. 80
Mettinger, T.N.D. 69
Meyers, C.L. 48
Meyers, E.M. 48
Michalowski, P. 59
Mildenberg, L. 80
Millar, W.R. 47
Miller, J.M. 282
Miller, P.D. Jr 61
Mirau, N.A. 72
Miscall, P. 191
Mitchell, C.W. 60
Momigliano, A.D. 77, 170, 174, 180, 181
Moore, C.A. 48
Morkholm, O. 80
Mosis, R. 253
Movers, F.C. 234, 235
Mowinckel, S. 71
Moyer, J.C. 65
Mulder, M.J. 89
Mullen, E.T. 52
Müller, H.-P. 17
Müller, M. 316
Munslow, A. 18
Murphy, R.E. 48
Murray, O. 42, 132

Na'aman, N. 17, 49, 72, 333
Nelson, R.D. 87
Neu, R. 299
Neusner, J. 79, 137, 153, 176
Newsome, J.D. 226
Nicholson, E.W. 60
Nickelsburg, G.W.E. 89
Nicol, G.G. 300
Niehr, H. 17, 305, 306
Nielsen, F.A.J. 37, 49, 51, 81, 221
Niemann, H.M. 17
Niethammer, L. 107
Niewöhner, F. 227

Nissen, H.J. 71, 75
Nissinen, M. 58, 62
Noort, E. 17
Noth, M. 54, 109, 127, 206, 226, 231,
    240, 252, 253, 275, 278, 297, 298,
    334

O'Brien, M.A. 52
O'Connell, R.H. 73
Oded, B. 62
Oden, R.A. Jr 223
Oeming, M. 227, 241, 252
Olyan, S.M. 69
Oppenheim, A.L. 70
Orlinsky, H.M. 154
Osswald, E. 65
Otto, E. 60, 214
Ottosson, M. 302
Otzen, B. 291

Parker, S.B. 62
Parpola, S. 64
Parry, M. 113, 209
Paton, H.J. 157
Paton, W.R. 167
Paul, S.M. 59, 214
Pedersen, J. 314
Peels, H.G.L. 67
Peltonen, K. 25, 32, 38, 48, 152, 237,
    320, 329, 340
Perdue, L.G. 65
Perlitt, L. 207
Peters, M.K.H. 289
Petersen, D.L. 226, 311
Petzold, K.-E. 169
Polzin, R. 191, 232
Pomponio, F. 60, 68
Pope, M.H. 48
Popper, K. 216, 334
Porten, B. 33, 125, 150
Powell, M.A. 51
Preuss, H.D. 52
Proseckya, J. 65
Puech, E. 72
Pury, A. de 52, 77
Qedar, S. 80

Rad, G. von 278, 303, 317

Ranke, L. von 204
Raven, J.E. 327
Redford, D.B. 218, 300
Reiner, E. 70
Rendtorff, R. 110
Renz, J. 73, 87
Reuter, E. 69
Richards, K.H. 92
Riley, W. 228
Ringgren, H. 217
Roberts, J.J.M. 156
Röllig, W. 98, 99
Römer, T. 52, 77, 202, 280
Rösel, H.N. 54
Rossoni, G. 230, 231
Rost, L. 293
Rostovtzeff, M. 136
Roth, M.T. 59, 215
Rothstein, J.W. 231
Rudolph, W. 231, 252
Ruffing, A. 227, 240
Runions, E. 195
Rüsen, J. 80
Rüterswörden, U. 35

Sachs, A.J. 171
Saebo, M. 85, 159, 161
Said, E. 91, 106
Sandars, J.A. 289
Sarna, T.N. 109, 112
Sasson, J.M. 48, 301
Säve-Söderbergh, T. 116
Schmid, H.H. 64
Schniedewind, W.M. 226
Schofield, M. 327
Schramm, B. 47
Schramm, W. 170
Schürer, E. 117, 138
Schwartz, S. 178
Schwienhorst-Schönberger, L. 32
Scott, J.W. 18
Selman, M.J. 228
Seow, C.-L. 152, 179, 329
Seters, J. van 50, 81, 109, 157-60, 172-
    74, 188, 202, 203, 209, 220-22, 276,
    280, 281, 308
Seux, M.-J. 66
Sherwin-White, S. 328

Silberstein, L.J. 196
Skehan, P.W. 143
Smelik, K.A.D. 82, 87
Smend, R. 227
Smith, M. 58
Smith, R.H. 218
Soden, W. von 66
Soggin, J.A. 292
Sonsino, R. 59
Spencer, J.R. 67
Spengler, O. 163
Spinoza, B. 227
Spong, J.S. 98, 99
Stanford, M. 79
Steins, G. 152, 225, 227, 231, 241, 269,
    270
Stern, E. 138, 310
Stern, M. 32, 40, 42, 78, 79, 88, 114, 117,
    121, 132, 133
Stone, M.E. 78, 89
Strange, J. 201
Strout, C. 18
Strübind, K. 227
Sweet, R.F.G. 72

Tadmor, H. 61
Talmon, S. 143
Talstra, E. 63
Tatum, J. 166
Tcherikover, V. 122, 133
Thackeray, H.St.J. 140, 141
Thompson, S. 208
Thompson, T.L. 17, 24, 26, 27, 81, 82,
    84, 92, 100, 104, 110, 159-61, 182-
    87, 190-94, 197, 199, 202, 205, 213,
    274, 277, 280-83, 286, 298, 320,
    321, 324-26, 329-33, 340
Throntveit, M.A. 226
Tigay, J.H. 70, 278
Toorn, K. van der 66, 69, 86
Torczyner, H. 87
Torrey, C.C. 252, 310
Tov, E. 76, 148
Treves, M. 48
Tsumura, D.T. 66
Ulrich, E. 293
Ussishkin, D. 17

Veijola, T. 86, 87
Vermaseren, M.J. 86
Vermeylen, J. 124
Veyne, P. 174, 175
Vries, S.J. de 227

Wacholder, B.Z. 79, 177
Waddell, W.G. 223
Walton, F.R. 44, 297
Walz, R. 219
Warner, R. 165
Weber, M. 306
Weeks, S. 58
Weidner, E. 70
Weinberg, J.P. 26, 217, 242-51, 261-64,
    267, 270, 271, 311
Weinfeld, M. 61
Weippert, H. 310
Weippert, M. 17, 58, 61
Weiser, A. 293
Welch, A.C. 231
Wellhausen, J. 109, 241, 313
Welten, P. 227, 230, 240, 253, 259
Wesselius, J.-W. 36, 37, 49, 50, 81, 220,
    221
West, W.L. 326, 327
Westbrook, R. 59, 214
Westermann, C. 48
Whitelam, K.W. 17, 193
Whybray, R.N. 110
Widengren, G. 67, 75
Wiesehöfer, J. 35
Will, E. 138
Willi, T. 253
Williamson, H.G.M. 48, 72, 82, 227, 235,
    252, 253, 265, 266, 268
Willoughby, B.E. 226
Windschuttle, K. 19
Wiseman, D.J. 216
Wittgenstein, L. 100
Wright, B.G. 143
Wright, D.P. 59
Wright, J.W. 293
Wyatt, N. 69

Yadin, Y. 143
Yardeni, A. 33, 125, 150
Young, I. 88

Younger, K.L. 61
Younger, K.L. Jr 210

Zeev, M.P. ben 142

Zenger, E. 225
Zerubavel, Y. 195, 197, 198
Ziegler, J. 143
Zunz, L. 234, 235